A MARITIME HISTORY OF THE AMERICAN REVOLUTIONARY WAR

AN ATLANTIC-WIDE CONFLICT OVER INDEPENDENCE AND EMPIRE

For Christine

A MARITIME HISTORY OF THE AMERICAN REVOLUTIONARY WAR

AN ATLANTIC-WIDE CONFLICT OVER INDEPENDENCE AND EMPIRE

Theodore Corbett

PEN & SWORD
MARITIME

First published in Great Britain in 2023 by
PEN AND SWORD MARITIME
an imprint of
Pen and Sword Books Ltd
Yorkshire – Philadelphia

Copyright © Theodore Corbett, 2023

ISBN 978 1 39904 041 9

Typeset in Times New Roman 9.5/12 by
SJmagic DESIGN SERVICES, India.
Printed and bound in the UK by CPI Group (UK) Ltd.

Pen & Sword Books Ltd incorporates the imprints of Pen & Sword
Archaeology, Atlas, Aviation, Battleground, Discovery,
Family History, History, Maritime, Military, Naval, Politics, Railways,
Select, Social History, Transport, True Crime, Claymore Press,
Frontline Books, Leo Cooper, Praetorian Press, Remember When,
Seaforth Publishing and Wharncliffe.

For a complete list of Pen & Sword titles please contact
PEN & SWORD BOOKS LIMITED
47 Church Street, Barnsley, South Yorkshire, S70 2AS, England
E-mail: enquiries@pen-and-sword.co.uk
Website: www.pen-and-sword.co.uk

Or

PEN AND SWORD BOOKS
1950 Lawrence Rd, Havertown, PA 19083, USA
E-mail: Uspen-and-sword@casematepublishers.com
Website: www.penandswordbooks.com

Contents

Preface.. vii

Introduction.. ix

PART 1: THE ESTABLISHED ROYAL NAVY

Chapter 1   Royal Navy Dockyards 2

Chapter 2   Administering the Royal Navy...9

Chapter 3   Coping with Rebellion 15

PART 2: FORMING A NEW NAVY

Chapter 4   Colonial Maritime Tradition..22

Chapter 5   Congress Forms the Continental Navy...28

Chapter 6   Rebel Privateers Offer Profit...36

PART 3: CANADA PRESERVED BY THE ROYAL NAVY

Chapter 7   Congress wants Quebec 44

Chapter 8   Creating Squadrons to Control Lake Champlain 50

Chapter 9   The Battle of Lake Champlain and the Capture of Ticonderoga....................56

Chapter 10   Canada Sustained by Control of Lake Champlain 61

PART 4: BLOCKADING THE COAST AND ENVELOPING NEW YORK

Chapter 11   The Royal Navy Blockade 68

Chapter 12   Amphibious Operations take New York..75

Chapter 13   Clinton and Wallace Sail the Hudson..79

PART 5: RAIDING THE BRITISH ISLES

Chapter 14   American Commissioners and Captains in Europe...........................86

Chapter 15   A Scotsman Desires Command 95

Chapter 16   Whitehaven Attacked 102

Chapter 17   The British Isles React 107
Chapter 18   Whitehaven Defends Itself..111
Chapter 19   Jones Loses Command..114
Chapter 20   Jones Sails Again...118

PART 6: THE ROYAL NAVY SUCCEEDS IN THE SOUTH

Chapter 21   A French Fleet and a Southern Strategy....................................126
Chapter 22   Charleston Besieged..132
Chapter 23   British Initiatives in the Chesapeake...138

PART 7: NEW ENGLAND AND NOVA SCOTIA IN CONFLICT

Chapter 24   Massachusetts' Hubris...146
Chapter 25   Halifax's Crucial Careening Yard..152
Chapter 26   Defending Nova Scotia 157

PART 8: THE SIEGE OF GIBRALTAR

Chapter 27   The Spanish Obsession with Gibraltar.......................................164
Chapter 28   The Defenders Succeed..170

PART 9: THE CONTINENTAL NAVY IN TROUBLE

Chapter 29   Loyalist Privateers Expand the War 180
Chapter 30   Demise of the Continental Navy 189
Chapter 31   French Assistance..196

PART 10: FINAL CONFRONTATIONS

Chapter 32   Rodney Humiliates France...202
Chapter 33   Maryland and Virginia Humiliated...207
Chapter 34   Evacuation Becomes Migration 216

Affirmations...220
Notes 225
Index 263

Preface

Little has been written about the Revolutionary War from the maritime standpoint. Most American accounts of the war focus on two events: the Battles of Saratoga in upstate New York and the Siege of Yorktown on Chesapeake Bay, neither of which involved significant naval action. Land battles seem to be the essence of military history. Christopher Ward's classic account of the Revolution's military history, mentions the naval conflict in only a few of its eighty-four chapters.[1] American historians have also not been at their best in looking at the British side, which they regard as the inevitable losing side, standing in the way of the great American experiment. Nor have British historians stepped up to the plate, for other, more glorious episodes of eighteenth-century warfare, fit more easily into the rise of the British Empire. French and Spanish historians see the conflict against the coming of the momentous French Revolution. Rarely do these perspectives meet.

Instead of maritime possibilities, American interpreters have built their histories around the cult of naval personalities. What has been written about the Continental Navy and American privateers has been subject to a heavy dose of the 'gallantry' of American naval officers. One becomes suspicious if it is argued that every defeat had a silver lining as long as it was conducted gallantly and was later vigorously honored by friends and family. At least one American historian has realized that revolutionary gallantry has its limits: 'As in all wars ..., the real experience was a paradoxical combination of exceptional gallantry and shabby expediency, heroism and cowardice, existing amid a world of boredom punctuated by occasional excitement.'[2] This critical attitude is what will be found here.

My journey to writing this book has been long and indirect. I have always been interested in the Revolutionary War because I grew up in upstate New York among many historic sites from the conflict. I began working on the Revolutionary War in 2003, speaking on it at Fort Ticonderoga's war colleges, held annually before a broad audience on Lake Champlain. Ultimately, I published *No Turning Point*, covering the Saratoga Campaign. For this on several occasions, I used the manuscript collections of the National Library and Archives of Canada in Ottawa to add a British perspective. Its most welcoming staff provided much of the material in Part 3.

The next stop in my journey took me south to the NABB Center of Salisbury University, Maryland, where I became acquainted with Director Ray Thompson and his staff, who were ever helpful. It was here that I first read manuscripts covering Delmarva history. An instructive and pleasurable experience was lively discussion with students in my Eastern Shore Maritime History classes, sponsored by Salisbury University. I was also able to visit the Chesapeake Bay Maritime Museum at St Michaels, Maryland where a collection of documents on the life of Lambert Wickes had been assembled by Norman Plummer. Further south, Archivist Miles Barnes of the Eastern Shore Public Library, Accomac, Virginia proved to be supportive, not only with new sources on Virginia's maritime history but also in chatting at his home library.

I have drawn on the Hamond Papers at the University of Virginia, the most extensive source on Captain Andrew Snape Hamond's career. They are readily available at several research libraries because they were microfilmed in 1966 and a guide to the papers was published the same year. Most of Hamond's papers were put together by himself in a scrapbook, for he was interested in producing an autobiography, which never was completed or published. In the manuscript, pagination is often lacking and loose inserts exist, while Hamond inverted the notebook pages into which his material was placed. This collection also includes Hamond-Hans Stanley correspondence, the only personal papers, which were purchased separately by the university to enhance the collection.

As with any historian who wants to comprehend naval history, Britain beckoned. There, during the spring of 2017, I had the pleasure of working with staffs of several research facilities. In Greenwich, the Caird Library of the National Maritime Museum offered a rich collection of ships' log books. One Caird librarian in particular, Mark Benson, was especially accommodating. Across London at Kew, the National Archives provided access to the Admiralty Papers. I had planned to return for research in 2020, but the pandemic intervened. I was able to make up for this on line, discussing John Paul Jones' exploits with Andrew Connell, formerly with the Appleby School, Cumbria. Working with the Pen & Sword team of Tara Moran and Harriet Fielding as well as editor Gaynor Haliday has been magical as my manuscript has become a book.

One of the necessities of scholarships is time and funding for research and reflection. I am grateful for awards received from the Gilder Lehrman Foundation and the National Endowment for the Humanities.

Another necessity is to clarify that quotes have not been modernized, being reproduced as found, with exception of bracketed material to provide context.

Introduction

In the seventeenth and eighteenth centuries, the British Empire was built on Atlantic trade. Ports in Britain grew by purchasing colonial staples like tobacco or sugar and in exchange providing the British manufactures that colonials so dearly wanted. British merchants and their agents were so successful that consumption of English goods in the colonies skyrocketed. Small American farmers aggressively entered the consumer market, demanding amenities that the neighboring gentry now took for granted. Even in remote rural areas, stores selling merchandise now existed at cross roads. In this sense, the British Empire was bound together by trade in staple crops and manufactures on the most local level, which was protected by the Royal Navy.

This situation continued throughout the colonial wars, the last of which, the Seven Years' War, serves as immediate background for the American Revolution. The conflict began in the North American colonies in 1754, but two years later merged into a Continental European struggle in which Britain's support of Prussia led to its emergence as a central European power to rival Austria, the ally of France. Resulting territorial rewards came to Britain in North America, where France lost most of its colonies except for the West Indies sugar islands of Guadeloupe and Martinique. France was humiliated, but in fact it had never placed much stock in its Canadian and Mississippi River possessions, in diplomacy preferring the sugar islands and Newfoundland fisheries over vast stretches of wilderness.

Once Britain had won these expansive American territories it had to decide what to do with them. During the war, the mainland colonies, especially those of New England, had bent over backwards to join them in driving the French from Canada. Now they were no longer a threat to the New Englanders. In Britain, it was decided to keep a military presence in the colonies, meant to police the new frontier by protecting Native Americans from incessant white encroachment. In Quebec, British tolerance pervaded as the new subjects were allowed to continue their Catholicism and French civil law. While previously Britain had neglected its colonies, it was now taking a greater interest in them as part of its empire.

This led to an era, from 1763 to 1775, of intense political conflict between Britain and some of its North American colonies. American historians have seen this period as the beginning of their nation and have written more about it than the actual Revolutionary War.[1] It was an era of protest against the Stamp Act and the Boston Tea Party, opposing the British government's effort to raise funds to pay for the Seven Years' War and the occupation of British troops. The protest was strongest in New England and it led to draconian measures against Boston carried out by the British military. Even after bloodshed at Lexington and Concord, New Englanders had to strive to convince other colonies to join them in the conflict with the mother county. And its effort would ultimately fail in Quebec, Nova Scotia, West and East Florida, Bermuda and the Bahamas.

France also remained lurking in the background. After 1763, France and its Bourbon ally, Spain, were bent on revenge. In particular, they were concerned to develop their navies so that they could at least match and perhaps exceed the number of Royal Navy ships. The French noted the conflict between Britain and its North American colonies and tried to take advantage by cultivating colonial leaders like Benjamin Franklin. However, at that time he proved to be a staunch Briton, and French efforts became more subdued after 1768, although it remained clear that France was still waiting in the wings, biding its time for an opportunity to strike back.

To further tell this story, I will seek to connect British North America to the wider Atlantic world, describing the events of the American Revolution in a maritime context. The scope will not be limited to the Royal Navy and Continental Navy, which usually operated in deep water. Privateers of both sides, Loyalist raiders and state navies will receive their due. These entities operated best in the narrow waters of rivers, lakes and coastal marsh, which required craft of a shallow draft, like sloops, galleys and barges. Such vessels were also able to trade with local famers for grain and meat to supply larger ships. In fact, the interrelationship between trade and war will be constant, as warships sought and distributed supplies, while private transports were made into warships or privateers.

It should be no surprise that several traditional interpretations of the Revolutionary War will be overturned. Original research demands that this happen, challenging the reader's reliance on this venerable wisdom. Judgements have been made in terms of eighteenth-century norms, rather than later modern theorists.

PART 1

THE ESTABLISHED ROYAL NAVY

Chapter 1

Royal Navy Dockyards

The quality of shipbuilding in Royal Navy dockyards gave their ships superiority over their enemies, guaranteeing a ship's extensive lifetime of service.[1] The expansion and maintenance of the Royal Navy depended upon extensive facilities to refit, supply and repair its fleet. Five principal navy dockyards functioned in Britain: Portsmouth in the southwest; Plymouth in the west; Deptford and Woolwich along the River Thames to the east of London; and, also to the east, Chatham on the River Medway. Overseas dockyards such as English Harbor in Antigua and Halifax in Nova Scotia were also crucial to American waters. Together, they formed the onshore naval establishment, the result of the burgeoning and increasingly efficient navy administration, caused by the expanding British state.

These dockyards were centers of manufacturing production, working with raw materials like Scandinavian hemp to meet specifications for rope production.[2] They were administered by the Navy Board, which supervised the thousand-strong workers at each dockyard, who divided their time between fashioning materials and building or refitting ships. While fortified, the dockyards had the drawback of lax security, allowing both non-employees and employees to easily pass through their gates. They also faced the labor problems of any manufacturing enterprise, so strikes were not unknown.

The Roebuck

While a variety of ships were constructed at the dockyards, one has been selected for detailed examination because it was designed to serve in America and was not a large ship of the line. Chatham Dockyard would be the place the *Roebuck* first saw light. Construction for the ship was ordered on November 30, 1769.[3] It was laid down in October 1770 and after four years of building, it was launched. It measured 140 feet in length with a 38-foot beam, and weighed 886 tons. Its construction required 1,582 loads of oak timber. The building and outfitting would be directed by two shipwrights, Joseph Harris and then William Gay. It was larger than the usual frigate, with two decks on which the guns were displayed. It carried more ordnance than usual, the armament consisting of twenty 18-pounders, twenty-two 9-pounders and two 6-pounders. It was not so much the number of guns as the presence of the 18-pounders that gave the *Roebuck* superior fire power. It was meant to carry a crew of 300, including 75 to 120 marines. Smaller than a ship of the line, it was more capable of operating in the rivers and shallows of the American coast.

The four years of construction for the *Roebuck* was not unusual because the work of putting vessels together by men and horses was done without heavy machinery and was prone to delays. The extensive time was also the result of the First Lord, the Earl of Sandwich's expressed desire that ships be built of timber seasoned in water and of frames that had been aired on the stocks. To make this possible, Sandwich had to find more and cheaper sources of timber and he sought to build up a three-year supply of timber for seasoning. On his annual visit to Chatham, Sandwich proudly observed 'all the seasoning sheds filled, and the whole face of the yard covered with timber, ranged in proper order, and so disposed ...'[4] Such concern made the new *Roebuck* stronger and more durable so that repairs would be less and the ship would have a long lifetime, giving the dockyards more time to build rather than repair ships.

The *Roebuck* was a prototype vessel, serving as a model for similarly designed ships. It was named for the small but agile deer found in the British Isles and these qualities were reflected in its lines. Its class of fifth rates was described by the Admiralty as 'built upon new principles and burthen than any which have been built these many years'.[5] By 1750, the Admiralty strictly defined frigates as ships carrying all their main battery of twenty-four to twenty-eight guns on the upper deck, with no guns or openings on the lower deck. A frigate might carry a few smaller guns – 6- or 9-pounders – on their quarterdeck and on the forecastle. In contrast, the *Roebuck*-class ships were two-deckers with complete batteries of forty-four guns spread on both decks, hence more firepower than usual frigates. Although sea officers casually described them and other small two-deckers as frigates, the Admiralty officially never used that term, considering them a class of ship above the frigate.

Seven years after the *Roebuck* design was first produced, the Admiralty reused the design for a second batch of nineteen ships. By this time, so many 44-gun two-deckers and smaller vessels had been sent to North America that more were needed for the British Isles, which were now threatened by French and American ships.[6] The first five vessels of this batch had two rows of stern windows, like larger two-deckers though actually only a single level of cabin was behind. Most of the other ships of the class had a single level frigate-type stern. Perhaps the most famous of this class was the *Serapis*, contracted in 1778, but taken by Captain John Paul Jones at Flamborough Head. A replacement of the same name was launched two years later.

Beyond the Revolution, the *Roebuck* would have a distinguished military career, but it was longevity by which it was judged a success. After thirty-six years and several changes in its use, the *Roebuck* finally faced the inevitable when at Sheerness at the entrance of the Medway, it was taken apart piece by piece, not far from where it had been built.[7] Its duration would be the result of the skill of the craftsmen at Chatham, the teamwork of its ship's company, and its adaptive reuse in later years.

Turmoil at Chatham

As the *Roebuck* was being completed, a strike took place at Chatham, the latest reaction to a reform that the Earl of Sandwich had begun twenty years earlier. He believed that dockyard employees would work faster if paid by the task, as in private yards, rather than the day.[8] The dockyard strike concerned hostility to task work, as Sandwich had initiated payment by results, which today is known as piece rate. He hoped that the introduction of this rate would increase wages for many dockyard workers, making them as productive as private yard workers.

Sandwich's reform was acceptable to most dockyard workers, but not to shipwrights. They feared dismissal as the Navy Board would not need as many shipwrights and that task workers might find themselves in gangs of old or worn-out workers. At Chatham, shipwrights began to work by task in the early summer and when the Admiralty and Navy Boards inspected, the experiment appeared to be going well. However, the shipwrights soon complained that task work had made them 'more miserable and wretched still', and they sought to have all task work removed.[9] To demonstrate, they went on strike, along with shipwrights in Plymouth and Portsmouth dockyards, although the rest of dockyard workers did not join them. In fact, the rest of the workforce seemed pleased with task work. To enforce its authority, the Admiralty dismissed 129 shipwrights, but subsequently readmitted all but a few ringleaders, and abandoned forcing task work on the unwilling. While their strike at Chatham went on for five weeks, most shipwrights eventually accepted task work. By mid-August, the shipwrights began to return to work, allowing Sandwich's task work to be eased into place. It was none too soon, for Sandwich had promised to send reinforcements to America. Still, this issue was never completely resolved and would continue to be a bone of contention.

Fear of Arson

Other conditions would menace the shipyards. At the end of 1776, the Royal Navy's English dockyards were seriously threatened, not so much by French or rebel privateers as by a single terrorist, dubbed John the Painter.[10] His real name was James Aitken and arson was his specialty. Aitken believed the dockyards were vulnerable to arson, especially the hemp warehouses and ropewalks, as well as warships at dock, carrying ample supplies of munitions and powder.

Aitken was born and grew up in Edinburgh, Scotland and traveled as an indentured servant to Virginia, but as war clouds gathered in 1775, he decided it was safer for a Scot to return to England. He became a supporter of the American rebellion and noted that despite their fortifications, Royal Navy dockyards were vulnerable, as one could access their interior as security at their gates was lax. Convinced of the possibility of arson, he went to France in mid-October 1776, where, after three attempts, he met the American commissioner, Silas Dean.[11] Dean was there primarily to purchase military supplies for Congress. Still, he listened to Aitken's plan to burn the navy dockyards and responded to him with three incentives: a small amount of money, a passport signed by the Comte de Vergennes, and the name of the man in London that all American sympathizers could depend on, Dr Edward Bancroft, whom Aitken would meet twice. Bancroft would eventually become Dean's secretary in France, an ideal position for him to exercise his secret position as a double-agent. Thus, Aitken joined a long list of adventurers who sought Dean's support.

Aitken returned to England in December 1776 and despite being a convicted petty criminal, he traveled to and freely entered the gates of the Navy Board's Portsmouth dockyard to determine where to plant his incendiary devices.[12] Using his training as a painter in mixing paint solvents, Aitken solicited the help of others, who were unaware they were constructing crude incendiary devices. While he failed to start diversionary fires in the boarding houses where he stayed near the dockyard, he was able to get into Portsmouth's rope house and start a fire which destroyed the brick structure. However, the overall dockyard was saved by the quick action of firefighters and as the tide was in, nearby vessels with gunpowder were able to easily distance themselves from the blaze. Aitken fled to London, walking most of the way neither identified nor pursued. As rope-house fires were frequent in navy dockyards, at first the authorities thought the fire was an accident, but the remains of his fire-starting device were found in the ruins.

Aitkin moved on to Plymouth dockyard, but as a result of heightened security after the Portsmouth fire, he was unable to enter and continue his machinations. Moreover, he feared that Portsmouth ropemakers, who had been transferred to Plymouth as a result of the fire, would recognize him. In January 1777, he decided to focus on Britain's second port, Bristol, with a large merchant sailor population. He became convinced that setting fire to the city's merchant docks, warehouses and ships could be done as easily as at naval dockyards.[13] He placed four incendiary devices throughout the town, several of them on ships, but in his first attempt the fires failed to catch and the city fathers offered rewards to discover the culprit. Aitken continued to build devices and his next fire was more dangerous, burning several ships, warehouses and houses in the vicinity of Quay Lane. The city firefighters soon extinguished the fires, aided by soldiers and marines. As a result, Bristol's pro-war party was able to win elections over the Whig reconciliation party. This was the last fire that Aitken set, although he did spend two days at Chatham dockyard, making notes on its layout.

While Aitken worked alone, his movements had created the impression that a band of terrorists were operating throughout southern England. His trial revealed that he had received Dean's blessing.[14] In London, he had also disclosed his plans to Edward Bancroft, the double-agent who distanced himself from him. The North ministry did not pursue the trial evidence to its logical conclusion, hoping not to upset France into participating in the war. However, Aitken was hanged and a few days later, the Admiralty and the Navy Board paid out over £1,000 to several informers.

Recruiting Ship's Companies

It was far easier to build quality ships at the Royal Navy dockyards than to put together an experienced and harmonious ship's company. No problem was greater for the navy than manning, the only consolation being that it would be more of a problem for the French or American navies. Royal Navy officers had to draw on seamen, landsmen and volunteers from a variety of sources, no single method ensuring a complete ship's company.[15]

Competition for experienced seamen was fierce. The demands of merchant ships and the army, in addition to privateers, would cut into the pool of seamen.[16] Merchantmen and letters of marque offered wages that were far higher than the navy, whose low pay remained a constant. Within the navy itself, the transport service and the amphibious and inland North American operations absorbed numerous seamen who might have served on a warship.

In the distribution of prize awards from Admiralty courts, privateer owners and crews claimed to hold an edge. By one estimate, the number of prizes condemned in the American War were 1,312 for the privateers to 1,021 for the navy.[17] Even though it was not a primary duty, the Royal Navy's occasional prizes brought ships' companies rewards. Still, the lure of privateers' prize money made recruiting seamen for the wartime navy far more difficult. By February 1781, 19,465 seamen were employed by privateers, amounting to about 15 per cent of the seaborne labor force.

The shortage of seamen for the navy was also caused by dealers called crimps, who enticed seamen from their ships and sold them to the ship that offered the highest bid, usually from privateers or merchant ships. Crimps were free enterprise operators who took advantage of mariners in ports, where they spent their advances, wages or prize money. Crimps were men or women who kept taverns or lodging houses, encouraging every sort of dissipation so that seamen would spend themselves into debt and ultimately be offered a choice of debtors' prison or placement on the ship, which provided the crimp with the most lucrative return.[18] This was rarely the navy, for a press lieutenant had only 10 shillings to offer for an able seaman. Little could legally be done against the crimp because their crime was only a misdemeanor.

The navy's officers were responsible for raising the ship's company. Typically, in a new ship, no crew members were inherited. Recruits would consist of volunteers, impressed sailors and some sailors on loan from other ships. The impressed sailors were experienced seamen, while the volunteers were a mixed lot, some with experience, but many landsmen. The crews came from all over the British Isles and also included Cretans, Danes, Italians, Portuguese, Swedes, Hanoverians and Americans from every colony.[19]

At least a tenth of the crews were boys, apprentices and servants as young as 6, from all levels of society, who were in training to be future seamen or midshipmen. The need for boys was so demanding that a sea officer suggested that an institution be established 'for the education of sons of seamen, where they might be instructed in in reading, writing, accounts, navigation, drawing'.[20] It was to be erected near a dockyard so they would learn knotting, splicing and rigging of ships, and those boys who were inclined might be introduced to shipbuilding. At the age of 14, they would be either sent to sea or bound apprentices to shipwrights. Some historians see the boys as child labor, but it was the eighteenth century, where adolescence was non-existent, and caring parents wanted their young sons apprenticed to a trade. Service at sea was an opportunity, not only for poor orphans, but for parents who expected their son to become a captain or an admiral.

Impressment in Britain

Recruiting by impressment was the age-old right of the Crown to gain the labor of seafarers. Its role has been overemphasized because it could be abusive, with tales of men being physically forced to serve.[21] Established during the Seven Years' War, the impress service involved a lieutenant and a gang of six seamen seeking sailors that lived in a seaport or district. It was limited to existing sailors taken on shore and thus even in wartime, it contributed only about half of the necessary recruits – though they were the best seamen. More than half of the service's recruits were actually volunteers attracted by bounties and the fact that they could choose their own ship. When at peace, the press was scarcely needed to fill the reduced ranks. Most recruits who were pressed and kept, ultimately stayed on. Negotiations with the impress service were common. River Thames Watermen and others employed in marine activities were especially liable for impressment, but the guilds that represented them made arrangements to meet impressment quotas. While impressment was often condemned by civil authorities, no one cared to replace it. Thus, 'the haphazard tyranny of the press gang reflected the weakness of the government and the inability to impose any regulated system on the labour market for seafarers.'[22]

It is often overlooked that the Impressment Service not only was responsible for pressing seamen, but also collecting volunteers. In wartime they made up half of those manning ships.[23] Landsmen were usually offered bounties by their local communities to volunteer, and although they were untrained and inexperienced, they had the potential to eventually make a deck sailor. The poorer and remoter parts of Britain were ideal recruiting grounds for volunteers. Pay was never an attraction for volunteers since it remained the same from 1653 to 1797. Instead, volunteers were lured by a captain who had a reputation for fairness or a ship known for taking prizes. Officers appointed to a command were sent to their home districts to attract recruits. Some actually led their tenantry to join, much as had been done by lords in the Middle Ages. One other source of willing volunteers were prisoners of war and debtors' prisoners, although criminals were never accepted.

Roebuck Sails

Despite the difficulties of forming a ship's company and the turmoil at the dockyards, the *Roebuck* completed its fitting out at Chatham. On August 4, 1775, Captain Andrew Snape Hamond 'came aboard and took charge and made sail down the river to Sheerness where it anchored', signifying the Roebuck was being readied for its maiden voyage.[24]

Hamond had experience in American waters. Three years earlier, he had sailed as captain of the *Arethusa* to the North American Station, renewing his acquaintance with Boston, New York, Philadelphia, Cape Henry, Williamsburg, Charleston and Halifax.[25] While the *Arethusa* was repaired in Gosport, Virginia, he met Lord Dunmore and George Washington. As a mark of favor, Dunmore approved a claim for Hamond to receive almost 20,000 acres in western Virginia, although the claim was eventually disallowed. Probably as an escort for a tobacco convoy, Hamond returned to England in the *Arethusa,* which was paid off in November 1773.

Luckily, in the peace after the Seven Years' War, Hamond had Admiral Richard Howe as a patron, who saw to it that he had ships and moved through the ranks to become captain. It was difficult because in peacetime, the number of navy ships would be much reduced. Still, as violence in the colonies increased in 1773, the navy was not expanded and Hamond was placed on half pay, unemployed until June 1775, when he was saved by being assigned the command of the newly completed *Roebuck*. He wrote to a close friend that he had not solicited the position, but as problems in North America were festering, his experience in those waters had been a deciding factor in obtaining the command.[26]

In July, the Admiralty ordered that 'a small detached squadron under an able and discreet officer' should be sent south to Delaware Bay, Chesapeake Bay and the Bar of Charleston. They were to open up a new area to the blockade and also receive governors who needed their support and protect 'any of His Majesty's subjects who may require it'.[27] This would be Hamond's first assignment.

The Press Continues at Sea

In the American War, too many obstacles existed for the Royal Navy press to fully operate on shore, but at sea the blockade of the coastal waters allowed the press to be effective. Moreover, those pressed at sea were more likely to be skilled seamen than those taken on land. In September 1775, operating in Chesapeake Bay, navy sloops like the *Otter*, under Captain Squire, made impressment a routine part of inspecting inward-bound ships. Squire stopped a ship coming from the Eastern Shore carrying a man identified as 'raising men to fight against the king'.[28] To punish and make use of him, Squire 'Prest him to raise men for the Otter'. A week later, Squire confronted two merchant vessels, one bound for Bristol, the other for Glasgow, with cargos of rum, sugar, coffee and beeswax. While the cargos were tempting, what Squire really wanted was seamen, so he impressed one man from each ship's crew. The *Otter*'s press would take no more than a few experienced mariners directly from ships it encountered, so as not cripple the ship's ability to continue its voyage. If this method was too slow, the possibility of recruiting the crews of captured prizes also existed. In 1776, Hamond impressed the entire crew of the private schooner *Betsey*, the schooner itself being left in the owner's care.[29]

After their arrival in Chesapeake Bay and the Delaware River, Hamond, Squire and other Royal Navy captains used the press, chiefly to man their tenders and smaller galleys and barges. The advantage of pressing by tender was that the officers and men taken stepped directly into their new positions, without the usual distribution delays. While it was soon realized that smaller vessels were needed for control of the shallows, their need for the crews caused further contraction in the pool of seamen. When aggressive Matthew Squire of the *Otter* outfitted his second tender, Hamond was not pleased because he felt the *Otter* was too small to have more than one tender.[30] This rivalry over crews for Royal Navy tenders was further complicated when Virginia's Governor Dunmore created additional crew shortages by purchasing five more ships to serve as his tenders. Technically, these new commissions were Loyalist privateers serving under Dunmore as Admiral of the Virginia navy. The need for crew members and outfitting these new ships could not be filled by Hamond, forcing Dunmore to go to the Maryland and Virginia Eastern Shore to recruit his crews. The creation of even a small ship's company was a complicated process.

Chapter 2

Administering the Royal Navy

As the American crisis deepened, it forced Frederick, Lord North and his ministry to defend the English constitution, fundamentally the King in Parliament. At the time, the ministry was not unified, for true cabinet government had yet to emerge. North's weak leadership meant some ministers did all they could to further their own interests at the expense of others. In November 1775, the person who was placed in charge of the American War, Lord George Germain, the Secretary of State for the Colonies, fitted this description perfectly.[1] While he was an able administrator and supportive of crushing the American rebellion by any means, his personality prevented him from working with the rest of the cabinet. His cold and arrogant demeanor isolated him from the others. He was certainly not a team player, as he worked to obstruct and undermine his colleagues, and he felt that every disappointment in the war was caused by his fellow ministers, not him. His chief obstacle in the cabinet was the Earl of Sandwich, First Lord of the Admiralty. While Germain realized how important the navy was to operations in America, it was not in him to cooperate with Sandwich. Sandwich would have to leverage his leadership of the Royal Navy to work within this difficult situation.

Admiralty

The most renowned naval administrative board, the Admiralty, initiated policy and as its First Lord was a cabinet member, thus he was involved in debates, consensus and the monarch's approval of military policy. It was in the cabinet rather than at the Admiralty that strategy was hammered out. The first and junior lords of the Admiralty were political appointees, holding office only as long as a particular administration was in power. As the North ministry survived for most of the war, Sandwich's continuity made him the key figure in the navy's strategy. His reputation suffered afterwards because he was regarded as a man of pleasure, having had a mistress who was murdered by an unhinged admirer.[2] He was also a politician rather an experienced naval officer, which made admirals suspicious of him. In fact, he was a man of tireless duty to the navy, who displayed a necessary flair for international diplomacy. He was also a skilled parliamentary manager and a tactful distributor of Admiralty patronage, including the promotion of admirals.

The Admiralty focused on the sea service, especially the discipline of officers and crews, and also the improvement of ship design.[3] Secretaries of State in the cabinet conveyed orders from the cabinet to the Admiralty. It met three or four times a week to formulate orders, which were then sent by its two secretaries to related entities like the Navy Board. Occasionally, the secretaries actually wrote letters directly to commanders at sea.

The Admiralty would be concerned to provide timely escorts for the supply convoys that plied the Atlantic.[4] A few navy warships served as escorts, attempting to hold convoys together by firing cannon as signals. This was nothing new; navy ships had been protecting tobacco convoys from the Chesapeake against French and Spanish privateers in the century before the American conflict. At first, the Admiralty underestimated the number of escorts necessary as the demand for convoys grew. Escorts often were delayed for weeks before transports were completely loaded. In May 1779, the *Roebuck* arrived at Cork, Ireland to escort a convoy of victuallers, but was forced to wait for over three weeks before it could sail for New York.

While the Admiralty may have appeared to be at the top of naval administration, its staff was actually small compared to that of other boards which assumed the responsibility for specialized support, leaving the Admiralty dependent on them, but without the ability to override them. Separate boards existed for Victualling (purchase, packing and storing food and drink), Sick and Hurt (caring for the navy's sick and wounded as well as prisoners of war), and Ordnance (issuing guns and warlike stores).[5] The largest board in terms of staff, the Navy Board, was a very rival to the Admiralty.

Navy Board

Although subordinate to the Admiralty because it lacked the political prestige of a cabinet seat, the Navy Board was an older institution, having been established by Henry VIII.[6] It oversaw the sinews of the navy, being responsible for the maintenance of the dockyards, the building of ships, technological improvements to ships and the financial records and expenditures for these activities. Sandwich could intervene, as we have noted, but the Navy Board had its own comptroller and members. During the war, it would become more powerful because of its responsibility for transport, which led it to absorb the responsibilities of rival boards involved in that business.

The Navy Board was responsible for the supply system that had first responded to the American rebellion. Its responsibilities were the transport of troops, naval stores, military clothing and equipment and, after 1779, provisions. Supplies were gathered in and shipped from the British Isles, usually the port of Cork or Isle of Wight port of Cowes.[7] Despite the difficulties of supplying military forces across the Atlantic, most convoys would arrive at New York or Halifax, where a surplus of supplies would be maintained for distribution.

The Board's staff directly supervised the transport service, hiring merchant ships under long- and short-term contracts. Those under long-term contracts as transports, storeships and victuallers, were 'the backbone of the transport service'.[8] As the war progressed, short-term contracts multiplied for ships or cargo space in British merchant ships, which were chartered for a single voyage to meet a specific military goal. The private owners of hired ships were required to have their ships properly manned, equipped, and repaired according to a charter. They were further charged with preventing fraud, such as carrying private cargos that violated their charter.

The Board conveyed orders to the masters of these hired ships and it was agents who made sure they were carried out. Transport agents were navy lieutenants with considerable experience.[9] While those in England were recommended by the Navy Board, in American waters, military and naval commanders might appoint their own agent locally. Agents were concentrated in three areas: those at British Isles dockyards and ports; those that traveled back and forth across the Atlantic with convoys and flotillas; and those stationed overseas, especially in New York and Halifax.

Agents at Deptford, Portsmouth and Cork dockyards were directly under the command of the Navy Board. Deptford on the River Thames was the major base for measuring, fitting and storing transports, victuallers and storeships. Once transports were made ready at Deptford, they were sent to other ports for loading. The Deptford agent was chief enforcer of the Board's orders. The Portsmouth agent became important during the war because many convoys began their journey from there. From 1779, Cork became a crucial link in the convoy system because it was the final place of inspection in the British Isles, especially for victuallers, who carried Irish farm products.

Early in the war, supply had been the responsibility of the Treasury Department, which was under the control of Lord Germain, who operated it to the detriment of the Navy Board by outbidding them for ships. In 1779, in a major administrative reform, the Navy Board took over the duty of providing the Victualling Board with transport at the right time and place.[10] The Treasury still defined the amount and type of provisions. Although the transition took more than a year to be effective, in the long run the Navy Board was able to supply the army, navy and their Loyalists and Indians for the rest of the war.

Convoys

In the beginning, victuallers had been allowed to travel the Atlantic on their own, but with the added French threat from 1778, the Navy Board required them to join an escorted convoy.[11] The bulk of the King's troops were raised and equipped in Europe and convoys carrying them, their gear and munitions became the best means of pursuing the war. Private ship owners were attracted to participate in convoys because profits, while small, were steady as the Board paid a monthly rate according to the ship's burden and their investment was protected by the navy escort.[12] The Board also compensated convoy owners, whose ships were taken or destroyed by the enemy.

The convoys had their problems. The victuallers did not immediately return from America, causing a shortage of transports in England.[13] The victuallers were detained in America for various reasons: they were asked to serve as floating warehouses, prisons or hospitals; their crews were impressed or they were forced to become troop transports on expeditions; and customs officers periodically delayed them for unloading infractions. Even if empty and ready to sail, they had to be organized for the return in a convoy protected by the navy.

Although the convoys would be the chief target of rebel privateers, few soldiers were actually lost at sea or captured by the enemy. The long Atlantic voyage was the chief cause of casualties in reinforcements because of the sickness experienced by troops and crews.[14] Mortality on transports sometimes approached those of slave ships. Rations provided by the Victualling Board were only two-thirds of what they would be on land, with the exception of rum which was a full ration. It was felt the sedentary life on board did not require so many calories.

Suppling a Squadron

Returning to the *Roebuck*'s first voyage across the Atlantic, we see Hamond was immediately enmeshed in this supply system, linking British resources to his own squadron. He sailed the *Roebuck* from Sheerness to Spithead and Yarmouth and then Guernsey Island before venturing out into the Atlantic alone.[15] By the end of September 1775, the *Roebuck* was following the northern convoy route toward New England, the shortest distance from the British Isles. Its destination was Halifax, Nova Scotia, then the only North American naval yard and supply base. The *Roebuck* carried crusty Marriott Arbuthnot, who had accepted the positions of commissioner of the careening yard, commodore at Halifax, and Lieutenant Governor of Nova Scotia. Arbuthnot and Hamond become friends on the voyage for their paths would cross often as the war continued. It also carried £10,000 in coin from the Navy Board to support the operations of Halifax's careening yard.

When the *Roebuck* arrived at Halifax on November 1, Arbuthnot was immediately upset by the lack of troops he found there. He detained the *Roebuck* as he feared the port would be attacked, ordering it to cover the shore in front of the careening yard. Arbuthnot found that the garrison numbered only 300 men, so that he needed the *Roebuck*'s 120 marines. Thirty-two of them were sent to guard the careening yard and storage. So short-handed was he that he had Hamond initiate a press of European seamen in Halifax, 'taking care not to enter Americans except a few good seamen, nor to take any but able-bodied healthy men …'[16] The Nova Scotia General Assembly had appealed to the previous governor, Francis Legge, that 'Seamen belonging to the Vessels in Nova Scotia may not be impressed', but Arbuthnot ignored this plea as he needed seamen to man his ships.

While Arbuthnot would have kept the *Roebuck* indefinitely, on Christmas Day, Admiral Samuel Graves, commander of the North American station in Boston, ordered Hamond to gather stores and leave Halifax. Following orders from the Admiralty, his assignment was to sail to the Delaware and Chesapeake Capes and take command of a squadron of navy ships already there. When Hamond left on January 14, 1776, Halifax could provide him with twelve months of sea stores and six months of provisions. It included 600 pieces of beef, ten barrels of limes and oranges to prevent scurvy, and 100 pounds of matches, but no butter because it was rancid.[17] Throughout 1776, this food would not only be used by the *Roebuck* but its squadron and even Governor Dunmore's Chesapeake fleet of 100 sail. Acting as a provisions transport, the *Roebuck* was able to reach the squadron guarding the entrances to Delaware and Chesapeake Bays.

In early February 1776, Hamond began distribution of the Halifax supplies in the Chesapeake. He first ordered his purser to provide the *Kingfisher*, the ship in greatest need, with 1,500 pounds of bread, eight bushels of pease and fifty pairs of shoes. The *Kingfisher* also received from the *Roebuck*'s 'Gunner … 5 barrels of powder, 100 pairs of Paper Cartridges, and 28 pounds of No Match', while its 'Carpenter offered a few nails and some Tin & Leather'.[18]

On the *Roebuck*, it was the purser, James Mason, who was in charge of maintaining and distributing food and drink.[19] The purser had to keep good accounts of these supplies because he was responsible for the entire value of the stores issued in England by the Victualling Board. His records covered every officer and man of the ship's company for each day, but he was only paid when food was actually consumed. The purser also issued clothes, which he had obtained from a clothing contractor. He could act as a private merchant, selling items not provided by the navy, such as tobacco. He worked closely with the cooper, monitoring the number of casks in the hold that were maintained by the cooper. He shared the responsibility for the mess book with the cooper, recording the consumption of food in the different messes onboard.

The *Roebuck*'s gunner was a warrant officer, who had risen from the ratings to become responsible for ordnance and powder.[20] His duties were unusual in that he rendered his accounts and received warrants from the Ordnance Board, separate from the Navy Board. On the ship, the gunner and carpenter acted as naval officers and might even stand watch. In battle, the gunner and his mates made up cartridges for each gun, which boys carried to them in sparkproof cases. The carpenter was also a warrant officer, responsible for the maintenance of the ship's hull, masts and spars. On board, carpenters were unique because their career had developed at a Royal Navy dockyard, and to qualify, they had to have been a shipwright of a year's standing. A crucial duty for them was to plug holes in the ship's sides as quickly as possible to prevent flooding.

In the next months, Hamond would have few problems with food supplies. He actually had food to spare for other British posts. When he was informed that the garrison at distant St Augustine, Florida was 'in the greatest distress imaginable for want of 10th Provisions', he dispatched a tender to Florida with flour, beef and everything that could be collected.[21]

Hamond would be most concerned to fill his fresh water casks, a commodity which only could be obtained locally. He would risk military confrontation to get the precious water. It was not exactly for drinking, as most fresh water was regarded as contaminated. Instead, water was mixed with wine, rum or spirits to produce a beverage, which seamen consumed alongside their ration of beer.[22] Water was also crucial for cooking meat and dried vegetables, which had to be soaked. Mixed with vinegar, fresh water was the favorite means of the weekly cleaning of the ship's deck and hold. Another commodity Hamond sought was wood, the chief use being as cooking fuel, although it was supplemented by available coal. Wood was also needed for ship repairs and making barrel staves.

Fresh provisions were known to make a heathier crew and ultimately, they could only be obtained locally. Rebels 'saw Cattle [o]n the Decks' of the *Roebuck*, showing that livestock was present, even in hostile waters.[23] It was not practical to ship live cattle from England, so crews spent time locally searching for a few cattle, which were driven on board, slaughtered and eaten immediately. The salting and barreling of meat on land was too arduous a process for naval foraging parties, who were unlikely to have enough time for the processing.

An undated story exists of a Hamond forage party meeting with a true Whig and worthy farmer, named Israel, residing with cattle on the banks of the Delaware River. He was, for a short time, held on board the *Roebuck*, directly opposite his house and land. While on board, it was reported by Loyalists that he had said that 'he would sooner drive his cattle as a present to George Washington, than receive thousands of dollars in British gold for them'.[24] Hamond sent a detachment of sailors to drive his cattle down to the Delaware River and have them slaughtered. 'Mrs Israel, who was young and sprightly, and brave as a Spartan', seeing the movements of the sailors as she stood in her doorway, and realizing their purpose as they marched towards the meadow where the cattle were grazing, called a boy about 8 years old, and started off to stop them. They threatened and she defied them, till at last they fired at her. The cattle, more terrified than she, scattered over the fields; she called on the boy 'Joe' the louder and more earnestly to help with the cattle, determined that the assailants should not have even one animal from the herd. She drove them all into the barnyard, and the sailors, 'out of respect to her courage, or for some other cause', ceased their efforts and returned to the *Roebuck*. Such incidents were commonplace in the *Roebuck*'s career, usually with more success than in this story from the pen of nineteenth-century American feminist author Lydia Howard Sigourney.

Here was the process of supplying a squadron on the most local level. Still, it should be clear that the Navy Board was able supply not just Halifax but places as widely dispersed as New York, the West Indies, the Mediterranean or even India. This was an indication of the superiority of the British war machine, which made the Royal Navy and British army independent of most local supply conditions.

Chapter 3

Coping with Rebellion

In February 1775, before Lexington and Concord, a young student at King's College in New York penned a pamphlet, *The Farmer Refuted,* opposing the right of Parliament to tax its colonies without their consent. However, Alexander Hamilton had to admit:

> Great-Britain is a maritime power; that the present flourishing state of her trade and of the trade of her colonies depends, in a great measure, upon the protection which they receive from the navy; that her own security depends upon her navy, and that it is principally, a naval protection, we receive from her, there will appear a peculiar propriety in laying the chief burthen of supporting her navy, upon her commerce; and in requesting us to bear a part of the expence, [*sic*] proportional to our ability, and to that protection and security which we receive from it.[1]

Hamilton tells us that a respect had developed for the Royal Navy during the colonial era because it protected trade. Thus, he was willing to make an exception and have the colonies pay toward support of the Royal Navy because it facilitated their trade. Such respect would be undermined in 1775, as in the eyes of many colonials, the Royal Navy had turned from being protector into a destructive enemy.

Policing the Rebellion

After Lexington and Concord in April, the North ministry faced the difficulty of choosing the best options to quell the rebellion.[2] The issues at stake were political rather than military for they concerned the relations between the ministry and the governed colonials, which demanded a political solution. This seemed impossible until order was restored in Massachusetts. Police action by the army to restore order in Britain had become common in the eighteenth century and this was what the ministry contemplated. The rebellion was seen as an internal affair in which the military would bring peace to the riotous Bostonians.

In the colonies, the Royal Navy had been policing smugglers and maintaining customs duties and regulations, avoiding outright military conflict. In October 1774, Captain James Wallace with the 20-gun post ship *Rose* was sent to Boston. He became engaged in inspections of the coastal towns between Boston and Long Island, where signs of rebellion existed.[3] He was ordered to Narragansett Bay in Rhode Island to put an end to the smuggling that had made slave-trading Newport one of the wealthiest cities in America. Wallace was an effective commander, pressing sailors from merchant vessels and seeking provisions for the British garrison at Boston, as well as bringing smuggling to a standstill. His success led Rhode Island's merchants to petition their legislature to create a navy to deal with him. They backed up their petitions with the cash to fit out merchant vessels for naval service. They commissioned the sloop of war *Providence*, which would be John Paul Jones' first naval command.

Wallace was born in Loddon, Norfolk in 1731, the son of Thomas and Mary Wallace. In 1746, he had entered the Royal Navy at age of 15 and was promoted to lieutenant and then commander in 1762. He was an experienced 44-year-old when the Revolution broke out. In 1775, as he returned to winter at Newport, he found that Fort George had been cleared of artillery and stores and he was informed that his continued berthing at the port was likely to be met with difficulty.[4] Nevertheless, he remained, maintaining peace and order. Forming a landing party of sailors and Royal Marines, Wallace bombarded Bristol, Rhode Island, and threatened to do the same to Newport unless it met his demand to re-provision his ships at their expense. In early 1776 he fell in with two rebel privateers consisting of twenty and sixteen guns respectively, and after an action at long range off Rhode Island, he rammed the smaller, causing her to sink and obliging her compatriot to flee. His boats collected survivors who were taken into the service.

While Wallace's efforts provided an uneasy standoff at Rhode Island's ports, he was bound to fall short because the navy had only a very few small ships to cover the expansive New England coast. Admiral Samuel Graves in Boston was blamed for this in the cabinet, and Sandwich informed him of the complaints, although he did not remove him. Graves decided to avoid his removal by a more aggressive policy, concentrating his slender resources on nine Massachusetts ports northeast of Boston.[5] Graves got no immediate reaction from the Admiralty, so he decided, uncharacteristically, to proceed on his own. What he wanted was an attack on the insurgents in these Massachusetts ports, using the threat of naval bombardment as a last resort.

To carry out this port pacification, Graves needed the cooperation of General Thomas Gage, military commander in Boston, from whom he requested troops, transports and artillery. Gage was less than enthusiastic, sparing only two transports, so that Graves was forced to bring about his effort on a shoestring. To command the tiny force, he selected Lieutenant Henry Mowat of 8-gun *Canceaux,* and added the 6-gun schooner *Halifax* and an armed transport, *Symmetry,* and the sloop, *Spitefire.* In addition to their crews, the vessels carried 100 marines.[6] Mowat, a Scot, who had entered the navy at 18, had come to the region in 1764 when he conducted a hydrographic survey of the New England coast, giving him an exceptional knowledge of its waterways. He would command the *Canceaux* for the next twelve years.

On October 11, Mowat's squadron left Boston, arriving at its first objective Cape Ann.[7] Following the advice of his artillery officer that the Cape's buildings were too far apart to be effectively bombarded, they sailed on, passing Newburyport, Ipswich, Portsmouth and Saco, so that they were just south of Falmouth (now Portland, Maine) in Casco Bay.

Falmouth's 2,000 inhabitants in 300 houses were known for their mast and lumber exports, shipbuilding and trade. The town had also acquired the reputation of being 'Boston's younger sister in rebellion'.[8] This epitaph was an exaggeration, as places like Brunswick, 30 miles to the north, were far more united in support of the rebellion. There, Samuel Thompson headed the local enforcement committee for the Continental Association to boycott British manufactures. In March 1775, he had intervened in Falmouth, attempting to enforce the boycott, demanding that Falmouth shipbuilder Captain Samuel Coulson have the English sloop *John and Mary* leave the port without unloading its ordered sail, rope and rigging. Falmouth was ambiguous on the boycott and Coulson requested delay while the English ship completed needed repairs after its transatlantic voyage.

Meanwhile Falmouth's sheriff, William Tyng, had written to Boston for help and in response Graves ordered Mowat's *Canceaux* to Falmouth to assist Coulson. Mowat arrived at Falmouth on March 29, protecting Coulson who offloaded his maritime goods.[9] Mowat's presence bolstered support for the British and the customs officials, who begged him to remain as long as possible. Meanwhile in Brunswick, the militia – inspired by the news of Lexington and Concord – laid plans to capture the *Canceaux*, disregarding the request of the Falmouth Committee of Correspondence to stay away. Thompson's militia landed near Falmouth and concealed themselves in the woods. When Mowat came ashore to arrange for religious services for his crew, he was taken prisoner by the Brunswickers. His officers on the *Canceaux* threatened to shell the town if Mowat were not returned. Thompson's surrounding militia now numbered 600 and Falmouth townspeople expressed their displeasure, so he agreed to free Mowat. Back on his ship, he wanted Thompson arrested, but his demand was refused, and the drunken militia began to loot the homes of possible Loyalists, including those of Coulson and Sheriff Tyng. The militia left on May 12, complaining of their treatment by Falmouth's inhabitants. After being assured that Falmouth had done all it could to resist the invading militia, Mowat left Falmouth a few days later.

The Thompson incident is context for Mowat's October arrival before Falmouth. The Falmouth authorities assumed that his squadron was a mere foraging expedition intending to take some of the town's livestock and hay. Mowat anchored abreast the town but made no effort to fire his guns, instead sending a junior officer to explain why they had returned. He said he would give the inhabitants time to clear out of town in preparation for an unspecified 'just Punishment', although he would receive on board his ships any who would accept the king's protection.[10] While his orders forbade him to delay further, he received three leading citizens who came to negotiate. He revealed to them that he was to 'burn, sink and destroy' the town and they pleaded with him to spare the town or at least allow time to remove their valuables. Moved by their pleas, Mowat stipulated that if they would deliver their arms and ammunition to him, he would send an express to Boston to clarify Graves' instructions. If at least some arms were sent to him that evening, he would hold off a decision until the next morning. Only a few muskets were delivered, however, and the inhabitants spent the night leaving, with their possessions, to safety away from the coast.

Not having received the required arms, at 9.40 a.m. the next morning, Mowat's vessels begun bombardment of the town. At first, a strong wind prevented their artillery from doing damage and at least one of his ships was damaged by its own artillery recoil. He was forced to send parties of seamen and marines ashore to spread fire. Little opposition came from the local militia and ultimately a strong wind burnt two-thirds of the town and ships in the harbor.[11] When Mowat left, he carried no Loyalists with him because the rebels had threatened to shoot them if they boarded his ships. He had delayed his action by negotiating with the town fathers, avoiding bombardment till the last. He realized his bombardment required larger ships and heavier ordnance to be successful. No other Massachusetts port would suffer Falmouth's fate from Mowat's expedition.

Graves had hoped that Mowat's expedition to the Massachusetts ports would change the perception of him in London; in fact his recall had been sent but did not arrive until after Mowat left. Graves was replaced by Rear Admiral Molyneux Shuldham, who would not continue his bombardment policy. Graves completed a straightforward report of the Mowat's expedition in January 1776 and little more appeared in British periodicals.[12] By February 1776, day and night guards were in place in Falmouth, as were procedures to identify all ships before they entered the harbor.

Norfolk Destroyed

In contrast with Falmouth, a few months later, an even more complicated bombardment situation developed in Virginia's chief port of Norfolk. With a population of 6,000, Norfolk was the colonies' most northerly ice-free port. By the mid-eighteenth century, it was the home of many mariners and had a waterfront workforce, including blacks. It had its own crimps, acting as middle men for the merchants and privateers in recruiting crews, as they did in England. Crimps ran the taverns and lodging houses, which were the chief places of enticement. The 'Very sensible and artful' slave Mary was seen on her way to Norfolk as 'she likes much to be on board of vessels, and in the company of sailors.'[13] Runaway slaves could pass for free persons in Norfolk.

On November 15, 1775, to raise more troops, Virginia's Governor Dunmore had issued a proclamation calling on all able-bodied men to assist him in the defense of the colony, including slaves and white indentured servants, who were promised their freedom in exchange for service in his army. In December, the Virginia Convention replied to the proclamation by branding his offer of freedom as a blow to the foundations of Virginia's plantation society.[14] It sent Virginia militia and Continentals under Colonel William Woodford and Colonel Robert Howe to occupy Norfolk. Many of its inhabitants had joined Dunmore and a Royal Navy squadron led by the 20-gun frigate *Liverpool,* moving from their homes to their own vessels in Norfolk's harbor. This was before the *Roebuck* arrived at the Chesapeake Capes. Dunmore retained a certain authority with his fleet and politely sought permission from Howe to purchase provisions in Norfolk and also to protect Loyalist property. Howe was responsible to the Convention in Williamsburg and while he requested their advice, he seems to have not waited for it, and as Norfolk's municipal government had ceased to exist, in practice Howe conducted a strictly military occupation.

On New Year's Day, responding to 'shirtmen' who sniped at his fleet and paraded, Dunmore began an unsuccessful bombardment, which forced him to send parties to the dockyards to flush out rebel marksmen. Howe and Woodford had already requested permission from the Convention to burn Loyalist properties, and when a dockyards fire broke out, they encouraged it rather than attempting to put it out. For the next three days, the Virginia troops were out of control and looted and burned, not just Loyalist properties but also those of rebels. The log of the *Liverpool* showed the destruction lasted on and off for the rest of January, ultimately the rebels destroying 863 structures valued at £120,000, while briefly, Dunmore had only burnt nineteen worth £3,000.[15] Howe went to Williamsburg to report to the Convention, requesting that his men be allowed to destroy the remaining town, failing to mention the destruction his men had already wrought. The Convention agreed and he returned to destroy 416 more structures. Norfolk was gone and the rebel leadership put out the word that Dunmore had burnt the city, when in fact it had been done by rampaging militia and Continentals.

The Royal Navy had gone from being the protector of the colonial trade to being charged with destroying colonial ports. Norfolk and Falmouth were but the first victims of a civil war which now seemed inevitable. The use of bombardment, especially if the ships were small, had proved ineffective. However, land-based arson made up for it. In this activity, rampant militia and even Continentals were best, although Royal Navy sailors would do it if ordered. Massachusetts newspapers called the destruction of Falmouth savage and brutal as they sought support for the rebellion that started there. The responsibility for the burning of Norfolk would be hidden from the public by the Virginia Convention.

PART 2

FORMING A NEW NAVY

Chapter 4

Colonial Maritime Tradition

During the colonial wars, under the protection of the Royal Navy, the rebellious colonies had developed a strong maritime tradition, based on Atlantic trade. The British Empire was bound together by trade in colonial staple crops and British manufactures on the most local level. For instance, by the 1740s, the tobacco trade originating in Chesapeake Bay ensured that nearly half of British exports went to Maryland and Virginia.[1] Annual tobacco convoys were organized by merchants from Chesapeake ports like Norfolk to Liverpool and Glasgow in Britain. Maritime historian Arthur Middleton has described the convoys leaving Chesapeake Bay:

> Nowhere else in the British Empire could an observer see a more important demonstration of the old colonial system. Here, stretching before him, was a vast, richly laden fleet of two hundred ships bound for England with the annual produce of two of her most prosperous colonies. Here, indeed, was the embodiment of maritime intercourse between colonies and mother country upon which the economic structure of the empire rested.[2]

Colonial Merchants

Alongside the tobacco trade, increasingly in the eighteenth century was the grain trade, which focused on wheat and corn being sent to the West Indies. This trade was not limited to the Chesapeake but also involved New York, Pennsylvania and Delaware, where wheat flourished. Increasingly, merchants in upper Chesapeake began to look toward nearby Philadelphia's merchants to facilitate this trade. As early as 1737, Philadelphia was the usual port for Chesapeake merchants to cash bills of exchange for the hard currency needed for trading in the West Indies.[3] Because Philadelphia merchants could collect grain from several areas they were able to load their vessels at once, while Chesapeake merchants were delayed in putting together a cargo. By the 1770s, Philadelphia firms had taken over the long-distance grain trade.

As the Revolution approached, an influential Philadelphia merchant was Robert Morris Jr. Born in Liverpool, England on January 20, 1734, he had been raised by his maternal grandmother until the age of 13, when he immigrated to the port of Oxford, Maryland.[4] He lived with his father, Robert Sr., who provided him with a tutor, but he quickly learned everything that he could and his father sent him to Philadelphia for further experience. He stayed with Charles Greenway, a family friend, who arranged for young Robert to become an apprentice at the shipping and banking firm of British-born merchant Charles Willing. Robert inherited his father's estate when he died and by 1757, he was a partner in the firm of Willing, Morris & Company. The firm traded in India, the Levant, and the West Indies and participated in the slave trade. Thus, the Morris merchant family became a fixture in Philadelphia's mercantile establishment and later, Robert would play a leading role in the administration of the Continental Navy.

Transatlantic Families

Merchant families with ties on both sides of the Atlantic were fundamental players in the empire of trade. New York's Cruger merchant family had come from Bristol, England, appearing in the city in 1698. By the 1750s, the family had its own docks on the East River, but it was also still involved in Bristol's trade, sending trawlers from there to the West Indies. Henry Cruger Sr. managed the selling of Hudson Valley flour in the West Indies. His sons, Henry Jr., John Harris, Teleman and Nicholas acted respectively as his factors in Bristol, Jamaica, Dutch 'Curassow', and Danish St Croix, creating a transatlantic family enterprise.[5] Unaware of the future, Nicholas had hired a bright 12-year-old named Alexander Hamilton as a clerk. The family business came to depend on sending English manufactures from Bristol to New York City and from there exporting fine flour and importing mahogany from the Bay of Honduras. In old age, as the Revolution raged, Henry Sr. would join his son Henry in Bristol, where he died in 1780 and was buried in the center aisle of Bristol Cathedral.

Henry Cruger Jr. became the family's most renowned member because he eventually became Mayor of Bristol and was elected as the port's representative to the Parliament. Born in New York in 1739, he attended King's College and at the age of 20 went permanently to the family counting house in Bristol. He was known as New York's largest exporter of flax seed and oil to Bristol, his ships returning with linen, candles, manufactures and bills of exchange. He made the rounds of the coffee houses and found friends he had made earlier in New York, who were now in semi-retirement, notably General Robert Monckton and his former aid, Captain Horatio Gates. How much influence disillusioned Gates had on Cruger is seen in that later political rivals called Cruger a 'hot Wilkite', a title which his moderate views did not match.[6] He did, as with his entire family and most Bristol merchants, oppose the Stamp Act of 1765. As a member of a Bristol merchant delegation, he spent three weeks in London, advocating the repeal of the act and his effort was rewarded by Bristol's citizens with a silver hot water urn. Later, he opposed the non-importation movement by the colonial legislatures because it stifled trade in general, remarking that one of his vessels from Boston had returned in ballast, 'unable to procure a freight for Love or money'. Cruger embodied the sentiments of both New York's and Bristol's merchants in the era leading to the Revolution, opposing measures that would restrict trade but stopping short of supporting the colonies' independence.

Slave Trade

In the eighteenth century, Newport, Rhode Island had the distinction of being more heavily involved in the slave trade than any other colonial port.[7] The trade required rum, either distilled in Newport from molasses or imported from the Caribbean. This liquid currency was used to purchase slaves on the West African coast, which then were sold in the Caribbean or southern American colonies. Rum was in great demand in Africa, giving Newport an advantage over English competition from Bristol or Liverpool, whose merchants traded for slaves in fabrics or East India goods. Vessels constructed for the slave trade were swift and small because a number of slaves had to be collected at several ports and then exported quickly to reach market without the impediments of slave sickness, injury or rebellion. The trade also meant that Newport's population in 1774 was one-ninth black, a high percentage for a New England community. Additionally, the number of adult males involved in the trade or lost at the sea was high, so the Newport's sex ratio was heavily in favor of women. While women were brought up to be dependent on their men, this maritime circumstance forced them to be independent in making day-to-day decisions while their menfolk were at sea. Many future Continental Navy captains began their maritime career navigating a slave ship.

Timber Economy

Beyond merchant trade connections, timber resources allowed for the development of the colonies maritime sector.[8] While lumber was abundant, it was not inexhaustible, so American communities and the Royal Navy attempted to restrict use of it. New Hampshire guarded its timber resources so as to protect its shipbuilding enterprises. In 1724, the New Hampshire General Assembly supplemented existing laws by fixing fines for cutting trees on another person's land or common land.[9] Even the making of barrel staves for sale outside of Portsmouth, New Hampshire was prohibited.

Building Warships

From the late seventeenth century, the trade between Britain and its colonies was jeopardized by pirates as well as French, Spanish and Dutch privateers. Armed escorts for the convoys were needed. Building warships, however, did not come easily to New England shipbuilders. This was because

> American shipwrights knew a good deal about building vessels for the merchant and fishing fleets but much less about building warships … Not only were they of greater size, but they also had to be more sturdily built to accommodate the weight of their armament and more heavily sparred to move their great bulk through the water.[10]

Unseasoned timber and slightly built frames could be built quickly, but such ships were by no means suited to the needs of the protecting Royal Navy.

Portsmouth, New Hampshire was one the few places with facilities considered sophisticated enough to build warships for the Navy Board. The colony's largest city, with a population of about 5,000, was located on the south side of the Piscataqua River before it entered the Atlantic Ocean. Fishing and West Indies trade had been the community's early sources of wealth.[11] A merchant oligarchy dominated Portsmouth, erecting substantial mansions and holding household slaves, reflecting a cosmopolitism born of trade. The lower orders consisted chiefly of mariners, who lacked property, in some cases probating none at all.

Proximity to waterways and standing timber made the Portsmouth area a center of shipbuilding. It built three of the four warships constructed in the colonies before the

Revolution: the *Falkland* and *Bedford* in 1695 and 1701, and the *America* constructed as compensation for the successful Louisbourg expedition in 1745.[12] The Navy Board considered these three contracts to be experiments as to the quality of ships produced in New England in comparison to those produced in private British yards. On the whole, the Board came to believe that New England timber was untreated and thus rotted quickly and therefore lacked the longevity the navy expected. This certainly was the case of the *America* and it would continue to be a drawback for ships built in the Revolution. The only way that New England timber became acceptable to the Board was in masts, and it appointed mast agents to mark selected trees with broad arrows and collect and finish them for use of the Royal Navy. They were exported to naval dockyards in large vessels with stern ports, although they had to compete with masts exported from Nova Scotia and the Baltic.

Maine's Falmouth region was also popular for shipbuilding, attracting shipwrights from the mother country. One example is Daniel Brocklebank from Whitehaven on the Irish Sea. He was born, son of the curate of nearby Torpenhow, Cumberland County in 1741 and apprenticed, aged 14, as a carpenter to a Whitehaven shipbuilder.[13] He became involved in shipbuilding by providing ships for the coal trade and purchased the Isaac Little & Co. Ropeworks. He married Whitehaven's Anne Cupperage at Holy Trinity Church. At the age of 28, Daniel decided to immigrate from Whitehaven to New England with his wife, baby daughter Sarah and his own carpenters and seamen.

Settling at Sheepscot, northeast of Falmouth, he had enough capital and resources to set up his own shipyard.[14] Two sons were born there, Daniel Jr. in 1773 and Thomas a year later. Between 1770 and 1775 he built five ships, including the *Castor*. When the American War began, he chose to be loyal to the crown, deciding to return to Whitehaven with his family. He sailed in his *Castor*, which had not completed its fitting and was forced to leave cargo behind. With insufficient supplies to complete an Atlantic voyage, he first headed for Newfoundland's fisheries. With the fish he caught and preserved in salt, extracted from between his ship's timbers, he arrived back in Whitehaven on June 11, 1775. Here he would begin his life anew by leasing the Brantsy Ropeworks.

Water-borne Employment

Just behind New England for shipbuilding was Chesapeake Bay. There, carpenters and shipwrights could prosper if involved in several projects, from erecting houses, to the fashioning of plows, carts and barrels, as well as the building of ships. Like New England, timber was abundant, but other necessities like nails were lacking. As early as 1641, on the Eastern Shore of Virginia, William Stevens claimed he had furnished a shipbuilder with 'nails of various size, six gallons of tar, and four days' work upon a shallop'.[15] Often, however, these items were not available, so that after construction, the fitting of ships was much delayed.

In the seventeenth century, few whites claimed to be mariners in the Chesapeake because of a lack of trade, competition from the northern colonies for sailors, and the conviction that tobacco planting was a surer way to prosperity. The crews of small sloops employed on the rivers were largely made up of slaves or a few free blacks.[16] After 1730, the number of native mariners increased because of expanding West Indies' trade. Three years later, in Maryland they numbered 106, rising to 480 by 1756, but declining after that as result of the Seven

Years' War. With the war over, trade revived and Chesapeake mariners rose to 1,200, while British-owned vessels in the Chesapeake employed almost 4,000 British mariners.[17] These increases were brought about by diversification away from tobacco and toward grain.

British sailors found the Chesapeake to be 'a very plentiful country' after their arduous voyage.[18] In the first half of the eighteenth century, however, the tobacco trade forced sailors to be stevedores, fetching and rolling the cumbersome nearly half-ton hogsheads to landings where they could be placed on ships. Furthermore, in the summer, as the sailors rolled the hogsheads, they drank spring water and cider to excess and were soon ill with fluxes and fevers. Mariners faced this strenuous work because ports were small and had no free labor force.

In 1747, Maryland passed the act establishing its tobacco warehouse system, relieving ship masters of the liability of sending crews to fetch tobacco from inland plantations, making it the responsibility of the plantation owner to get it to the warehouse for shipment.[19] The lack of free workers in the Chesapeake made it possible for mariners to demand higher wages, and the dispersed work places made it easier for them to desert, following the highest wages. Colonial governments did protect seamen's rights in the courts, where it was common for them to successfully sue for back wages.

Desertion of sailors on merchant ships became a problem for colonial governments and great planters because if crews were depleted, tobacco could not get to European markets in a timely fashion.[20] To prevent the threat of desertion in Chesapeake waters, mariners were prohibited from going ashore without leave. Also, they were only allowed limited credit at taverns and they could not cross a ferry or travel overland without permission from their captain. These local restrictions sounded almost like a slave code. To tide themselves over, some seamen took work on plantations. They could always be found congregating at the nearest tavern, where brawling was common as sailors took on each other, soldiers and locals.

The condition of Chesapeake mariners was different from the larger port cities of Boston, New York and Philadelphia, where their grievances led them to participate in riots. Eastern Shore mariners resided in a few small places like Chestertown, Oxford and Cambridge, which were too small for an urban crowd.[21] True, in Chestertown in 1757 a brawl developed which included sailors, British soldiers and town boys of good family. Casualties were limited to a single sailor and those charged were pardoned at the request of the ships' captains. Thus, while the possibility of mariner discontent existed, such incidents were rare because urban conditions were lacking.

In addition to sailors, trade offered employment to maritime support services. Crucial for seaborne commerce were the cooper's skills. Larger Royal Navy ships actually employed one, for on board food and water were stored in casks. The copper used staves, supported by wooden rims, to make the hogsheads in which tobacco was packed.[22] Levers, weights and screws were used to pressure as much tobacco as possible into the cask. The size of the Maryland hogshead grew in the eighteenth century to meet competition from Virginia and reached a point where it weighed between 950 and 1,400 pounds. The casks were stored tightly in the hold of a ship and accounts were registered in the number of casks rather than their weight. Many of these casks were made on plantations by slaves, who, because they were not experienced coopers, sometimes produced an inferior product. In rolling casks over rough trails, poorly made ones could fall apart. Planters, therefore, sought the best coopers to ensure the protection of their exported tobacco or grain.

The need for pilots was essential for Chesapeake Bay and the Delaware River, which abounded with treacherous shoals. Those captains who tried to navigate without a pilot often found themselves grounded on a sand bar. In Virginia, pilots were regarded as professionals and were licensed by the government, while in Maryland and Delaware, pilots were left unregulated.[23] Maryland's Calvert proprietors' efforts to license them were unsuccessful because they failed to prosecute unauthorized pilots; anyone with a knowledge of local soundings and a compass could claim to be pilot. When the Revolution began, the rebel authorities in Philadelphia feared that pilots in Sussex County, Delaware would guide the Royal Navy through its Delaware River defenses to the very gates of their city.

Impressment a Necessity

Some American historians make it seem that shore-based impressment was the only way the Royal Navy recruited and thus a key cause of colonial rebellion. To them impressment was an abuse that Atlantic sailors struggled against. These historians claim that this hostility 'first took shape among the buccaneers of America'.[24] Thus pirates and sailors are linked in protest in the early eighteenth century, to the violence against taxation of the 1760s and 1770s, which caused the American Revolution.

Most Chesapeake trade with Britain was not carried in colonial vessels, the tobacco convoys being made up of British merchant ships, whose seamen did not remain in the Chesapeake but were lured to New England's ports by lucrative privateering. Colonial merchants found their crews depleted by desertion and thus were unable to sail. They petitioned Maryland or Virginia governors for relief and in response the governor ordered Royal Navy warships to supply the petitioner with seamen.[25] To make up for its loss, the navy ship was then empowered by the governor to conduct an impressment. Governors granted requests to carry out presses to refill the navy's crews, so long as they met prohibitions like not appropriating men from crews with fewer than a dozen members. Unfortunately, some Royal Navy commanders were too desperate for sailors to wait for credentials to carry out impressment.

Impressment by colonials became a regulated and well-established practice by the Seven Years' War. When in 1767, Captain Jeremiah Morgan of the sloop *Hornet* attempted a night-time impress in Norfolk to obtain sailors, town authorities, including the mayor, calmly confronted him and forced him to leave empty handed.[26] In this case, the rioters were the Royal Navy pressmen, not sailors. In New York, the local magistrates organized New York militia to serve as press gangs in recruiting sailors for the hired transports that plied between the city and the British Isles. The press was an accepted necessity of maritime trade.

Narratives of impressment of sailors as a cause of the Revolution stop cold as the war commences because both sides were forced to use the impress more extensively than before. In Massachusetts in 1779, not only sailors but ships' cargoes of pork, beef, flour and bread would be impressed to feed a growing fleet. These historians now admit that sailors 'were read out of the settlement at the revolution's end'.[27] While dissident mariners may have helped to cause the Revolution, their early motives do not continue into the war. Mariners were not predisposed by the impress to support the rebel cause. In fact, as late as October 1783, Philadelphia seamen, blacks and 'loyalist leather-aprons' tore down the Stars and Stripes from Captain Stewart's vessel and triumphantly carried them through the streets.

Chapter 5

Congress Forms the Continental Navy

The creation of the Continental Navy was not so much a matter of political independence, but rather of economic necessity. In 1775, Congressional political leaders, merchants and supply commissaries supported the formation of the Continental Navy, believing its importance was to obtain materials to carry on war. The new navy was not charged with confronting the Royal Navy but rather to avoid its superior ships in an effort to continue trade. Typical efforts would involve salvaging stranded cargos of munitions and valuables before Royal Navy tenders could. The committees hoped that a substantial portion of the navy's revenue would somehow come from its ships taking prizes. At its birth, then, confusion existed as to whether the Continental Navy was primarily a military or trade endeavor.[1]

It would be overseen by Congress's Naval Committee, which in 1776 was renamed the Marine Committee. Top-heavy with New Englanders, its original members included John Langdon of New Hampshire, Silas Dean of Connecticut, John Adams of Massachusetts, Stephen Hopkins of Rhode Island, Richard Henry Lee of Virginia and Joseph Hewes of North and Christopher Gadsden of South Carolina.[2] Eventually, the committees would be phased out and the names of Robert Morris in Congress and Benjamin Franklin in France would dominate the navy's administration.

Building Ships

Even if Congress could not create a navy to confront the Royal Navy, it did commission and build warships. Most of the ships commissioned were converted merchantmen, although a few warships would be purposely built. Portsmouth, New Hampshire on the Piscataqua River was the home of several purpose-built ships for the Continental Navy, including the 18-gun sloop *Ranger*. It was the third ship built for the navy at John Langdon's shipyard, Badger's Island, Kittery Point, today's Maine.[3] He was a merchant, who had profited from trade to the West Indies and London. In 1777, he would be Speaker of the New Hampshire General Court and his state's representative to the Continental Congress. Fittingly, Langdon planned to name the new sloop *Hampshire,* but Congress preferred *Ranger*.

The *Ranger* was launched on May 10, 1777. Construction had been delayed because a warm January had made the delivery of hewn timber impossible. Further construction and outfitting would last until October. While twenty-six guns had been purchased for the *Ranger*, it was discovered that the ship was incapable of bearing the weight of that number and the complement was reduced to eighteen 6-pounders.[4] Also, thirteen swivels were purchased to supplement the armament. Its crew of sailors and marines had already been gathered and by August, rum had become an import expense meant to please them.

Construction continued as the bowsprit was placed by early June. Still to be found were an anchor, sweep oar, lanterns, thumbs, poles, pails, bolts of duck, medicine, axes, hinges, oakham for caulking and two pump hammers and two hawsers. Items needed for war included cartridge paper and boxes, powder horns, grape shot and cannisters.[5] Daily necessities would be tallow, candles, cabinets and lockers. Finally, a set of colors were required to identify or disguise the ship. Not until the last would it have a crucial suit of sails, of which half were made of inferior loose-woven cloth.

The construction quality of American ships like the *Ranger* had been debated before and continued to be at this time. A review of its later repairs shows that its captain had to make changes to the ship in Portsmouth before it ever sailed. As built, the vessel was oversparred, meaning the masts were too large for the ship, so that it needed a lower topside weight and center of gravity.[6] The best means of doing this was to reduce the ship's heavy armament. Also, on its Atlantic voyage the tiller rope broke, causing broaching. In France, thanks to Nantes' dockyards, it would be repaired, its masts shortened, more ballast added and new sails cut to replace those battered in the Atlantic crossing. To clean the *Ranger*'s already foul bottom, it was careened in a graving drydock, found only in France's most sophisticated dockyards. On the *Ranger*'s return Atlantic voyage, the fore topmast and main top gall mast were carried away, another sign that the ship was top-heavy. Finally in 1781, after it had been captured, the decision of the Royal Navy to sell rather than adopt the *Ranger* showed that it was not a durable vessel.

The *Ranger*'s situation was not unique. Of the original frigates authorized in 1775, none got to sea until 1777 and eight of those rendered no service while incurring considerable expense.[7] This situation would debilitate the navy for the rest of the war.

Continental Manning Problems

The Continental Navy also had difficulty in putting together crews. Often, navy ships were stranded in port for months, facing debilitating desertion and sickness, while they continued to lack sufficient sailors.[8] Stiff competition existed, not just from the Royal Navy, but state navies and privateers. Even the Continental army took its share when Colonel John Glover, a sea captain from Marblehead, Massachusetts, formed a 'Webfoot Regiment' for Washington to transport his troops by bateaux.

Marblehead, northeast of Boston, had conditions which allowed their fishermen to join crews not just of Glover, but of Continental and Massachusetts ships, privateers and even a local coastguard. Settled in 1629 by fishermen from the Channel Islands and Fowey in Cornwall, Marblehead developed as a fishing and shipbuilding center, replacing Boston as the Massachusetts' port of entry after passage of the Boston Port Bill in 1774. Built on a granite promontory, the community of 5,000 was known as a 'brawling, smelly [because of the drying fish], irreligious town'.[9] It was notorious for its population of growing boys, 'attributed to their feeding on Cod Heads, which is their principal diet'. Among them was Samuel Tucker, who would rise to become a merchant captain and go on to a career in the Continental Navy.

When the war came to Marblehead, unemployed fishermen looked on service in the Continental or state navies favorably because they could gain a share of prize money, although the former service required a long-time commitment. Privateers also offered shares, but they did not have regular pay. Marblehead's coastguard was singular. It was responsible for building and manning sea-coast defenses at its harbor entrances, guarding inbound and outbound vessels and challenging British vessels that attempted to enter. Marblehead maintained three 'Sea Coast Defense Companies' of fifty men each.[10] While the pay was low, men in these companies could remain in town and supplement their wages. These units also sustained vessels to patrol harbors. Still, the Marblehead situation was unique.

Inevitably captains and states were forced to turn to unpopular impressment. The Massachusetts General Court issued a press in 1779 for its expedition to Penobscot. A year later in Philadelphia, when Captain John Young began a press to man his sloop *Saratoga*, he was thrown in jail. In 1777, Captain James Nicholson desperately tried to man the *Virginia*. He decided to use the press on the Baltimore waterfront to fill his crew, adding thirty men to his rolls. However, Governor Johnson of Maryland had not been consulted and he demanded that the pressed men be released. Nicholson replied that he was under pressure from Congress to get his ship underway, that impressment had been going on in Philadelphia while Congress was sitting, and that he did not give a whit 'for the threats of any Council of Maryland'.[11] Congress backtracked and suspended Nicholson from his command, but he was reinstated after he made a grudging apology to Johnson. A year later, Nicholson sent a request to the Marine Committee asking that he be able to recruit mariners and naval officers in the West Indies, showing how desperate he remained for seamen. The request was not far-fetched because late in 1780 the American community at Dutch St Eustatius numbered 2,000.

After a ship's company was formed, Continental captains still lacked the support of their crews and it was commonplace for crews to mutiny.[12] The crews' polyglot makeup meant diverging reasons for going to sea. Loyalty to their hometown and by extension to shipmates from the same place was a primary motivation. Some historians have seen New England sailors' propensity to mutiny as a result of their commitment to democracy, meaning less inclination to take orders from officers.

Continental Captains

Due to Congress's emphasis on political appointments rather than sea experience, a top-heavy ratio of one officer for every ten men developed. As most of them had previous experience on privateers or transports, they felt the new navy would be most effective if its ships acted as privateers, combining self-interest with public service. They also seemed to be emotionally a bunch of jealous school boys and their personal antics have earned them the designation of being dystunctional.[13]

James Nicholson would block John Paul Jones' lobbying with Congress to become commander of the United States Navy because he felt Jones lacked seniority and that his exploits were as an adjunct to the French navy.[14] Nicholson had different qualities; while he was not a great sailor he did obey the orders of his superiors and he was respected in both the Maryland and Continental navies.

While court martials by their peers were regarded by captains as a chance to clear blots on their reputations, Continental captains fared badly. From 1776 through 1780, at least seven Continental captains were dragged before a court martial.[15] Five were dismissed and one, Abraham Whipple, was found guilty of poor judgement but remained in the service. Only one, John Manley, whom we shall hear about later, was exonerated.

Esek Hopkins

These conditions were first evident in 1775, when Congress designated Esek Hopkins commander-in-chief of the Fleet of the United Colonies and gave him command of eight converted merchantmen, the largest, his flagship the 20-gun *Alfred*. Esek's brother Stephen, a member of Congress's Naval Committee, was responsible for his appointment.[16] Their home, Rhode Island, was the first state to petition the Congress to form a navy to rid Narragansett Bay of Captain James Wallace's smuggler-seeking *Rose,* which was crippling Newport and Providence merchants.

Known as the 'Father of the American Navy', Esek was born in Scituate, Rhode Island where his family was prominent. At the age of 20 he went to sea and proved to be a good sailor and skilled merchant. He sailed to nearly every quarter of the Atlantic and commanded a privateer in the Seven Years' War.[17] In the interval between voyages, he was engaged in Rhode Island politics, serving as a deputy to the Rhode Island General Assembly. In September 1764, Hopkins took command of the slave ship *Sally*, owned by the influential Nicholas Brown and Company. Hopkins had no prior experience in sailing a slaver and as a result the fifteen-month voyage would cause the death of 109 out of 196 slaves. When *Sally* arrived in the West Indies, the surviving African captives were in such poor condition that most sold below expectation. Hopkins' failure with the slaver contributed to the Brown brothers reconsidering their participation in Rhode Island's slave trade.

Hopkins' orders from the Naval Committee on January 5, 1776 read: 'Proceed directly for Chesapeake Bay … and if …you find that [the enemy] are not greatly superior to your own you are immediately to enter the said bay, search out and attack, take or destroy all the naval forces of our enemies you may find there.'[18] A few days later, the Committee added that he was to seek information on 'Lord Dunmore's fleet and land forces'. Clearly Congress wanted him to shadow Dunmore's fleet and protect rebel shipping in Chesapeake and as far south as the Carolinas.

However, Hopkins completely ignored his orders without informing Congress or making any effort to ascertain the strength of Dunmore. At his court martial in August, he defended himself by stating his orders could be dispensed with, on account of 'bad winds, or stormy weather, or any unseen accident of disaster discernable to you …'[19] Still, the committee had assumed that he would make every effort to protect rebel shipping in the South.

Hopkins feared a confrontation with the Royal Navy, believing the preservation and profitability of his fleet was primary. Since his ships were converted merchantmen, he also seems to have assumed that he was a privateer, primarily concerned to use his ships to take enemy merchantmen as prizes. In fairness to Hopkins, the committee had not yet formulated a naval policy for prizes. Clearly, Hopkins and Congress's Naval Committee had rather different perceptions of the role of the Continental Navy.[20]

From here the story of Hopkins' squadron is well known. He sailed from Philadelphia directly to the Bahama Islands, skipping Chesapeake Bay and the Southern colonies altogether.[21] He chose to go to Britain's weakly defended Bahamas, which in previous colonial wars had been a center of piracy and privateering. Nassau was easily taken, and among other booty, Hopkins did obtain a small amount of ammunition. Leaving after a few days, he headed for New London, Connecticut, rather than the destinations suggested by the committee, although he did send a ship to Philadelphia to report his whereabouts. In his home waters, the Nassau booty was sold and proceeds divided by Hopkins among his officers and crew. Admiralty courts were only in the process of being set up and Hopkins avoided them so that he and his crew would not have to share their prize money with Congress, state authorities or ship owners.

By April 1776, Hopkins' squadron of six warships was at the east end of Long Island near Block Island.[22] The squadron cruised off the island and began to take merchantmen as prizes. At night on April 6, they caught sight of a single ship, the *Glasgow*, a 20-gun Royal Navy dispatch carrier on its way from Portland, Rhode Island to Charleston, South Carolina. Under Captain Tryingham Howe, it turned about to investigate Hopkins' squadron, closing to within hailing distance. Hopkins gave no signals to the *Glasgow* before it confronted his ships individually. With the *Cabot,* after a few broadsides, it killed the master, wounded the captain and disabled its steering. Next came Hoskins and Dudley Saltonstall in the *Alfred*, where the gunnery was even, but the *Glasgow* broke the lines to the *Alfred's* tiller and it drifted as it was raked by fire. Then it was the turn of the *Andrea Doria*, which was entangled by the Hopkins' drifting ships. The *Providence* stayed out of range and the *Columbus* came up, but its fire was ineffective. The squadron operated in what was described as 'Helter-Skelter'.

Outnumbered, the *Glasgow* drew off and distanced itself, and in the morning, Hopkins called off a pursuit for fear they would encounter Captain James Wallace's squadron at Newport. The *Glasgow* had sustained one killed and three wounded while the Continental squadron had at least twenty-four casualties.[23] Hopkins' ships had depleted crews, many of whom were sick, and after the debacle they sought a complete refitting. The *Glasgow's* destination was changed as it was sent to England to be honored.

The young captain of the *Andrea Doria,* Nicholas Biddle, a former Royal Navy officer, charged that 'a more imprudent, ill-conducted affair never happened before.'[24] Even Lieutenant John Paul Jones of the *Alfred* surmised, 'the unfortunate engagement with the *Glasgow* seems to be a general reflection on the officers of the fleet.' As noted, Captain Abraham Whipple of the *Columbus* asked for a court martial, which condemned him but allowed him to remain in the navy. John Hazard of the *Providence* was not so lucky; a court martial convicted him of neglect of duty and he was forced to resign. A single Royal Navy mail ship had almost demolished Congress's first squadron. Hopkins had been correct in advising never to confront a Royal Navy ship, even if your force outnumbered it.

Some of Hopkins' officers went to Congress to protest his command, and in August 1776 he was censured by Congress for taking his squadron to Nassau.[25] However, he had support from New Englanders in Congress like John Hancock and they opposed removing him from command. Finally over their objection, in January 1778, Congress voted to permanently relieve Hoskins of his command.

Before he was relieved, Hoskins had been in more trouble as commander of the frigate *Warren*. On February 19, 1777, officers of the *Warren*, led by Third Lieutenant Richard

Marven and Midshipman Samuel Shaw, met under the deck and drafted a petition to the Marine Committee accusing Hopkins of calling Congress 'damned fools', of obstructing the recruitment of crews because he 'had such a spleen', and of torturing British prisoners.[26] An inquiry was conducted, and Hopkins retaliated by bringing criminal libel proceedings against both officers. In July 1778, Congress responded to Hopkins that they would legally defend the petitioning officers, as it was their duty to report misconduct and fraud, this commitment being the first Congressional Whistleblower law. Thus ended the saga of Congress's only commander of the Continental Navy, showing Hopkins' propensity to act like a privateer, rather than protecting trade and supporting the war effort.

List of Captains

In October 1776, Congress produced a seniority list of its top twenty-six captains.[27] No Admiral would ever be designated and the list would never be updated, so it shows who they felt counted at the time. Hopkins was not on the list as his star had faded, but his critical subordinate, Nicholas Biddle, was ranked fifth. Captains like Hopkins' brother-in-law Abraham Whipple, John Paul Jones and John Young were well down the list at numbers twelve, eighteen and twenty-three respectively. Remembering the egos of these captains, here was the basis for complaining for the rest of the war. The top position belonged to Marylander James Nicholas, followed by two Massachusetts captains, John Manley and Hector McNeill. Here was political balance, the Southerners in Congress wanted the top spot after Hopkins had ignored them. Still Manley and McNeill represented the continuing influence of New England.

James Nicholson

James Nicholson was the product of a Chesapeake family that made a reputation in the Revolution through naval service. From Chestertown, Maryland, three members of the Nicholson family – James, Samuel and John – would have careers in the emerging Continental Navy. The Nicholsons were not gentlemen planters; before the war, their ships were hired by planters for trade with England.[28] The patriarch was Joseph Nicholson, a colonel of Kent County militia and a member of the first Committee of Correspondence in 1774.[29] He had been in Chestertown since the 1730s and he and his wife ran the White Swan Tavern, a hangout for sailors.

James was born in 1737 and had the advantage of serving in the Royal Navy, participating in the Siege of Havana in 1763.[30] Earlier, he been accused, but pardoned, of killing a sailor in Chestertown. It was his cargo that caused Chestertown's Tea Resolves of 1774, but he also served with his father and brother Joseph on the resulting Committee of Correspondence. He supported the sending of flour to the poor of Boston.

From October 1776, he would have dual responsibilities in the Maryland and Continental navies. In his first action, when the Royal Navy blocked his squadron in Baltimore Harbor in October 1776, he was forced to abandon his ships and march his men overland to serve with Washington in New York.[31] In 1777, he was made commander of the Maryland navy and was given command of its first outfitted ship, the *Defense*. He was ordered to watch the movements of British and Loyalist ships and escort rebel merchantmen in Chesapeake Bay, a duty rated foremost by Congress and the Maryland Assembly.

Congress's Marine Committee continued to focus on obtaining war materials from overseas sources and the diplomacy it believed would win the war. When the Maryland Assembly built the powerful 28-gun Continental frigate *Virginia* in 1777, James Nicholson was given its command. His orders from the Committee in April stated that the *Virginia* was to sail to French Martinique, the West Indies, where William Bingham the rebel agent resided, and it was believed he would supply the Continental ship with stores.[32] Bingham hoped that when the ship came, it could cruise in the West Indies, showing the new nation's colors. If possible, the *Virginia* was to capture ships to add to the navy, to obtain valuable seamen and even attempt to seduce Royal Navy petty and warrant officers to desert. Prizes that were taken would be exempt from court reviews as they could be sold on the spot because their cargos were 'perishable or particularly suited to the West Indies markets'. Nicholson was to return to the middle colonies, where he would be under the instructions of the Philadelphia Naval Board. However, these ambitious instructions were never implemented.

Instead, for the next eleven months, the *Virginia* was unprepared to sail from Baltimore. Delays were caused by shortfalls in the manning of the ship, the lack of a lieutenant, which Joshua Barney was sent to fulfill, and by the need for a tender to service the ship. In December, it was suggested that the *Virginia's* primary duty was financial, to carry tobacco to sell in the West Indies. Finally, she was underway, but on March 21, 1778, she ran aground on Middle Shoal, between the Chesapeake capes, and was easily captured by Royal Navy ships.[33] Thus, all the effort came to naught; Nicholson was blamed for this by his rivals, a situation typical of his career.

Manley and McNeill

In Congress's seniority list, after Nicholson, John Manley and Hector McNeill were ranked second and third. They were both from the Massachusetts coast, had connections with the Royal Navy in the colonial wars, and had shepherded the outfitting of the new ships designated for them, in preparation to sail against the Royal Navy blockade.[34]

McNeill was born in County Antrim, Ireland on October 10, 1728, the son of Scottish migrants to Ulster. At the age of 9, he immigrated with his parents to Boston, arriving there in 1737. In the Seven Years' War, he entered the King's service, claiming that he was 'acknowledged' by 'Admirals Boscawen, Saunders, Durrell and Colvill', commanding an 'armed vessel of war'.[35] He probably was in the transport service, in April 1755, taking General Robert Monckton to Nova Scotia, where he remained during the siege of Fort Beausejour. Later, he commanded a vessel that was captured by French allied Indians in Passamaquoddy Bay and taken as a prisoner north to Quebec. After an exchange, he was able to acquire another ship and participated in the New England coastal trade. This experience made him highly regarded by Congress and even John Paul Jones, a dear friend, who felt he had more 'Marine Knowledge' than any other officer in the service. McNeill was living in Quebec when the Revolution began and Governor Carleton demanded that he either join the militia or leave the colony – so he left.

In June 1776, McNeill went before the Continental Congress to lobby for a commission as captain in the Continental Navy. By September, he was granted the position and given command of the new frigate *Boston*, which was outfitted at Newburyport, Massachusetts.[36] After a year preparing the ship and finding a crew, the *Boston* joined John Manley's *Hancock* to form a squadron to be commanded by Manley.

Manley was born in 1733 near Torquay, the Devon port. He eventually settled in Marblehead, Massachusetts, becoming the captain of a merchant vessel.[37] John Paul Jones claimed that Manley had also served as a boatswain's mate on a Royal Navy warship. In November 1775, Manley sailed from Marblehead and captured a valuable prize, the brigantine *Nancy,* carrying ordnance and military stores for British troops in Boston that were needed by the Continental army. As a result, he was named captain of the *Hancock,* a new frigate in building.

On May 21, 1777 the *Hancock* and *Boston*, minus their absconding privateers, sailed to the Grand Bank fisheries.[38] From the beginning, however, McNeill and Manley did not get along and this would endanger their enterprise. Early in June, they captured the frigate *Fox*. In the confrontation, Manley's ship did most of the fighting, but McNeill was able to position his ship to take possession of the British frigate. Manley would not allow it, ordering McNeill to relinquish the *Fox* to his prize crew. Tempers began to flare.

By July, the two ships made landfall in Nova Scotia and encountered two Royal Navy ships, Captain George Collier's *Rainbow* and the *Flora*, only frigates though Manley and McNeill thought they were larger.[39] It was decided that the best way of avoiding them was for the three ships to disperse in different directions. Manley sailed ahead of the other two ships but had navigational problems and after a thirty-nine-hour chase, the discipline of Collier's crews allowed them to capture the *Hancock* and recapture the *Fox* from its prize crew. McNeill did not support Manley's flight, instead withdrawing to the safety of the Sheepscot River, Maine, where he remained, as criticism of his leadership mounted. In contrast, Manley and his crew were sent to Halifax and then imprisoned in New York until March 1778. After a prisoner exchange released Manley, both he and McNeill were court-martialed, with the result that McNeill was dismissed from the navy while Manley was exonerated.

McNeill spent the rest of his career trying to get Congress to expunge the blot on his career, writing appeals, including sympathetic letters to John Paul Jones, who had recently lost command of the *Ranger*. Manley and McNeill would end up commanding privateers. In answer to petitions by the investors, McNeill would be named by Massachusetts authorities as the captain the privateers, *Pallas* and *Adventure*.[40] Even though exonerated, Manley also became a privateer, commanding the *Marlborough, Cumberland*, and a prize, the *Jason*, until 1782, sandwiched between two more periods of imprisonment, one for two years in England's Mill Prison. Their fate was not exceptional.

The names of these four early captains are not well known, with the possible exception of Hopkins because he was so infamous. All had served in ships in the Seven Years' War. Only Nicholson had a documented appearance in the Royal Navy, while the other three commanded privateers or transports. Hopkins, Manley and McNeil were New Englanders and they shared a regional distain for Congress's command of the navy, which imperiled its ability to conduct the war. Nicholson was better in obeying the Congressional orders, although he seems to have been so unlucky that he rarely was able to put to sea. All parties sought to gain prizes, but the New Englanders felt the proceeds belonged to them, while Congress expected that the proceeds would support their war effort.

Chapter 6

Rebel Privateers Offer Profit

It was no accident that Manley and McNeill ended their careers as privateer captains. Popular accounts of the American naval effort tend to focus on privateers since they provided the best opportunities for success, even for Continental Navy officers. As with their British counterparts, privateering was a business venture in which profit dominated, justifying the cupidity of the owners and captain. Privateers were said to combine 'freedom and fortune' – goals associated with pirates.[1]

During the Seven Years' War, privateering had given investors a stake in war. In New York City, the list of privateers was a social register of its finest families as seventeen of them were members of the Vestry of Trinity Church, the city's most prestigious house of worship. Only the wealthy like the Livingston family could afford the expense of outfitting a privateer. They preyed upon the annual French fishing fleets that came or left the Grand Bank fishery, hoping to cut out stragglers. Altogether, over 200 New York ships would be privateers, manned by 15,000–20,000 men.[2] Chesapeake Bay also had privateers. Chestertown gentry fitted out a privateer, the *Sharpe*, named for the governor. It carried twenty-six guns and twenty swivels and was manned by a crew of 200. It was the first of several privateers that caused havoc among French and Spanish shipping. When the Revolution came, these examples were not lost on merchants seeking to continue profitable trade.

Following British American precedent in the colonial wars, from March 1776, Congress's Marine Committee issued letters of marque to privateers. Vessels already involved in trade saw the letters as a way of maximizing the profits from a voyage at little cost. As they remained most interested in cargo space, they had only to add five or six guns to be ready for prizes and booty. Over the entire war, Congress would issue letters of marque to 1,697 vessels.[3] Fewer vessels were commissioned as private warships as they were much more expensive, often carrying at least fifteen guns, usually financed by a syndicate of merchants to spread the expense in case the ship was lost. In fact, these were warships that Congress and the states could not afford to build, outfit or maintain. Congress also authorized its naval agents in the West Indies and the American commissioners in France to issue privateer licenses. All these licenses had limitations: they did not justify land raids or the taking of property from those who supported the rebellion. Congress further regulated privateering, including the reporting of prizes and treatment of prisoners. Bonds were required of owners, amounting to $5,000 for a vessel under 100 tons and $10,000 for those over it.

The commissioning of privateers was at first slowed by the lack of new Admiralty courts to adjudicate prizes. At the end of 1775, Washington, who had experienced problems in using his own ships during the siege of Boston, requested that the states create 'tribunals to govern the disposal of captured enemy vessels'.[4] Congress authorized the states to create new ones. The Maryland convention established such a court on May 25, 1776. While privateer captains and their crews sought to have British ships captured and their cargos declared prizes and sold, these courts often prevented them from gaining as lucrative a share as they expected.

Why were privateering results often disappointing? It was the cargo that made a ship a prize and some ships taken carried only ballast or insignificant cargos.[5] Moreover, only enemy ships could be taken and the identity of ships at a distance was confusing. The cases before the courts were complicated: was, for example, a privately owned vessel, captured by the privateer a prize? Or did it belong to the original owner and therefore should it be returned to him? On investigation many ships turned out to be owned by neutrals like the Danes or later allies like the Dutch. Many had a checkered ownership and all of the non-British owners could claim a share of the prize. Congress and the states also claimed a share. Many claimants were unhappy with the court's decisions and appealed to Congress, which was simply not set up to handle such cases until 1780, when it created its first Federal Court to adjudicate prizes.

By 1778, all states licensed privateers, even Delaware which never authorized a navy. New York and Connecticut licensed their privateers to operate only in their home waters, while other states allowed them to sail anywhere on the high seas. Massachusetts is thought to have had the most privateers: 1,000 privateers under her commission and 626 under Continent papers.[6] From 1776 on, Maryland offered letters of marque to 280 privateers.

While attempts have been made to estimate the number of prizes American privateers took, the figures remain guesses and are compromised by the fact that some privateers held licenses from all of these authorities. It has been claimed that the most prizes by a single captain were secured by Gustavus Conyngham operating successfully in European and West Indian waters, although not in American.[7] While Conyngham thought he was a Continental captain, British and French authorities and even Congress felt he acted as a privateer or even a pirate. His and his ship's commissions were so confused that it is amazing he had such success.

Privateering was a business venture directly related to shipbuilding. While at first, shipbuilding was depressed by scarcity of cordage and canvas, lack of skilled workers and the Royal Navy blockade, in time merchants were able to recover from these conditions by turning to construction or modification of ships for privateering. As an investment, vessels were built for speed and weatherliness, so that they could avoid the Royal Navy. Even if the British took two out of three ships, the one that got through could be quite profitable.

In 1776, the privateer *Sturdy Beggar* was built at Richard Graves' Worton Creek yard in Maryland and was described as the 'handimost vessel ever built in America'.[8] She would carry eighty men, fourteen carriage guns and fourteen swivels. Privateers were expected to have a large crew so that it could be dispersed into prize crews to navigate captured ships to friendly ports. To recruit her crew in August, the *Sturdy Beggar* put in at Vienna on the Nanticoke River and, among others, lured away 18-year-old John Kilby. It then operated successfully out of Baltimore and New Bern, North Carolina for a year, when it was chased by the Royal Navy's *Resolution* and perished in a storm with a loss of all hands. Kilby, however, survived in the crew of a prize, retaken by the *Resolution* and was sent to an English prison until he was released and went to France, where he fortuitously joined the crew of John Paul Jones' *Bonhomme Richard*.

By 1777, Robert Morris, the father of the Continental Navy, decided that privateering might be worth a try and he invested as a silent partner in a ship with agent William Bingham on Martinique. Their next venture, however, ended in a total loss for them as the successful privateer captain refused to pay their shares. Soon Morris warned of 'that kind of irregular conduct on b[oar]d the Am[erican] privateers that savours more of Moorish piracy than Christian forbearance.'[9] He saw that privateers seduced American sailors, who should have been serving in the Continental or state navies. He complained that Continental and state ships dedicated to public defense rather than profit languished in port because they could not obtain crews or complete their outfitting.

By preventing the Continental and state navies from operating effectively, privateers actually obstructed the war effort. They advertised extensively, luring men to make fortunes at one stroke. This happened even to men who had signed the Continental articles, as privateers offered short-time commitments and lucrative voyages.[10] In the last years of the war, Continental and state naval commanders had no ships and faced unemployment unless they became privateer captains.[11] The demand for privateers affected even those appointed to protect the concerns of the Continental Navy. Nathaniel Shaw, while the Continental agent at New London, Connecticut, owned and operated at least ten privateers, which as a business interest took a priority over his agent's position.

While privateers became more numerous as the war continued, they did not perform well when joined with the Continental or state navy ships. They were best when operating singly or with one or two compatriots, rather than in a squadron, especially if it was not devoted to taking prizes. In May 1777, the *Sturdy Beggar* was part of the Manley-McNeill squadron that sailed the Grand Banks, but it soon left the squadron to pursue its own interests.[12] Privateers avoided warships so as not to damage or lose their investors' property. They were also useless in a prolonged siege, as there was little opportunity to take prizes.

Later State Commissions

In areas of intense trade, states commissioned raiders that were different from privateers. After New York was taken by the British in 1776, the western portion of Long Island (Kings and Queens Counties) was strongly occupied by the British, while eastern Suffolk County was not held so closely and there a substantial rebel opposition reappeared. Trade to the city and across Long Island Sound to New England ports had always been a regional feature and would continue, despite the efforts of the governors and legislatures of New Jersey, Connecticut and rebel New York to treat it as trading with the enemy.[13] At first, most of the state laws were embargoes on exports, chiefly foodstuffs, which were enforced by local militia. Like embargoes everywhere in the thirteen colonies, these efforts failed as self-interest prevailed over even the most patriotic Whig. Congress was so upset by illicit trade that by 1780 it urged the states to institute the death penalty to curb the criminal practice. Connecticut had allowed Long Island refugees from across the Sound to return to their former homes in the British-occupied sector, but by 1778, they were involved in this illicit trade. Long Island became a major source of British manufactures so desired by New Englanders, who had been deprived of them by embargoes and wartime interruptions.

Separate from privateering, commissions were given by the Governors of Connecticut and Rhode Island to the owners of private ships to seize British goods locally. This was popular late in the war, as crews received a part of what was seized in booty, although the ships were limited to single cruises on enemy shipping within Long Island Sound.[14] It is against this background that the records of Connecticut and Rhode Island county courts, acting as vice-admiralty courts, show the role of these specially commissioned vessels.

In 1776, raiders from Connecticut were usually Long Island refugees, most interested in rescuing their own property left behind when the British invaded. Two years later, however, raiding had become a land enterprise, not traditional privateering.[15] In certain cases, Connecticut raiders left their boats on Long Island Sound and traveled overland as far as the southern shore of Long Island. No longer was the object to seize a sugar ship from a convoy, instead focusing on retrieving British manufactures found in the middle and eastern areas of Long Island. Investors sent their crews to scavenge for goods in ports or inland at well-stocked shops or homes. While their crews were armed, most ships carried no ordnance, space for cargo being maximized, as they were not meant to confront British ships.

By 1781, the Connecticut Council of Safety had asked Governor Johnathan Trumbull, Sr. to empower the schooner *Weezel,* belonging to Nathan Steadman and Company of Connecticut, to use 'force of arms on the coast of this state above high water mark or islands adjoining the said coast apprehend, seize and take all kinds of British goods, wares and manufactures, the property of the subjects of Great Britain'.[16] This private commission allowed the schooner to take British manufactures on Long Island Sound, but whether Long Island itself qualified as an adjoining island is not clear from the commission. The question of how Johnson was to identify subjects of Great Britain was presumably left in his hands. Later, Captain Edward Johnson of the *Weezel* received clarification from his superior, Captain William Leyland, which instructed him 'not to enter the dwelling house or molest or rob any peaceable inhabitants on Long Island or elsewhere'.

Johnson did the opposite of Leyland's order, heading to Southold and seizing the goods in Nathaniel Finning's store.[17] Johnson carried the goods to a Connecticut port, where they were adjudicated by a Connecticut Court. The court ignored Fanning's claims, ruling in favor of the owners of the *Weezel*, but ultimately the court's decision was overturned by Congress and Fanning's property was ordered returned. It was evident that profit from the sale of goods was the paramount goal of the *Weezel*, even if the goods belonged to rebels.

This raid led to Trumbull being censured by Congress as he had assumed that everyone living on Long Island was a Loyalist and thus fair game. He defended himself by implying that the British manufactures had not been sent by the North ministry to supply New York's military and civilians, but rather to purposely disrupt the rebel cause. He saw the situation as a plot by the ministry:

> For this end the British ministry have sent large quantities of goods to New York; large parcels of them have been brought along the whole length of [Long island] ... agreeably to a plan systematically laid, to introduce them ... to various places on our seacoasts, to care and disposal of inimical, evil, & artful men, fit tools for their turn, to catch hold of the avarice, luxury, pride and vanity of some persons who are designing and others who are unwary ... with

the allurements furnished them, spread the contagion of corruption, falsehood, unreasonable jealousies, a cry of intolerable taxes, and artfully seduced young men to enlist [in] the associated loyalists, and they secretly hand out the declarations of General Clinton and Admiral Arbuthnot offering pardon.[18]

Thus, the rights of property had to yield to combat this inimical plot.

Another raid the same year was carried out by East Haddam, Connecticut's Captain Amos Judson, commander of the *Revenge,* which marched with premediated speed inland to the Southold home of Captain Jeremiah Wells. Judson claimed that he had a right to Wells' property because all inhabitants of Long Island were subjects of the King, while Judson held a permit from Governor Trumbull, similar to that of the *Weezel.* When a Southold Justice of the Peace demanded to see it, Judson refused, mumbling a few phrases. Wells was a respectable Southold merchant and a captain in Fanning's regiment of New York militia. His family made a living in the local trade of goods such as 'broadcloth, calico, chintz, flannel, holland, gauze, cambric, poplin, silk, knives and knife and fork sets'.[19] Judson moved on from Wells' house to that of David Gardiner Jr. and robbed him of similar goods. It was these manufactures that Judson took back to Connecticut and at a Hartford hearing, despite ample evidence that Wells and Gardiner were rebels, the goods were awarded to Judson. Wells and Gardiner knew they were in the right, however, and appealed to the Congressional Court of Prize Appeals and after two years, it reversed the lower court decision and ordered the goods returned to them.

Rebels like Fanning, Wells and Gardiner were victims in these commissioned raids because governors and prize courts did not attempt to review the loyalty of their Long Island victims. They found it convenient to believe that all inhabitants of Long Island were Loyalists. It was left to Congress to correct these miscarriages of justice. As the final arbitrator of these raids, its Court of Prize Appeals overturned the local decisions, proving that most of the victims were rebels.[20] Some of the local courts actually forbade appeal to Congress's court, knowing that their biased judgements would be overturned, but those rebels with a strong case were able to appeal.

Illicit Trade

Historians have seen the raids from across Long Island Sound as efforts to harass the British. This may have been true in the early years of the British occupation, but the commissioned raids were not aimed at crippling British trade as with the licensing of privateers. Commissioned ships preferred to establish illicit trade, carrying out trade contrary to the laws of their state. Often these commissions became the basis of purposeful smuggling operations, established to avoid Congressional and state embargoes on British goods.[21] These were purchased in New York and distributed to shops and homes in British-controlled areas or beyond. They were exchanged for food carried by Connecticut traders. The goods were then made up as cargo and taken to an obscure Connecticut or Rhode Island port, ignoring the militia enforcing the embargo. There, a local court adjudicated in favor of the original investors, avoiding the government's duty on British goods, so that fortunes were made in the sale of these goods. Rivalry between Connecticut and Rhode Island courts existed as raiders chose the court that would be most rewarding. Soon produce came to New York from far beyond Connecticut, as ships under flags of truce arrived from Massachusetts, Rhode Island, Maryland and Virginia. This illicit trade existed because the new United States remained as dependent on British manufactures as it had been in the colonial era.

In fact, historian Bernard Bailyn has claimed, 'what helped bind the widespread and intensely competitive Atlantic commercial word together – was the mass of illegal trade that bypassed the formal, nationalistic constraints.'[22] With the British occupation of New York City from 1776 to 1783, it became the great magnet for illicit trade in British manufactures that embarrassed Robert Morris. To counteract illicit trade, Congress recommended that the states make it unlawful to import any British manufactures except prize goods. While states and merchants tried to comply, they made little headway against market forces. Morris hoped to have French manufactures replace those of Britain, but the French navy could not protect its ships and illicit trade in British goods flourished until the end of the war.

American privateers will be found in action in coming chapters. It was privateers who sustained the central role of overseas commerce in the American war effort. Gustavus Conyngham's career will be described, explaining why he was called the 'Dunkirk pirate'. In 1779, we will see the failure of privateers to contribute to a fleet besieging Fort George at Penobscot, Maine. Two years later, similar conditions to those of Long Island Sound existed in Nova Scotia, encouraging New England privateer raids on its ports.

PART 3

CANADA PRESERVED BY THE ROYAL NAVY

Chapter 7

Congress wants Quebec

Throughout the Revolution, Congress entertained the illusion that Canada was ripe for the picking, hoping that freedom-craving Canadians would rally to the American call and join them in ousting their common British ruler. Strangely, Congress cast its rebellion against Protestant King George III as a struggle against the Catholicism that the British had allowed to continue in Canada. Rebels like Alexander Hamilton classified the tolerant Quebec Act of 1774 as an Intolerable Act because it had recognized the right of French Canadians to practice their Catholic faith and civil law. He asked, 'Does not your blood run cold to think that an English Parliament should pass an Act for the establishment of arbitrary power and Popery in such an extensive country?'[1] He warned that religious tolerance in Quebec would draw Catholics from throughout Europe, who would eventually destroy America. Sam Adams told a group of Mohawk Indians that the Quebec Act 'to establish the religion of the Pope in Canada' would mean that 'instead of worshipping the only true God', they would pay their dues to images made with their own hands. The rebel propagandist Thomas Paine claimed, 'It was once the glory of Englishmen to draw the sword only in defense of liberty and the Protestant religion, or to extend the blessings of both to their unhappy neighbors ...' therefore 'popery and French laws in Canada are but a part of that system of despotism, which has been prepared for the colonies.'

Massachusetts' silversmith, engraver and artilleryman, Paul Revere, elaborated on this perspective by creating a cartoon for the *Royal American Magazine* called 'The Mitered Minuet'.[2] It was meant to tie detested popery to Britain's Anglican Church. It depicted four contented-looking mitered Anglican Bishops, dancing a minuet around a copy of the Quebec Act to show their 'approbation and countenance of the Roman religion'. Standing nearby are the authors of the Quebec Act – Governor Guy Carleton, the Earl of Bute, Lord North – while a devil with bat ears and spiky wings hovers behind them, whispering instructions.

This perspective motivated Congress to raise expeditions to make Canada the fourteenth colony of the American confederation. The key to Canada was control of its inland waterways, beginning with the St Lawrence River penetrating westward from Quebec to Montreal. At Sorel, the St Lawrence was joined on the south by the Richelieu River, which when rapids were passed, connected to Lake Champlain, and from its south end by Wood Creek to the Hudson River, creating a water route which since the Seven Years' War had been dubbed the 'Warpath of Nations'. Congress hoped that control over this route below Sorel would lead to the fall of Canada.

Congress put its first Canadian expedition together only five months after Lexington and Concord. An aggressive rebel army led by Brigadier General Richard Montgomery was sent up Lake Champlain into Canada. Quebec was totally unprepared for this invasion and thus the rebels carried all before them.[3] The crucial fort and boatyard on the Richelieu at St Johns fell after a fifty-six-day siege, then Montreal was bloodlessly taken – Governor Carleton barely escaping down the St Lawrence River to defend Quebec. There he was besieged by Montgomery, joined by another force under Colonel Benedict Arnold that had reached there by way of Maine.

Carleton Defends Quebec

The British forces defending Canada against this rebel invasion were led by Governor Guy Carleton, a military man with talent for dealing with civilian matters. Carleton was born in Strabane, County Tyrone, Ireland, in 1724.[4] At the age of 18, he was commissioned a naval ensign, but then joined the First Foot Guards and by 1757 he had risen to lieutenant colonel. He first served in Canada during the Seven Years' War, where he was a protégé of the brilliant James Wolf. For the Louisburg expedition of 1758 and the siege of Quebec a year later, Wolf chose Carleton as respectively his aide and quartermaster general. During Wolf's siege of Quebec, Carleton provisioned the army and acted as an engineer, supervising cannon placement. He was wounded in the head and after Quebec's fall, he returned to England to recuperate. Two years later, he was designated commander of the 72nd Regiment in an amphibious attack on Belle-ile-en-Mer, an island off the French coast. While the island was

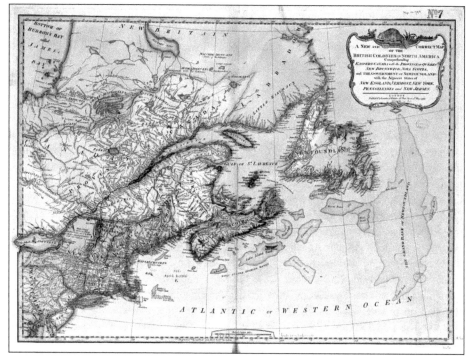

Canadian Waters.

taken, Carleton was again wounded, this time seriously. A year later, he was a colonel in the British expedition that captured Havana, where he was wounded again, forcing his retirement from active service as the war came to an end.

It was a surprise in April 1766, when Carleton was named acting Lieutenant Governor of Quebec as he was retired and lacked administrative experience.[5] However, he had influence with the Duke of Richmond, the new Secretary of State for the North American Colonies. Carleton's appointment included the title of commander of all troops stationed in Quebec. Still, he was only to assist the Governor of Canada, James Murry, also a veteran of Wolfe's Quebec campaign. Carleton soon was at loggerheads with Murray. All Quebec officials, from the governor down, were unsalaried, forcing them to seek income from charging for services. The system naturally led to corruption and Carleton sought to reform it by introducing salaries for officials. Upset, Murray resigned in 1768 and Carleton replaced him. Four years later, he was promoted to major general and it was then that he drafted his thoughts on Canada, including toleration for Catholics, and restored French civil law, which became the basis for the Quebec Act. On his return to Quebec in September 1774, he carried the act with him to promulgate.

A year later, Carleton had just received word of Lexington and Concord, when he was informed that Ticonderoga and Crown Point had been taken by rebels. He had previously sent two regiments to help General Gage in Boston, leaving him with only 800 regulars in Quebec, whose boundaries extended to the Mississippi River.[6] While mission Indians might support his forces, Carleton was reluctant to use them because he believed Indian support would help the rebels, as the Indians could not fight without committing atrocities. Many rural French Canadians, whom he had courted with the Quebec Act, failed to rally in their local militias and he soon learned not to depend on them. While the authorities in London had promised reinforcements for Canada, none arrived in 1775.

Quebec's Defense

The city of Quebec had a history that was inseparable from the St Lawrence River, which connected it to the Atlantic world. The town's location was chosen for its maritime qualities: the large basin on the edge of the city could accommodate more than 100 ships annually, the narrowness of the St Lawrence at the city made it easy to control navigation. Toward the end of the seventeenth century, the first concessions were established along Quebec's shoreline, where the landowners designated their property with cedar post fencing.[7] Here the early port developed, protected by two cannon platforms constructed in 1660 and 1690 at Pointe aux Roches. A Royal Battery was built a year later. An attack by the English in 1690 justified these defenses.

Quebec became divided between an Upper and Lower Town, the former being the administrative and religious center, while the latter hugged the waterfront, the domain of merchants and sailors. The harbor front grew in the eighteenth century as two batteries were installed on private wharves: the Dauphine Battery in 1709 and later the Pointe à Carcy Battery. The port took on a rectilinear shape, with a small cove in the west, the Cul-de-Sac, where a shipyard was developed from 1746.[8] Here were warehouses and at least two dockyards, one in the Cul-de-Sac and the other in Palace Quarter along the St Charles River. After 1759, the Royal Battery would be abandoned and the land sold for warehouses and a quay, reflecting the city's increasing interest in trade.

An idea of who the defenders of Quebec were can be gleaned from a proclamation issued by Carleton on November 22, 1775. He asked that all persons who wished to leave Quebec do so by December 1 to cut down on the number who would have to be fed during a siege. Still, 5,000 non-combatant civilians remained. The defenders included 873 militia, the majority of them French Canadians, 230 Loyalists of the Royal Highland Emigrants and only 70 Royal Fusiliers. An important contingent, serving onshore from the ships were 400 mariners and 35 marines, a combined group which rose to 480.[9] Essentially, the defense of Quebec depended on French Canadian militia and sailors.

As to the navy, Captain Thomas MacKenzie of the sloop *Hunter* had been sent from Boston to Quebec by Admiral Samuel Graves.[10] The escort, *Lizard*, Captain John Hamilton, had come to protect the *Jacob,* which brought supplies to the defenders and agreed to stay after it was unloaded. During the siege, the *Hunter* and *Lizard* would be the chief navy ships, operating around the city, returning fire from rebel batteries.

Rebel Invasion

From November 1775, through the winter and spring, Major General Philip Schuyler attempted to supply the rebel armies besieging Quebec with reinforcements, food and powder. His chief staging area above Albany was Fort George, at the head of Lake George, from which supplies could be portaged at Ticonderoga and loaded on vessels to sail up Lake Champlain.[11] Schuyler fumed that his army was rife with corruption. When Seth Warner recruited his second Continental regiment for the relief of Canada, Schuyler provided bounties for 736 recruits, yet when they arrived in Canada, Warner's men numbered only 417. Warner was not the first rebel officer who was forced to pad his accounts.

Previously, in September, Schuyler had led the invading army against the Richelieu River defenses, but his ill heath intervened and he was forced to return to Ticonderoga, leaving Montgomery in charge. By December, Montgomery was besieging Quebec from the Plains of Abraham and made fun of Carleton's defensive force: 'the wretched garrison [consists] of sailors unacquainted with the use of arms, of citizens incapable of soldiers' duty, & of a few miserable emigrants.'[12] He was soon to learn how wrong he was. A rebel attack on the city on New Year's Eve in a snow storm was soundly defeated. It focused on the lower town, where Montgomery was killed and Benedict Arnold wounded. The command of the attackers was left to a group of officers of whom Captain Daniel Morgan was most conspicuous. With their firearms too wet to discharge, the rebels surrendered, though Morgan, in tears of rage, refused to give them his sword and would have been killed had he not handed it to a priest, who was a bystander in the crowd.

At the beginning of 1776, Arnold held on stubbornly outside the city, continuing the siege of Quebec with the remains of his army as Carleton still had only sailors and city militia to defend Quebec's extensive fortifications. He was unsure that his forces were capable of dislodging them.

Saving Canada

On the Bristol-bound merchantman, *Polly*, in late December, Lieutenant Thomas Pringle had carried Carleton's dispatches to London.[13] They contained the news that he was defending

Quebec against two rebel armies that besieged it. Since this was the last dispatch received from Carleton, at the beginning of the year the Admiralty was unaware of whether the city had fallen or not.

Rescue Fleets for Quebec

At the Admiralty, First Lord Sandwich and Rear Admiral Hugh Palliser decided to respond immediately, equipping a small squadron to reach Canada quickly. It consisted of the 50-gun *Isis*, the frigates *Surprise* and *Triton*, the sloop of war *Martin*, three victuallers and two large navy transports with supplies; enough to support 3,000 men for three months. The squadron carried only 200 regulars of the 29th Regiment, as supply and naval support were regarded as most needed at Quebec. The commodore was Charles Douglas, who was ordered by Sandwich to put to sea immediately 'as the fate of Quebec depends on it'.[14]

This first relief squadron left in early February 1776, facing the dangers of an Atlantic winter crossing. Ice would be abundant in the Gulf of St Lawrence, so the squadron had to force its way through thick pack ice – which many thought was impossible. Passing through icebergs in April, the ships' ropes were frozen, so that they 'appeared as if rigged with ropes of crystal, nearly four times their usual diameter', requiring that they be thawed.[15] Once on the St Lawrence River, the dispersed ships made for the small port of Kamouraska on the southern mainland and then reformed at Isle Coudres in the river. Douglas was at Coudres by May 3, 1776 and took command of the ships as they arrived. The *Surprise* was sent ahead to Quebec three days later and was welcomed by a boat from the *Lizard.* Soon Douglas with the *Isis* and *Martin* arrived at the city. The entire mid-winter voyage had taken only seven weeks. It has been argued that the navy's relief of Quebec 'was a momentous victory, arguably more significant than the original capture of 1759 …'.[16]

With the arrival, Carleton marched out of Quebec's gates with 850 of the garrison into the Plains of Abraham, driving the besieging rebels before him. They fled, leaving stores, ordnance, and General John Thomas' 'dinner which he had left at the fire, [which] served as a refreshment to the [British]'.[17] The *Surprise* and *Martin* were sent above Quebec to annoy the rebel's retreat westward along the St Lawrence. Carleton kept pressure on the fleeing Continental army, sending ships up to Trois-Rivières on May 22, carrying troops from his garrison under Loyalist Allan Maclean.[18] Further reinforcements would appear at Quebec when the *Niger* and three transports arrived from Halifax, carrying the 47th Regiment, sent by General William Howe from his Boston evacuation army. General Thomas would command the rebel retreat (until his death from smallpox), as Benedict Arnold was now charged with the defense of Montreal.

Second reinforcements

After the first relief force left Britain, a more substantial force was organized in late March to carry an extensive army and battery train from Ireland to Canada. The escort warships for the thirty-nine transports were the *Carysfort, Pearl, Juno* and *Blonde.*[19] The army included about 3,000 German troops furnished by the reigning Duke of Brunswick and the Prince of Waldeck. Carleton was to use the reinforcements as he sought fit, although General John Burgoyne, commander of these troops, was to advise him on the invasion of Lake Champlain. Among those in this rescue fleet would be Lieutenant Pringle, now in command of the armed ship *Lord Howe*.

By June 1, ships of the second relief convoy begun to appear at Quebec. Burgoyne in the frigate *Blonde* was amongst them.[20] Some of them did not even anchor at Quebec's basin but carried on up the St Lawrence. Those soldiers that had gained their land legs were sent on ships under General Simon Fraser to Trois-Rivieres, so that five days later, the pursuing British force numbered almost 1,000. Their St Lawrence supply line stretched back to Quebec. At last, Carleton had enough troops to chase the rebels from Canada.

In two weeks, navy ships were at Sorel, which the rebels promptly abandoned. Carleton then forced the rebel army to St Johns. The navy reached Montreal, though it failed to bag the main rebel army, which escaped by way of St Johns to Lake Champlain. Lieutenant William Digby of the 53rd Regiment observed:

> Thus was Canada saved with much less trouble than was expected … We [now] had everything to build, battows to convey the troops over, and armed schooners and sloops to oppose theirs [and] the undertaking was … persevered with the greatest dispatch possible.[21]

Rebel army retreats

As the Continental army retreated down Lake Champlain, it disintegrated. By July 2, the rebel army was back at Crown Point. Continental army doctor Lewis Bebee explained the disaster in these terms: 'God seems to be greatly angry with us, he appears to be incensed against us, for our abominable wickedness.'[22] When the army retreated further to Ticonderoga, Bebee found an epidemic of smallpox raging, while British Indian raiders were nipping at their heels. Thus ended the only invasion of Canada Congress would be able to mount.

Chapter 8

Creating Squadrons to Control Lake Champlain

The American expositor on seapower, Alfred Mahan, commented on how the narrow settled strip of the thirteen colonies was 'intersected by estuaries of the sea and navigable rivers', reducing individual Revolutionary colonies to the conditions of islands. Such a place was the navigable corridor formed by the north–south expanse of Lake Champlain and the Hudson River, where he noted 'ships-of-war at intervals and accompanying galleys' supported a sufficient army, ... themselves preventing any intercourse by water between New England and the States west of the river.'[1] Throughout the war, this region would be the scene of naval conflict for control of the corridor.

The Rebel Squadron

It was Philip Schuyler who built, fitted out and manned the Lake Champlain squadron, although he would not actually command it in action.[2] Congress had named him a continental major general, commander of the Northern army, and he had earned the support and friendship of George Washington. Before the race began to build squadrons for control of Champlain, Schuyler had already established a naval force during the rebel invasion of Canada. It consisted of the 8-gun schooner *Liberty*, stolen from Philip Skene's plantation at the south end of the lake; the sloop *Betsey,* renamed the 12-gun *Enterprise*, taken by Arnold in the first attack on St Johns; two unfinished schooners, which were being built at St Johns, and when completed became the 12-gun *Royal Savage* and 8-gun *Revenge*. Also, three flat-bottomed, double-ended gondolas had been built for the advance up Lake Champlain. In the retreat from Canada, most of these ships had been converted to transports, their guns removed to employ them as 'floating wagons'.[3] Thus, they needed to be rearmed. These ships would form the nucleus of the American squadron that began to gather at Crown Point in late August 1776.

Schuyler's Albany

As a wealthy merchant of Albany, Philip Schuyler had the connections in and around the city to support the building of a navy on the lakes. In the past, locally built smaller ships, canoes and bateaux had carried products, produce and people cross-river and between Albany and settlements at Greenbush, Kinderhook, Coeymans, Catskill, Esopus, Poughkeepsie and points south.[4] The legendary Hudson River sloop had evolved to become commodious and durable, able to take bulky cargoes south and return with imported goods and a growing number of passengers, destined for new homes beyond Albany. More than a dozen Albany-based sloops, each owned by a prominent merchant or his kinship network, were best at carrying farm and forest products down the river to New York. Schuyler also looked northward, having his own schooner to carry boards and grain from his Saratoga plantation on the Hudson to Albany.

Skenesborough

Above the Schuyler's Saratoga plantation at the south end of Lake Champlain was Skenesborough, where the bulk of the Continental squadron would be constructed. It had been sacked in 1775 at the same time as Ethan Allen had taken Ticonderoga. Captain Samuel Herrick, a Bennington tavern keeper, led the men who, among other thefts, took owner Philip Skene's schooner and watercraft.[5] Skenesborough was not a fort, but a New York estate with a stone manor house and barn, saw and grist mills, a bloomery, a coal house, a shipyard, supported by the rents of his tenants. A British officer at the capture of Havana in the Seven Years' War, Skene had acquired twenty-three slaves, whom he brought to Lake Champlain to operate his enterprises. He was not there to defend his property and his son, two daughters, elder sister and overseer were sent to Connecticut, where the daughters and overseer were released to return home by the embarrassed Connecticut Assembly. Still, Skene would never get his property back.

Early in 1776, Schuyler called for shipwrights to construct sloops and bateaux at Fort George at the south end of Lake George. Then he found Skenesborough, better equipped, making it his chief naval yard.[6] His cousin and neighbor at Stillwater, Hermanus Schuyler, was named the superintendent at Skenesborough. Experienced in the lumber business, Hermanus ran Skene's sawmill day and night, as log supplies were tallied at sunset and sunrise to be certain the sawyers were meeting their goals.[7] Another member of an old Albany family, Philip Van Rensselaer, was asked to send spades and axes from the Albany Public Storehouse to Skenesborough.

Hermanus built two types of ships at Skenesborough: gondolas and row galleys. A gondola was decked over in places and carried a sailing rig, with a flat bottom and the pointed bow and stern. Fundamentally, it was an oversized bateau dependent on oars. It carried a single bow gun meant to be fired over the gunwales. The only shelter for the crew was an awning or perhaps tree boughs, for the vessel was too shallow to offer better protection. In all, eight were completed; when they arrived at Ticonderoga to be rigged it was noted that the gondolas were 'very unwieldly to move'.[8]

The galley was an improvement on the gondola, although fewer were completed. It was longer, with a round bottom and square stern, and also a raised quarter deck and gun deck, where gunports were cut in the bulwarks. Crew quarters existed in the hold below the deck, with about 5 feet of headroom. The galley had two masts rigged in triangular lateen sails, a condition popular in the Mediterranean, hence they were called a 'Spanish galley'.

In June, the first gondola was ready for caulking and a second was being planked, although caulking material was lacking. Later, Schuyler urged Hermanus to closely supervise his loggers, mill hands and carpenters. He hoped for harmony between the workforce of Yankees and the Yorkers, who often did not see eye to eye. He made a plea to Connecticut's Governor Jonathan Trumbull to send General David Waterbury's militia and ship carpenters from Connecticut ports.[9] They arrived in July along with carpenters from Massachusetts and Pennsylvania. By the end of July, 200 carpenters were working at Skenesborough. Altogether, a dozen gondolas and row galleys would be under construction.

Ticonderoga Outfitting

At Ticonderoga, Horatio Gates, promoted in June to major general, was in immediate command of the defenses, which he expanded well beyond the fort. While he had been a competent British army officer in the Seven Years' War, he admitted he had no experience with naval matters and actually had traveled on Lake Champlain no further than Crown Point. He needed a person to serve as his naval advisor, someone who was not within Schuyler's rival network. This was where Benedict Arnold came in, as Gates called him to Ticonderoga, where he arrived in July.[10] Arnold had some claim to be a merchant sailor, for before the war at his home in New Haven, Connecticut, he had his own ships which traded in the West Indies. Having failed to take Quebec and participated in the retreat of the army from Canada, he was now looking for a new challenge.

Arnold had nothing to do with the construction of the squadron at Skenesborough. He was more concerned with ships after they were built and sent up South Bay to Ticonderoga to be outfitted. For this purpose, Albany seamen were mustered by Richard Varick, Schuyler's secretary, while the aforementioned Philip Van Rensselaer tried to collect blocks, rigging, cables and anchors from Albany ship owners. It proved to be difficult, for 'Neither the Love of money, virtue to their country or persuasive eloquence of officers will induce some persons to part with a single article.'[11] Varick also obtained light artillery and shot from Robert Livingston's iron works below Albany. Yet in August, the schooner *Liberty* and gondola *Spitfire* had not been completely rigged; also waiting were another gondola and a 'Spanish-built' row galley. The squadron would not be ready until early October, when three row galleys, the 8-gun *Congress*, the 11-gun *Washington*, and the 10-gun *Trumbull*, were finally launched.

Crews

With both navies, the manning of ships would prove to be a stumbling block. Unlike recruiting for the Continental Navy or privateers, no prize money was offered on the lakes. In February, Schuyler sent reinforcements to Fort George and Ticonderoga, consisting of five companies of Colonel John De Haas' First Pennsylvania Battalion.[12] They were 'much thinned by sickness and desertion', but they would be drafted to serve as seamen in the squadron, although De Haas had difficulties in dealing with Arnold. Schuyler hoped that the Northern army at Ticonderoga would be the chief source of sailors and a draft from it was initiated on July 23 with the promise of an increase in their monthly pay of 8 shillings, but at the end of July, instead of hundreds, only seventy men were found for naval duty.

Schuyler turned to familiar Governor Trumbull of Connecticut, asking him for 200 to 300 mariners. Trumbull sent Stamford's Brigadier General David Waterbury and his militia to the lakes, many of whom had maritime backgrounds. In mid-August, however, Schuyler found that the Connecticut militia were spreading smallpox. He ordered Waterbury 'to dispatch three or four trusty Officers to the different roads which the Militia take on their way to Skenesborough, with positive orders to remove all Officers and Soldiers infected with the Small Pox to a distance from the roads'.[13] He also forbade officers or soldiers who had lately had the smallpox from joining the army, unless the person could produce a certificate of immunization. Waterbury would be influential at the Skenesborough dockyard, where one of the last ships constructed was the lateen-rigged galley *Washington*, which he would command. Despite many obstacles, in August, ten vessels were manned by 350 sailors, which mounted fifty carriage guns and seventy swivels. Not until October were seventeen craft ready, with 102 guns, 176 swivels and 900 sailors and soldiers acting as marines.

Command of the Squadron

Confusion would develop over who was to command the lakes squadron. As early as February 5, 1776, Congress granted a request from Schuyler that Jacobus Wynkoop, a 55-year-old captain in the 4th New York Regiment, be given command of the squadron being outfitted on Lake Champlain.[14] Wynkoop had been master of merchant ships and had served in the Seven Years' War on both land and sea. At first Congress made Wynkoop a subordinate to its choice for commander, William Douglass of Connecticut, who was designated commodore. However, Douglass avoided the command, proving reluctant to go northward, instead joining Washington in the defense of New York City.

On April 13, the New York Committee of Safety, wishing to expedite matters because of Douglass' ambiguity, ordered Wynkoop to enlist sailors in New York City and proceed north to take temporary command of the vessels on Lake Champlain. The Continental Congress endorsed the committee's action a month later by empowering Schuyler to appoint Wynkoop to the command in place of Douglass.[15] Washington recognized Wynkoop, asking him to enlist mariners and proceed with them to Albany and then the lakes. He continued in this capacity until August when Horatio Gates, as commander at Ticonderoga, named Benedict Arnold commander of the Lake Champlain squadron. Gates and Arnold had been hatching this promotion for some time, ignoring Congress, New York's government and Philip Schuyler in making Arnold commander; on top of it no one informed Wynkoop. On Lake Champlain, unaware of being superseded, Wynkoop challenged orders Arnold made to two vessels, firing across their bows to stop their movement.[16] Defending Arnold, Gates had Wynkoop arrested. Arnold's promotion must be seen against the background of Gates' effort to supersede Schuyler as commander of the Northern army, a future contention that Congress would decide in Schuyler's favor.

The trial over the Arnold-Wynkoop incident opened at Ticonderoga on July 20, 1776, but was adjourned because Arnold claimed he was now too busy with the Lake Champlain squadron to attend. Gates asserted to Congress's President John Hancock that Arnold had appeared at Skenesborough to be the 'life and spirit to our dock-yard'.[17] In contrast, Colonel William Maxwell, who had served under Arnold at the siege of Quebec, told New Jersey

Governor William Livingston that Arnold was 'our evil genius to the north'. After the Battle of Lake Champlain, Wynkoop still remained active. In March 1777, Schuyler reinstated him as commander at Fort George, employed in building two armed schooners. A year later, he was directed to prepare bateaux to defend the Hudson River. With the support of Gates, however, the controversial Arnold was now in command of the Lake Champlain squadron.

Royal Navy squadron

Meanwhile in June, Governor Carleton had asked Commodore Douglas to coordinate the vessels going to the lakes with the British army. Douglas realized that the Royal Navy's presence had to expand beyond the dockyards of Quebec and Montreal on St Lawrence River and into Lake Champlain and even Lake Ontario 'in order to accelerate the passage of the army'.[18]

Douglas' immediate problem was reaching Lake Champlain from the St Lawrence, as the route from Sorel was obstructed by the Chambly Rapids. When his ships moved southward on the Richelieu River, these rapids forced a significant portage. By early July, he had Captain Harvey of the *Martin* return to Sorel 'to examine into the means of floating between camels (as is practiced in Russia and Holland) through the Rapids of Chambly into Lake Champlain ...'[19] Bateaux could be drawn on rollers by horses around the rapids, but when an effort to do this with two stripped-down sloops was attempted, it was necessary to take them further apart, removing planking down to the waterline, before they could pass the rapids. The entire squadron had to be deconstructed above the rapids and then after passing them, be rebuilt again and equipped at St Johns. An observer noted 'A great many gunboats, the frames of which had come from England, were rebuilt, as was also a ship large enough to carry 20 guns, the frame of which was built in Quebec.' In addition, the schooner *Carleton* was launched below the rapids at St Johns on September 2. Originally constructed at Quebec, the frigate *Inflexible* was the last to be taken down and moved around the rapids to be rebuilt at St Johns. Douglas expressed 'unspeakable joy' that carpenters had reconstructed the 300-ton *Inflexible* and it was able to sail with eighteen 12-pounders, only twenty-eight days after its keel was laid. He believed it offered 'the prowess of which will give us the dominion of Lake Champlain beyond a doubt'.[20]

Douglas also faced the problem of 'our paucity of proper hands'.[21] To support the Champlain squadron, he took carpenters and materials from his St Lawrence fleet. Artificers also came from different army regiments. After a long passage, twenty Glasgow shipwrights and ten English house carpenters arrived and he hurried them to Chambly on transports. Guns for the vessels were taken down the Richelieu River, including twenty-eight 12-pounders and ten 6-pounders.[22] The *Inflexible*'s heavy armament was troubling, for the ship had to be floated in the deeper water below Isle aux Noix on the Richelieu before they could be placed. Guns were also needed for a few of the largest longboats.

Experienced sailors were sought for the Lake Champlain service. Douglas had the *Triton, Lord Howe, Juno* and *Isis* lend as many seamen as they could spare. On September 1 at Chambly, he sent an order to the *Triton* for thirty-seven seamen to serve on the lakes. To this was added twenty more men from the *Triton*, twenty-five from the *Isis* and twenty from the transports. Later, above 200 prime seamen from the transports 'did most generously engage themselves' to serve in the Champlain vessels.[23]

The British naval force that was finally gathered consisted of the *Carleton*, *Lady Maria*, *Inflexible*, and the radeau *Thunderer*.[24] The latter had been built for firepower and strength, as it was capable of firing six 24-pouders and six 12-pounders. It was actually a flat-bottomed barge with two masts, similar to future Chesapeake war barges, although its 90-foot deck was larger than usual. While it was a great gun platform, it was unwieldly and thus it failed to play an important role in the coming confrontation. On September 27, Captain Thomas Pringle of the *Maria* was named commodore of the Lake Champlain fleet. A week later, most of the fleet was at or below the Richelieu's Isle aux Noix.

In July, Carleton asked Douglas for the longboats from his transports and ordnance ships to convey his army down Lake Champlain. Douglas responded, 'The Masters of the transports were willing to leave their longboats and hoped that the carpenters of such vessels would also stay.'[25] He estimated that such boats could carry 1,800 men, with arms, accoutrements, tents and provisions for ten days. To get provisions to Lake Champlain, Douglas would 'drug up the [Chambly] rapids, thirty Long boats, his flat bottom boats, a Gondola weighing about thirty tons, and above four hundred Battoes'.

Douglas' command would keep him at Quebec, from where he assessed the building and equipping of the Champlain squadron. He maintained, 'The Rebels did by no means believe it possible, for us to get upon Lake Champlain this Year.'[26] Certainly, this was a squadron to be reckoned with.

Chapter 9

The Battle of Lake Champlain and the Capture of Ticonderoga

On October 5, Carleton's fleet, without the frigate *Inflexible* but including the bateau transport for the army, was on Lake Champlain. Five days later, the *Inflexible* arrived. The squadron, with Captain Pringle commanding, consisted of twenty-five vessels: the 28-gun *Inflexible*, schooners 14-gun *Maria* (the flagship with Carleton, Burgoyne and Pringle on board) and 12-gun *Carleton*, the powerful *Thunderer*, and a gondola the *Loyal Convert* (captured from the rebels and rechristened) and several gunboats.[1]

Completed at the same time, Benedict Arnold's squadron consisted of the *Royal Savage*, *Revenge* and *Enterprise*, schooners; the row galleys, *Congress* (Arnold's flagship), *Trumbull*, *Washington;* a galley cutter, the *Lee*, and gondolas: *Philadelphia, Spitfire, Boston, New Haven, Providence, New York, Jersey* and *Connecticut.* In all fifteen vessels with 800 effectives.[2]

The action between the two squadrons developed over three days: on October 11 at Valcour Island; the next day when the wind was contrary and both fleets struggled to sail down the lake; and the third day in which the British pursued the remainder of Arnold's ships, taking or forcing the abandonment of all but a few.

Initially, Arnold's fleet hid behind Valcour Island so that Pringle's ships went by them and had to tack back against the wind, having difficulty in coming close enough to fire on Arnold's ships. As General David Waterbury had warned Arnold, the rebel vessels were now boxed in Valcour Bay by Pringle's squadron. The action commenced at 11 a.m. The first casualty was the *Royal Savage,* which came out to fight and was mauled by the *Carleton* and *Inflexible.* Guillaume, Chevalier de Lorimier and a party of Indians brought the *Royal Savage* under withering fire from shore, which sealed its fate. It ran aground, the crew abandoned ship, the British boarded and turned its guns on Arnold's ships, but eventually *Royal Savage* was burnt and blew up.[3] The *Philadelphia* began to sink. Both the *Congress* and *Washington* suffered from the British guns. The only chance for Arnold was when the *Carleton* was blown into the American center and hit, but then British gunboats pulled her out of harm's way.

By 5 p.m., the fire had slackened and the British created a line across the bay to prevent Arnold's battered fleet from escaping that night, assuming they would finish them off in the morning. However, in the dark, Arnold's squadron – minus the *Royal Savage* and *Philadelphia* – escaped.[4] They made for Crown Point, but their vessels were damaged and unseaworthy, and with the wind against them, they scarcely moved, only sailing 10 miles from Valcour, by 7 a.m.

Upset the rebels had escaped, Pringle's squadron went after them on October 12. However, the wind was contrary and both fleets were forced to row, so that they remained in sight of each other but could not close the distance.[5]

The next day, the wind changed and the chase was renewed so that the British caught most of Arnold's ships. Pringle's *Maria* was fresh, having scarcely been involved at Valcour, and moved to the front of the British squadron.[6] The *Inflexible* caught General Waterbury's *Washington* near the Island of the Four Winds and forced it to strike its colors. The *Boston, Providence, New Haven, Connecticut* and *Spitfire* were abandoned. Soon the *Congress* and four gondolas were all that was left. Three British ships caught the *Congress* and knocked her main mast off, forcing Arnold to scuttle and burn it in Ferris' Bay. Arnold and his crew made their way overland to Ticonderoga. Canadian parties found the gondola *Jersey* and the cutter *Lee* abandoned and brought them to Carleton at Crown Point.

Of the original fifteen ships in the rebel squadron, only the *Trumbull, Revenge* and *Enterprise* survived. Of the gondolas, the lone survivor was the *New York.* Arnold's fleet had lost over eighty sailors, either killed or wounded, and a further 110 were captured by the British. Most of these prisoners were sent by Carleton to Ticonderoga on October 15 under a flag of truce for exchange. They, including Waterbury, were paroled as long as they returned to their homes and did not take up arms against the British for the rest of the war. Carleton was trying to foster reconciliation with the rebels, who had recently declared their independence. The British losses were insignificant and they would refit and use several of Arnold's ships in the future. A German officer concluded 'Thus, Lake Champlain was free again as most of the enemy fleet had been transformed into nothing.'[7] In the Revolution, the rebels would never again confront the Royal Navy on Lake Champlain.

Crown Point was occupied by Carleton and Pringle, although the rebels had 'set fire to and demolished everything'.[8] The post was now more of a settlement than a fortification and the inhabitants fled into the woods, leaving their household goods to the flames. Carleton would use Crown Point as a base for his attack on Ticonderoga. On arrival there, however, Carleton still had no reserve of supplies, with none coming from Canadian sources as they were hoarded to survive the coming Canadian winter. He also did not have enough men to undertake a siege of Ticonderoga, for Gates' army was more than twice as large as his. Gates had spent many months strengthening Ticonderoga in preparation for a British siege. Even Carleton's base at St Johns had not yet been rebuilt from the damage done when Montgomery had besieged it. Moreover, if Carleton had taken Ticonderoga, he faced garrisoning it over the winter – a debilitating task as the rebels would find out during the winter of 1776–1777.

As Lake Champlain began to freeze over, it was proposed that General Simon Fraser's corps remain at Crown Point over the winter, but the post offered no shelter. With the lateness of the season, Carleton felt it was prudent for his forces to retire to St Johns and prepare for a spring offensive, without the winter burden of defending Crown Point. Burgoyne, who was the ranking army officer, agreed with the retreat. In fact, his army would be rested and healthy in the spring of 1777 because they wintered in Canada.[9] Lieutenant Darcy was sent as Carleton's envoy to Quebec and then London, with his account of the naval victory and occupation of Crown Point.

Carleton had enemies in Quebec and the British Isles. He would be criticized for his conduct of the entire campaign, regardless of the fact that he had driven the rebels out of Canada and won control of Lake Champlain.[10] He was blamed for taking the time to build an excessively large squadron so that he did not reach Ticonderoga until it was too late in the season. Still, Carleton had done an excellent, if not spectacular job, in carrying the war to Ticonderoga. Considering that the Siege of Quebec had only been broken in April and by October, Carleton occupied Crown Point, controlling Lake Champlain, the criticism seems unfounded. British control of the lake would last for the rest of the war.

Canadian Winter

The victorious Royal Navy fleet returned to St Johns, where the ships were pulled on to the banks of the Richelieu to avoid the growing ice. They included the *Maria, Carleton, Inflexible, Thunderer* and the gondola *Loyal Convert,* among others. Prizes from Arnold's fleet included the galley *Washington*, cutter *Lee* and the gondola *New Jersey*. At St Johns dockyard they were refitted over the winter. Governor Carleton was concerned to keep as many warships over the winter in Canada so as to have some of their crews available for Lake Champlain in the spring. Construction of a new vessel at St Johns, the *Royal George*, would be completed over the winter.[11] It was a frigate of twenty-six guns and was to be the most powerful vessel on the lake. It and the *Inflexible* alone would carry more heavy guns than the entire remains of the American squadron at Ticonderoga.

Carleton's army at Crown Point had been small because he lacked bateaux for transport, but the army forming in the spring of 1777 would have over 100 bateaux. A German soldier praised the bateaux for 'They can carry from seven to eight thousand pounds of weight and twenty-eight or thirty people. Our soldiers, who have learned the art perfectly since they have been in Canada ...'[12]

Burgoyne's Invasion

The commander of the British spring invasion would be General John Burgoyne. He had left Canada and spent the winter in the comforts of England, lobbying for the position. This paid off, as Lord Germain was Carleton's enemy and it was easy to subtly criticize Carleton when he was not there to defend himself.[13] Carleton would not be removed but rather continue his role as governor and commander of all Canadian forces, while Burgoyne was raised to commander of the invasion force that might reach as far south as Albany.

Charles Douglas had left for England, leaving the naval command of the St Lawrence to Captain Richard Pearson, who had arrived on a convoy escort, the *Garland*, and would make a name for himself capturing rebel privateers. Below him, in April 1777, Captain Skeffington Lutwidge of the *Triton* was appointed commodore of the Lake Champlain squadron.[14] On May 28, the larger ships of Lutwidge's squadron entered Champlain without Burgoyne's army as it would not be ready for another month.

Fall of Ticonderoga

At the beginning of July, Burgoyne landed at Ticonderoga, as the rebels did not occupy Crown Point. He attempted to surround the fortifications and cut off their escape routes.

Their defenses had been expanded across the lake from the fort to Mount Independence so that it proved impossible to cover the routes completely. In looking for places to mount his artillery, Burgoyne had his chief engineer scale the undefended Sugarloaf Mountain, which, it turned out, commanded both the fort and Mount Independence. Seeing the guns above them, on July 5, General Arthur St Clair's council of war voted unanimously to abandon Ticonderoga and retreat by way of Vermont or Lake Champlain's South Bay to Skenesborough.[15]

St Clair was confident the iron chain and log floating bridge in front of the fort would prevent the British squadron from following them in their retreat down South Bay. However, Lutwidge's gunboats approached, and with a few shots broke the chain and cut through the floating bridge. Lutwidge had the *Maria, Carleton, Inflexible* and *Washington* with him and he followed the rebels, catching up with them at Skenesborough's harbor. The rebels attempted to burn the place, destroying survivors of Arnold's fleet, the *Revenge* and *Liberty*, although the British were able to salvage the latter.[16] The *Trumbull* was already in their hands as it had been left at Ticonderoga. Skenesborough, where their navy on lakes had begun, now proved to be its final demise as no ships remained from Arnold's fleet.

As Burgoyne's army moved south from Skenesborough to the Hudson River and down it to Schuyler's plantation, it became necessary to establish a supply chain back to Ticonderoga. Naval stations manned by 220 sailors were established at the Lake George Landing and Diamond Island in the middle of lake and on the Hudson River near Burgoyne's army. Later as Burgoyne's fortunes sank, at Quebec, Captain Pearson feared that 'Lieutenant Brown of the *Apollo,* Lieutenant Schank of the *Canceaux* and three or four petty Officers that had crossed Lake George with [Burgoyne] to Hudson's River … are either killed or fallen into the Hands of the Rebels.'[17] This was not so.

Within Burgoyne's army on the Hudson, a 'batoe service' had become crucial as they moved south.[18] It was chiefly made up of Loyalists, though it also contained Canadians and Royal Navy seamen. Brigadier Fraser had organized them in August, first placing them under command of Loyalist Captain Hugh Munro. It was a popular force and it soon numbered seventy. Their earliest duty was to ferry supplies between Fort Edward and Burgoyne's various camps. The Hudson was not without rapids and at times their bateaux had to be pulled out of the river and moved by land on log rollers. The corps had a gun boat, which gathered intelligence, and they were called upon to construct floating bridges over the Hudson.

At Ticonderoga by mid-September, the manning of Royal Navy ships was again a problem. Lieutenant Starke on the *Maria* reported, 'from the Sickness so predominant here, hardly any of the Vessels have, for one week together the same men or the same numbers'.[19] Lacking a surgeon at St Johns, the sick had been sent to Montreal, causing 'the number of Men employed in the Lake Service [to be] greatly shortened'.

Raids by rebels on Ticonderoga's outer defenses, including its naval stations, unnerved its commander, Brigadier Henry Powell. Seamen were captured at the Lake George Landing, leading Lieutenant Starke to feel 'it should be thought necessary to have the other Vessels mann'd and arm'd', with more seamen and officers there.[20] The raid's commander, Colonel John Brown, appropriated the vessels at the landing, moving south on Lake George, where he attacked the British base at Diamond Island. This time, in the words of a rebel sailor, the engagement 'was a very severe one. A considerable number of our men were killed and colonel [Brown] ordered a retreat, the sloop being very much disabled by the shots of the enemy.' Two gunboats and the island's garrison of the 47th Regiment had been on the alert.

Hearing of Brown's raid at St Johns, Captain Pearson immediately set out for the lakes with a relief force, consisting of Captain Graves of the *Viper* and sixty men from the *Garland,* but on arrival at Ticonderoga they found that Brown had disappeared. When news of Burgoyne's difficulties came, Pearson was prepared to offer him protection if he retreated. He 'thought … that as many Officers and Men should be sent from His Majesty's Ships … [to] give Assistance in securing the Retreat of [Burgoyne's] Army across the Lakes.'[21] He proposed to send more seamen under Captain Lutwidge, including one lieutenant, three mates, three midshipmen and eighty seamen from the *Garland* and *Triton.* However, Burgoyne was uncooperative as he considered retreat to be a blot on his reputation.

Rumors that Burgoyne's army was in serious trouble came to Ticonderoga as Loyalists and Native Americans from his auxillaries appeared. General Powell reported them to Carleton on October 19. Burgoyne had actually surrendered at Saratoga, near Schuyler's plantation, two days before. Powell added that, 'The [Trumbull], Washington, & Liberty are to sail this Day for St Johns, with some sick, who require a Change of Air, some Families belonging to the Mohawk Indians, and some Loyalists who are desirous of going to Canada.'[22] Powell wanted Carleton to order him to give up Ticonderoga, but Carleton was unwilling and continued to send reinforcements to Pearson, preventing Powell from leaving. Carleton did ask that Lutwidge be recalled to command the *Triton* and cruise about Cape Breton to protect trade.

Lutwidge was replaced on October 4, 1777 by Captain Samuel Graves. By the end of the month, the squadron was spread from Mount Independence to Crown Point, with vessels moving back and forth on the lake between Ticonderoga and St Johns. Powell finally gained enough courage to meticulously plan the evacuation of Ticonderoga, Diamond Island, Crown Point and Chimney Point.[23] On November 8, his 2,000 evacuees headed for St Johns by water and land. The navy's ships again would winter over at St Johns.

Powell's men and ships would have a future as the nucleus of a striking force that would defend Canada. His evacuation was the beginning of a Loyalist exodus from New York and Vermont to Canada that would continue for the rest of the war. The British would retain control of Lakes Champlain and George, a situation which would be exploited as they continued to send expeditions from Canada.

Chapter 10

Canada Sustained by Control of Lake Champlain

Many assume that the British evacuation of Ticonderoga late in 1777 brings an end to contention over Lake Champlain. Nothing could be further from the truth, as the lake continued to be the key to the conquest or defense of Canada.[1] After Burgoyne's surrender at Saratoga, Congress's desire to seize Canada was stronger than ever.

A forgotten part of the Articles of Confederation, which served as the rebellious colonies' first constitution, was an open invitation exclusively for Canada to join the United States, with no strings attached. Drafted only a month after Burgoyne's surrender, Article XI stated 'Canada acceding to this confederation, and adjoining in the measures of the United States, shall be admitted into, and entitled to all the advantages of this Union; but no other colony shall be admitted into the same, unless such admission be agreed to by nine States.'[2] While never taken up, the invitation stood open until the proposed US Constitution was ratified in June 1788.

Possibilities of Attacking Canada

Canada reappeared as an issue in February 1778, when France completed a Treaty of Alliance and Commerce with the rebellious colonies, ratified by Congress two months later. Congress assumed that the French would be interested in their former Quebec colony. However, two secret clauses in the alliance stated that British territory conquered by the United States would become part of the new nation and that Louis XVI renounced forever the right of possession of any British territory. The French government desired the clauses, as it did not want to be involved in a reconquest of Canada. In fact, France wished to see Canada retained by Britain as its presence constituted 'a useful source of anxiety to the Americans, which [would] make them conscious of their need for the friendship of the King [of France] and for an alliance with him'.[3] Thus when French authorities in the United States were called on to support an invasion of Canada, they would equivocate, contending it was necessary to guarantee the thirteen colonies' independence before any consideration of that issue could be made.

Congress, the Marquise de Lafayette, and even Washington remained ignorant of these secret clauses, especially the French favoring British retention of Canada. Congress continued to hope for a possible invasion of Canada with French military support.[4] As the war continued, Congress would draft several plans for an invasion, which sought French support and ignored the Royal Navy's control over Lake Champlain, blocking any invasion.

Gates' Invasion

Even before the alliance with France, late in 1777, from Pennsylvania, Horatio Gates had hatched his own plan for an invasion of Canada, which was meant to further his efforts to replace Washington as commander-in-chief.[5] It was an about face, since in 1777 Gates had made no effort to move against Powell's evacuation of Ticonderoga. Without consulting Congress, Washington, or Governor Chittenden of Vermont, Gates planned his invasion with Continental Colonel Moses Hazen and former Continental Colonel Timothy Bedel, now of the New Hampshire militia. They were to gather a force in northern Vermont, coordinating with support from the Abenakis at Odanak Mission. Bedel was an unsavory character, who had been expelled from the Continental army for his cowardly behavior, which in 1776 had caused the rebel defeat at the Battle of Cedars. Hazen's influence was dependent upon his supposed ability to raise French Canadian volunteers. The recruits in his regiment did open a road from Newbury, Vermont to the Quebec border that could serve as an invasion route.

In fact, Gates' expedition never got off the ground. He found himself isolated from Washington, and in April 1778 he was removed from the Board of War, an appointment that Congress had given him to support his interests.[6] Congress ordered Gates to Fishkill on the Hudson from where he was to administer the Northern Department. This was well below Albany, from where any Canadian invasion would have to be organized.

Lafayette's Invasion

In the aftermath of Burgoyne's surrender at Saratoga, Congress originally offered the victor of the Battle of Bennington, John Stark, the command of the 'secret' army to invade Canada.[7] Born in 1728 into a Scots Irish family in Derryfield, New Hampshire, he had performed legendary feats serving in Rogers Rangers during the Seven Years' War. He was 49 when he led the New Hampshire militia that defeated a foraging and Loyalist recruiting expedition from Burgoyne's army near Bennington, Vermont. Now, Stark had already raised volunteers at considerable expense in New Hampshire and had them ready to march for a raid to destroy the Royal Navy ships at St Johns, just as he had recruited troops for his Bennington foray.[8]

In a matter of a few days, however, Congress changed its mind, dumping Stark and adopting the Board of War's plan for a Canadian invasion, which depended upon French cooperation, by designating young Marie Joseph, Marquis de Lafayette as the invasion commander. Congress felt that Lafayette's French nationality would appeal to French Canadians. Stark learned of his removal from Gates in a letter of January 1778 in which Gates struggled to maintain his goodwill after he had been slighted by Congress. Gates claimed that Congress 'for wise and prudential reasons', had 'appointed Major General the Marquis de Lafayette in command, and [Gates' protégé] Major General Conway, second in command, who will set in concert with you in promoting the interest and political views of the United States in Canada'.[9] How Stark received his demotion from Gates is not recorded, but certainly he felt exploited by the fickle Congress.

Lafayette was inspired to lead as he hoped to win over Canadians by emphasizing the common ties of French blood. He even offered to pay for the expedition out of his own resources. Washington, who had not been consulted on the invasion plans, was not impressed by the fact that Congress wanted 'an irruption to be immediately made into Canada'.[10] He promptly labeled the expedition a 'child of folly'.

Lafayette soon discovered that he and the expedition were pawns in the effort of the Board of War and some in Congress to oust Washington from command. Lafayette needed a minimum of 5,000 troops, but when he arrived in Albany in February 1778, he found only 1,200 'naked' men, not even fit for a summer campaign.[11] This force was judged inadequate by John Stark, Benedict Arnold and even Moses Hazen, now deputy quartermaster general for the expedition. Lafayette ordered Bedel not to come to Albany, but to keep his troops to defend the frontiers of northern New Hampshire.

From the beginning, Layfette had dealt with his friend Washington rather than Gates on plans for the expedition. On February 19, 1778, Lafayette revealed to Washington that he had been told:

> I was to find General Stark with a large body, and indeed General Gates had told to me, General Stark will have burnt the [British] fleet before your arrival. Well, the first letter I receive in Albany is from General Stark, who wishes to know what number of men, from whence, for what time, for what rendezvous, I desire him to raise.[12]

Washington consoled Layfette, noting that the success of an attack on Canada would depend on troops located and readied so that they could surprise the enemy. On March 2, 1778, Congress ordered an end to the under-resourced fiasco. With the expedition on hold, Layfette left Albany to join Washington, wiser about the political intrigue of Horatio Gates. By August, Lafayette had decided to take a leave from the Continental army and return to France. Congress could not resist asking him to talk to Franklin about soliciting French support for a joint expedition against Halifax and Quebec.[13] France was preoccupied with other matters, but it is evident that Congress was still infatuated.

Stark's Invasion

On April 18, 1778, Congress again named John Stark commander of the Northern Department. Stark arrived in Albany a month later, without his New Hampshire volunteers, as they had failed to receive their promised wages. He reported that 'we expect an invasion, for the enemy's vessels are now at Crown Point, cruising along [Lake Champlain].'[14] In July, Washington continued to make Stark's chief objective the burning of the British naval base at St Johns. Simultaneously in Fishkill, Gates funneled his orders to Stark. Now Gates confided to Stark that any initiatives against Canada were impossible. Actually, he argued, an expedition would not be necessary for 'The period is not far distant when [Canada] must join the great confederation, without any force being raised to effect it; or if any, such only as is merely necessary to take possession.'[15] A bewildering statement, Gates was soon removed and dispatched by Congress to the South, where in August 1780 at Camden, his army was crushed by General Charles Cornwallis. Such was the fate of a general who had defeated Burgoyne but involved himself too much in Congress's political machinations.

In June, Stark became convinced that his fellow officer, Timothy Bedel, had defrauded the earlier planned expeditions. In Bedel's regiment, which Gates had put so much hope upon, Stark found that 'no man knew where it was' because as soon as it was mustered, the whole immediately retired to their homes and yet claimed Continental 'wages and provisions'.[16] Bedel had been collecting pay and rations for twice as many men as were actually enlisted in his regiment. Stark complained about him to Gates and asserted that the only way to ascertain the size of Bedel's regiment was to order the entire unit to proceed to Albany, where Stark could see them for himself. One hundred of Bedel's men were already at Albany and were extremely unhappy with the terms of their enlistment. The discovery of Bedel's corruption was Stark's chief contribution to organizing an invasion of Canada – which never happened.

Invasions Lack Naval Support

The realization that an invasion of Canada was an impossibility had already come to those who were most knowledgeable of the region: Schuyler and Washington. At the end of 1778, Washington wrote to Schuyler about the further chances of invading Canada. He admitted to the New Yorker that 'the emancipation of Canada is an object, which Congress have much at heart.'[17] Schuyler had proposed the building of two large vessels on Lake Champlain in preparation for a future invasion. At the moment, however, Washington was 'clear that neither force nor stratagem can give us a well-grounded hope of decisive superiority in naval strength upon Lake Champlain, where the enemy are, at present, so powerful'. He was only able to instruct his quartermaster general to gather materials for the building of the two vessels, although neither of these would ever be constructed.

Not till the end of 1780 would Congress finally abandon plans for an invasion of Canada as it had no ability to transport an army over British-controlled Lake Champlain. It now found that the New York frontier was continually being invaded from Canada; until this was prevented, any idea of an expedition against Canada was impossible.

Haldimand's Continuous Forays

Aggressive British raids over Lake Champlain from Canada also prevented Congress's invasion plans from 1778 to 1781. In Canada, Governor Frederick Haldimand was able to unleash a series of raids which reached as far as Saratoga, only 20 miles north of Albany. He used the Royal Navy on Lake Champlain to carry raiders that ravaged New York and Vermont settlements. On March 21, 1778, three local Loyalists and 100 mission Indians came from Canada and surprised Skenesborough, the rebel's only toehold on Lake Champlain, capturing the garrison of thirteen and burning several buildings before retiring up the lake on the ice.[18] Then in August, Loyalists John Peters and Justus Sherwood raided into Vermont, with thirty-four men of the Queen's Loyal Rangers and some Indians. They hid their bateaux on Lake Champlain and advanced through the woods to seize the garrison of the Onion River blockhouse, which they burnt, and they returned to St Johns with their prisoners and loot.

A more substantial foray came in October/November 1778, when Haldimand tapped Major Christopher Carleton, nephew of Guy Carleton, and Commodore William Chambers to lead a squadron of ships, gunboats and bateaux from Ile aux Noix southward. The *Maria* under Lieutenant William Adler, the *Carleton* under Lieutenant Hercules Harrison and the captured cutter *Lee* were the largest vessels.[19] The troops consisted of 324 to 390 regulars – including Hessian Jaegers – 30 soldiers of Johnson's Royal Regiment of New York and 80 to 100 Mission Indians of Kahnawake and Kanesetake. Haldimand planned the foray to take place as late in the season as possible because he predicted the rebels would weaken their guard by then and would be unable to respond. It also had to be done before Lake Champlain froze over.

Christopher Carleton's three-week foray put the Vermont and New York militia on the defensive. On November 6, a detail attacked Reymond's Mill on Beaver Creek in New York and Middlebury and New Haven on Vermont's Otter Creek. More raiders were sent to Monkton and Moore's Mill near Vergennes, as they skirmished with the Vermont militia. Then thirty regulars took captives on Putnam's Creek, just south of Ticonderoga. From St Johns, Brigadier Powell bolstered Carleton's force with additional men for the gunboats and a smith, familiar with the area, to set up shop at Ticonderoga.[20] A number of Loyalist families from Albany County and the Connecticut River Valley were rescued and taken to St Johns.

On November 14, Carleton reported that his force had destroyed 'enough supplies for 12,000 men for a four-month campaign'.[21] He had taken 79 prisoners and destroyed 1 saw mill, 1 grist mill, 47 houses, 48 barns, 28 stacks of wheat, 75 stacks of Hay, and over 80 head of cattle. Except for the drowning of seventeen men in a bateau on Lake Champlain, his losses were insignificant. The rebels had no navy or strength to oppose him. On both sides of the lake, places that had been attacked would remain devastated and would not be rebuilt until after the war.[22]

Haldimand would send further forays down Lake Champlain in 1780 and 1781. The use of ships from Carleton's 1776 squadron made it unnecessary to bear the expense of permanently occupying Ticonderoga and Crown Point. The 1780 force would again be led by Christopher Carleton and William Chambers, sailing on the *Maria* all the way to Skenesborough, where on debarkation the raid would extend to Saratoga.[23] In October and November of the following year, Ticonderoga and Crown Point were occupied by a Royal Navy flotilla and troops under Barry St Leger and Chambers. They were unaware of what was happening in Chesapeake Bay at the same time.

Despite the fact the rebels could not even defend their own border with Canada, the desire to add Canada to the union was still alive to Benjamin Franklin in France, who asked that Canada be ceded to the United States in negotiating the peace.[24] These overtures were not considered by British negotiators, and the Peace of Paris in 1783 recognized Canada as belonging to Britain.

In fact, the British continued a fortified presence on Lake Champlain far beyond the Peace. On the American side of the border, Point au Fer in New York and Dutchman's Point on North Island, Vermont remained British posts after the war.[25] During the Revolution, both had been fortified with barracks, stockades and entrenched cannon and were garrisoned by Loyalists. Not until 1796, thanks to John Jay's controversial treaty, were these posts abandoned by the British and their territory at last given to the new republic. This was the legacy of the Battle of Lake Champlain, the fall of Ticonderoga and Haldimand's forays over Lake Champlain, all of which asserted British control over this entrance to Canada.

PART 4

BLOCKADING THE COAST AND ENVELOPING NEW YORK

Chapter 11

The Royal Navy Blockade

In 1775, Lord Barrington, the Secretary of War, argued that the navy alone could bring the rebels to terms, for the army in Boston had already found itself in such trouble that it would be best if it were withdrawn. He suggested that a naval blockade would hit rebellious New Englanders in their pocketbooks and cut them off from external relief.[1] From a political perspective, however, critics pointed out that such action might encourage rather than suppress rebellion as it caused hardship for the population.

Moreover, it was a momentous task for the Royal Navy to blockade the long Atlantic coastline, stretching from Labrador to Barbados. The task was further complicated by the navy's other duties, from protecting troop and supply convoys across the Atlantic, to participating in amphibious military actions.[2] Just in the first two years of war, the navy would reinforce Boston, evacuate the army to Halifax and then transport it to New York, while it relieved Quebec at the same time.

Originally limited to the police action in Massachusetts, this expanded blockade would remain a long-term solution that the navy would enforce throughout the war. In July 1775, Captain Andrew Hamond had been chosen to command the squadron that would blockade the Delaware River, its port of Lewes, and the city of Philadelphia. Hamond believed 'the principal means of putting an end to the war was to put an entire stop to the trade of America, which was only to be done by having a great number of cruisers, and a constant succession of clean ships.'[3] Here he followed his superiors – Admiral Samuel Graves, Admiral Richard Howe, Admiral Marriot Arbuthnot – in advocating the establishment of a naval blockade over the entire North American coastline to strangle trade.

Replacing Admiral Graves as commander of the North American Station in July 1776, Admiral Richard Howe arrived to direct the blockade. He claimed to have too few ships to successfully maintain it, as ships had to be detached to support British army operations.[4] He teamed with his brother William to conduct joint expeditions with the army, which interrupted the continuity of the blockade. Still, Howe felt his blockading ships had successfully disrupted trade in the colonies below New York. After he left American waters in 1778, the blockade would continue. The ministry renewed it and it proved more promising than ever, as it led to a decrease in rebel seaborne trade beyond the coast and caused the prices of foreign goods to rise in their markets.

Disrupting Trade

The enforcement of the blockade from early 1776 was chiefly in the hands of the Royal Navy. Its ships were now allowed to take merchant ships as prizes and share in the spoils just like privateers – although it was a secondary activity, meant as an inducement to attract sailors, not a regular duty. Often navy ships simply chased suspected vessels and went aboard to investigate, convincing them to return to their home ports rather than taking them as prizes.[5]

Support of the blockade depended upon adapting to local conditions. Crucial to Hamond's blockade of Chesapeake and Delaware Bays was his ability to move seamlessly from water to land, as 'on account of the navigable rivers, there is no part of the continent where ships can assist land operations more.'[6] The numerous tributaries allowed smaller ships, tenders and barges to penetrate deeply into the interior. By emphasizing these smaller craft, the Royal Navy could sustain the blockade over a broader geographical area.

Historian Richard Buel Jr has shown that from March 1 to August 22, 1776 the Royal Navy blockade caused the number of ships entering Philadelphia from the Delaware River to plummet by two/thirds. This situation would continue and actually the blockade would become most effective late in the war in 1782, as peace was being negotiated.[7] By this time, Royal Navy ships at the Delaware Capes were augmented by privateers from New York, which were soon selling confiscated Delaware Valley flour in the city's markets. The blockade had continued to cause Philadelphia's overseas entries to fall and even its trade with minor Delaware River ports had declined. The city also suffered a credit crunch, bankrupting many merchants. As Philadelphia's trade declined, illicit trade with the British in New York rose. The blockade also effected the states' compliance with Congress's requisitions of men and supplies to carry on the war. With commerce brought to a standstill and specie (money in the form of coins, more trusted than paper notes) from the outside cut off, the states were broke or unwilling to meet their Continental obligations. Thus, to the very end, the blockade contributed to the overall distress of the rebel economy.

Blockading the Delaware and Chesapeake

The blockade required numerous small confrontations, creating a collective effect. What follows is a detailed account of Hamond's blockade of the Delaware River and Chesapeake Bay. He believed that a forceful blockade would prevent Philadelphia's munitions trade with the West Indies.[8] He explained:

> The Merchants in the French and Dutch West India Islands tell the Merchants at Philadelphia … that if they will send them very small fast sailing Pilot boats, they can supply them amply with Powder, Arms and Clothing at very little risk, but as they have no money to send in return, and these Vessels will not convey the bulky commodities of America, they can not devise any mode for remittances to be made, and unless that can be done the trade must drop. Therefore the necessity of shutting up the Ports is obvious …[9]

In March 1776, Hamond outlined the state of the blockade at the Delaware Capes, where the task was to cut Philadelphia's trade. His ships had already been frustrated by shoals and tides at the mouth of Delaware Bay, which had prevented them from getting two rebel privateers. Other rebel privateers had confounded his tender the *Lord Howe*, but it had been able to take the *Grace*, a Philadelphia ship bound for Virginia, at Cape Henlopen.[10] Earlier, the *Lord Howe* had also captured the *Stockholm* out of Dutch St Eustatius bound for Egg Harbor, New Jersey with 745 barrels of powder and bale goods.

Hamond had arrived just after the destruction of Norfolk, and Governor Dunmore asked him to organize his diverse fleet in the Chesapeake. On his way, Hamond sent the *Stockholm* to Norfolk to be refitted as the tender *Maria*. He 'manned and armed' her with an officer and four men and sent her, with the *Lord Howe*, after two small sloops coming down the bay destined for North Carolina, which they took, one in ballast and the other, the *Polly*, with groceries. Hamond distributed the food amongst his ships' companies.[11] Next, Lieutenant George Ball sent Hamond the *Dove*, a vessel bound for Philadelphia from Plymouth, Massachusetts, which Hamond scuttled as it was in ballast.

The *Roebuck* then left Dunmore, returning to Cape Henlopen on March 25, and renewed the Delaware blockade. In late March and April, it remained between Cape Henlopen and Cape May, along with its tenders and ultimately the frigate *Liverpool* and sloop *Otter*, inspecting ships, searching for pilots and taking numerous prizes. Shipping from Philadelphia would attempt to evade his blockade by maneuvering in the shallows and by running their ships on to the land, where the cargo might be unloaded by local militia. Realizing the difficulty in confronting enemy ships in the shoals, Hamond would let them pass the capes into open water, where the *Roebuck* could freely give chase and easily catch them. He also continued to perform a balancing act in placing ships at both the Delaware and Virginia Capes as he was 'desirous to keep the little footing we have in Virginia secure'.[12] He did this so well that rebel authorities reported that the *Roebuck* was in both bays simultaneously.

The day after his return to Delaware Bay, Hamond sent his ships in pursuit of a Lewes pilot schooner owned by Henry Fisher, agent of the Pennsylvania Committee of Safety. The schooner wanted to get to Philadelphia with the news of the *Roebuck*'s arrival.[13] Hamond's squadron had no difficulty in taking the vessel, but in the fog the crew escaped in a skiff and disappeared. This schooner was the first prize that Hamond would convert to serve in his squadron, because it would be useful in chasing enemy vessels. On March 28/29, he decided to destroy three of his prizes off Cape Henlopen – the *Dove*, *Dolphin* and *Betsey* – as he assessed they offered no advantages.

The Continental Navy posed no threat to Hamond's blockade, as its ships aimed to avoid him, getting into the Atlantic at any cost. The *Roebuck* and the tender *Maria* confronted their first Continental warship, the 10-gun sloop *Hornet* under Captain William Stone, which fled and was able to elude them.[14] A week later, the *Roebuck* chased the Continental brig *Lexington* under Captain John Barry, but it escaped.

Hamond had to gauge the performance of his new tenders like the *Maria* and *Lord Howe* in supporting the squadron. On its own, the *Maria* brought in a small Philadelphia-bound sloop laden with oats. At least twice, however, Hamond was forced to tow the *Maria* behind the *Roebuck*, probably because its crew was unable to manage it in difficult waters. On April 7, he sent a tender and two armed boats after a vessel, which they drove ashore, but were unable to bring off because a rebel shore party kept up a constant fire against them.[15]

Refitted merchant prizes like the *Lord Howe* did not necessarily make good tenders. Its capture of the *Grace* was not profitable because it had no cargo. Hamond also felt the *Lord Howe* had failed in its principal task, which was to acquire a Philadelphia pilot. He wanted something larger than it to serve as a tender, ideally a vessel that could carry ten guns. Finally, on April 9 he decided to disarm the *Maria* and *Lord Howe* and send them to be laid up at Norfolk. It made more sense to take recruits from the *Lord Howe* and *Grace* to fill the gaps in the *Roebuck*'s crew.[16] Lewes' rebels were puzzled by the tenders' disappearance and assumed that they had been taken by their land forces.

Without its tenders, during April, the *Roebuck* had a successful run in blockading shipping. It captured a vessel 'laden with shot & stores for a battery erecting in North Carolina'.[17] Then, it took the sloop *Sally* from North Carolina, 'laden with pitch tar & turpentine, which the rebels are in great want of', and the *Roebuck*'s tenders, after removing the cargo, destroyed the ship. Six days later, the *Chance,* under Philadelphia's Captain Cropley Rose, laden with flax seed and staves, was boarded as it came down from Philadelphia. Rose argued with Hamond, claiming that the vessel belonged to an English merchant and that the cargo was shipped legally according to an Act of Parliament. On examination of the ship's papers, however, Hamond discovered that it belonged to a rebel, Mr Carson of Philadelphia, who had been importing powder and arms from the Netherlands. Hamond seized the mostly English crew and replaced them with a prize crew that was to sail the ship to be condemned at the Halifax Admiralty Court.

On April 12, four vessels and a pilot boat came to Delaware Bay steering for Cape May.[18] The *Roebuck* was at the opposite side near Lewes and rather than immediately chasing them, it purposely allowed them to pass out into the Atlantic. The *Roebuck* then pursued them in the open water and took the schooner *Dolphin* with a cargo of hams and bread, bound for Dutch St Eustatius. Hamond also took the pilot boat. While he did not know it, the two vessels that eluded him were the first commissioned Philadelphia privateers *Congress* and *Chance.*

A few days later, the *Roebuck* intercepted a brig under Danish colors from St Croix headed for Philadelphia. As she had no valuable cargo, Hamond decided to send her back to St Croix with a warning to the governor that if they continued to allow such shipping to go, it would be considered 'a breach of the neutrality'.[19]

The acquisition of tenders was an ongoing project. While Hamond discharged many of his tenders, he complained about 'the great misfortune that has attended my not having a small sloop or two with me, which I have now been in daily expectation of arriving from headquarters'. Continuing to look for suitable tenders, he took the pilot schooner *Ranger*, and armed and adopted it as a tender, keeping its name. Then the sloop *Little John*, with a cargo of salt, limes, molasses and rum, was taken as it arrived from Bermuda.[20] Hamond adopted the ship, arming it and renaming it the *Pembroke,* and placed a midshipman with a crew on it.

Not for the last time, the *Roebuck* was twice endangered by being stuck on a shoal. The rise of tide and wind got her off without damage on both occasions.[21] Hamond was only delayed a day and was able to continue taking prizes.

Overall, the capture of numerous prizes would not in itself make Hamond or his ship's company rich. In practice, Hamond had to adopt or scuttle more ships than he was willing to keep as prizes. He admitted the *Roebuck* and its tenders had 'taken 6 or 7 small vessels, but as none of them … had cargoes of much value, [he] rather chose to destroy them than weaken [his] ships company by sending men on board to navigate them'.[22] To go to a distant Admiralty court required precious sailors and avoidance of the captive crew's efforts to retake its ship.

The blockade experience would cause one of Hamond's sister ships to be better organized to profit from capturing prizes. The entire ship's company of the sister frigate *Liverpool* produced a document of October 7, 1776, in which they designated 'Capt. Henry Bellew of the said ship and Mr George Sherry of the Bugle our agents for all such prize or prizes as shall have been sent or may hereafter be sent by us to the Port of New York'.[23] The two were to act as their attorneys to recover all sums, goods and merchandise belonging to the company, representing them before governors and judges. The transaction was signed by Bellew, two lieutenants, the master, the boatswain, the gunner, the lieutenant of marines, the clerk, two master's mates, and three midshipmen, representing eighty-five seamen, landsmen, boys and marines. It was sent to the Vice Admiralty Court at New York.

Hamond would have been amused to know that his blockade had earned his squadron the epitaph of being 'British Pirates' from Major Henry Fisher of Lewes. The *Roebuck*'s blockade threatened not only trade but opened the possibility of his squadron combining with Delaware's Loyalists. On account of the *Roebuck*'s success, the rebels in Lewes felt they were surrounded by Loyalists and found it necessary to seek outside help. The Lewes area soon became a Whig fortress surrounded by 1,500 'Disaffected' (the term used by many rebels to describe Loyalists). From April to July 1776, Lieutenant Enoch Anderson of Haslet's Delaware regiment confronted Loyalist patrols on his way to Lewes and Dover. While he claimed to be in fear of being taken captive to the *Roebuck*, he was able to arrive in Lewes unscathed and noted that the 'Loyalists were willing to remain neutral and keep the peace'.[24] Anderson demonstrated that the *Roebuck* was working with local Loyalists, who had not yet drawn hard lines between themselves and rebels like himself.

On to Philadelphia

While Hamond's official duty remained the blockade, in mid-January 1776, he had also been given leeway 'to destroy those floating batteries, and to weight up or otherwise render useless the machines sunk in the channel of the [Delaware] River' to protect Philadelphia.[25] Here was authority to leave the Delaware Capes and push northward on the Delaware River and test the defenses immediately below Philadelphia.

In late April, Hamond decided to move his squadron northward on the river in search of fresh water to fill his casks. He anchored and got the water at Fenwick Island, which he used as a base for the next weeks, his ships visiting Bombay Hook, Port Penn and finally Newcastle.[26] The squadron's presence on the Delaware prevented ammunition from being sent to the rebels at Lewes and it ended the shipping of wheat from local farms to mills on the Brandywine River. As the squadron moved up the Delaware, Fisher reported on it, alarming Port Penn. This was one of thirteen alarm posts the Pennsylvania navy had created, stretching from Cape Henlopen to Bombay Hook, Delaware and then to Chester, Pennsylvania in Philadelphia's vicinity.

On May 4, Hamond admitted to General Henry Clinton that

> Without a body of troops to act in conjunction with me, I confess, I see no
> great advantage that would arise in clearing the passage of the [Delaware]; it
> would only afford an opportunity of cannonading [Philadelphia] for a short
> time, and the navigation can be stopped without it.[27]

Hamond realized that bombarding Philadelphia would be useless without troops, especially as the blockade at the Capes had already brought the city's trade to a standstill.

The next day, the *Roebuck* moved up the Delaware River, chasing the Continental warships *Lexington* and *Wasp*. Its squadron now consisted of the *Liverpool* and two tenders. The chase went on for two days, until the *Wasp*, commanded by Charles Alexander, escaped up the Christiana River, while the *Lexington* hid near Wilmington. There they remained; neither of these Continental warships would figure in the confrontation that was coming. Two days later, Hamond's squadron was off Wilmington, where a rebel vessel was driven ashore and its cargo of bread and flour confiscated. It was claimed that Wilmington's citizens were attempting 'to ingratiate themselves with' Hamond.[28]

Confrontation

On May 6 at 1 p.m., a confrontation began (which lasted for two days) between the *Roebuck*'s squadron and the newly created Pennsylvania navy. Hamond was still thinking in terms of the blockade, his decks were covered with filled water casks, not cleared for action. He reported, '[The rebel] fleet consisted of 13 Row Galley's [*sic*], each carrying a Gun, from 18 to 32 Pounders, a Floating Battery of 10 Eighteen pounders, and a Sloop fitted as a fire ship.'[29] Actually neither the fire ship nor the floating battery would be in the confrontation, which would be carried out exclusively by the galleys. They kept their distance and remained on the river's edges so that Hamond admitted, 'being such low objects on the water, it was with some difficulty that we could strike them, so that we fired upon them near two hours.' The rebel galleys responded with an ample expenditure of ammunition, but their distance was so far from his squadron they failed to damage his ships. John Emmes, a rebel captive on the *Roebuck*, confirmed that most of the galleys' shot failed to reach the ship. George Read, New Castle attorney and Whig, commented similarly on the first day's encounter, 'I suppose it will be thought that too much powder and shot have been expended by the gallies ..., but I am well satisfied they have produced a very happy effect upon the multitudes of spectators.' The expenditure of powder was watched by Wilmington crowds along the shore, who were entertained as if it were a fireworks show.

In the evening, to get closer to the galleys the *Roebuck* moved forward but was grounded on the New Jersey shore. Hamond had the *Liverpool* and the tenders form a protective screen to warn him if the galleys returned. Plans went as far as the abandonment of the *Roebuck* and the transference of the crew to the *Liverpool*, but the galleys did not appear and must have been unaware of the vulnerable state of the *Roebuck*. She healed so far that her gun ports had to be closed to prevent flooding. (Healing is the dangerous situation in which the ship tilts to its side and does not return to an upright position.) The *Liverpool* finally got the *Roebuck*'s stream cable on board by 4 a.m. and the ship was freed, moving into deeper water. It was undamaged because the bottom mud was soft.[30] This was not the last time the *Roebuck* was stuck in the mud. Rebel authorities claimed it had been stuck on shoals only a few days before in the vicinity of Odessa, although it had managed to free itself and made its way to New Castle. Still, the close call near the rebel galleys was a lesson neither Hamond nor his crew would forget.

The following day, Hamond found that the galleys 3 miles above him had been supplied with fresh ammunition. With the wind in his favor he moved against them and they 'industriously played their oars & sails to avoid us'.[31] As the British moved north, the wind slackened and the river narrowed so that Hamond was wary of the possibility of being again stuck and he decided instead to move south hoping to lure the galleys closer to a wider part of the river. In the late afternoon, he noted, the galleys 'followed us, and kept up a smart fire, but cautiously remained at their usual distance'. As night came, the galleys stopped their pursuit near New Castle and Hamond anchored his squadron. The galleys had inflicted some damage on the *Liverpool*, but not all of their galleys had been able to reach this New Castle anchorage.

Later, Hamond summed up the confrontation with the observation, 'they fired away seven tons of powder at us, without doing us the least mischief, except the loss of one man in the *Roebuck*.'[32] The damage discrepancy between Hamond's and rebel sources may be attributed to a difference of perspective: Royal Navy ships were always prepared for combat or bad weather and routinely expected to receive and repair damage. The *Roebuck*'s carpenters applied a compound called plaster to effectively plug holes. The boatswain routinely knotted and spliced rigging to repair it. Rebel vessels often had no one to do this.

Afterwards

Hamond's squadron continued southward to Reedy Island, where it spent three days filling its water casks.[33] George Reed noted that the squadron still blockaded the river and that powder and lead destined for Lewes would have to be carried overland to avoid it. Moreover, small farmers continued to be unable to use the Delaware to ship their grain to the Brandywine mills. In Philadelphia, Congress sent Lambert Wickes, captain of the 18-gun Continental ship *Reprisal*, to confront the *Roebuck*.[34] However, before *Reprisal* was able to find the *Roebuck*, it collided with her sister ship, the 24-gun *Montgomery*, which carried away her 'Jibb boom'. Wickes had to return to Philadelphia to repair his ship, thus ending his effort to shadow the *Roebuck*.

While the *Roebuck* had not penetrated Philadelphia's defenses, its squadron remained at the mouth of the Delaware, effectively blockading the city's trade, making it seem that the colonies' largest city was under continuous siege. On September 10, 1776, much after these events, the Dutch newspaper *Middelburgsche Courant* reported that the *Roebuck* 'and two war barges' had aimed an attack on Philadelphia.[35] The paper's source was two Philadelphia ships with a load of corn in the harbor of Cadiz, Spain. Clearly this news was old and exaggerated. The routine activities of the blockade had somehow turned into an invasion.

The formal capture of Philadelphia by General William and Admiral Richard Howe took place a year later. William Howe was brilliant enough to leave the advance against the city's extensive naval defenses till last, after the city had already fallen to him. The Delaware River defenses south of the city were formidable, including at least four *chevaux de frizes*, the Billingsport gun battery, and Forts Mercer and Mifflin.[36] It took from October to mid-November 1777 to destroy them and the navy suffered the loss of a ship of the line, the *Augusta*, and another vessel, while the army was exposed to heavy casualties. However, the Pennsylvania state navy and three Continental frigates, *Effingham, Washington* and *Delaware*, proved ineffective in the defense and were forced to flee north above the city. With other priorities, Washington suggested several times that they should be scuttled, but Pennsylvania captains and Marine Committee members could not face such a draconian end. They finally accepted Washington's advice and the ships disappeared into Delaware ports, though the *Washington* and *Effingham* were caught and burnt by the Royal Navy. When Admiral Howe decided to leave to winter at Newport, Andrew Hamond replaced him as commander of the occupation fleet with the duty of keeping Philadelphia's Delaware River supply lines open. On the basis of his earlier experience with the blockade, he would again be a success in the narrow Delaware waters.

Chapter 12

Amphibious Operations take New York

In mid-August 1776, the largest British expedition of the war was gathered against New York, the crucial port, halfway between Boston and Philadelphia. New York had a superb harbor, was at the southern end of the Hudson–Champlain corridor, and was a center of Loyalist sentiment. William and Richard Howe commanded the army and the navy that had been gathered at Staten Island to capture the city. The *Roebuck* joined a fleet of twenty-five men-of-war and 300 transports under Lord Howe. Hamond expressed, 'the pleasure [he] received in finding my friend Lord Howe entrusted with the conduct of the American business ... because I know his abilitys for carrying on a war are not to be excelled.'[1]

The New York expedition required a great battle fleet, a concentration of resources which also exposed shortcomings. Hamond noted that

> the Ships [in the New York fleet] are ill mann'd & very short [in numbers]. You ... have no Idea of the Number of Men it takes to attend upon such an Army as this is; with the Ships we have here (which is two-thirds of those employed in America) when all the Flat Boats, Galleys, Gondolas ... are mann'd, there is scarce Men enough left on board many of the Ships to move them.[2]

Even then, six or eight more ships of the line were needed, not so much for their fire power as 'for their large complements of Men'.

Hamond identified the lack of skilled seamen in the larger ships as being critical. He was also not pleased that the New York expedition took him away from the blockade of the Virginia and Delaware Capes:

> Unfortunately this expedition against New York has necessarily required the attention of so many ships, that all the Southern Ports are now left open, and there is no doubt but [the rebels] will embrace this opportunity – to send away their Tobacco and Grain.[3]

Washington Defends New York

Washington's defending army was soon trapped in the city because there was no navy to carry on amphibious operations and thus it was easily outmaneuvered by General Howe. In September at daybreak, the *Roebuck* was among the ships covering the unopposed landing of flat-bottomed boats with 15,000 men and an artillery train at Gravesend Bay, Long Island. General Howe's army then attacked the entrenched rebels, outflanking their position and winning the Battle of Long Island. Although separated from Manhattan by the East River, Washington reinforced his army in fortified Brooklyn Heights. In an effort to cut off his defenders from Manhattan, the *Roebuck* moved up the East River. Despite contrary winds, it was able to fire on the Red Hook battery, which guarded the East River entrance, and destroy it. However, without additional help the *Roebuck* could make no further progress.[4] Admiral Howe sent five more warships to sustain the *Roebuck*, but a strong north wind and an ebbing tide kept the warships back and overnight Washington's Brooklyn army was able to escape to Manhattan.

On September 13, the *Roebuck* was in a squadron with the *Orpheus, Carysfort* and *Phoenix* that moved up the Hudson River in a demonstration of the navy's distain for fixed fortifications. They wanted to gain control over the river, which was an important source of supply for Washington's army. Commanded by Captain Hyde Parker, the squadron contemptuously did not even return fire when the rebel forts' guns opened upon and damaged their ships.[5] The squadron succeeded in moving past the guns and up the river. Two days later, several warships covered General Howe's landing of 12,500 soldiers on Manhattan at the East River's Kips Bay. General Henry Clinton, William Howe's second in command, went aboard the *Roebuck* to reconnoiter the landing.[6] From the river, the squadron bombarded the rebel entrenchments for an hour and the rebel militia units facing the landing fled. The rebels soon evacuated New York City and it was occupied without British casualties.

The focus was now on where Washington's army would go. To continue the navy's effort to control the Hudson, plans were made to invest the strong rebel battery at Paulus Hook, New Jersey. The plans were delayed as it was discovered that New York was ablaze in a fire blamed on the rebels. Two days later, the *Roebuck*, *Tartar* and *Emerald* bombarded Paulus Hook, softening its defenses, and troops from New York in flat boats, landed and took possession of the works, as the rebels fled.[7] The British would continue to hold the Hook using it as a row guard base on the Jersey side of the Hudson.

General Clinton felt that controlling the Hudson River was the key to bagging Washington's army before it escaped to New Jersey. To stop Hudson Valley foodstuffs from reaching Washington and to prevent his army's access to New Jersey, a further naval demonstration was necessary. The rebels had laid a *chevaux de frize* and stretched a boom across the Hudson between Forts Washington and Lee to obstruct naval passage. On October 9, again Hyde Parker of the *Phoenix* led the squadron, followed in a line by the *Roebuck*, the *Tartar*, a schooner and two tenders in the face of cannonading from the forts. Parker had a pilot with him who was supposed to open a channel, but he lost his nerve and Parker on his own found deep water to carry the squadron through. Then Parker chased four rebel galleys, two sloops and a schooner toward Dobbs Ferry, moving almost 30 miles up the river as far as Tarrytown. Two rebel galleys and the other vessels ran ashore and became prizes. Parker's fleet then returned, again running the gauntlet of the forts' guns. The navy ships suffered damage and casualties. Hamond described how 'The shot that did the ships the most damage was from the Jersey shore [and] we were upwards of an hour in passing.'[8] Hamond praised Parker's leadership in the affair as the navy continued to be contemptuous of the forts' guns.

Washington reported that the British fleet 'ran up the [Hudson] River without receiving any interruption from our *chevaux de frize* or apparent damage from our batteries, tho a heavy fire was kept up against them from each side of the river'.[9] Ultimately, General Howe's army would capture both Forts Washington and Lee, including over 2,800 men at Fort Washington, as well as ordnance and munitions. A month later, Royal Navy ships were at Tappan Bay on the Hudson, 30 miles above New York City. The rebel river obstructions, batteries and ships had proved to be only a minor obstacle in establishing control of the Hudson. However, despite a victory over Washington at White Plains, General Howe failed to pursue him and Washington's army crossed the Hudson without opposition at Peekskill, escaping into New Jersey. The navy's Captain George Collier showed 'inexpressible astonishment and concern' in witnessing General Howe's failure to destroy Washington's retreating forces after many brilliant maneuvers.

In early October, the *Roebuck* with the *Phoenix*, *Tartar* and *Rose* seized the galley *Crane* with its cannon, apparel and furniture; its crew had abandoned it in the Hudson River.[10] The captains asked that it be declared a prize by the New York Admiralty Court and that the proceeds be equally distributed among their ships, including the seamen, marines and soldiers. The Royal Navy was then with much competition in taking prizes, but it would take two years for the court to make a favorable decision.

Occupation

The British military occupied and governed New York under martial law until November 25, 1783. While the restoration of civilian government was often proposed and Mayor David Mathews retained his title, it never actually happened. This caused friction between the military and the municipal authorities. For instance, British officials found it difficult to control Royal Navy sailors on land. In December 1779, General James Pattison forbade seamen off the East River from going ashore on Long Island because their plundering would deprive the city markets of produce.[11]

The military came to depend on officials who were not respected by the city's Loyalist leadership. Andrew Elliot, customs collector, made himself indispensable to the military, accumulating positions of importance in the city, but not admiration.[12] At first exiled in New Jersey, he had returned to New York by late September 1776, as the British re-occupation of the city began. Elliot resumed his position as customs collector and in July 1777, he was appointed by General Howe as the superintendent of imports and exports of New York's port. He was charged with issuing licenses that restricted trade in favor of military objectives, causing Loyalists to accuse him of using his position to wallow in luxury, acting like a 'Turkish Bashaw'. From the navy's standpoint, he collected the monthly sixpence from seamen's pay for the support of Greenwich Hospital. By March 1780, he was lieutenant governor of the Province of New York under James Robertson, who had succeeded William Tryon as governor. When Robertson returned to England in April 1783, Elliot became acting colonial governor of New York, a post he held for about eight months. He worked with Guy Carleton on the evacuation from the city of British troops, government officials, and white and black Loyalists. In December 1783, he finally returned to his native Scotland.

Despite these problems, the city's population grew to 33,000 civilians in 1779, the largest it had ever been. Illicit trade between the city and surrounding rebel-held areas fostered the growth. As Alexander Hamilton calculated in 1782, New York rebels were spending £30,000 on British manufactures from New York merchants and the other rebel areas in proximity to the city were purchasing an additional £8,000 worth. Its merchants 'scorned [Robinson] Crusoe-style isolation from the world's traffic and applauded material plenty, fuller employment, and maturing settlements'.[13] Founded in 1768, its Chamber of Commerce at the beginning of the war was divided between Whigs and Loyalists. When the Whigs left the city during the occupation, the Chamber became the leading civilian body, representing community concerns to the British. It cooperated with the military, especially when called upon to recruit sailors and encourage privateers.

In 1776, the New York area already had the largest black population north of the Mason–Dixon line. On Staten Island one-fifth of the population was black and the use of slave labor was so widespread that non-propertied white men were unable to find employment there, being forced to make a living by going to sea. Shipbuilding expanded, employing blacks, while the masters of ships, especially privateers, had crews which drew from the city's free blacks' population. In turn, blacks were willing to welcome the growing number of black refugees who made their way to the city during the war.[14] As a result of the capture of New York, it replaced distant Halifax as the chief base for North American operations.[15] While Admiral Howe preferred to winter at relatively ice-free Newport, Rhode Island, he would not neglect the New York area to refit ships for southern stations. The largest North American careening yard was re-established near the city in 1776 at Turtle Bay, the best harbor on the East River, where a careening facility and store houses already existed. At the southern entrance to New York Bay, fortifications were erected around the lighthouse at strategic Sandy Hook, New Jersey; these would play an important role in the city's future defense. New York would be held by the British for the rest of the war and future chapters will round out this account of the city's occupation.

Chapter 13

Clinton and Wallace Sail the Hudson

After New York fell to the Howe brothers, it became the home of an Admiralty court, a center of privateering, and a magnet for Loyalist refugees. With these attributes, it was the place from where British expeditions were organized and sent out. Our focus is on an expedition up the Hudson River, which was part of a strategic effort to separate the New York and New England colonies, preventing unified action along this corridor.

In late June 1777, in New York, Henry Clinton received a letter from William Howe, who had been at sea a week with his army on his way to capture Philadelphia, suggesting to Clinton that 'If you can make a diversion in favor General Burgoyne's approaching Albany, I need not point out the utility of such a measure.'[1] This was Howe's attempt to make up for the fact that Minister George Germain had originally hoped he would cooperate with Burgoyne's army (which had run into deep trouble near Schuyler's Saratoga plantation), coming down from Lake Champlain. Howe had with him 15,000 troops, leaving Clinton to believe that he had too few men to do more than defend New York City.

The man on the spot, Henry Clinton, was born into the British aristocracy and his family and professional connections were so significant that no government could afford to ignore him.[2] Although he had never held a field command, he knew his business as a soldier. He had a keen analytical intelligence, which could fit details into an overall pattern, seeing always the form of the strategic wood through the tactical trees. His bent was aggressive and as a military planner he had great gifts. This was offset by his paranoid suspicions, always in fear of real or imagined enemies among the British military.

The Hudson Highlands

Among other objectives, Clinton had contemplated attacking the rebel fortifications in the Hudson Highlands, 50 miles to the north of New York. Here, the river was not only dominated by mountains on both sides but it was a narrow spot, control of which effectively blocked the route to the north. In addition to the forts, a *chevaux de frize* had been sunken in and an iron chain and log boom stretched across the river.[3] The defenses were crucial to Washington to ensure east–west movement of New England recruits and militia around New York City to support his army in New Jersey and Pennsylvania. Moreover, the rolling land north of the Highlands was wheat country, one of Washington's best sources of foodstuffs for his army.

In early June 1777, Washington had gone to defend Philadelphia from the Howes, leaving General Israel Putnam, the legendary Seven Years' War hero, at Fishkill on the Hudson to command rebel forces. Putnam sensed that Clinton in New York was preparing a strike, although he was unsure of where. He described how a single enemy galley was constantly cruising up and down the river at pleasure and had been as far as Fort Independence, stopping the ferry because 'we have nothing on water that can oppose her.'[4] Moreover, enemy crews could land and plunder the inhabitants for more than 50 miles on the river 'without molestation'. As no naval force was strong enough to challenge them, the Royal Navy and Loyalists could even prevent Putnam's forces from crossing the river.

Putnam hoped the river's Continental squadron would be bolstered by the New York Council of Safety's forwarding of its frigates, *Montgomery* and *Congress,* to Fort Montgomery. Instead, the Council of Safety voted on June 5 to pay off the crew and put the *Montgomery* up for sale, defending the sale as a matter of economic necessity.[5] While the *Montgomery* was not immediately sold, in effect, the forts in the Hudson Highlands were left on their own, without naval support.

Clinton's Hudson River Diversion.

In September, Clinton received reinforcements and a request from Burgoyne at Saratoga for help as the rebel army he faced was increasing.[6] Before leaving, Howe had recommended that Clinton concentrate on the defense of New York and make no diversions, with the exception of a request from Burgoyne. Thus, Clinton felt he could act, although he did not think he could reach Burgoyne, but that his presence in the Highlands would take pressure off Burgoyne's army.

New York's Royal Governor William Tryon had already produced a plan that allowed troops to travel up the Hudson to rapidly reach the Highlands, alternating water transport with marching. Clinton brought together nearly 3,000 men and moved them by stages to Stony Point, on the same side of the river as the forts.[7] He had flatboats and bateaux sent down Spekendevil Creek. Captain Powell with 1,100 troops proceeded to Tarrytown and another equal division marched from Kingsbridge. Besides the Royal Fusiliers and the Trumbach Hessians, the force had numerous Loyalists – from the Westchester County Light Horsemen to Emmerick's Chasseurs. The galleys and armed vessels carrying them were under Captain Onmarney. The squadron was immediately commanded by Sir James Wallace, under Commodore William Hotham, who remained in the city. After the squadron arrived at Tarrytown, they reached Verplank's Point and Wallace went north to cut off the rebels at Peekskill Ferry on the east side. This was part of a feint to make Putnam think that his force was the object of the expedition. Putnam would remain under this delusion for the entire campaign and timidly keep his troops on the east side of the river far from the action.

For the success of the campaign, Clinton would find Commodore James Wallace, captain of the *Friendship*, indispensable. Early in the war, (as we have seen) he had made a reputation by reducing smuggling in Rhode Island. In 1777, he had become the captain of the 50-gun *Experiment*. Sent to England with military dispatches, he would be knighted there before returning to New York.[8]

Forts Attacked

Leaving 400 troops at Verplank's Point to distract Putnam, the bulk of Clinton's army marched from Stoney Point inland to approach Forts Clinton and Montgomery from the rear.[9]

They marched 12 miles north over the rugged terrain that had convinced the rebels to build the forts at this natural defensive spot. The force was split so that each fort could be attacked simultaneously. The forts' garrisons were under the command of the two Clinton brothers, George and James, who sent out parties to harass the British in the rugged terrain. Sir Henry finally got both his armies in place at 4 p.m., and after that the action was swift and decisive. Using the bayonet, the British took the forts by the end of the day. A total of sixty-seven guns and considerable stores fell into their hands.

Meanwhile, Wallace's warships, galleys for the shallows and transports for supplies, moved above Peekskill Landing. In the afternoon, the squadron advanced and opened fire on Fort Montgomery to divert rebel attention away from the fort's rear, from where the attack came. Wallace got near enough with two galleys to throw shot into the fort. Next, the boom and chain across the Hudson from Fort Montgomery were destroyed.[10] Above them, rebel galleys and two sloops were taken, while the retreating rebels burnt the still existing frigates *Montgomery* and *Congress*.

Further up the river on October 7, the British sent a joint summons to Fort Constitution opposite West Point to surrender, but as 'our Flag meeting with an insolent Reception', they embarked in Wallace's galleys to attack but found the fort had been evacuated in the greatest confusion, the store houses burnt, although the cannon were unspiked.[11] From there, Wallace's squadron went up the river to pick its way through another *chevaux de frize* between Polypus Island and the main river channel.

Two days later, Tryon was detached to destroy the Continental Village, a base designed for 1,500 men, where he burnt the barracks, several storehouses and loaded wagons.[12] It was the only establishment in the Highlands from which Continental troops could draw supplies. Certainly, the British victory was complete.

Wallace & Vaughan's Expedition

Clinton had achieved his goal in taking the Highland fortifications, but the fear that Washington's army might return from Pennsylvania forced him to leave the expedition, returning to defend New York City. He now found that Burgoyne was trouble, so much so that he requested orders from Clinton as to whether he should attack the enemy at Saratoga or retreat to Canada. On October 6, Clinton answered him in third person: 'Sir Henry Clinton cannot presume to send orders to General Burgoyne.'[13] He had never been privy to Burgoyne's orders and Burgoyne was obviously attempting to shift the blame for his troubles on to Clinton.

Still, Clinton was willing to leave Commodore Wallace, Major General John Vaughan and Governor Tryon to lead the expedition further north to relieve pressure on Burgoyne. This territory was wheat country, produced from large manorial estates, owned mostly by New York's rebel elite. It was a commercially oriented agricultural environment similar to the Delaware River Valley or upper Chesapeake Bay. Wallace's squadron now included the 14-gun *Raven*, the 22-gun *Friendship*, twenty galleys and flat boats, while some ships remained at the captured forts. Vaughan's force of 1,600 consisted of 7th Royal Fusiliers, and the 26th and 63rd regiments.[14] Wallace's galleys and schooners were already within 3 miles of Poughkeepsie, where he burnt Van Keuren Mills, buildings and vessels. By October 14 they had destroyed Poughkeepsie's shipyards and a number of small villages and large houses, including that of William Livingston. William was the son of Philip Livingston, the second lord of the vast Livingston Manor, who had moved to New Jersey in 1772 and during the Revolution became governor of that state.

Advance to Esopus

After the loss of the Highlands, New York's Governor George Clinton and General Putnam had retreated north, shadowing the Vaughan-Wallace expedition. Clinton reported to his legislature in Esopus and requested that they order out the Ulster and Dutchess County militia. By October 10, Clinton proposed to head off the British, but found 'The militia do not join me as I could wish ... They are anxious about the immediate safety of their respective families ... who are moving further from the river.'[15]

The British force of 'eight large square rigged vessels' proceeded up the Hudson, destroying a number of vessels as they sailed, until they arrived at the mouth of Esopus Creek, where two batteries and an armed galley fired on them.[16] Wallace realized that such an obstacle could not be left in his rear. The next day, the *Friendship*, supported by the ships' boats, attacked the Esopus batteries, driving the rebels from them, spiking their guns and burning two brigs, several armed sloops and stores upon the shore. In this action, he felt the officers and men 'behaved with great spirit'.

The village of Esopus lay above the creek and it was the most populous place between New York and Albany. It was the seat of New York's rebel government, including the New York Committee of Safety. General Vaughan noted that 'Esopus being a nursery for almost every villain in the country, I judged it necessary to proceed to the town.'[17]

From 1775, Esopus had been dominated by its Committee of Observation, which opposed disaffection from the first, stating that Loyalists should 'be punished ... as enemies to the liberties and privileges of American subjects'.[18] The town censored opposition to the Revolution by burning copies of *A Westchester Farmer's Resolves,* which condemned the Congress sitting in Philadelphia. Beginning in August 1776, the town was divided by demonstrations caused by wartime privations. In front of its meeting house, women announced that if food shortages were not resolved 'their husbands and sons shall fight no more'. The women felt it was their place to influence the government because these were issues of family and domestic concern. In November, Esopus was the scene of a resulting riot when a crowd broke into warehouses and stores, seizing tea.

By the time Vaughan's troops entered Esopus on October 16, the New York government had fled to nearby Hurley. However, rebels remained and they fired upon the British from the houses, 'which induced [Vaughan] to reduce the place to ashes ... not leaving a house'.[19] Thus Esopus joined a litany of war burnings, like Falmouth by the British or Norfolk by the rebels.

Livingston Manor

A day later, Vaughan pushed forward on board the *Friendship* off Livingston Manor, the river's east side, a place where the desire for better leases and avoidance of militia service had led tenants to rebel against the Livingstons only few months earlier. Vaughan ravaged several properties belonging to the Livingston family.[20] They included: the house, storehouse, barn, and outbuildings of Petrus Ten Broeck, a rebel general; the house, barn and out-houses of Robert Gilbert Livingston, jun., son of Gilbert Livingston of Esopus; and a house and mill belonging to Robert Livingston Jr., the third and last lord of the manor, who represented it in the New York Assembly. The next day, as they moved north, Vaughan destroyed another Robert Livingston house, one belonging to Mr John Livingston, and three others. Onshore parties burnt the Clermont homes of Margaret Beekman Livingston and her son Robert, who had just been named New York's first chancellor, as well as tenant houses. Margaret fled with her daughters to Salisbury, Connecticut. Robert Livingston Jr. moved his family to Ancram, although his own house and outbuildings were spared. Raiding the rebel aristocracy's substantial properties from the water had become an accepted part of the British war effort.

Unaware that Burgoyne had surrendered, on October 22, Vaughan's expedition reached its northern limit, as he wrote to Clinton, 'From the accounts I had received of Burgoyne's situation, I found it impracticable to give him any further Assistance.'[21] Still as the expedition returned, two houses were burnt, one the property of Mr Smith. A sloop and barn, likewise two more houses, with their appendages, were also burnt. Back at Esopus, a quantity of powder and a large number of firearms, together with many valuable stores, were burnt. Altogether the expedition had destroyed 1,150 stands of arms, 44 barrels of powder, 800 small vessels and 400 houses, barns and mills. Vaughan concluded, 'I can't be too thankful to Sir James Wallace, Captain [Henry] Stanhope, and the rest of the Officers of the Navy for their great Attention and Assistance upon that Expedition.'

Forty miles to the north in Albany, the burning of Esopus and the proximity of Wallace's fleet caused consternation. The city fathers sent a delegation to Gates at Saratoga to confer with him on the city's protection, but he was not about to detach a single soldier from Saratoga, claiming that the city's defenses were adequate.[22] Albany leaders then ordered local militia to join Putnam's army along the banks of the upper Hudson and to have flour sent to Albany.

Vaughan now noted a gathering opposition on shore for Putnam had finally taken post with 5,000 men on the east side, while Governor Clinton with 1,500 was on the west. Vaughan continued southward unopposed to Fort Vaughan where he arrived on October 26. General Howe in Philadelphia had requested reinforcements. Thus, Clinton had 'ordered [Vaughan's] Troops [now] destined for Philadelphia to sail immediately for New York'.[23]

Putnam's Failure

On October 18, Governor Clinton had warned Putnam, that,

> The enemy is eight or ten miles above [Esopus] burning away, … with my present force I can't advance to oppose them with safety to my artillery … I imagine the enemy will not proceed higher up the river and that on their return they will attempt to lay waste the places they have passed.[24]

Governor Clinton had to look to Putnam for troops as he had 6,000 spread along the Hudson, although they were chiefly militia. Most were held on the east side of the river because they lacked the vessels to cross it, which anyway was controlled by the British. Putnam had failed to produce promised troops to save Esopus.[25] He became aware that he had to prevent the progress of the British northward as it was meant to relieve Burgoyne. Still, he found a lack of spirit among his militia – who wanted to go home: 'The general is surprised to hear that any … militia who have come into the army in defense of their country should be so lost to all sense of honor and of regard to our general's safety as to abandon their posts or think of deserting the army in this critical moment. …'[26]

A court martial would look into Putnam's lethargy, but as expected he was exonerated. His inability to control the Hudson River had frustrated his ability to act.

The effect of the Vaughan-Wallace expedition on New York's food supplies would be evident in the winter of 1777–1778. From Valley Forge in February 1778, Washington wrote to Governor Clinton of New York about how 'For some days past, there has been little less than a famine in camp.'[27] He affirmed that his army would disband if it did not receive provisions, although he recognized that the Hudson Valley had been the scene of military devastation. Clinton responded that New York had no 'material supplies' to send him and he feared if the war continued 'a very fertile part of this state will be depopulated – The shores of the Hudson River will be deserted.'

Alfred Thayer Mahan, in his classic *The Influence of Seapower upon History*, singled out the importance of the 1777 expedition up the Hudson as an example of 'how a British amphibious force could have easily controlled the Hudson River and severed Washington's communications with New England'.[28] Crucial to the British success was Clinton's decision after the Highlands were taken to continue the expedition under Wallace and Vaughan, showing 'what might have been done under a better system'. They had come within 40 miles of Albany, which Burgoyne claimed to be his objective. If Howe had remained in New York and followed Clinton's example, using his naval power to dominate the Hudson, Albany would have easily fallen to him, and Gates at Saratoga would have found himself sandwiched between two British armies.

PART 5

RAIDING THE BRITISH ISLES

Chapter 14

American Commissioners and Captains in Europe

While conflict unfolded in New York, American commissioners in France would send two ships' captains to raid the British Isles in the summer of 1777. Captains Lambert Wickes and Gustavus Conyngham faced difficulties that later captains would not. No French alliance existed for them as France and Spain remained neutral, subject to British threats, which made them ultimately expel these two American raiders from their ports. While both raiders would be successful from the standpoint of taking merchant prizes, this emphasis would be

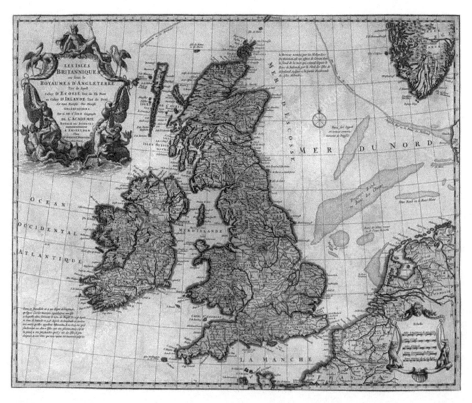

The British Isles.

dangerous to the commissioners who promoted them. The French court was not ready for Wickes and Conyngham and it would take another year for France to ally itself with the rebellious colonies.[1]

American Commissioners

In October 1776, Captain Lambert Wickes of the *Reprisal* was ordered by Congress's Marine and Secret Committees to carry Benjamin Franklin and his two grandsons to France. Wickes' orders directed him not to digress from getting Franklin to France by taking prizes. Franklin was so sick from the voyage that he had Wickes allow him and his grandsons to disembark at the first fishing boat they could find, which landed them at Auray.[2] It was the beginning of a career in Europe in which Franklin could claim equal honors with Robert Morris as being the father of the Continental Navy.

Franklin was to join Silas Dean of Connecticut and Arthur Lee of Virginia to form the commission whose goal was to obtain a political and commercial alliance with France. It never seemed to bother them that France was an absolute monarchy without an English constitution to prevent the arbitrary power of a monarch.[3] The initial expenses of the new commission were to be paid for by a cargo of indigo which had been shipped to Nantes, France; Franklin was to see to its sale. It was at this time that Dean met with James Aitken, the incendiary who planned to burn British dockyards. Here was the inauspicious beginning of the American Commissioners in France, who would become the focal point of American naval activity in Europe.

While seeking an alliance with France, the American commissioners could not resist the pleas of Continental and privateer captains to raid the rich pickings in European waters. Even if some French were sympathetic to the American cause, the commissioners had to be careful because the French Foreign Minister, the Comte de Vergennes, was determined to remain neutral. It was Vergennes opinion that France was not ready for war with Britain. Thus, he would impound ships and imprison crews operating under the auspices of the commissioners.[4] The diplomatic crisis created by these two captains angered Vergennes and made him break off contact with the commissioners, and their threats to begin negotiations with Britain did not help.[5]

The commissioners did facilitate less blatant activities. Munitions were always in short supply in the colonies and, whenever possible, Continental warships were to return to America with them. Congress hoped that this would be done quickly as the war effort was constantly stalled without them. From the standpoint of its captains, however, delays in Europe made speed impossible and the munitions trade was not lucrative. Higher aspirations existed among some commissioners that proved impossible to fulfill. In May 1777, Benjamin Franklin dreamed, 'We have not the least doubt but that two or three of the Continental frigates sent into the [North Sea] with some lesser swift sailing cruisers, might intercept and seize a great part of the Baltic and Northern trade.'[6] He was referring to seizing naval stores, which Royal Navy dockyards depended upon, from Baltic convoys. Linen trade convoys in Irish waters might also be targets. The disruption of any trade in the British Isles proved enticing.

The commissioners could offer Congressional privateer letters of marque to merchant vessels in France. Silas Deane specialized in privateers and, with French business partners, actually selected privateer captains in whom they might invest.[7] Of course, the more privateers, the less able were Continental ships to gather crews and devote themselves to operations that profited from the sale of prizes. In Europe, this created the impression that Continental warships were in fact privateers because the commissioners' limited funds led them to act as such.

Ultimately, Franklin, Deane and Lee did not get along.[8] Lee exposed several of Dean's dubious financial transactions. Lee bombarded Franklin with written allegations of corruption to the point that Franklin admitted he did not answer them and had some burned. Lee threatened he would report on Franklin's disloyalty to Congress where he had the strong support of his brother Richard Henry Lee. The dissention was finally solved in February 1779, when Congress dissolved the commission and named Franklin alone minister plenipotentiary to the court of France.

Lambert Wickes

Captain Lambert Wickes followed his orders from Congress to the letter, informed the American commissioners of his location often, and meticulously kept his ship's log. He would be an ideal Continental captain because he respected Congress and did not embellish his deeds. From an old Maryland Eastern Shore family, he was born in 1735 at the family homestead Wickcliffe, near Shipyard Creek and Chestertown.[9] From his few letters it appears that he was not well educated. He became captain of the for-hire merchant ships *Neptune* and *Ceres*, trading wheat, flour and staves from the Chester River, Annapolis and Oxford to Spain's Canary Islands, Falmouth, Cornwall and London. He returned to the Chesapeake with European manufactures and indentured servants; he had become familiar with the British Isles' waters and would make his reputation through wartime cruising, most of it in Europe.

In May 1776, with the support of Robert Morris, Wickes had been made captain of the 18-gun, 130 men, Continental brig *Reprisal*. After returning to Philadelphia for repairs from a collision with another frigate, Wickes' *Reprisal,* with two other ships, was able to elude the *Liverpool* and get to Cape May by traveling in shoal water 'where [the *Liverpool*] could not follow them'.[10]

Wickes was then ordered by the Secret Committee to transport young Philadelphia merchant William Bingham to French Martinique in the West Indies. There he would act as the crucial agent responsible for getting the best prices for colonial staples and the lowest prices for munitions. On his return, Wickes was to carry munitions for the Continental army.[11] He sailed from Philadelphia, but his cruise was interrupted in the Delaware River, where he came upon the Continental 6-gun brig *Nancy*, which was being chased by six Royal Navy ships. It carried 400 barrels of needed gunpowder and its captain decided his only option was to run the *Nancy* aground and try to salvage as much of the cargo as possible. The *Reprisal* and another Continental ship begun to unload the gunpowder on to their ships as the British closed in. Wickes' brother Richard, his third lieutenant, led the unloading, during which, however, the remaining powder exploded, killing him. Still, the *Reprisal* continued on, clearing the Delaware Capes and ultimately delivering Bingham to Martinique. *Reprisal* did have to escape the challenge of HMS *Shark* at Martinique, but it had the support of the French fort's guns in St Pierre Harbor because Captain General d'Argout felt the *Shark* was the aggressor, disturbing the peace.

Wickes' next assignment from the Secret Committee was the aforementioned delivery of Franklin to France, but he could not stay for long as French authorities, under pressure from the British, asked him to leave. He returned to Philadelphia by way of Martinique, carrying not only the munitions Bingham had obtained but goods like rum and molasses that Bingham had acquired on account for Willing, Morris & Co. Of course, Robert Morris was a member of both the Marine and Secret Committees and, along with Bingham, reaped a personal profit from this sale.[12] The mixing of public and private interests would continue throughout the war.

From Philadelphia, the Congressional committees now sent Wickes and the *Reprisal* back to France, hoping to foster trouble between France and Britain. Early in 1777, based in France, the *Reprisal* cruised to the Bay of Biscay. After a forty-minute battle and the loss of one killed and two officers wounded, it took the mail packet *Swallow,* which traveled between Britain and Portugal.[13] The *Swallow* was not a merchant ship but rather part of the mail service and thus the British described the attack as piracy because they did not recognize American independence. When Wickes attempted to return to France with his prizes and put in at Lorient, French authorities ordered him to leave within twenty-four hours. He claimed his ship was in danger from a leak and it needed to be careened for hull repairs, an excuse, but also a reality.

On April 27, the Lorient authorities again ordered the *Reprisal* out and forbade Wickes to take any prizes on the French coast – 'on any pretense whatsoever'.[14] However, Wickes refused to sign the French orders, claiming they were not consistent with his orders from Congress and asserting that he had never taken prizes on the coast of France. Clearly his arguments were an effort to delay, but he knew he could not stay and finally he proposed to go to Nantes.

While at Lorient, Wickes faced an all-too-common experience: the mutiny of *Reprisal*'s crew. After his arrival, the entire crew had refused to go to sea until they received their prize money. He prevailed upon them to go to Nantes for the prize money and he affirmed that they would be paid there. As their one-year service had now expired, Wickes hoped the commissioners would be punctual in 'giving orders to Mr Morris for paying them', as he hoped 'to prevent any dispute between me and Mr Morris'.[15] The crew did promise to continue on the *Reprisal*, provided they received their compensation. If they were not paid, however, Wickes felt he would have to sail directly to America with only a portion of the crew, perhaps thirty or forty men.

Wickes gained his crew's trust and late in May 1777, he followed orders from Franklin and Deane to sail from France to Ireland, with the aim of capturing the Belfast linen convoy. His squadron consisted of the *Reprisal*, 14-gun *Lexington* under Captain Henry Johnson and 10-gun *Dolphin* under Captain Samuel Nicholson. Samuel, James Nicholson's brother and Wickes' Maryland neighbor, had been unemployed in London when the war broke out, but at the end of 1776, Congress commissioned him a lieutenant in the Continental Navy. They went around Ireland's west Atlantic coast and entered the Irish Sea by way of the North Channel, cruising southward along the eastern Irish coast. The squadron sailed between Dublin and Holyhead on the Welsh coast and then south to the port of Wexford on the Irish coast, avoiding the Royal Navy patrols. In a month, while they missed the linen convoy, they took eight prizes, including the sloop *Jason* from Whitehaven, the *Peggy* from Cork with butter and hides, a Scottish sloop with wheat from Prussia, and the snow, *Lizard*, with a load of cork from Gibraltar.[16] The only valuable prize amongst them was the *Grace* from Jamaica with sugar, rum, cotton and tobacco. One prize was actually stolen by a French prize master and three vessels belonging to smugglers were released. Seven vessels, including three in ballast and three coal brigs heading for Dublin were scuttled, after taking their crews on his ships. Finally, he sent one of his prizes to Whitehaven with 110 captured mariners. In response, Whitehaven authorities requested the Royal Navy send warships, but by that time Wickes was gone.

On July 4, 1777, Whitehaven's *General Advertiser* commented how restrained Wickes had been in his cruise, especially as he had never raided the English coast:

> We are told, that vessels were frequently seen, and passed without molestation. The people in general speak in the warmest terms of the humane treatment they met with from the commander of the Reprisal and Lexington, both of whom endeavoured to make the situation of their prisoners as easy as their unhappy circumstances would admit.[17]

On June 26 near Ushant, the 74-gun Royal Navy *Burford* gave chase to Wickes' squadron and he drew off in the *Reprisal* to enable the other ships to reach port safely. The *Reprisal* narrowly escaped the *Burford* by jettisoning its cannon and swivels so that it could sail more rapidly.[18] The *Dolphin* arrived at St Malo, but it had been so heavily damaged by the *Burford* that it was beyond repair and had to be converted into a packet ship.

Wickes obtained refuge at St Malo, where he was detained by French authorities as they feared his further cruise would cause Britain to declare war. On August 19, British Ambassador Lord Stormont demanded that Wickes' squadron be expelled, threatened France's Newfoundland fishing fleet and ordered a blockade of shipping in the French West Indies. Wickes was concerned to sell his prizes illegally and Franklin suggested that they might be sold along the coast outside of a regulated French port. When the prizes were finally sold it was at a great loss, and Silas Deane admitted the cruise had not been profitable. While Wickes waited, he replaced *Reprisal*'s lost ordnance and had it careened. Finally in September, Wickes was allowed to leave France for Boston or Portsmouth. He wrote to Johnson, who was at another French port, hoping they could meet and sail together. However, the *Lexington* was captured by the cutter *Alert* near Ushant and Johnson was sent to Mill Prison at Plymouth. *Reprisal* sailed alone across the Atlantic and on October 1 it foundered off the Grand Banks of Newfoundland, with the loss of all hands except the cook.[19] After only eighteen months, Wickes' distinguished career as a Continental captain was over. British diplomats were elated; Wickes was gone and the commissioners' path to an alliance was blocked as upset Vergennes broke off contact with them.

Gustavus Conyngham

Gustavus Conyngham was a most controversial captain. Like John Paul Jones, he came from the vicinity of the Irish Sea, where he had been a merchant mariner. He was born in either 1744 or 1747 at Larganreagh, near Londonderry, County Donegal, Ulster.[20] As a teenager, he moved to Philadelphia, where he worked for his cousin Redmond Conyngham in partnership with John Nesbitt, and then was apprenticed to Captain Henderson, who indulged him, giving him command of the merchant ship *Charming Betty*. In the fall of 1775, as a private citizen, Conyngham took that ship to the Dutch Republic, where he quietly arranged to purchase arms for the rebel cause. However, Conyngham and the *Charming Betty* were picked up by the British on a tip from one of his sailors and ordered to England under a prize crew. He and his crew were able to overpower the prize crew, escaping to the Dutch Republic. There, they were stopped from sailing by Dutch authorities and he was forced to sell the *Charming Betty* to the Dutch government. However, the Dutch never paid him for the ship and he languished in Holland, having failed to obtain any munitions. He might have given up, but instead he decided to find another ship.

Conyngham headed for the French port of Dunkirk, which was notorious for smuggling and raiding, so that in negotiations at the end of the Seven Years' War, it had been forced to destroy its fortifications and accept a British agent to watch its waterfront. He contacted Franklin, who had blank commissions for captains in the Continental Navy, and he supposedly offered one to Conyngham on March 1, 1777. Franklin then sent him back to Dunkirk to discreetly find another ship. This was a small swift lugger, which Conyngham named the *Surprize*.[21] He actually purchased the lugger in Dover, England and recruited its crew from idle American sailors, detained in French ports, plus an assortment of French nationals, although the French government had refused to allow him to recruit. While Conyngham believed the *Surprize* was a Continental warship, legally it turned out to be no more than a privateer or even a private ship, as the American commissioners could only offer a ship a letter of marque. Even Conyngham's commission from Franklin had been limited to this single voyage and his name did not appear in Congress's October 1776 list of Continental captains.

The *Surprize* sailed from Dunkirk into the English Channel and was at the mouth of the River Thames in early May 1777, capturing a British mail packet, *Prince of Orange,* and the brig *Joseph* carrying a cargo of wine. Conyngham ordered his prize crews to make for land with them, where they were to be refitted and sold.[22] When *Surprize* and the prizes approached Dunkirk's harbor, however, they encountered a pair of Royal Navy ketches. The British vessels rammed the *Surprize* multiple times, trying to goad Conyngham into a fight, but he proceeded into the protection of demilitarized Dunkirk.

France had a treaty with Britain that forbade the selling of commandeered goods in French ports, and Lord Stormont protested Conyngham's prizes and demanded that France return the *Joseph*.[23] To emphasize the point, the British sent the 18-gun sloop *Ceres* to blockade Conyngham. What Conyngham did not realize was that the Comte de Vergennes was equally upset. He bowed to Stormont's demands, turning over the *Joseph* and arresting Conyngham and his crew. They were sent to prison under charges of piracy. The French seized the *Surprize* and confiscated Conyngham's Continental Navy commission. This document was crucial to him because without it, Conyngham was illegitimate. It was never again found and for the rest of his career Conyngham remained open to charges of being a pirate. Moreover, both British and French authorities referred to the *Surprize* as a privateer, not a Continental warship.

While Conyngham languished in prison, Franklin set about obtaining a new ship for him. Royal Navy ships were watching the construction of new ships and were prepared to destroy vessels that were being built to aid the American cause. In mid-1777 at Dunkirk, Franklin arranged the building of a cutter called *Greyhound* for Conyngham, which had false buyers to confound British authorities. One of these investors, William Hodge, had it outfitted and armed with fourteen carriage guns, as it awaited an opportunity to slip past the British. On July 16 it sailed, its guns having been removed, but once outside the port they were returned and Conyngham boarded it, taking command and renaming it the *Revenge*.[24] For Hodge's part in the subterfuge, the French threw him into the Bastille.

Conyngham and his crew had been allowed to sail by Vergennes with the stipulation that *Revenge* would leave Europe and sail to America. Conyngham received written instructions in July 1777 from a commissioner stating that he must sail directly to America and 'do nothing which may involve your security or occasion Umbrage to the Ministry of France ...' and only 'if attacked first by our Enemies', could he defend himself.[25]

Conyngham ignored these orders, instead raiding the British Isles for the next two months, going into the North Sea and then the Irish Sea.[26] His journey carried him to Irish waters almost at the same time as Wickes. Yet, no evidence of coordination between them exists. And while Wickes was always a Continental captain, it is not clear Conyngham was one or even a privateer. It has been argued that arrogant William Carmichael, a protégé of Silas Deane, had verbally countermanded Conyngham's original orders. As Carmichael was hostile to the French, he may have become a British agent, using the countermand as a means of undermining the commissioners.

As Conyngham's voyage around the British Isles developed, he went first to the North Sea and then pretended to be a private vessel going to Bergen, Norway in order to shake Royal Navy ships shadowing him. They drew back as they thought him to be a French privateer and they wanted to continue French neutrality.[27] Conyngham scoured the shipping lanes off the English coast for prizes, finally capturing the schooner *Happy Return*, two brigs *Maria* and *Patty*, and the merchantman *Northampton*. This last prize proved to be his undoing because it was recaptured and taken to Yarmouth, England. There the British authorities found that the majority of the *Northampton*'s prize crew were Frenchmen and they protested to French authorities. They also discovered a new commission for Conyngham from Congress's president John Handcock, evidently having been sent to support the commission Franklin had given him; one that he would never receive.[28]

Unaware of this, Conyngham sailed north, rounded Scotland's Shetland Islands and sailed south on Ireland's west coast. Like Wickes, he was not interested in ravaging communities and when he stopped at Broadhaven Bay on the Atlantic coast, it was for supplies, which brought him close to his boyhood home.[29] He then returned to the Irish Sea and blatantly landed at Kinsale, a little-used naval dockyard near Cork, to take on water. When the *Revenge* was badly damaged by a storm, he sailed it into an English port to be repaired, reverting to his native Irish brogue to maintain anonymity. He was able to disguise his ship and hide its intentions, acting as an unmarked smuggler. At this moment, he had kept only five prizes, several ships having been burnt as not being prizeworthy.

Finally, Lord Stormont asked French authorities to issue orders to arrest the 'Dunkirk pirate' if he returned to France.[30] British warships were placed to prevent his return. Conyngham also remembered from his earlier voyages that he had been unsuccessful in disposing of prizes in neutral France, so that rather than returning to France with his prizes, he decided to head for Spain. He was pursued by a Royal Navy ship, which exchanged shots with the *Revenge,* damaging her maneuverability. Feeling vulnerable, Conyngham avoided a fight with the unidentified ship and then sailed to Ferrol, Spain to resupply and replace his crew. Manning was a problem because prize crews had depleted his ship's company and most of his crew, being Europeans, lacked respect for his unknown republic. He claimed the crew overruled him, forcing him to act like a pirate, seizing several prizes in Spanish waters, including a French brig. He also became a confidant of Silas Dean, who was pleased to help dispose of his prizes in neutral Spain. British authorities protested to the Conde de Floridablanca, who assured them that Conyngham's abuses were known and that he had been sent out of Ferrol and would not be permitted to enter any Spanish port.

Shut out from Spain in February 1778, Conyngham decided to sail for Spain's colonies in the West Indies, where he continued to act against the British as a privateer. This ended when he captured a ship carrying munitions, which, remembering his original reason for his European voyage, he deemed worthy of escorting to American shores. He arrived in Philadelphia on February 21, 1779 with his prizes and goods in tow. Though some local newspapers hailed him as a returning hero, the Continental Congress was less than pleased with his disobedience to orders and his loss of his commissions, which opened him to charges of piracy. Congress's Marine Committee had already met to discuss his voyage and it found he had sold prizes in foreign ports without paperwork to back up the sales.[31] Former crewmen who preceded him home claimed that they had not been paid their promised wages. And his involvement with Silas Deane, now accused of various financial wrongdoings in France, did not help him. Richard Henry Lee of Virginia alleged that both *Surprize* and *Revenge* were privateers and several partners along with Deane had profited handsomely from the prize money derived from Conyngham's cruises. Conyngham claimed he had only sought to harass British commercial shipping in their home waters, a priority which Congress had yet to make. Adding to this, as Conyngham was not the owner of the *Revenge*, Congress took it from him and it was sold at a private auction, further indicating that it had been a privateer rather than a Continental Navy ship.

Conyngham's only consolation was that the *Revenge* was bought by none other than his cousins in the Conyngham and Nesbitt Company. They again gave him command of the *Revenge* to sail as a privateer, as he no longer claimed a position in the Continental Navy.[32] In April 1779, he and his crew were unable to outrun the British frigate *Galatea* off the coast of Delaware and were taken prisoner. Since he held no commission at the time, he was arrested on charges of piracy and sent to the English Pendennis Castle prison. He escaped from there, only to be caught again and transferred to Mill Prison, Plymouth. He was kept in irons continuously, although he was able escape to Texel, the Dutch Republic, where, despite being blockaded, John Paul Jones was able to find him a place for a few months on his *Alliance*. While returning to America on board the *Experiment* in March 1780, he was recaptured by the British and sent back to Plymouth's Mill Prison. He remained there until his release in a prisoner exchange in June 1781.

Although a firm count is impossible, it appears that Conyngham had been able to keep more prizes than any other navy commander. He was not an articulate self-promoter like John Paul Jones and thus his feat in accumulating prizes went unrewarded. Before the French alliance, Conyngham was an embarrassment to both the French and American governments. 'The only party that had anything to gain by publishing [his activities] was the British', because they were regarded his efforts as illegal.[33]

The Prize Game in Europe

Wickes' and Conyngham's cruises introduce us to the early prize game, which requires further explanation. Congress's Marine and Secret Committees consistently made it clear to their captains that trade in munitions and the fostering of alliances with France or Spain took precedence over cruising for prizes.[34] They might order warships to cruise in specific areas like the Irish Sea – where the possibility of taking prizes was great – but were pleased only if revenue came to the navy from the sale of prize cargos.

Congress hoped for prize money to finance the war. In Europe, conditions for the sale of American prizes and their cargos were difficult. It was not only that no courts were available to adjudicate, but that until France declared war on Britain in mid-1778, all prize transactions had to be done illicitly. This meant that sales opportunities were clandestine and returns were only a fraction of expectations. Furthermore, one of the American commissioners, Silas Dean, was accused of personally profiting from these sales.[35]

The failure for prize money to meet expectations also affected Continental crews, who were recruited with the promise of pay for a year, although not coming till the end of a voyage. Crews found even this in arrears, their only realistic hope of remuneration being a share of a prize. The failure of a captain to obtain prize money was a cause of discontent among crews, as we have seen with Wickes' crew at Lorient. Prize money was especially important if a mariner had a family he was supporting at home.[36] If a crew was kept beyond the year of service, far from home, without compensation from prizes it had risked its life in taking, it understandably became mutinous.

Prize claims actually continued after the war. Of the three captains in Wickes' Irish expedition, only Samuel Nicholson would live to witness the post-war effort of the three crews to share in the prize money they felt due them. The Marine Committee found the commissioners had no records of the sales of their ships and cargos.[37] Congress finally agreed to compensate them for only the Irish cruise and the figure was much lower than the value of the prizes taken. Wickes' estate never collected any prize money from Congress.

Similarly, when Conyngham returned to the United States, he sought to obtain his share of the thirty-one prizes he claimed to have taken. But he was plagued by his lost commission and by Congress asserting that it had intended his commission to be 'for temporary expeditions only and not to give rank in the navy'.[38] And the case was delayed so long that his best witness to counter that claim, Benjamin Franklin, passed away.

Overall, Lambert Wickes in the *Reprisal* and Gustavus Conyngham in the *Revenge* had separately sailed around the British Isles and into the Irish Sea. The disguised object of the two squadrons was to take enough British merchant shipping to cause war between Britain and France. As France and Spain were still neutral, they had to be restrained enough to capture only British ships and make no effort to attack British ports. Wickes' and Conyngham's activities were often secretly financed by the French, but this did not mean they could expect French government support when they needed refitting and supplies. Their efforts would not add much to the reputation of the new Continental Navy, instead being confused with the action of privateers and even pirates.[39] It was their reputation that the next important Continental captain in Europe, John Paul Jones, would seek to avoid.

Chapter 15

A Scotsman Desires Command

Wickes and Conyngham had established the Irish Sea as an ideal place to raid. It separated the island of Great Britain from Ireland. To the north was the Irish Channel, forming a deep strait between Northern Ireland and southwestern Scotland, connecting the Irish Sea with the Atlantic Ocean. The strait was narrow enough to allow easy movement of migrants and goods between Scotland and Ireland. In the eighteenth century, it was also a haunt of diverse privateers and smugglers causing the disruption of British merchant shipping.

It was here that John Paul was born in July 6, 1747, the son of the head gardener of Arbigland Estate, near the southern Solway Coast of Scotland.[1] Originally the family was from Fife and John Paul Sr. was born at Edinburgh's port of Leith, where William Craik, the owner of Arbigland met him and hired him to lay out his gardens. John's mother was Jean Duff. Arbigland was fortunate to have Craik, a polymath, as its laird, who had inherited the rundown estate in 1736 and decided to revive it by putting new ideas into practice. Craik designed and completed Arbigland House in the Adam style in 1755, as well as building the kirk for nearby Kirkbean. He was also an agricultural improver in the manner of Charles Townsend, draining the land, reclaiming low-level marsh from the sea, and laying out a park and fields protected by drystone dykes. The money for his enterprises is thought to have derived from smuggling brandy from the Isle of Man.

John Paul might have become a gardener like his father or uncle. The Pauls' fourth child, he was sent to live with his uncle, who was Lord Selkirk's gardener at St Mary's Isle, 25 miles to the west of Arbigland. John came back to go to Kirkbean School but spent much of his time at the nearby port of Carsethorn on the Solway Firth, which served as the port for the region's largest town, Dumfries, 10 miles northward.[2] In later life, William Craik's son recalled that John would run to Carsethorn whenever his father would let him off, talk to the sailors and clamber over the ships, and that he taught his playmates to maneuver their tiny boats to mimic a naval battle, while he, taking his stand on a cliff overlooking the roadstead, shouted shrill commands at his imaginary fleet.

It was from Carsethorn, at the age of 13, John Paul Jr. boarded a vessel to go to Whitehaven across the Solway, where he signed up for a seven-year seaman's apprenticeship.[3] He sailed out as ship's boy aboard the *Friendship* under Captain William Benson, traveling annually from Whitehaven to Barbados and then Virginia. He went especially to Fredericksburg, Virginia, where he visited his older brother William. William was a tailor, living in a corner house, and was married, although it was an unhappy relationship, leaving no children. The *Friendship* was at the Chesapeake port for several months, where John spent the time learning navigation.

After his return to Whitehaven, John found that the *Friendship's* owner, John Younger, was in financial difficulty and he released him from his apprenticeship. When the Seven Years' War ended, the *Friendship* was sold and her crew let go.[4] Sixteen-year-old John Paul had sailing skills, but like most seamen he was out of work. A year later, he went into the slave trade as third mate on the King George of Whitehaven. Slavers were still taking advantage of the legality of exporting slaves from Africa to America.

In 1766, John Paul transferred as first mate to the brigantine *Two Friends* of Kingston, Jamaica. Only 50ft long with a crew of six, it carried seventy-seven blacks from Africa in a slaving voyage. The smell from 'black-birders', as the slavers were called, could be detected for 10 miles distance. Still a teenager when paid off in Jamaica, he quitted the slave traffic calling it an 'abominable trade'. He was given free passage home by a friendly Scot on the new brigantine *John* of Kirkcudbright.[5] During the voyage, Captain Samuel McAdam and the mate died of fever. Paul took command as the only qualified officer and brought the ship safely back home to Kirkcudbright, the Scottish port at the mouth of the River Dee. The owners Currie, Beck and Co were so pleased they appointed him master and supercargo (in charge of buying and selling the cargo) for the *John*'s next voyage to America.

Unfortunately, John Paul had a violent temper which became evident at this time and would manifest itself throughout his career. At the age of 21, while serving as captain of the *John*, he was accused in Tobago by Mungo Maxwell, the ship's carpenter, of having flogged him excessively with the cat-o-nine tails.[6] Maxwell, the son of a prominent Kirkcudbright worthy, was examined by a court, but his complaint was dismissed as frivolous. Later, when Maxwell died of Yellow Fever while returning home on a Barcelona Packet, it was his father who claimed that his son had been 'most unmercifully, wounded on his back … and of which wounds he soon afterward died'. On this accusation, John Paul was arrested when he returned to Kirkcudbright and was charged with murder and placed in the seventeenth-century tollbooth.[7] However, evidence from Tobago and a declaration from the master of the Barcelona Packet that Maxwell was in perfect health when he came on board was sufficient to acquit Paul.

Captain John Paul tried to put this behind him and in October 1772, he took command of the *Betsy*. He traded back and forth between England, Madeira, the West Indies and Tobago and seems to have accumulated some wealth. A year later, however, whilst in Tobago, Paul's crew became mutinous over pay and the ringleader swung at him with a club.[8] In a rage, Paul ran him through with his sword. Since his assailant was a Tobago local, Paul's friends urged him to leave the island quickly, not trusting a local jury to give him a fair hearing. He fled, leaving his affairs and property in the hands of his partner and agent. Having been accused of killing one crew member and now this second obvious one, concerns about his treatment of his crews increased dramatically. It became difficult for him to put or hold a crew together. He was forced to evade the law by changing his name to 'Mr John Jones' and in 1774 he escaped to Fredericksburg, Virginia to find refuge in his brother William's modest estate, as he had recently died. Here John hoped to be incognito until his Tobago incident blew over.

Jones' Path to Command

Coming out of hiding in 1775 at Fredericksburg, John Jones was still basically a Scot when he volunteered to serve in the new Continental Navy. After a strenuous self-promotion campaign lasting a year, he was appointed a first lieutenant of the *Alfred*.[9] This was followed by serving as captain of the *Providence* in Rhode Island and then as captain of the *Alfred*.

By October 10, 1776, Congress had a listed John Paul Jones as eighteenth among its Continental captains, behind James Nicholson, John Manley, Hector McNeill and Lambert Wickes. Jones reacted negatively to his low place on the list, claiming, 'there are characters [on the list] who are truly contemptible – with such, as private gentlemen, I would distain to sit down.'[10] He argued, 'until [the officers above him] give proof of their superior abilities, I never shall acknowledge them as my senior officers – I never will act under their command.' He went on to claim that many of his fellow officers were illiterate 'characters so rude & contracted'. He shared his disappointment with Robert Morris, who would support an improving role for the Continental Navy to the very end of the war.

Meanwhile, in Portsmouth, New Hampshire finding a captain for the Continental sloop *Ranger* was a controversial process. In September 1776, New Hampshire Congressional delegate Josiah Bartlett was lobbied by John Roche, an Irish captain in the West Indies trade, to command the *Ranger*. Earlier, John Langdon had given Roche his recommendation for the position to present to Congress and he had returned to Langdon with orders to build the *Ranger*. Roche would be involved in its construction and Langdon called it 'Roche's ship'.[11] Roche rented a house in Portsmouth from where he searched for ordnance, sails, canvas, cordage and bunting. Despite Bartlett's and Langdon's support of Roche, however, Massachusetts' authorities claimed they had evidence of his unlawful misconduct. He was suspended from command in June 1777 until the Navy Board had made an inquiry into his character, an activity which was never completed and he subsequently disappeared from the record. At the same time, John Langdon and William Whipple in Congress were given authority to appoint most officers of the *Ranger*. Only the appointment of the top command was reserved to Congress, and in February 1777 their choice was an outsider, now named John Paul Jones.

Jones would complain to the New Hampshire commissioners that his appointment to the *Ranger* had been 'rendered abortive by the jealousy of the then Commodore Hopkins'.[12] Jones had served as a lieutenant on the *Alfred* and his experience with Hopkins had not been fruitful. Hopkins had joined Bartlett and Langdon in opposing Jones' command of the *Ranger*. Jones' designation as captain was seen as an act of hostility by New Englanders in Congress. However, as Hopkins star was falling, Jones' was rising, although New Englanders would never allow him to assume the position of commodore that Hopkins had held.

Ranger's Officers and Crew

Jones arrived in Portsmouth in July and he picked Mathew Parke and John Gizzard Frazer as officers for the *Ranger*. Parke was soon aiding him in procuring supplies for the ship. Other officers' appointments were in the hands of New Hampshire's commissioners.[13] Langdon and William Whipple had been approached by numerous New England candidates to serve as the *Ranger's* officers. One possibility for lieutenant was New Hampshire merchant Captain Thomas Simpson, who was older than Jones. Simpson was Langdon's brother-in-law and a cousin to the Quinceys, the Wentworths, the Wendells, and even John Handcock, the president of Congress.[14] He and Elijah Hall were selected as lieutenants by the commissioners. Born in Raynham, Massachusetts, Hall had been appointed lieutenant in the Continental Navy on

June 14, 1777. The ship's surgeon would be Dr Ezra Green of Dover, New Hampshire. John Wendell, Portsmouth merchant, wanted a midshipman's place on the *Ranger* for his son, Daniel. These Portsmouth friends of Langdon or Whipple were mostly landsmen.

The choice for Marine commander was Samuel Wallingford, captain in the fourth company of a New Hampshire regiment and a friend of Langdon's. After Jones had been named captain, he wrote to Wallingford from Portsmouth that he had been

> nominated as Lieutenant of Marines in the Service of these States, [and was] directed forthwith to Enlist as many Able Bodied Men as possible to Serve in the Navy under my Command – You are to enter All the good Seamen who present themselves – as Sundry petty Warrant Officers will be Appointed from Among them.[15]

To get them to the *Ranger*, the men would be entitled to wages from the date of entry and also their travelling expenses and 'a bounty of Forty Dollars for every Able Seaman will be Paid on their Appearance at the Ship'. Having done this recruiting, Wallingford would be ready to sail with the *Ranger* in November 1777. To further make up the crew, Jones requested that the New Hampshire House of Representatives allow him to enlist matrossmen from the batteries in Piscataqua Harbor, and they allowed him up to twenty. Jones sent officers to scour not just New Hampshire but Boston, Salem and Marblehead, Massachusetts, and Providence, Rhode Island. A March 1777 broadside called on all 'gentlemen seamen and able-bodied landsmen' to make 'an agreeable voyage in this pleasant season of the year'.[16] It was explained they were not to immediately be given Congress's advertised advance on their recruitment, but they would receive the advance and their travel expenses once they arrived at the *Ranger*. Petty officers were to be appointed from 'the most deserving seamen'. Recruiters hid the possibility that the *Ranger* would not be sent to France as Jones felt it would dampen the effort. The call enticed recruits from Wells and York (now in Maine but at that time part of Massachusetts), making the Massachusetts contingent nearly as large as that of New Hampshire.

When recruits arrived at the *Ranger* in Portsmouth, they found that Jones had no funds for the advance, as Congress had not meant it for those who signed for a single cruise, it being only for those who signed for three years during the war. Jones could only offer half their monthly wages if they left wives or attorneys to receive it, provided they signed for a year, not a single cruise. For those who signed only for the cruise, he could advance no more than one month's pay besides a clothing allowance. Clearly Congress did not have the funds to be generous to recruits for a single cruise. Many of the recruits felt they had been hoodwinked by 'false promises' and 'deceitful advertisements'.[17] New Hampshire's commissioners passed on their local prejudices to the *Ranger's* crew. It had been recruited at Langdon's Shipyard by Simpson, who they felt was a 'Fatherly officer', while Jones would be seen as 'deceitful'.[18] Later, the crew felt that Jones had altered the *Ranger*'s articles to extend their enlistments and had stalled payment of prize money. As a result, they would tend to obstruct rather than follow Jones.

Sailing as a French Ally

During the *Ranger*'s late November cruise across the Atlantic to France, John Paul Jones was on the lookout for 'English property'.[19] Finally, he met and took two merchant ships from

Malaga bound to Yarmouth and London with cargos of raisins, figs, lemons and wine, which he felt could be sold when they arrived in France. His Continental warship was acting like a privateer, although its ability to profit from the sale of these prizes would be delayed. It was also evident in the crossing that the *Ranger* had sailing problems. It arrived and traveled up the Loire River to the dockyard at Nantes, where Jones arranged for changes to its rig, the addition of ballast, and careening.

In France, Jones thought his responsibility for the *Ranger* would be over as he would be immediately transferred to command the frigate *L'Indien,* being built in Amsterdam, the Dutch Republic. But he would be frustrated as the commissioners could not afford to build, rig, man and provision such a large ship. The French government had stepped in and taken over the expense as well as the ownership of the new ship.[20] Jones learned this when he traveled to Paris in November, where Franklin suggested that instead he use the *Ranger* to capture a British nobleman to be exchanged for American prisoners. Jones thus became concerned to take prisoners for a naval exchange. Franklin had visited Whitehaven more recently than Jones and the two may have discussed it as a possible target. This raid was to be different from those of Wickes and Conyngham since ports were now targets. Jones tantalized his crew by claiming that they would be paid for any ship they burnt in Whitehaven harbor as if they had captured it.

The *Ranger* would spend the winter and early spring having its masts set further aft and the sails shortened. Meanwhile, France signed two treaties with the commissioners in February 1778, one a commercial and the other a military alliance.[21] The second was regarded by the commissioners as most crucial since they wished France to go to war immediately with Britain. France had never been anxious to declare war on Britain, however, not just because of a lack of preparation, but because the Dutch alliance with Britain required them to come to Britain's aid if she were attacked, so that France did not want be seen as striking the first blow against Britain. France also hoped that Spain would join the alliance with the United States, a situation which never happened. With the French alliance in place, Jones now had the opportunity to raise the stakes and do something that Conyngham and Wickes could not. He could operate openly from France against British Isles, even though France had yet to declare itself a victim of British aggression in order to declare war.

Jones faced officer problems as he was forced to dismiss Marine Captain Matthew Parke over prize money and Major John Frazer was a casualty of excessive drink, making Jones believe he was 'surrounded by enemies'.[22] He decided he would have to command his crew 'by persuasion'. His worst fears were realized at Brest when, on March 10, some of his crew took the *Ranger*'s cutter, went to the shore and deserted. Three days later, Jones found them and had them brought back under guard and confined in irons. It now appears that the New England crew had been augmented so that it also included 'blacks, Spaniards, Swedes, French escapees from convict galleys, and a few Americans'. Both the pilot and barber were French. Later petitions show that two-thirds of the crew was still from New England.

Jones wrote to Silas Dean in late March about preparing the *Ranger* for an undisclosed project, as he attempted to maintain secrecy. Jones admitted he had cruised the *Ranger* in Camaret Bay, France 'in disguise', although he had 'now pulled off [the] masque as the face of affairs are altered', a reference to the change the alliance with France had made.[23] Jones hinted that he would abandon his project if word came of the availability of the Amsterdam ship.

Because Britain's warships were concentrated in the Channel Fleet, Jones faced a Royal Navy that was spread thinly in patrolling the English coast. When Wickes and Conyngham had cruised in July 1777, only the Royal Navy's *Pelican* and *Cameleon* were stationed off Scotland's Shetland Islands.[24] The *Hound, Alderney* and *Drake* were between England and the Dutch coast. Smaller vessels were stationed about the Irish Sea at Waterford, Dublin, Milford, Liverpool and Glasgow, though none were at Whitehaven. As seen, warships were stationed to watch the French ports, especially Dunkirk and Brest. More important to the Admiralty, it had initiated a system of protected convoys in British coastal waters.

On April 11, Jones sailed the *Ranger* from Brest toward the Irish Sea, confident that he knew the waters from his boyhood. Eight days later, he made an attempt to fool the 8-gun Whitehaven revenue cutter *Hussar*, under Captain Gurley, into thinking the unmarked *Ranger* was a merchant ship, the *Molly* of Glasgow. A mystery ship to Gurley for it never identified itself, Jones asked for a pilot as he claimed to be unfamiliar with the waters, to which Gurley answered that he could not spare one as he was chasing a smuggler. Suddenly, Gurley reported,

> in a threatening manner, [the Ranger] ordered him to bring to, or they would sink him – in an instant the ports were knocked open, the decks filled with men, and a tier of guns run out, several vollyies of small arms were fired into the Hussar, and such of the great guns as could be brought to bear upon her.[25]

The cutter tacked several times, getting out of reach of the *Ranger*'s guns and while it was damaged, there were no casualties. Although the *Hussar* had recognized Jones' ruse, Gurley remained uncertain as to the identity of the ship.

In the morning of the 20th, near the Isle of Man, Jones sank a Scottish coasting schooner laden with barley and oats, and in the evening, a sloop in ballast from Ireland suffered the same fate. The next day, the *Ranger* was near fortified Carrickfergus, Ireland, another familiar place to him. When a fishing boat came out, Jones detained it and they volunteered that the Royal Navy 14-gun sloop *Drake* was now in port. Jones determined to attack her secretly at night by overlaying her cable and falling upon her bow, so as to have her decks open and exposed to his musquetry. However, the wind was high and his anchor was fouled so that the hanger was brought to upon the enemy's quarters at the distance of half a cable's length and 'the crew was unwilling to undertake it.'[26] A second effort was prevented as 'The weather now became so very stormy and severe, and the sea ran so high, that [they] was obliged to take shelter under the south shore of Scotland.' Those on the *Drake* seem not have been aware of any of Jones' maneuvering. Thus far, Jones' cruise was much like that of Conyngham or Wickes, but that would soon change.

Whitehaven

In the eighteenth-century British Isles, between vast London and numerous fishermen's villages were medium-sized ports like Whitehaven. Looking out on the Irish Sea from the Cumberland coast, Whitehaven was unusual in that it was a planned community built on a grid pattern in the seventeenth century. Landowner and MP Sir Christopher Lowther had taken a tiny fishing village and erected a town around a harbor to export coal from Cumberland coastal mines to Ireland.[27] It also had transatlantic families who had developed trade in Chesapeake tobacco. As a result, an elaborate system of stone quays was constructed, ultimately divided between an outer and inner harbor. By 1762, its population reached 9,063, about the size of Charleston, South Carolina. A considerable number of merchant seamen, who had been crucial to the Atlantic and slave trades, resided there. Another consistency in its trade was smuggling, which for many had become a way of life.

Eighteen years earlier, John Paul had gone to Whitehaven to serve a seven-year seaman's apprenticeship and while there he sailed to Jamaica, Tobago, Barbados, Virginia and West Africa. It would be his next target.

Chapter 16

Whitehaven Attacked

After its brush with the *Ranger,* the *Hussar* went to Carrickfergus hoping to join Royal Navy ships, but having failed to find them, it bore away for Whitehaven, where it arrived at the Customs House on April 19. It would remain there for four days, after which it would clear the port. Captain Gurley thought the *Hussar* had encountered the usual smuggler and his routine report 'threw the inhabitants, in some degree, off their guard ...'[1] In Whitehaven, while it was known that the rebels had formed an alliance with France, a declaration of war by France on Britain had not yet come, so it was assumed that Britain was still at peace with France. During that duration, a Whitehaven newspaper ran a contest with a 10-guinea prize as to whether war would be declared by either country by April 1. It is evident there was no winner and it must be assumed that many in Whitehaven did not think war with France was inevitable.

Whitehaven was a modern town, having no existing walls, castle or keep. Its defenses were limited to a corner of its harbor. There, a gun platform battery, surrounded by a perimeter wall with a guardroom and powder magazine, had been constructed from 1741.[2] An armament of ten 18-pound guns stood in a line, commanding a view out to sea. Sods laid grass-side down were placed along the top of the wall, leaving embrasures for the guns.

During the scare of the Jacobite Rebellion in 1745, Whitehaven had raised ten companies of fifty men each and erected breastworks on the streets, but when it heard of the capture of strongly defended Carlisle, it removed its ordnance and placed them on the ships in its harbor to prevent them from falling into the hands of the Jacobites. After their defeat, the guns were returned to the battery. Seventeen years later, during the Seven Years' War, recommendations for improvements of the defenses by the Board of Ordnance were never fulfilled as the war ended before they were initiated. With the war over, the town council had most of the guns dismounted, laid in beds in a shed and their carriages placed in storage houses.[3]

When the Revolutionary War broke out, it is assumed that the guns were brought out of storage and were present in 1778, although it was reported that many were rusty.[4] As to soldiers, Whitehaven's innkeepers complained about the excessive number of militiamen occasionally quartered on them, but evidently no garrison existed for the fortifications. Whitehaven seems to have been far more concerned about the nearby Jacobite Rebellion than the far away American War.

Jones' Plan

Leaving Carrickfergus on the clear and frosty night of April 22, the *Ranger* arrived 2 miles off unsuspecting Whitehaven. From the beginning, this raid was carried out in face of opposition from the officers and crew of Jones' command. He wanted his raid on Whitehaven to be an exercise in military strategy and he aimed to take the prisoners Franklin had requested for the sake of diplomacy. He felt the *Ranger* should not act in anyway as a privateer, for 'privateers ... let their prisoners go [so] that they immediately augment the strength of their enemies'.[5] This attitude still allowed him to plan to burn some of Whitehaven's shipping. In contrast, the crew's priority was for the promised personnel remuneration from taking prizes and booty in the harbor, not strategy, prisoners, or the burning of ships.

Two longboats were let down from the *Ranger* and filled altogether with thirty to forty sailors and marines with pistols and cutlasses, who had volunteered from a crew of 140.[6] They carried combustible 'candles' made of canvas dipped in brimstone, which could be ignited by flint and steel. Jones took charge of one longboat, while the other was under Lieutenant Wallingford of the Marines and Midshipman Ben Hill. The two longboats rowed against the tide for three hours to reach the harbor, an arduous beginning. Jones wanted to set alight the hundreds of ships in the harbor, as with the tide out, they lay stranded on the beach, packed tightly together, several abreast, against the piers.

The two parties first attempted a landing on the coast near Saltom Coal Pit, in order to run along the shore and attack the guns of the lunette battery, but the sea was too rough and the shore too rocky.[7] They lost half an hour and then they rowed past the battery around the New Quay and into the harbor as first light was appearing over the hills, so they had lost the element of surprise. The plan would become unstuck because of this delay and Jones' increasingly mutinous crew.

Jones had intended that Wallingford and his men would be the arsonists, burning the ships in the northern half of the harbor, while he, almost alone, would spike the battery's guns. This last was important because the guns of the fort covered the harbor entrance and could have blasted Jones' two longboats when they made their escape. Jones landed first, near the upper battlements. He had left trustworthy Lieutenant Meijer guarding his boat, which was wise, for it turned out that most of his crew had concocted a plan to take the boat and leave Jones behind if it appeared the attack was failing. Jones had to stand on the battlements to encourage a few men to join his mission.[8]

As it was a cold night, the Whitehaven guards had gone into the guardhouse at the back to keep warm.[9] It is unclear as to who they were, but they were not navy sailors, militia or regular soldiers, or members of an artillery company. By climbing on each other's shoulders, Jones' men managed to silently scale the walls, enter the fort, burst into the guardhouse and secure the surprised guards without bloodshed.

Having secured the upper fort, only Jones and Midshipman Joe Green went to spike the guns at the Half-moon Battery, which lay on the shore, behind Tom Hurd's rock.[10] It contained 32-pounders that could fire over a mile, capable of hindering their escape. While he was spiking the guns, Jones expected Wallingford's men to burn the shipping in the southern part of the harbor. However, when Wallingford and his men landed at the Old Quay slip, they headed straight for Nicholas Allison's pub and began drinking, although they did not allow Allison to raise an alarm. They later told Jones that they needed to find lights for their candles, but they failed to do this. It appeared that they did not want to be arsonists or harm the shipping.

Attempting Arson

When Jones returned, he was upset to find that no ships had yet been set on fire, apparently because his own crew as well as Wallingford's had no more lights, their candles having burnt out.[11] With daylight growing, they gave up on the North Harbor and after securing a light from a house, headed along the quay. The arsonists got to the nearest ship, the *Thompson* belonging to Captain Richard Johnson, which was full of coal destined for Dublin. They roused out of bed the boys left aboard to look after the ship and tried to bribe them with money to go with them.[12] The boys refused and were taken prisoner in just their shirts, gagged with handkerchiefs, under the threat of being shot.

Finally, 'Matches' made from canvas covered in sulphur appeared and were set alight and thrown into the holds of several ships.[13] Wallingford's men threw down a barrel of tar near the *Thompson*'s main mast and started a fire. It took hold in the steerage of the ship and eventually burnt out the cabin. However, the matches thrown down into the other ships failed to ignite so that only the *Thompson* was damaged.

Twenty-one-year-old Loyalist David Freeman of Jones' crew deserted and started knocking on the doors on Marlborough Street to warn the town's folk that a fire had been started at the *Thompson* that might spread. Jones did not later report Freeman's defection, although according to the *Ranger*'s log, he would be 'left on shore voluntarily because he gave information at several houses that fire had been set to the ships'.[14] As in the case of Portsmouth and Bristol, sailors, mechanics and colliers moved quickly to extinguish the only fire. Besides leather buckets, several pumping devices existed to douse the flames. Built of oak, they consisted of a cistern, two single-acting pumps, wheels and drag handles. The largest could throw water a distance of 50 yards. The exertions by all classes of inhabitants working together extinguished the flames on the *Thompson* before they reached its rigging. Thus, no fire spread to the ships or town.

Having failed to burn the ships, Jones decided that it was time to escape. He had two or three prisoners, for whom there was scarcely room in his longboats. The boy from the *Thompson* was one, the other boy having escaped. Another was George Jefferson, the former master of the *Isaac* and *Barbary* from a maritime family, who had unsuspectingly gone down to the pier for late night fishing.[15] Such ordinary people, Jones knew, would be disappointing to Franklin.

By the time Jones and his men started rowing for the ship, Whitehaven sailors had occupied the forts and started working on the guns in the Half-moon Battery, for some evidently had not been spiked. They managed to get them in working order and fired upon the retreating longboats, but failed to sink them.[16] The *Ranger* had not been directly involved in the raid and was facing north, ready to escape as the crew started to think the mission was a failure and began to worry that Jones had been captured. Then they spied the longboats leaving harbor and smoke from the *Thompson*.[17] The firing of shots from the battery alerted them that Jones was in retreat, and they turned *Ranger* around to receive the longboats. After they were picked up, the *Ranger* fled northwestward towards the Scottish coast, Jones' boyhood home.

Later from Brest, when he reported the raid to the commissioners, Jones claimed that 'had it been possible to have landed a few hours sooner my success would have been complete ... and all the world would not have been able to save the town.'[18] Considering Jones' inside knowledge and the unprepared nature of the town, these claims bear no relation to reality. Jones did not mention that he failed to have control over his officers and crew, who warned the town about the burning and spent much of the time drinking in a local pub. Despite his organizing for arson, only one ship was partially burnt, as the town was alerted and able to put it out. Marine Lieutenant Wallingford explained that his crew had refused to 'destroy poor people's property'.

Embarrassment at the Selkirk Mansion

In the afternoon of April 24, the *Ranger* arrived on the Scottish coast and anchored near Kirkcudbright on the Mull of Galloway at St Mary's Isle, where Lord Selkirk had his home. Having lived with his uncle, the gardener of the Selkirk estates on St Mary's, Jones knew of the Selkirk family. Jones and Wallingford, with twelve men, landed on the beach with the design to take the lord as an important prisoner, making up for the ordinary Whitehaven prisoners. Lord Selkirk, born Dunbar, Hamilton in 1722, had adopted the name Dunbar Douglas upon his succession as the fourth Earl of Selkirk in 1744.[19] He attended Glasgow University from 1739 and in six years he was granted the honorary Doctorate of Civil Law and later he became rector of the university. Selkirk was a supporter of the government during the 1745 Jacobite uprising. He also served as Lord Lieutenant of Kirkcudbright. To Jones, he was the needed star prisoner.

Still, Jones must have felt uneasy about kidnapping the lord because he remained on the beach, refusing to go further, as he may have heard that Lord Selkirk was absent. Instead, Wallingford and another lieutenant with a few sailors insisted on taking a boat to the Selkirk mansion.[20] Their concern to obtain booty, which they had failed to get in Whitehaven, outweighing Jones' interest in prisoners.

At the mansion, the servants had assumed the strange party was the navy's impress service and had accordingly disappeared. A governess saw the invader's boat and removed 7-year-old Thomas, Selkirk's son and heir, to safety. The raiders were greeted at the front door by the butler. Lady Selkirk invited the officers into the drawing room for tea, while whisky was found for the sailors who remained outside surrounding the house. Carrying 'two horse pistols' at their sides, the officers explained that they had come to kidnap her husband; Lady Selkirk replied that Lord Selkirk was not at home, apparently being in London. When Lieutenant Wallingford suggested that instead, they might take the young Thomas, Lady Selkirk replied that they would have to kill her first. They then claimed to 'have orders to ask for your plate'.[21] Lady Selkirk agreed that they might have the family silver and she ordered the butler to provide it in a sack, which actually had only silver on top, the rest consisting of coal. After drinking a toast to Lady Selkirk, the party returned in their longboat to the *Ranger* and gave Jones the silver.

Undenounced to Jones, the *Hussar*, with an additional number of men, had shadowed the *Ranger* to Wigton Bay, seeking to inform Royal Navy ships of its location. Having lost sight of the *Ranger* in the evening, however, she was unaware of what transpired at the mansion and, after warning the coast, returned to Whitehaven.[22] Afterwards in early May, Jones seemed to be embarrassed by the Selkirk mansion incident, as he wrote an apology to

Lady Selkirk commenting that 'his heart' did not approve of his crew's actions.[23] He went on that while he esteemed Lord Selkirk's private character, he had wished to take him and make him part of a prisoner exchange and he asked her to facilitate a general prisoner exchange. While he was not party to the taking of the plate, he claimed that when it was sold he would purchase it and restore it to her. He concluded that he waged, 'no war with the fair', that he was not to be regarded as an enemy, that he was 'ambitious of her esteem and friendship'. He begged her to respond to him in France. She was not impressed by his chivalry and Lord Selkirk refused his offer to return the silver and it did not come back until after the war.

On the whole, Jones' Whitehaven experience was disappointing. What the Selkirk raiding party thought of his failure to join them and his surprising attitude toward Lady Selkirk was unclear. The *Ranger*'s Surgeon Green attempted to minimize the Selkirk mansion incident by stating that 'As Selkirk was not at Home and no man was in the House, for the sake of his Lady Selkirk & her Company they came off with 160lb. of silver plate.'[24] Thus ended the raid; it was evident that his crew had much different priorities to those of Jones. His raid belonged with previous American privateers in European waters, as they were recognized 'not so much for their military effectiveness as ... their success in envenoming relations between Britain and France'.[25]

Chapter 17

The British Isles React

While admitting the Whitehaven raid was a failure, American historians like Samuel Elliot Morison have claimed that its 'moral effect was stupendous'.[1] He and others emphasize that Jones' carrying the war to the Irish Sea was unique, as if the British Isles had remained untouched by enemies since 1066. Actually, these historians are simply following Jones himself, who made similar boasts after he returned to France. One is supposed to assume that Morison and Jones thought the Whitehaven raid caused widespread panic in the British Isles.

In fact, English newspapers were modest in their coverage of the *Ranger* because such attacks had happened before. The British Isles had an extensive coast that was impossible to defend and thus in their past they had been continuously raided and invaded. If we look at the history of British smuggling, the coast was as porous as the nearest deep inlet. A typical moment remembered by Royal Navy officers was the Dutch invasion of 1667, when the dockyard and fort at Sheerness were burnt.[2] More obviously, in the southern extreme of the Irish Sea, Lundy Island was located on the Bristol Channel, the entrance to that large port. Forty years earlier, pirates known as the Salé Rovers, from the Republic of Salé, an Atlantic Moroccan port, after raiding the coast, occupied Lundy for five years.[3] Under the command of a Dutch renegade named Jan Janszoon, they flew an Ottoman flag over the island. They specialized not so much in seizing plunder as in taking entire English families to be sold as slaves in North Africa. As many as 1,400 Devonshire captives were held on Lundy before being sent to be sold in Algiers. Throughout the seventeenth century, Lundy was also plagued by pirate ships of French, Basque, English and Spanish origin. These incursions were ended by Sir John Pennington, but from 1660 to 1700 the island still fell prey to French privateers. People on the coast of the British Isles had long suffered from the most disgraceful depredations.

Another reason for the press's neglect was the cloak of secrecy over Continental ships leaving French ports and cruising the British Isles. Intelligence about stealthy Continental warships was usually lacking for the British press. While the Continental captains paraded the Stars and Stripes to be saluted by the French, they did not display these colors in the Irish Sea unless the ship was immediately confronting an enemy. Conyngham had actually used a 'Don't Tread on Me' flag in red and blue stripes with gold trim, in itself a mystery to most Englishmen. A rare exception came when Captain George Bowyer of the *Burford* gave chase to Wickes' *Reprisal*. After twelve hours of forcing it into St Malo, Bowyer was able to describe its eighteen carriage guns and sails, including the fact that its 'fore studding sail looks blacker than the other sails'.[4] Here was a matter of naval intelligence, however, not news coverage.

Eighteenth-century media popularity is complicated. An opposition to the North ministry's conduct of the war always existed, not only in parliament but beyond it in newspapers, petitions and broadsides.[5] The British Isles possessed more than sixty newspapers, with some papers primarily devoted to news, domestic and foreign. They reprinted letters and reports on current events without editing or any attempt to check for veracity. Often several papers would run the exact same report. Other newspapers were of a purely political bent, promoting an agenda without any attempt to be objective. Thanks to John Wilkes, freedom of the press was widely accepted and in 1772 the right to publish Parliamentary reports was established to further transparency.

James Aitken's arson scare of 1776–1777 had received newspaper coverage. Advertisements placed by the Admiralty in consecutive issues of *The London Gazette* or *The Hue and Cry*, spread descriptions of Aitken and his whereabouts, contributing to the search for the culprit.[6] As a result, in less than a week, Aitken was in custody. While it was possible for newspapers to incriminate both Silas Dean and Benjamin Franklin in Aitken's incendiary plot, they followed the government line and downplayed the connections because they did not want to encourage war with France. They covered Aitken's time in jail and his hope for a pardon. *The Public Advertiser* let its readers know that Aitken had 'made a genuine discovery of the persons who set him to set fire to Portsmouth Dock … and that the parties are some of them of eminence, and are in France'. None of this was true.

Conyngham's and Wickes' previous raids of the Irish coast in 1777 had set a precedent for lack of English coverage. It was limited because the ships and their captains were unidentified. Yet, Conyngham was celebrated on the Continent by French engravers, one showing him as bearded, with no uniform, a scarf tied at his neck, waistcoat, stripped pants, five pistols in his belt and a sword in hand – certainly a perfect corsair. In contrast, no contemporary portrait or caricature of Wickes was printed.[7] It became imperative to Jones that he was not associated with the image of Conyngham's piracy.

Jones' effort to burn ships in Whitehaven Harbor received attention in the press, and coverage of the raid on the Selkirk Mansion received equal billing. The most extensive and freshest coverage of the Whitehaven incident was in the April 25 issue of *The Cumberland Chronicle and Whitehaven Public Advertiser,* which introduced David Freeman as a source from within Jones' crew, who had testified before Whitehaven magistrates.[8]

More succinct and typical was the April 28 *Gazetteer and New Daily Advertiser* reporting:

> Last Tuesday part of the crew of the American Ranger privateer landed near the head of the Old Quay at Whitehaven, proceeded to the public house and drank much liquor, then set fire to, and greatly damaged a collier, but the fire was extinguished; they afterwards made off to the Scots shore. One of the crew was taken who says she mounts 18 six-pounders and six squivals, and has 140 men.[9]

While it identified the 'privateer' *Ranger* it did not mention Jones, even though he had a local background.

As the local newspaper, *The Cumberland Packet and Ware's Whitehaven Advertiser* was the common source for several newspapers. It had only begun publication the year before.

On January 6, 1778 it had reported in confidence about the government's preparations for the American War in the coming year. It commented:

> We are assured from good authority, that the most vigorous exertions will be made in the coming campaign. A new army and new commanders are to be sent to America. The militia are to be called out in this kingdom. New corps are already put on the establishment, many others are in contemplation; and the Scotch brigades are to be recalled from the services of the States of Holland.[10]

It went on to list newly contemplated Scottish regiments, a concern for Whitehaven, as they were likely to be transported from its harbor to America. Clearly these overall measures were meant to inspire confidence.

On April 28, Whitehaven's *Morning Post and Daily Advertiser* would appropriate an article from the *Cumberland Packet* covering Jones' raid in some detail. This newspaper was the first to mention 'alias John Paul', blaming him for 'this infernal plan, unprecedented except in the annals of John the Painter'. It claimed that the French had offered Jones 'a considerable sum of money' to burn Whitehaven.[11] It further described the raid as 'diabolical' and 'infernal', having led to warnings being sent to all ports in the kingdom. John the Painter had the support of American envoy, Silas Dean, as did Jones, a sign that the French were connected to the foray. British newspapers viewed the raid as a continuation of plots that aimed to foster war between France and Britain. The same day, the twice-weekly *Edinburgh Advertiser* published a detailed account of the raid based on David Freeman's deposition.

On April 29, news of the 'pillage of Selkirk House' by an American privateer reached the *Morning Chronicle and London Advertiser* by way of a letter to Edinburgh's Provost.[12] Jones was not identified with the incident, although a later periodical claimed that he insisted a silver teapot was missing when he perused the sack taken from Lady Selkirk.

Virtually all the English newspapers identified the *Ranger* as a privateer, although Jones wanted it seen as part of the Continental Navy based in France. Jones wrote to Robert Morris from Nantes late in 1777 on his misgivings about privateers, especially in their failure to keep prisoners:

> Public virtue is not the characteristic of the concerned in privateers, no wonder then that they let their prisoners go, in such a manner, that they immediately augment the strength of the enemies fleet, their selfishness furnishes them with reasons for this conduct, were they to keep their prisoners, their provision would be the sooner consumed; which might perhaps obliegh them to return home before they had sufficiently glutted their avarice.[13]

Jones complained to Franklin that some part of the English press had unfairly accused him of having been paid 'a Capital sum ... by the Court of France' to attack Whitehaven.[14] Not until May 8, 1778, did the *Morning Chronicle and London Advertiser* note that John Paul had previously lived around Kirkcudbright and it dug up the old accusation that he had murdered the ship's carpenter Mungo Maxwell, causing him to change his name.

Not pleased by the coverage he received in England, Jones may have been happier with American papers like the Baltimore's *Maryland Journal,* which, however, had no news of his raid until July or August at the earliest, long after the fact.

Visuals also enrich our knowledge of how Jones was perceived. They required additional time to be printed, thus it was more than a year after the Whitehaven raid that three etchings of John Paul Jones appeared. One of Captain Paul Jones from London in October 22, 1779 shows him with a cutlass, pistol, open jacket and plumed hat, the garb of an ordinary seaman or petty officer.[15] It is similar to a contemporary French engraving of Gustavus Conyngham and implies that Jones was a privateer or at least a smuggler.

While Jones was remembered differently on the Continent, he continued to be remembered in the British Isles, even after his death.[16] The French Revolution broke out in 1789 and Jones experienced its early years, but he died in Paris in 1792, before renewed war with Britain.[17] However, Jones' reputation now took a turn for the worse. During the American Revolution he had been called a privateer; now he was portrayed in caricature by an English engraver as a pirate, with a beard and skull and cross bones. This portrayal fit him easily into the tradition of Irish Sea smugglers and raiders.

Insurance Rates

American historians have also claimed that during the Irish Sea expeditions of Conyngham, Wickes and Jones raised British insurance rates on shipping. It is difficult to project economic changes from their minor actions, when it is admitted the haul from the sale of their prizes was never what was expected. In the case of Jones, the speculation involves only northern Irish Sea insurance rates. Usually, insurance rates might rise on the basis of losses in an expected convoy, but the actions of unknown raiders taking individual prizes were too scattered to make an impression. In eighteen months in the West Indies, Conyngham's seizing and scuttling of ships was said to have caused a 10 per cent rise in British shipping insurance rates, but not in the West Indies, rather in the English Channel between Dover and Calais. This could not be, for events in the Atlantic and West Indies set insurance rates, not those in European waters. We know that pre-war insurance for transatlantic routes ranged from 2 to 2.5 per cent. As a result of France's declaration of war on Britain in mid-1778, the rates more than doubled for ships in convoy, and for those risking sail without protection the rates were even higher.[18] Lloyds of London was Britain's leading, but by no means only, underwriter setting national rates. At the end of the war, it released its best estimate of the number of merchant vessels and privateers captured by both sides. They showed a loss for Britain's large merchant marine of 2,208 to its enemies: France, Spain, the Dutch Republic and the United States. However, British ships took 1,106 enemy merchant vessels and also, thanks to the Royal Navy, recaptured an exceptional 39 per cent of British ships taken. In contrast, the allies could recapture only 2 per cent. The effect of Jones' Whitehaven raid on insurance rates is not clear.

Chapter 18

Whitehaven Defends Itself

The *Ranger*'s attack awakened Whitehaven magistrates and gentlemen as to their lack of defense. These leaders met in Haile's Coffee room where they admitted they had been lax in believing reports that the *Ranger* was a commonplace smuggler. However, Whitehaven was not a gathering point for militia – that honor belonged to inland Penrith. Whitehaven also had limitations on the use of the navy's press gang, as it protected its merchant mariners, meaning that navy ships were not always welcomed. Still, leaders were able to establish their own proper watch to secure the town and harbor. A subscription was opened by the gentlemen for the harbor defenses and 'so great was the ardor of the people that a company of two hundred seamen and mechanics were embodied in less than an hour … to man the batteries.'[1] The subscription was organized by street and included donations from Captain Daniel Brocklebank, the privateer, Nicholas Allison of the public house, and William Benson, master of Jones' first ship, the *Friendship*.

Expresses were sent to the Admiralty, the militia at Penrith, and the mayors, magistrates and officers at Glasgow and Liverpool.[2] Smacks and the *Hussar* with intelligence to take the privateer were sent to the Lord Lieutenant of Ireland, the magistrates of Belfast, and the commanders of the Royal Navy ships. Three companies of militia left Penrith at four o'clock in the afternoon, arriving at Whitehaven about noon, having traveled all night to assist the town. It was at this time that David Freeman explained that he had joined the *Ranger*'s crew in New Hampshire in order to return to his beloved homeland. As noted, he was the first to identify the *Ranger,* Jones and the crew to the authorities.

Not only Whitehaven but the British coast needed to have its fortifications manned and more volunteers were needed for the militias. To patrol the Irish Sea, a Royal Navy frigate *Thetis* was sent from Greenock, Scotland and the privateer *Heart of Oak* came from Liverpool.[3] On May 9, the *Morning Chronicle and London Advertiser* noted that a letter from Belfast reported that the *Heart of Oak* had been taken by the *Ranger* off Lough Foyle. Two days later, the *Gazetteer and New Daily Advertiser* confirmed that the *Heart of Oak* was safe at anchor at Lough Foyle, demonstrating what to expect from eighteenth-century newspapers.

With the immediate success of the subscription, within two weeks a new battery was made on the north side of Whitehaven's harbor. It was on a small hill known as Jack-a-Dandy, which gave its name to the battery.[4] Initially four 42-pounders were placed there and another six of the same weight came from the other batteries. By September, the number of new batteries had risen to six. Two of these were placed on the projecting edge above the Half-moon Battery to give it cover and prevent any seaborne attack from around St Bees head. The other battery was placed on the brows at Redness Point preventing attack from the northern side. The command of the batteries was given over to Colonel Moore of the Westmoreland Militia and the regulating to Captain Thomas Pemble. Although the guns were mounted, 100 men were still working on completion of the parapets.

By November, ten 18-pounders had arrived from the government.[5] The year after, the new batteries were finally demonstrated to the public. Two shots were fired at a ship a mile away: the first shot fell short but in line, while the second nearly hit the target much to the satisfaction of the onlookers.

Privateers

Privateers had become crucial to the British war effort as Royal Navy ships were spread thin. Whitehaven's privateering expanded as a result of three political events. In April 1777, privateering commissions were first authorized by Parliament, which had delayed the action because it did not want to recognize the rebellious colonies as a sovereign nation.[6] A year later in June, France finally declared war on Britain, opening its nearby coast to British privateers. At the end of 1780, Britain declared war on the Dutch Republic, which proved to be unprepared, opening it to a rush of British privateering in the last years of the war.

After 1777, Whitehaven's merchants joined those of Liverpool and Bristol in firm support of the ministry's war. While in the rebellious American colonies trade in staples declined, Whitehaven was still able to send cargos to British-occupied ports; these included cheese, flour, porter, salt, bricks, coal, wrought iron, woolens, linens and osnabrigs. It made sense that privateering be added to these ventures. Even as Jones was planning arson, privateers were commissioned in Whitehaven. The Whitehaven trader *Earl of Sandwich* under Captain Hutchinson received its letter of marque, as it was 'properly armed and manned and expected to sail tomorrow on a cruise'.[7] Meanwhile, Jacob Fletcher, born in Whitehaven in 1726, became a privateer of renown. In 1776, his brig *Nelly* was burned by rebels in the Savannah River, Georgia, but he managed to escape. In November, 1778, the 14-gun *Catcher* under Captain Fletcher, owned by Messrs. Salisbury & Co., brought into [Liverpool] a French ship from Cape Francois, Haiti, bound for Nantes, with '130,300lbs of sugar, 115 barrels of coffee, 7 barrels of indigo, and 12 bales of cotton'.

Having returned from Maine, Daniel Brocklebank was attracted to privateering and sailed the Atlantic in his *Castor*. From New York, with the help of another ship, he recaptured a British merchant ship, *General Sullivan,* that had been taken by the American privateer, and was rewarded by the Cork owners. This led him to apply for a letter of marque in 1779 to legalize the *Castor*'s privateering activities. Brocklebank set out in *Castor,* now improved with twenty-six guns and an armed crew of forty-five.[8] After *Castor* sank near Jamaica, he replaced it in 1782 with the 18-gun brig, *Castor 2,* which traded as far as Bengal. In all, he made twenty-five voyages across the Atlantic under his letter of marque.

The War Effort

Beyond its six strong batteries, improvements were made in Whitehaven in 1781 with an eye to preventing attacks. Its streets were lit with oil lamps to discourage night-time raids.[9] Two years later, a dispensary was opened where the poor could obtain free medicines.

Regardless of the Franco-Spanish invasion threat in 1779, Whitehaven's port continued to function as base for troops and supplies being sent to America. The Navy Board sought to hire Whitehaven merchant vessels as transports. As it required that such hirers be inspected at a Royal Navy dockyard, compensation was offered to cover that voyage. In the spring of 1776, Whitehaven merchant ships went to Spithead to be part of a convoy carrying Hessian troops to Staten Island, New York. On March 31, 1779, the transport *Mermaid* left Whitehaven with 200 Scottish soldiers and supernumeraries for Halifax. From there they traveled to New York, but were blown off course into the New Jersey shore and the transport wrecked, only forty-five surviving.[10] Other transports, however, followed and made up for the decline of trade between America and Whitehaven. A month earlier, Whitehaven had the unusual experience of being the refuge of navy tars who had broken out of a prison at Brest. They brought intelligence that a French fleet was due to sail to the West Indies.

Whitehaven's shipbuilding industry was encouraged by the Navy Board, which wanted it to compete for contracts to build warships. During the peace between the Seven Years' War and the American War, navy ships had suffered because they had been hastily built during the earlier conflict using green timber, and while laid up in peace time, their plank had not been taken up to be properly ventilated. Stocks of treated timber and naval stores had also declined.[11] When war came, the naval dockyards could not afford the time to produce a ship like the *Roebuck*, instead being overwhelmed by repairing and refitting the existing ships. From 1778, Comptroller Charles Middleton had the navy dockyards concentrate on refitting ships, while he wanted private dockyards to build new ships (all but the largest ships of the line). He advertised the specifications and bargained over the offers that were received. This led to private dockyards all over the British Isles competing to obtain contracts to build ships in terms that were advantageous to the Board.

Post-War

Daniel Brocklebank developed a post-war trading empire as a result of his privateering. In 1784, he sailed to the West Indies and later he added merchant ships *Precedent* and *Cyrus* to his fleet, which traded broadly. Another couple of ships were purchased from Stockdale and Co. and then in 1785 he purchased his own yard, restarting shipbuilding, which led to building another twenty-five ships, some of which he sold.[12] In addition, he had shares in a rope-making facility. By 1788 he had retired from the sea to devote his time completely to his shipyard.

Brocklebank shipping eventually merged with the famous Cunard Line. What had begun as a wartime defensive matter had led to the creation of one of world's great maritime lines.[13]

Chapter 19

Jones Loses Command

Carrickfergus in Ulster, in the north of Ireland, was Jones' goal after Whitehaven. It had not been panicked by the presence of either Conyngham or Wickes in their previous raiding of the Irish coast. Jones thought Carrickfergus had received news of his attack on Whitehaven and he claimed he would have attacked the port had he not seen the Royal Navy sloop *Drake* in the harbor. Originally, the merchantman *Resolution*, the *Drake* was purchased in early 1777 and commissioned in April and fitted at Plymouth dockyard.[1] Smaller than Jones' *Ranger,* it carried fourteen 4-pound guns.

Carrickfergus was a different town to Whitehaven. With a single quay extending from its castle, it did not have the Atlantic trade of Whitehaven, but its defenses were more extensive. It was much older than Whitehaven, having a medieval and Tudor past. In addition to its mighty garrisoned castle, in the early seventeenth century, modern walls with a series of gates and bastions were built to surround the town. Carrickfergus had changed hands often in the conflict for sovereignty over Ulster. A professional soldier and natural leader, Arthur Chichester built the town walls, settled the countryside and populated the town with English and lowland Scots.[2] By 1621 the first Presbyterian meetinghouse was established. In 1688, the town and castle were held by James II's garrison, despite the population's overwhelming sympathy for the Williamite cause. A year later, Williamite forces landed and besieged Carrickfergus, breaching the walls, and bringing about the surrender of the Jacobite garrison a week later. Finally, William of Orange stepped ashore at Carrickfergus, destined for the Battle of the Boyne where he defeated his father-in-law James II and, with his wife Mary, claimed the English crown.

In 1759, as the Seven Years' War raged, the French had planned three attacks on Britain, one aimed at Ireland, one at Scotland and one at England. This plan was thwarted at the Battle of Quiberon Bay, which was a disaster for the French navy. Before that battle took place, however, François Thurot with a French fleet of four frigates, carrying an army of 1,360 men, conducted the proposed diversion against the Scottish coast and the Irish Sea.[3] Thurot was a French privateer and smuggler, who had lived in the sailors' towns along the River Thames, becoming fluent in English. He flew British colors to seduce British merchantmen, a figure not unlike John Paul Jones. Sailing around Scotland in mid-February 1759, Thurot managed to get supplies at Claggan Bay on the Isle of Islay and repair the broken rudder on his own frigate at Belle-Isle. It seems that the local islanders were not hostile towards the gallant Thurot and his French squadron. They continued to cruise off the north Irish coast and the possibility of taking Belfast was discussed, although it was assumed that Carrickfergus had to be captured first.

By February 21, Thurot was at Carrickfergus Bay. He landed unopposed at Kilroot and from there marched to the Scottish fishing quarter just outside Carrickfergus' walls and then attacked.

The British garrison of fewer than 200 men of the 62nd foot held for a while, but then retreated to and attempted to defend the crumbling castle, but the task was hopeless and they surrendered with generous terms.[4] It proved much easier to capture Carrickfergus than to hold it, as Thurot's extensive army had suffered many casualties in the siege and needed to be fed. The surrounding countryside and nearby Belfast offered few supplies. Although the surrender terms had included a clause not to loot Carrickfergus, the hungry French soon took the silver from the Church of St Nicholas and the warrant and jewels of the local Orange Lodge and threatened the populace. After occupying Carrickfergus for about a week, Thurot decided to leave.

By then the Royal Navy had sent three frigates to confront his fleet. They caught up with him between Galloway and the Isle of Man. In the ensuing battle, Thurot and 160 men, mainly soldiers who were packed below, were killed and his three remaining ships taken.[5] His body was quickly interred in the sea, but was later found on the shore near the Mull of Galloway and buried with full military honors by sympathizers. His expedition demonstrated that the coastal Irish Sea could be invaded and looted by privateers, while the Royal Navy could only belatedly protect even the strongest towns. Two days after the battle, a Whitehaven delegation arrived at the Isle of Man with a present to honor the success of the frigates' commander, Captain John Elliot.

With this in mind, on April 24, 1778, Jones would hover outside of Carrickfergus, not up to attacking it. He had already been turned away from the town just before his attack on Whitehaven, though not without taking Scottish fishermen he encountered as prisoners. With the fishermen as his guides, he crossed the Irish Sea and made a second effort to lure the *Drake* outside Carrickfergus harbor, despite the opposition of his crew. The *Drake* routinely came out and sent a boat to inquire who Jones' ship was, as it was not flying colors, but when the boat drew alongside it was seized. The *Drake* followed slowly and 'after the usual compliments', the *Ranger* suddenly fired a broadside into the sloop.[6] The action continued for more than an hour until the *Drake*'s commanding officer, Captain George Burdon, was killed and second in command Lieutenant William Dobbs was mortally wounded, along with twenty others killed or wounded. Her rigging and sails very much damaged. Having no colors to strike, they 'called for quarters', signifying the *Drake* was taken. On the *Ranger*'s side, Marine commander Lieutenant Wallingford was killed by a musket shot, John Dangle was cut in two in the fore top, Nathanial Wells died of his wounds, Midshipman Pierce Powers lost his right hand, and James Fells and Thomas Taylor were wounded by musket shots. Captain Burdon was buried at sea the next day with the honors of war, as was the body of Wallingford. Jones now released the fishermen he had previously taken, as they had helped him with his approach to Carrickfergus. The *Drake* would have to be taken to France.

Jones Loses Command of the *Ranger*

On the *Ranger*, John Paul Jones had been trying to create a sense of military duty, which if it had existed, was disappearing from the crew. To his subordinates, Jones seemed overbearing because he was motivated by fame, the desire to rise his social status, and delusion that he could be a European nobleman. His Scottish background contributed to his desires. In Virginia, he had attempted to purchase a landed estate and had a coat of arms concocted to falsify his background, as a result of Louis XVI's naming him a 'Chevalier'.[7]

When writing to Lady Selkik soon after the incident at her mansion, Jones described himself in terms that would not have endeared him to his crew. He claimed to want peace:

> I am not in arms as an American, nor am I in pursuit of riches … I profess myself a citizen of the world, totally unfettered by the little mean distinctions of climate or country, which diminish the benevolence of the heart … And I am ready to sacrifice my life also with cheerfulness, if the forfeiture could restore peace and goodwill among mankind.[8]

Was this simply bombast to a lady he had never met or was their truth in his profession?

When the *Ranger* arrived in Brest on May 7, Jones found that the American commissioners' finances in France were in dire straits. The prizes he had taken previously had not been sold and no cash existed for his crew's provisions. The commissioners had no credit and no authority to use public money to pay officers or men.[9] Jones was forced to mortgage his prizes to feed his crew. Despite his best efforts, these financial shortfalls were making his crew hostile.

During the return from Carrickfergus, a misunderstanding developed between Jones and First Lieutenant Thomas Simpson, who had been placed on the towed *Drake* as commander. At one point, Jones needed to break away from Simpson so that the *Ranger* could pursue what Jones hoped would be a prize, although it turned out to be a neutral Swede.[10] It appeared to Simpson that Jones' release of the *Drake* left him to make his own way to Brest while Jones pursued the prize. However, Jones claimed he wanted the *Drake* to follow him. Simpson was chased by an enemy brig and was unable to rejoin the *Ranger*. Jones saw it differently and had Simpson arrested for 'insubordination', giving Elijah Hall the responsibilities for bringing the prize into Brest. Remembering Simpson's conduct at Whitehaven, Jones felt he was still plotting against him. Over the next months he sought to destroy Simpson's reputation.

Simpson wanted a court martial to clear his name, but there were not enough Continental officers in France to hold one and Jones put Simpson in prison, where he languished. Much of the *Ranger*'s crew became incensed over the situation as they were loyal to the officers that had recruited them like Simpson. In May and June, petitions came from the crew and petty officers in favor of Simpson's release from 'a lousy, dirty French goal', accusing Jones of being nasty and vain. The officers claimed Jones' 'government [is] arbitrary and his temper and treatment insufferable, … threatening to shoot the person or persons he … choses [sic] to call ignorant or disobedient'.[11] The crew had enlisted for year, but as they were delayed in leaving, Jones had disregarded the original dates because he needed them for his unending enterprises. The expedition to the Irish Sea had failed to produce the promised lucrative booty. They asserted that he had been unable to sell the prizes, which had been the impetus for their signing and believing they could support their famished wives and children in New Hampshire. It was now their goal to return to them.

Commissioners Benjamin Franklin, Arthur Lee and John Adams found that Jones' treatment of Simpson 'was too harsh' and that Simpson be sent back to America for a court martial.[12] In late May, Franklin wrote to Jones hoping that he could obtain a new command to counter 'The Jersey Privateers that do us a great deal of mischief, by intercepting our supplies'. Franklin suggested that with the support of French frigates at Brest, the *Ranger* should draw out and attack these privateers. Jones stayed ashore, however, not daring to return to the *Ranger*, still hoping for *L'Indien*, which because of its enormous draft could not be transported to the North Sea and was actually rotting at anchor. To add insult to injury, the prize crew of the *Drake* plundered the captured ship, even taking the uniforms of the British prisoners and selling them. Jones' personal effects, also stored aboard the *Drake,* were tossed out or trashed.

Under orders from the commissioners, Jones was forced to release Simpson on parole. Simpson replaced him as captain of the *Ranger* on July 27 to the 'joy and satisfaction of the ship's company'.[13] Meanwhile, the *Drake* was sold for a fraction of its worth to Jean Peltier-Dudoyer, the most successful shipping manager in Nantes.[14] He was a friend of Jones and Franklin, having sent arms to the colonies before the French alliance and in this process he had lost thirteen ships to the British. Later, he would be involved in fitting out the *Amphytrite* once promised to Jones and the *Bonhomme Richard,* which Jones would command. None of this helped Jones' relations with his crew. In October, the *Ranger* returned to America under Simpson.

Loyalty of Continental Crews

Jones' problems with his crew were faced by most Continental officers. Captains struggled to maintain discipline in the face of desertion and mutiny, even on the part of their officers. They succeeded in recruiting if they developed a reputation as a good officer for sailors to serve under.[15] The captain was expected to nurture the sailors and boys who sought a position on his ship. He would have to advance their careers, get them timely wages and prize money, and protect them when they were in harm's way. In turn, they would enhance the captain's influence among the crew, giving him their respect. It is evident that Jones had failed to do this with the *Ranger's* crew and his success was consistently limited because of this lack of respect among his crews.[16] Their polyglot makeup and diverging reasons for going to sea made it difficult to develop loyalty. They were proud of their hometown and loyal to their shipmates from the same place. With the *Ranger*, this meant New Hampshire and Massachusetts, the epicenter for the recruiting of the crew. Some historians have seen New England sailors as less inclined to take orders from officers.

American ships based in Europe, like the *Ranger*, inevitably became more diverse in the makeup of their crews. Some sailors gave up their American citizenship and ties to their family to serve on a French privateer.[17] Other American seamen were penniless, in a foreign country whose language they did not speak, and they hoped to end up at home. After a year with Jones, a majority of the *Ranger*'s crew could not wait to get home, even though they returned largely empty handed.

It was the *Ranger's* petty officers who had led the crew's revolt against Jones. They included gunners, carpenters, stewards, quartermasters, cooks, armorers, the boatswain, the coxswain, the prize master and the master's mate. In their petition, they claimed to have served on the Irish Sea cruise to 'maintain their families', a reference to the fact that they were far more likely than the average crew member to be married with children.[18] This made their desire for earnings more noble, not simply a matter of looting. They also claimed a measure of patriotism, desiring to serve their 'injured country'. It was their crucial position in the makeup of the ship's company that allowed them to bring the crew along in standing up to Jones. This would not be the last time that Jones would lose command of his ship.

Chapter 20

Jones Sails Again

After Jones' raid on Whitehaven, conditions in Europe improved for the Franco-American alliance as Spain joined France in the war against Britain. This alliance, signed by the Bourbon monarchs on April 12, 1779, upset the balance of sea power in the Channel, as the two powers assembled a fleet, which was larger than any the Royal Navy could put together, to invade Britain.[1]

England Saved by 'Admiral Scurvy'

Spain was anxious for quick and decisive stroke against Britain rather than a prolonged war. The Bourbon invasion of England with a fleet of sixty-six ships of the line would be the largest since the Spanish Armada. This force set sail in June 1779, commanded by Louis, Admiral d'Orvilliers for France, and for Spain, Admiral Don Luis de Cordoba y Cordoba.[2] The original aim of the fleet was to land at the Isle of Wight on England's south coast, in proximity to the Royal Navy's Portsmouth dockyard. From the beginning, however, there was a lack of coordination and planning. When d'Orvilliers, who was already late, arrived at the rendezvous near La Coruna, he found no Spanish ships. He was forced to wait six weeks for the Spaniards, while his water and provisions were largely consumed. The allied fleets also needed to standardize their signals, so an entire signal corps had to be improvised.

The French navy had been able to recruit 23,750 sailors for the invasion.[3] Back in 1669, renowned marine minister Jean-Baptiste Colbert had improved the navy's training and morale by instituting a system of classes for the service to ensure loyalty. Every seaman would provide six months of service once within a four-year period, in which he would receive full pay and then receive half pay and a pension when these conditions were met. Still in place, young men were taken from their farms and families to be sailors under these conditions. Only about 10 per cent of recruits were volunteers. As for boys, at the age of 12, orphans were designated as cabin boys and sent aboard ships to be apprentices and servants. Many sailors in the invasion force come from Brittany, which was the staging ground as it was immediately across the Channel from England.

In 1779, however, the Bourbon sailors were exhausted by the invasion fleet's continual maneuvers, forcing them to come into port, where they lost discipline and become sick, drinking wine in the cabarets. Scurvy and other diseases spread quickly as the ships sailed back and forth, requiring that stops be made to discharge the sick, rather than heading directly toward the southern English coast. Soon half the sailors in the fleet were ill, meaning there were insufficient well men to carry out maneuvers.[4] Unfortunately, it was not policy for the

A Plan of His Majesty's Naval Yard at Chatham, 1774.

No. 1: Cabin-Boy, London, Pub. Feb. 15, 1799, Rudolph Ackermann.

Commodore Hopkins, Commandeur en Chef der Ameri. Flotte, Thomas Hart, 1781.

The Mitered Minuet, Paul Revere.

British Troops landing at Kip's Bay, 1776, artist unknown.

Above left: *Captain Paul Jones, "original drawing taken from life on board the Serapis," Tho Macklin, no. 1, Lincolns Inn Fields (London), Oct. 22, 1779. Cutlass, pistol, plumed hat, open jacket.*

Above right: *Eighteenth-century French engraving of Augustatvs Kuningam, Commodore of the United States of America in the English land.*

PAUL JONES THE PIRATE.

IOHANN PAUL IONES,
Befehlshaber einer Schwadron in Diensten
DER 13. VEREINIGTEN PROVINZEN VON NORD - AMERIKA. 1779.

Above left: *Paul Jones the Pirate,
nineteenth-century English engraving by
Archibald and Arthur Park, 47 Leonard
St., Tabernacle Walk, London.*

Above right: *Sketched in Amsterdam,
Oct. 9, 1779, attributed to Simon Folcke
of Amsterdam, this is engraved portrait is
the earliest likeness of John Paul Jones.
Epaulets of an officer.*

Left: *John Paul Jones, engraved by Elias
Haid, Augsburg, ca. 1780.*

'To the Merchants trading to Russia, this print representing the gallant defense of Capt. Pearson in his Majesty's ship, Serapis, and the Countess of Scarborough Arm'd Ship Capt. Piercy, against Paul Jones's Squadron, whereby a valuable fleet from the Baltic were prevented from falling into the hands of the Enemy, is with greatest respect Inscribed by their humble servant, John Harris' and showing 'English Force' and 'Enemy's Force' with numbers of men and guns. Engraving by John Peltro after a painting by Robert Dodd, London, Dec. 1, 1781.*

An Exact Prospect of Charlestown, the Metropolis of the Province of South Carolina, engraved by William Henry Toms, 1739, 1762, 1779.

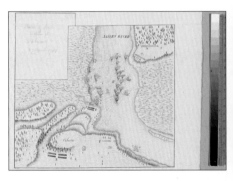

Above: *Benedict Arnold's greatest naval victory was not on Lake Champlain, but in the service of the British at Osborne's on the James River on April 27, 1781. From The Journal of the Operations of the Queen's Rangers, John Graves Simcoe, Huntington Digital Library.*

Left: *George Collier, John James Hinchiff, 1795.*

The Castle in the Moon.

The Duke de Crillon, giving orders for the Siege of Gibraltar. London printmaker, Thomas Colley, 1782.

Engraving by William Sharp of The Siege and Relief of Gibraltar, to the King's Most Excellent Majesty, originally painted by John Singleton Copley.

Sir Roger Curtis gallantly exerting himself in preserving the Spaniards at Gibraltar

Lord Rodney

Above: *Sir Roger Curtis gallantly exerting himself in preserving the Spaniards at Gibraltar, engraving in 1802.*

Left: *Admiral George Rodney by Thomas Gainsborough, 1782-1787.*

Bourbon ships to carry citrus fruit or fresh vegetables to combat scurvy, even though Spain was a source of lemons and oranges.

Finally, the invasion fleet lay off Plymouth, now aiming to land at rugged Cornwall. Le Havre, St Malo and Honfleur were bursting with supplies for the army once it landed.[5] However, foggy weather and continued sickness among the ships meant that the Bourbon fleet only once even sighted the Royal Navy. Under these conditions in late August, the allied threat melted away as its fleet was forced to return to Brest. Still, the fact that an invasion force was put together by the Bourbon powers showed how vulnerable the British coast and the Channel were.

Jones Makes a Diversion

Against this background, John Paul Jones spent the rest of 1778 in Paris, supposedly to be near Benjamin Franklin. He suggested Jones find a suitable prize to turn into a warship, realizing that *L'Indien* was no longer an option. Jones found a ship, built strongly in 1766, but slow and clumsy, which the French navy had just purchased. Fitted out with funds from Louis XVI, Jones named it the *Bonhomme Richard*.[6] He had difficulty in getting the forty, 18-, 12- and 6-pounders it needed from French arsenals. Even more problematic was the diverse crew which numbered 380. While many of the officers were Americans, they made up less than half of the petty officers and only forty-six of the seamen and boys. According to the Maryland gunner John Kilby, thirty-three of them had escaped from 'Fortune's Jail' in England, after being taken prisoner from the privateer *Sturdy Beggar.* French marines and sailors numbered 173, of whom thirty-six were landsmen. Britons, many who came from French prisons, were more numerous than Americans with fifty-four seamen and boys, and more than half of the petty officers. The rest came from almost a dozen nationalities, a mixture that was not unusual.

As Jones was completing the *Richard*, ambitious plans called for him to lead a French-financed naval squadron, carrying a landing force to make a full-scale invasion of Irish Sea ports like Liverpool. Franklin backed it and even the French seemed supportive. It was seen as a useful diversion to the north, taking attention away from the buildup for the Bourbon invasion of southern England.[7] The squadron's 1,500 men landing force would be commanded by none other than the Marquis de Lafayette, who been anxiously cooling his heels since Congress's expedition against Canada failed to materialize. Jones would command two Continental frigates, a French frigate, and two smaller warships. Lafayette, as a Continental major general, was given overall command of the expedition by Franklin, but Jones would be in command of the ships. The French, however, decided they needed their troops for the Bourbon invasion of England and Lafayette was diverted to a dragoon regiment. Jones was left with ships but with no expedition. The next plan was simply to cruise off Scotland and northern England, again to divert attention from the Bourbon invasion, but this also failed to materialize.

Finally, Franklin came up with a new cruise for Jones, from Lorient, up the west coast of Ireland, crossing to the North Sea and then down to the eastern English coast and across to the Dutch port of Texel. The French were paying for the expedition so that Jones would have to do their bidding, but Franklin pointed out that Texel was near to where *L'Indien* was still being built.[8] Jones would be joined by four ships. One of them, the *Alliance,* was actually a new American frigate, but it was commanded by Pierre Landais, a Frenchman, who had been made an honorary Massachusetts citizen. The frigate *Pallas*, the brig *Vengeance,* and the cutter *Cerf,* belonged to the French navy, although their officers had been given commissions in the Continental Navy. In June, Jones conducted a shakedown cruise with his squadron in which the *Richard* and the *Alliance* collided and were badly damaged, a situation that Jones blamed on Landais. Moreover, a plot was detected among his numerous British crew members to seize the *Richard* and take her to Britain. The mutineers' ringleader was supposedly sentenced to 250 lashes. None of this boded well for Jones' expedition.

Joined by two French privateers, Jones' squadron sailed on August 14, 1779, with high expectations because the Royal Navy had concentrated all available ships on the south coast to prevent the Bourbon invasion.[9] From the beginning, Jones found his French officers were uncooperative. His efforts to signal them and share in their prizes led them to completely ignore his authority.[10] The privateers soon disappeared with their prizes and the *Cerf* retuned to France, as the *Pallas* and *Alliance* went off on their own. While these two ships occasionally returned to the *Richard,* they refused to acknowledge Jones as squadron commander.

Jones' squadron sailed from the west coast of Ireland, north to Scotland's Orkney and Shetland Islands, taking prizes. He then decided to raid Edinburgh's port of Leith on the Firth of Forth. To get his French captains to support the attack, he claimed they could ask for a £200,000 ransom from the town fathers.[11] Jones got close to Leith, but a gale damaged his ships and drove him out to sea and Leith was left untouched. He cruised south along the northeast coast and hoped to force England's coal capital, Newcastle-on-the-Tyne, into similar terms, but again failed. After this, the captains of the *Pallas* and *Vengeance* refused to go further, fearing that it was only a matter of time before they would be confronted by Royal Navy ships.

In late September, having failed to raid an English port or to keep his fleet together, Jones' luck changed at Flamborough Head, a headland jutting out into the North Sea. Here Franklin's ideal, a Baltic convoy, appeared out of the mists, loaded with naval stores and timber for Royal Navy dockyards.[12] When they saw Jones, the merchant transports fled northward to the protection of Scarborough Castle's batteries, where they remained secure. The convoy's escort ships, the frigate *Serapis* under Captain Richard Pearson and the sloop *Countess of Scarborough* under Captain Thomas Piercy, interposed themselves between Jones and the retreating convoy. Pearson, you will remember, had replaced Douglas in 1777 as commander of the St Lawrence River and Lake Champlain naval force. To Jones' surprise, the *Pallas, Vengeance* and *Alliance* rejoined him.

Jones' squadron slowly closed the gap between them and the Royal Navy escort. Jones ordered the squadron to form a line of battle as they approached the British, but instead the *Alliance* abruptly left the *Richard* in the lead, alone against the *Serapis*.[13] The *Pallas* also turned away, although she would later attack the *Scarborough.* The *Vengeance* failed to come up. Flying British colors, the *Richard* pulled aside the *Serapis* and fired a broadside, which was immediately answered. The *Richard*'s main battery of 12-pounders was soon shattered or overturned. In the midst of this, the *Alliance* appeared and inexplicably fired two broadsides into the *Richard* and then disappeared. The *Richard*'s French marines were effective sharp shooters and they were able to sweep the *Serapis'* upper deck, both sides suffering heavy casualties. The *Richard* began to sink and some officers decided to surrender and pull down the colors, but Jones stopped them. The battle came down to which captain would give up first. The *Countess* had struck to the *Pallas* and the lurking *Alliance* was virtually undamaged.

Outnumbered, Pearson decided to pull down his flag. The *Richard* was so damaged that it sank the next day and Jones and the remains of his crew were transferred to the *Serapis.* In no condition to go after the Baltic convoy, his squadron, led by the *Alliance* and *Vengeance,* followed their original orders and went straight to the safety of Texel on the Dutch coast.

The squadron was followed by Royal Navy frigates, who promptly bottled Jones up at Texel, where he remained till the end of the year. While some crew members like John Kilby supported Jones, for the next two months, desertions from his crew increased, as many were angry because they had taken no prizes from the escaped convoy.[14] Although the Dutch were technically neutral and delayed in expelling Jones, British protests soon had their effect. To protect Jones' squadron from expulsion, the French ambassador claimed that it was French and ordered the replacement of its colors with those of France, believing that the Dutch would not order a French squadron to leave. Jones refused to cooperate, but Franklin rebuked him, 'As the [French] Court is at chief expense, I think they have the best right to direct.' Jones was forced to give the *Serapis* and *Countess* to the French. The French tried to placate Jones by offering a commission as a privateer, a great mistake on their part because he considered it an insult to be a privateer. In the meantime, Jones carried on a vendetta with Captain Landais of the *Alliance,* whom he accused of trying to subvert the expedition. Franklin realized that Landais had been insubordinate, but he dared not punish him as it would strain his relations with France. He was able to get Landais to leave the *Alliance* and have Jones replace him as captain.

While Jones was blockaded in Texel, the Dutch printed engravings of him, which are a great contrast to his English likenesses. The first Amsterdam engraving shows a burial stone, with its image of 'Paul Jones' at the top and the epitaph: 'sketched in the theatre in Amsterdam, October 9, 1779'.[15] His uniform has epaulets and he is surrounded by the paraphernalia of naval glory. The second Amsterdam print appeared a year after in London, taken by Sayer and Bennet from a Dutch original. Here Jones was in the service of France as well as America and he was in an officer's uniform, but not one that followed Congress's uniform regulations. He had petitioned in 1777 to wear the uniform portrayed, consisting of white small clothes and blue coat with white facings, but it was never approved by Congress. The reasoning against it was that it was almost identical to Royal Navy officers' uniforms. He wore this uniform in Amsterdam and as late as 1780, when he tried to lure the privateer *Triumph* into thinking his ship was British. Was this a subterfuge so that Jones could approach British ships or did he want to be mistaken for a Royal Navy officer? Both these likenesses reflected the way in which Jones preferred to be portrayed.

As for the Jones' taking of the *Serapis* with the *Bonhomme Richard,* surprisingly little was immediately done by Americans to commemorate it. While American painters lined up to portray incidents from the Siege of Gibraltar, none painted the battle until well into the nineteenth century. The earliest effort to show the confrontation was by England's Robert Dodd. Born in 1748, he was a marine and landscape painter as well as an engraver and publisher, known for his portrayal of naval battles, including Flamborough Head. His work was engraved by John Peltro and published by John Harris, etcher and line engraver, in London, December 1, 1781.[16] Six years after Jones' death in 1798, a French edition of his writings, entitled *Memoirs de Paul Jones* was published with a frontispiece captioned 'Bonhomme Richard on Fire'. This French perspective on the action seems to emphasize the loss of the *Bonhomme Richard.*

Jones Loses Command

When the British frigates were called elsewhere, Jones left Texel with the *Alliance* and at the beginning of 1780 he was in the English Channel from where he would sail to the northern coast of Spain before returning to Lorient. Instead of acquiring prizes, however, he found his crew to be completely divided.[17] The *Alliance*'s officers and crew and those of the former *Richard* were at loggerheads with one another. Most of the ship's company was angry because they had received neither pay nor prize money from the previous expedition. Jones had been unable to dispose of the prizes before the French government took over. This was not the first time that he had difficulty in keeping his crew together.

When Franklin heard of Jones' return, he wrote to him that Congress's Board of Admiralty wanted the *Alliance* sent home with a cargo of arms, powder, uniforms and cannon.[18] Jones was also asked to take back Commissioner Arthur Lee. His return caused problems because he had a coach and other property, which he wanted to go with him, although the *Alliance* was already filled with the needed munitions.

As preparation for the voyage went on, Jones suddenly disappeared. Instead of staying with his ship, he spent April and May as a social lion at the French Court. He was inducted into the Order of Military by Louis XVI, who gave him a sword. From then on, he demanded that he be recognized with the title of 'Chevalier'.[19] Even when he was finished at court, Jones refused return to the *Alliance* until mid-June. During this time, the still unremunerated crew were pleased at the return of their former Captain Landais. With the support of Lee, Landais was named captain of the *Alliance* and Jones made no effort to intervene. After delays in July, Landais was able to leave with his precious munitions for Philadelphia. Even Franklin was disgusted with Jones, writing, 'If you had stayed on board where your duty lay, instead of coming to Paris, you would not have lost your ship.'

While Jones preferred to remain in France, the need for munitions remained Congress's priority. When Jones was given command of the 20-gun sloop *Ariel*, on loan from the French, it was to bring munitions across the Atlantic.[20] In mid-December 1780, he took the *Ariel* from France to Philadelphia, heavily loaded with arms and equipment. On the way, they encountered a mysterious ship which Jones thought to be British. He raised the Union Jack and dressed in the blue and white of a Royal Navy officer, inviting its captain to come aboard. However, the privateer *Triumph* would not take the bait and broadsides were fired. Jones claimed the privateer struck its colors, but no matter as the *Triumph* proved faster, pulling away from the *Ariel*.[21] After over three years in Europe, this was Jones' last action under the Stars and Stripes. Jones' cruises had been the last effort of the Continental Navy to sail around the British Isles.

Legacy

Jones' renown at the French court and in Texel was based on his squadron's action that led to the capture of the *Serapis*. More disappointed with Jones would be Franklin, who never got his nobleman for a prisoner exchange, never saw a Baltic convoy disrupted, and was wearied with Jones' habitual difficulty to command his crews.

How do we account for Jones as a commander? His education at Kirkbean and his apprenticeship aboard Whitehaven's *Friendship* must have given him useful navigational insight. He was a skilled sailor who could solve the deficiencies of his ships on their voyages.

Jones also could write. As one historian has put it: 'He seems to have enjoyed playing with his pen as much as a brace of pistols …. He was nearly as good an actor and penman as seaman.'[22] He made an art of flattering his betters with his pen, whether it was Congress, the American Commissioners, a Scottish Lady, or Louis XVI and his ministers. Anyone has to be wary in using his extensive correspondence because it was his chief vehicle of self-promotion. Objective criticism is simply ignored in his letters.

Jones' ability to flatter, however, did not impress his fellow officers and crew and it was here that Jones found only frustration. He failed to be able to reward his ship's company, who were constantly disobeying him. Unable to create a loyal crew, he twice lost command of his ship. It is possible that his situation was typical of the Continental Navy. Even the competent Wickes had to placate a mutinous crew and Conyngham claimed his crew took command of his ship during its most successful privateering.

Despite his service to the Continental Navy, Jones remained a European, not an American. Samuel Eliot Morison contends that his 'Pinnacle of Fame' was in Paris in 1780, where weeks slipped by as he received honors not only from Louis XVI, but the ladies. He was conscious of rank, proud to accept the title 'Chevalier', given by the king of France. He felt he was more genteel and skilled in war than most of his fellow Continental officers, even though he had a similar merchant marine rather than Royal Navy background. Rival American and French captains, of course, saw him as little better than a European mercenary.[23] Jones was clearly a misfit in the Continental Navy for he felt more at home in Europe and he eventually served as an admiral in the Russian navy.

Understandably, Jones was not even mentioned in Mahan's classic *The Influence of Seapower upon History*. Until the twentieth century, he was an obscure naval figure, rescued at the turn of the nineteenth century by an intensive search for his body, which was found in an unmarked grave in an abandoned French cemetery. It was exhumed and in 1905 brought to the Naval Academy at Annapolis. Three years later, the Naval Academy Chapel received the remains, which were placed in a bronze and marble sarcophagus in the crypt. Jones would certainly have appreciated the tribute, but it ignored the fact that he was a deeply flawed ship's captain. After his resurrection, his admirers produced what one historian calls an 'adulatory literature that repels the average reader'.[24]

PART 6

THE ROYAL NAVY SUCCEEDS IN THE SOUTH

Chapter 21

A French Fleet and a Southern Strategy

In mid-1778, the French navy was as yet uncommitted and had a choice of where it wished to go. It could concentrate on the English Channel, where its enemy was massed, and force a decisive battle. The Comte de Vergennes, however, preferred to fight a more limited war, which reflected the fact that despite improvements, the French navy still felt itself to be inferior to the Royal Navy.[1] Therefore he favored tying down the British home fleet in the English Channel, while sending out considerable forces to overseas' theaters like the West Indies or the rebellious American colonies. Many historians think that this was a mistake, arguing that Vergennes would have been wiser to concentrate on the Channel, rather than dispersing his strength overseas.

The Royal Navy's primary duty was now controlling the English Channel, especially observing the activities of France's naval base at Brest.[2] In July 1778, the classic showdown between the maneuvering British and French battle fleets in the English Channel finally took place. Admiral Augustus Keppel's ships met those of Admiral Comte Louis d'Orvilliers near Ushant Island off Brest. The battle was inconclusive, but the French performed well enough to shake British confidence in their naval superiority.

France had developed an important naval base at Toulon in the Mediterranean, which was much more difficult to watch than the Channel. Earlier in February, Vergennes had sent Admiral Charles-Henri-Hector d'Estaing to take command of the French fleet at Toulon and it became evident to the British that he would lead that fleet to a distant destination. A cousin of Lafayette, d'Estaing was a very thin man, having suffered from a severe bout of dysentery.[3] The 49-year-old had been a lieutenant general in the French army, but now received the position of vice admiral of the French navy, which would make him France's senior naval officer when he arrived in American waters. His land experience was thought to qualify him to lead amphibious operations, using sailors as marines. However, French naval officers resented outsiders from the army, who had been forced to find jobs in the navy after the army was reduced. D'Estaing may have been a brave soldier, but he seemed confused and indecisive as naval officer. In an ironic twist of fate, he would be guillotined during the French Revolution.

British intelligence usually knew all, but the French were able to keep d'Estaing's destination a secret. Were the British to remain concentrated in the Channel in case d'Estaing went there, or would they disperse if he headed for America? Sandwich believed that the Channel must remain the highest priority for fear of invasion, and he hesitated to create separate navy fleets for distant theaters.[4] Thus, no squadron was sent to Gibraltar or the Mediterranean Straits to determine d'Estaing's direction. Finally, Royal Navy ships found him in the Atlantic and it was realized that he was heading for America and a warning was sent to Admiral Howe, who received it off the Delaware Capes. In Britain, a relieving squadron was formed to follow d'Estaing, but it was delayed because of the usual manning and supply difficulties.[5]

Howe Foils d'Estaing

Having been warned, Admiral Howe had rushed the Philadelphia evacuation to be able to face d'Estaing's fleet as it neared New York. In reality, the French fleet greatly outnumbered and out gunned Howe's fleet.[6] Reinforcements for Howe from the Channel Fleet had not yet come. He had to make do with his New York resources, taking volunteers from the transports to fill the gaps in his crews, receiving marines from the army by lot, while New York's Chamber of Commerce and merchants offered recruits, provided fire ships and scouted for the admiral.

In early July, d'Estaing's fleet arrived off the Delaware coast and Congress's Marine Committee welcomed it by offering water and food. The French then moved north toward Sandy Hook, New Jersey, a notorious center of night-time smuggling. Inside the bend of Sandy Hook Island, Howe had double anchored his ships and springs were applied to the anchors allowing the ships to swing into position for a broadside. D'Estaing came within a mile of Howe, but dared not attack the shallows of the Hook as they were unknown to him.[7] He never seemed to have mastered the navigational skills necessary to command a great fleet. He sounded the harbor bar and maneuvered for several days, while Howe and Clinton strengthened Sandy Hook's land defenses. D'Estaing had not received the promised supplies from the Marine Committee, as they had been delayed because of a 'long land carriage'. Finally, he gave up, veering off from Sandy Hook's shallows and headed into the Atlantic.

D'Estaing eluded Howe's fleet and went to Newport to coordinate with a rebel army besieging the town. On August 8, the French fleet entered Narragansett Bay, but suddenly Howe's fleet appeared and positioned itself advantageously. Unfamiliar with the waters, d'Estaing again backed off from a confrontation. He then doubled back to threaten Newport, but a gale suddenly incapacitated both fleets. Admiral Howe's *Apollo* was completely dismasted and Hamond found Howe sitting by the rudder head of his damaged ship, so he had him transferred to the safety of another ship. The siege of Newport by the rebels failed. D'Estaing decided to take his fleet to Boston for repair as the *Roebuck* and other warships shadowed the limping fleet to the very edge of Boston Harbor.[8] D'Estaing would eventually sail to Martinique. Howe's fleet was back at Sandy Hook on September 11, the admiral having succeed in protecting New York and Newport from a more powerful enemy fleet.

Admiral Howe's feat in the face of personal danger would enhance his reputation when he returned to England. An admirer summed up his achievement:

> Thus, by a happy mixture of prudent and bold measures, by a series of maneuvers, which the naval tactic was scarcely thought capable of exhibiting; ... Lord Howe, having, with forces so unequal, defeated all the great designs of the enemy, protected the army and the fleet of transports at New-York, raised the siege of Rhode Island, and driven the French Squadron into the port of Boston, whence their shattered condition would not suffer them to venture for a length of time ...[9]

Southern Strategy

After the evacuation of Philadelphia and Howe's defense of New York, it appeared to Lord Germain and Sir Henry Clinton that the South, with its strong Loyalism among whites and blacks, was now the best place to carry on the war.[10] The policy was a reaction to the situation in the Middle Colonies where, despite the Howe's successes, Washington's army remained stubbornly at large. It recognized that New England was a bottomless source of recruits for the rebel military, thwarting any hope of restoring that region to the crown. The renewed assault on the South would begin at the furthest distance in Georgia and from there lead to the conquest of Charleston, and ultimately move north to Virginia and the Chesapeake.

St Augustine

At the outbreak of the Revolution, fortified St Augustine, Florida was strategically placed to serve as a British base on edge of the Southern colonies. It had been taken from Spain by the British at the Seven Years' War peace table. The commander of its garrison was Swiss-born Augustine Prévost, a colonel of the 60th Regiment.[11] The 60th had been raised in North America during the Seven Years' War and included many foreign and colonial Protestants and was dedicated to the forest tactics necessary in North America. Prévost and Governor Patrick Tryon of East Florida had their differences, but with its own vice-admiralty court, St Augustine attracted Loyalist privateers and a few Royal Navy ships. Its harbor was protected by a treacherous bar and channel, which could only be navigated with a pilot.

Southern Mainland States.

Savannah Taken

As the first step in the Southern strategy, Clinton sent 3,000 Germans and Provincials under Highlander Lieutenant Colonel

Archibald Campbell to Georgia, in a squadron under Hyde Parker. They arrived in late December 1778 and were guided by an elderly female slave through the swamps, surprising the rebel garrison at Savannah. Simultaneously, Prévost invaded Georgia from St Augustine. He crossed the St Marys River into Georgia and after token resistance, the rebel forces abandoned Savannah, leaving it to be occupied by both armies at the end of the year. On Prévost's arrival in Savannah, he took command of the British forces, as he was a brigadier general, outranking Campbell.[12]

Clinton wanted Savannah to be a secure post from which to invade the Carolinas. Campbell was charged with the occupation of city and the cultivation of Loyalist support. He showed a concern for the civil population that made him dreaded by rebel leaders. 'His immediate care was to soften the asperities of war, and to reconcile to his equitable government, those who had submitted, in the first instance, to the superiority of his arms.'[13] Inhabitants flocked to serve the British, altogether numbering 5,000 enslaved and free blacks and 2,000 whites.

Prévost left Georgia in March 1779 to advance into South Carolina as he felt that it was the center of the region's opposition to the crown. He defeated the rebels at Briar Creek and reached the outskirts of Charleston. It appeared the city was ready to surrender, as long as it was agreed that South Carolina would be neutral for the rest of the war. Prévost overplayed his limited hand, however, demanding unconditional surrender of the city. General Benjamin Lincoln's army arrived to oppose him and he was forced to lift the siege. According to Clinton, Prévost wisely retreated, leaving a force 'under Lieutenant Colonel Maitland at Beaufort for the purpose of securing a footing in Carolina'.[14] Governor John Rutledge of South Carolina painted a picture of chaos created by Prévost's invasion, requesting help from d'Estaing in the West Indies. He decided to respond to the request as he still needed to demonstrate the valor of French arms in a victorious action.

Savannah Defended

In occupied Savannah, rumors of the gathering of 1,500 rebel troops at Augusta, Georgia, were the first indication to the British that something was a foot.

By September 1, 1779, d'Estaing's fleet of forty-two sail and 5,000 French troops arrived from the West Indies, including black volunteers from Saint Dominque.[15] They were to cooperate with Lincoln's army. D'Estaing hoped the isolated British garrison would be easy prey, warning Lincoln that he could only be involved for a limited time. His ships had been at sea for too long and badly needed refitting, so that he had only a narrow window in which to take Savannah.

D'Estaing's fleet appeared at Tybee light house, which the British abandoned to concentrate on the defense of the city above it. They were surprised by the extensive French force, which captured their largest ship, the 50-gun *Experiment*. The remaining Royal Navy squadron consisted of the 20-gun *Rose*, the *Foley*, and the smaller brig *Keppel*, along with the *Germain*, *Comet* and *Thunderer*, all three galleys from St Augustine.[16] Also, the British armed two merchant vessels, the *Savannah* and *Venus*. At first, the squadron was ordered to shadow the French fleet as it advanced up the Savannah River. Considering the odds, however, it seemed best to sacrifice the squadron for the defense of the city. On September 20, the *Rose,* which James Wallace had commanded so effectively in Rhode Island, was scuttled and sunk to block the channel, while the *Savannah* and *Venus* were burnt, and three transports sunk to further obstruct the river. Responding to Prévost, Captains John Henry, Brown and Fisher came ashore and brought their seamen (of whom thirty were black), marines and cannon to support the town's batteries, leaving the remaining ships almost defenseless. Most of the batteries in the town would be manned by sailors and the marines were added to the 60th Grenadiers. Sailors on transports, privateers and merchant vessels volunteered to be assigned to posts. As at Quebec, the navy would provide an important segment of the onshore defense.

With the river blocked, it took d'Estaing two weeks to move beyond the lighthouse and he was unable to get close enough to bombard the city. The allies demanded that Prévost surrender, but he refused, instead strengthening the city's defenses as a siege became inevitable. Captain James Moncrief, the commanding engineer and a great asset, constructed an entrenched defensive line on the plains outside of the town, using slave and free black labor.[17] He secured the city's river front by throwing a boom across the river. Troops came in to defend the town from all over Georgia, including those of New York Loyalist Lieutenant Colonel John Cruger (brother of Henry). On September 16, Colonel John Maitland arrived with reinforcements of the 71st Regiment and New York Volunteers from Beaufort. The rebels were supposed to stop him before he entered the town, but they mistook his men for French troops. Maitland had left earlier, but had taken inland waterways to avoid the allies, delaying his arrival until just before a truce was called. At least 620 blacks were involved in erecting fortifications, as Black Pioneers, as volunteers and as seamen. Uniquely 250 black freemen were armed to serve as skirmishers.

Prévost's defense forced d'Estaing into a prolonged siege.[18] He was ill-prepared to establish land batteries, for his ship's cannon had to have their carriages modified for service on land and be manned by his sailors. In October, he was finally able to erect batteries with tools lent by Lincoln, and his sailors were able to bombard the town but were ineffective against the British lines, sheltering troops and gun crews. Desperate to end the siege and move his fleet as scurvy had broken out, d'Estaing decided to launch a frontal attack on October 9 on the Spring Hill redoubt. However, a counterattack by marines and two companies of the 60th drove him back with the loss of 700 to 900 Frenchmen, killed, wounded or taken prisoner, without counting the rebels. D'Estaing himself was twice wounded. Of the defenders, only sixteen were killed and thirty-nine wounded.

After the failure of the frontal attack, the besiegers gradually lost heart as many French and rebel troops deserted to the British. On October 20, d'Estaing left his camp, retreating down the Savannah River to return to France, leaving the North American coast for the second time. He was most concerned to save his fleet for another day, having momentarily brought French and American forces together. By the end of the year, he was back in Europe 'having achieved nothing in eighteen months cruising and fighting around the western hemisphere'.[19]

The failure at Savannah caused the French and Americans to blame each other, a condition that strained the alliance. It seemed to the rebels that the British were more than capable of coping with the new French presence in the war.[20] On news of the repulse at Savannah, Sir Henry Clinton would be able to continue his Southern strategy by preparing an expedition against Charleston, South Carolina. Savannah would be a base for that expedition as it would continue to be occupied by the British until July 1782.

West African Rivalry

As Savannah's slaves became freemen defending their city, ironically French and British forces struggled over West Africa, for decades the center of the slave trade. Among places they sought control of was Goree off the Senegal Coast, a notorious if not flourishing slave-trading island, from which slaves in Savannah may have come. Early in 1779, the French had taken it from the British, but only months later, Admiral Edward Hughes' reinforcements on the way to the Indian Ocean returned it to British control.[21] The slave-quarters had actually fallen into disuse as the war had interrupted the slave trade, leading Goree's merchants to diversify into peanuts, gum Arabic and ivory, providing a more secure future for the colony. The 1783 Peace of Paris restored Goree and Senegal to the French.

Chapter 22

Charleston Besieged

With Savannah saved, Sir Henry Clinton continued his renewed Southern strategy by seeking to take the South's largest city and port, Charleston. Lord Germain was enthusiastic over the objective, arguing 'The feeble resistance ... Prévost met with in his march and retreat through so great a part of South Carolina is an indubitable proof of the indisposition of the inhabitants to support the rebel government.'[1]

Clinton faced several delays in gathering the expedition to capture the city. Reinforcements finally arrived from the British Isles, allowing him to feel secure about leaving New York with an adequate garrison. His naval commander, Admiral Arbuthnot, remained more interested in the Chesapeake, where it was rumored a few French ships remained, so he advocated a diversion to the Chesapeake as part of the expedition. He sent Andrew Hamond and General Cornwallis to Clinton to convince him of the importance of the diversion. Clinton, however, was skeptical, opposing anything that blurred the focus from the proposed expedition against Charleston.[2]

By the day after Christmas 1779, the Charleston-destined fleet amounted to ninety-six ships, consisting of transports, supply ships, five ships of the line, and five frigates, including the *Roebuck*. It was readied at Sandy Hook, but faced a stormy path to its destination, the Tybee Light House at the mouth of the Savannah River, which had figured in d'Estaing's failed attack. Violent weather created confusion and ships actually returned to Sandy Hook on January 24, but were back in Port Royal after a few days. The fleet had to regroup at Savannah and replace much of its lost ordnance before it sailed northward toward Charleston. Arbuthnot had shifted his flag to the *Roebuck* so that he now was in daily conference with Hamond. Clinton attributed the success of the expedition's northward sail to 'the judicious arrangements' of Scottish naval Captain George Keith Elphinstone.[3] The troops were landed at Seabrook Island from February 17; they then moved closer to Charleston, positioning themselves on marshy James Island at one side of Charleston's harbor, where Fort Johnson would be taken.

Clinton and Arbuthnot's tempestuous relationship would continue, which Hamond, who knew Arbuthnot from Halifax, would attempt to mediate. Arbuthnot has been described 'as a rough old diamond' who would not have been appointed to the command in ordinary circumstances. He was in his late sixties, not in good health, and 'wrote in a style so muddled as to make his dispatches obscure and ambiguous.'[4] Arbuthnot felt that the navy's obligation was limited to transporting Clinton's army to the Charleston area and did not involve participating in a siege, except for leaving a few frigates and smaller craft that could maneuver in the shallows of Charleston's harbor. Obviously, Clinton expected the navy to remain and fully cooperate in the siege. Arbuthnot would refuse to follow up on Clinton's requests for naval support during the siege. Hamond got him to apologize to Clinton for ignoring his orders, ultimately bringing the two men uneasily together. It was a more thankless task than Hamond realized, for Clinton evidently resented his 'ascendency over' Arbuthnot.

Charleston was the rebellious colonies' fourth largest city, approaching 12,000 souls and also its wealthiest, with elegant planter and merchant households that were related through intermarriage.[5] Built on peninsula between the Ashley and Cooper Rivers, the port was on the latter side. To reach it, ships had to cross an extensive harbor or bay with occasional fortifications, the harbor being obstructed at its mouth by a bar. The rivers offered access to the immediate interior and along them were low country plantations growing rice and indigo (processed to make a blue dyestuff), the source of the city's wealth. It was no accident that over half the city's population was black and that the plantations required that its merchants be involved in the slave trade as much as those of Newport. In contrast to the other American ports, it had a decidedly West Indies flavor for that is where it had imported the bulk of its slaves, although some came directly from Africa.

Inside Charleston, the Continental army numbered over 5,000, commanded by General Benjamin Lincoln, while the civilian government was headed by Lieutenant Governor Christopher Gadsden, Governor John Rutledge and most of his council having fled. You will remember that Gadsden had been one of original members of Congress's Naval Committee. In his twenties, his enthusiasm for a navy had been motivated during King George's War, when he was the purser on the Royal Navy's 20-gun *Aldborough*. The city's fortifications had been improved, but the flat terrain to its north left it vulnerable to attack. Gadsden would insist that Lincoln not abandon the city, by taking his army in a strategic retreat.[6]

As we have seen with d'Estaing at Savannah, sieges were to be avoided, unless one had concentrated firepower and time to starve the enemy. These were challenges that Clinton's expedition would meet. From the naval standpoint, the first obstacle was the bar at the entrance to Charleston's harbor. The *Roebuck* and other frigates waited two weeks, until the spring tide with an easterly wind allowed an attempt to get over the bar.[7] To lighten the ships, crews had to work feverishly to remove the guns and supplies from *Roebuck*, the 50-gun *Renown*, and the 44-gun *Romulus*. Thus prepared, they moved over the bar unopposed on March 20, and for the next two weeks reinstalled their equipment and arms. After this was accomplished, even the largest British ships were able to slide past. From here they moved toward the inner harbor and port, firing on the rebel post at Point Pleasant, which commanded the first portion of the inner harbor.

By late March, Clinton's army moved from James Island to above the city, crossing the Ashley River unopposed on seventy-five flatboats and began digging siege entrenchments at the rear of the city.[8] In an act of cooperation, Captain Elphinstone had been detached with a party of sailors to aid the crossing.

Still, the impressive fortification on Sullivan's Island, Fort Moultrie, stood as an obstacle to Arbuthnot's squadron in reaching the inner harbor. The fleet would have to pass within a quarter of a mile of the fort as they came up the only channel.[9] Arbuthnot faced a stronger Fort Moultrie than had the previous British invasion fleet of 1776, in which the fort had inflicted heavy losses on them. On April 9, Arbuthnot's ships approached Fort Moultrie at 3 p.m. Knowing the fort's log-braced sand walls could not be breached by cannon fire, Arbuthnot decided against anchoring for a cannonade as the earlier British fleet had done; instead he chose to run by the heavily defended fort. As in the navy's effort to control the Hudson River in the New York campaign, he felt that once past the stationary fort, his fleet would no longer have obstacles.

The *Roebuck* and the frigate *Richmond* served as the van, withstanding the heaviest fire from Fort Moultrie's 24-pounders. They were followed by four more frigates, six transports, and the 50-gun *Renown* as the rear guard. From the steeple of St Michael's Church, an observer watched the passage of Arbuthnot's ships and remarked: 'They really make a most noble appearance and I could not help admiring the regularity and intrepidity with which they approached, engaged, and passed Fort Moultrie. It will reflect great honor upon the Admiral and all his captains, but 'tis pity they are not friends.'[10] After two hours, and extensive damage to the *Richmond* and twenty-seven casualties on the *Renown*, Arbuthnot anchored in the Ashley River, providing Clinton's army with supplies. On account of the shallowness of the inner harbor, the *Roebuck* continued to act as Arbuthnot's flagship.

Two days later, Clinton and Arbuthnot sent a formal summons into the city to surrender as further resistance would be 'indifference to the fate of the inhabitants'.[11] The document was drafted by the pens of Major John Andre and Hamond, now showing cooperation between the commanders. Nothing was unusual about the summons, although General Lincoln rejected it.

Having control of the Ashley River, securing the Cooper River and port on the other side of the city became a priority for Clinton. He found that it was blocked by a massive boom. Lieutenant Josias Rogers, commander of the sloop *Fury*, volunteered to sever the boom.[12] It took three night visits with only a boy to guide his canoe, but he was finally able to cut it. Despite Rogers' success, it turned out that a substantial portion of the Continental and South Carolina navies had been sunk behind the boom, effectively still blocking the main channel of the Cooper River. Clinton continued to urge Arbuthnot to approach the Cooper River by the narrow and exposed Hog Island Channel. Arbuthnot felt he could not attempt this channel unless batteries at Point Pleasant and Lampriere's Point were silenced. He based his conviction on a report by Hamond, who had difficulty in sounding the channel because he was fired on from these rebel strongpoints. Clinton fumed because he wanted to have the city completely surrounded, as Arbuthnot continued to delay an approach to the Cooper River.

Arbuthnot's fleet continued to be exposed to rebel artillery. While the Ashley River was now open, the fleet was under long-range fire from batteries in the city, although most of their shot landed short. Each time Arbuthnot's ships approached the city they were placed under fire; as a result, they were forced to stand off Fort Johnson for much of the remainder of the siege.[13] Shells were thrown into the city, chiefly for the psychological effect as the main portion of the city was almost 2 miles from Arbuthnot's ships.

Finally, Arbuthnot felt he could move in the direction of the Cooper River. He preferred not to use Clinton's soldiers, who anyway were heavily involved in the siege. Instead, he sent his sailors to take the Point Pleasant battery and word came that nearby Fort Moultrie was vulnerable. On May 4, Captains John Orde and Charles Hudson led 200 seamen and marines in ships' boats to Sullivan's Island. This detachment succeeded in passing the fort before daylight, unobserved by the rebels, and took possession of a redoubt on the east end of the island. After some negotiation, the fort's commander surrendered his garrison of 117 Continentals and 100 militia without resistance.[14] Fort Moultrie contained forty-one guns, four mortars and supplies of powder and ammunition. Charleston's principal fortification was now in the hands of the Royal Navy.

Clinton continued the siege using several heavy guns loaned from Arbuthnot's fleet. He gained control of the Cooper River's upper reaches using his own troops and Charleston was completely cut off. After negotiation, Lincoln capitulated on May 12, 1780, surrendering the garrison and the remaining warships, the largest military concentration in the South. One naval historian has called the Charleston Campaign 'the biggest and most successful British amphibious operation ever mounted'.[15]

The surrender brought an end to the careers of many Continental officers and ships. Among the losses was Captain Abraham Whipple of Rhode Island, who had been critical of Hopkins at the Glasgow affair, led the squadron that took prizes from the Jamaican Convoy in Newfoundland, and had brought the *Ranger* to defend Charleston. In fact, many of its guns had been transferred to the land to defend the city, while the *Queen of France, Notre Dame, General Moultrie, Bricole* and *Truite* were sunk at the mouth of the Cooper River in the effort to block it during the siege. Most of these ships were from the South Carolina navy, which disappeared with their loss. Those Continental ships that remained in the Cooper River were trapped when the city fell. Whipple was made a prisoner and paroled to Chester, Pennsylvania, the end of his service in the Continental Navy. The *Ranger*'s career under the Stars and Stripes had lasted only four years.[16] The Royal Navy converted it into HMS *Halifax,* which sailed to Portsmouth Dockyard, where it was immediately put up for sale. It was purchased by a Plymouth merchant, who paid only a small fraction of its original cost and used it for coastal trade. Its ultimate fortune is not known, but it is clear that the Royal Navy had no use for it.

Occupation

With the exception of New York, the occupation of Charleston would be one of the longest and most successful, especially in contrast to the difficulties the British would face in the rest of South Carolina. The Clinton–Arbuthnot expedition had viewed Charleston principally as a naval base from which Carolina trade could be controlled. Lord Germain, however, suggested that it should also be considered a base from which to encourage Loyalism and subdue the inland South.[17] It became the duty of the army, now commanded by General Charles Cornwallis, to move the war to the Carolina interior and see that it was pacified.

After the surrender, Clinton and Arbuthnot had been designated joint commissioners to administer Charleston, a situation which perpetuated their differences.[18] Arbuthnot urged immediate implementation of a city civilian government to enhance Loyalism, while Clinton hesitated, promising only that it would happen at a future date. In practice, for close to three years, the city would remain under Clinton's interim government.

Actually, Charleston had never had an incorporated city government, its civilian defense had been coordinated by the state, so that its previous governing experience was limited. Clinton's interim government established several boards of prominent citizens to administer the town. A Board of Police was created as an interim civil authority, a system that was an improvement over the colonial government's relatively negligent rule.[19] William Bull II, the former lieutenant governor and a plantation owner, returned and was named Intendant General of the Police Board. Commissioners were appointed to oversee the markets, internments, streets and address numbers, and civil suits. As cattle and rice were found in plantations around the city, Clinton created Commissaries of Captures to take charge of fresh provisions obtained from these sources. For Loyalists, the city was actually running smoother than ever and business opportunities were ample. Those who publicly pledged loyalty to the crown enjoyed greater personal and commercial freedoms, while those who secretly scorned the occupying power were ignored.

Charleston's port was revived as a center of trade. From July 1780, Cornwallis gave the Intendant General of Police and the superintendent of the port control over the city's trade.[20] Merchants who wished to export commodities had to present a certificate to the superintendent of the port and the captain of the ship exporting the goods had to document his intentions. Goods shipped without the certificate could be confiscated. Ships' captains pledged and posted bond that they would carry cargo exclusively to the British Isles. Vessels trading only locally were forbidden to land cargo any place but Charleston, and the penalty was seizure and sale of the ship and cargo. Initially, trade revived with the British Isles as well as locally with Savannah, Georgetown, South Carolina and St Augustine. Illicit trade between the city and the countryside also flourished as the rebels sought munitions to carry on the war and the popular British manufactures. In return, food appeared to feed the city's expanded population which now included the British military and large numbers of white and black Loyalists.

A Royal Navy careening yard was established in Charleston, known for its ample naval stores. Navy convoys carried supplies to Charleston, Savannah and St Augustine, and the navy's protection of trade continued as rebel privateers increased in Carolina waters. Along with Captain James Gambier's *Raleigh*, the *Roebuck,* under its new commander, Andrew Snape Douglas, left Virginia and returned to occupied Charleston on November 21, 1780 where the two ships spent months protecting the trade entering the city and patrolling its environs. By the end of the year, further assistance was requested as 'many vessels have been taken of great value within sight of the town'.[21] In February, additional protection came from two schooners, paid for by the contributions of Charleston merchants.

To dispose of captured prizes, the vice-admiralty court in Savannah sent a representative to take depositions on captured vessels and send them to the court to be tried. Finally, in October 1781, Charleston's own vice-admiralty court reopened, acting independently of the military authorities.[22] This was just in time, as several privateering raids originated in Charleston in the following year. To the south, Beaufort, half the size of Charleston, but better protected by the Outer Banks, dominated Port Royal Sound. In March 1782, Major Andrew Deveaux, son of a Beaufort Loyalist planter, planned the attack on his home town. Three Loyalist privateers, the *Peacock* (Captain Duncan McLean), *Rose* and *Retaliation*, left Charleston for the Carolina coast to take prizes and capture public stores believed to be in Beaufort. On April 4, the privateer squadron entered Beaufort Harbor without identifying itself and seized the pilots and townspeople who went out to greet them. The next day, Loyalist militia rowed ashore under Major Isaac Stuart and captured Beaufort, driving off local militia gathered by planter Lieutenant Colonel John Easton. The privateers spent the next five days plundering the town and vessels in the harbor, and skirmishing with local militiamen, who increased in numbers from neighboring communities. Having spiked the cannon in the town battery, the

Loyalists returned to their ships but remained in the harbor, where they were able to take an incoming sloop. The town sent two fire rafts against them, but they failed to do damage and an exchange of prisoners (whalers, townspeople, slaves) was negotiated. On April 17, the privateers returned to Charleston's vice-admiralty court with their prizes. Charleston would remain in British hands for the rest of the war.

Excepting only George Elphinstone, Clinton continued to feud with Royal Navy officers. His last bone of contention was over the valuable prizes surrendered in Charleston Harbor. Clinton claimed the navy took more than half of them, while they comprised only a third of the expedition. He complained that the £10,000 that the army had 'taken and lodged with their agents until His Majesty's pleasure should be known', had not been awarded, 'as the Lords of His Majesty's Treasury … have neglected it'.[23] Clinton had no idea that this was normal for the distribution of prize money, and he would continue to argue over the army's share of prizes even after he had returned to England and the war was over.

Chapter 23

British Initiatives in the Chesapeake

To take pressure off British armies in the Carolinas, from 1779 to 1781, Sir Henry Clinton sent four British expeditions from New York to Chesapeake Bay.[1] Each had a navy and army joint command, and they aimed to cut off supplies and troops from reaching rebel armies to the south and prevent reinforcements for Washington's army around New York. These operations had the effect of making the Chesapeake region one of the principal theaters of the war. While the Royal Navy was not able to establish a permanent base there, the expeditions were enough of a presence to debilitate the Virginia war effort and allow the British to cultivate considerable Loyalist support.

Collier and Mathew

Clinton's first expedition to the Chesapeake was in the aftermath of the capture of Savannah, but before it was besieged by d'Estaing. Clinton felt the Chesapeake should have a naval base to keep the adjourning provinces 'in constant alarm by desultory excursions along their shores', for the purpose of 'collecting together the well affected inhabitants'.[2] He was also convinced of the Chesapeake's strategic importance in 1779 when he sat down in New York with Sir George Collier and Major General Edward Mathew to develop a plan for coastal raids to curtail the region's ability to supply rebel armies and to destroy what was left of the Chesapeake tobacco trade. Ideally, a naval preserve of three men-of-war would be constantly stationed in the bay, one at Tangier Island, one at Smith Point at the mouth of the Potomac, and one in the middle.

In the spring of 1779, Collier had come from Halifax to replace James Gambier as acting commander of the North American Station. A very accomplished Royal Navy officer, at first he had disapproved of using privateers in the war. In New York, however, the strength of his squadron had been drastically reduced by ships joining the West Indies fleets, leaving him to need New York privateers to supplement his expedition. Collier believed 'that ... the shutting up of navigation of the Chesapeake would ... answer very considerable purposes and if not itself be sufficient to end the war', it would cause the rebels difficulty 'as [their] army was constantly supplied by provisions sent by water through the Chesapeake ... '[3]

Collier organized and carried out his foray to the Chesapeake in early May. He arrived near Norfolk and anchored twenty-eight sails, including the 64-gun *Reasonable,* the 44-gun *Rainbow*, the *Cornwallis* galley, a new *Otter* and 100 flat-bottomed boats. Among the privateers were those of John and Bridger Goodrich. Clinton had contributed 2,000 infantry, including the Loyalist Royal Volunteers of Ireland, under Mathew, a veteran of the Philadelphia Campaign.

Collier used his flat-bottomed barges to capture Portsmouth and the Virginia navy's shipyard at Gosport, which he turned into a base to prevent shipping from reaching rebel armies. Cattle and horses were taken, as well as 137 enemy vessels. The British occupied Norfolk and the Suffolk supply center. To prevent them from being captured, the rebels were forced to burn the frigate *Virginia* and two French merchantmen loaded with over 1,000 hogsheads of tobacco. Also lost were six ships in various stages of construction, including two frigates ordered by Congress. Collier reported, 'A great deal of tobacco, tar, and other commodities were found in the warehouses and some laden merchantmen were seized,' while rebel privateers that fled up the Elizabeth River were 'either captured or destroyed'.[4] Runaway slaves boarded his ships, which provided asylum to the distressed, whoever they might be.

The presence of Collier's squadron made Portsmouth a Loyalist town and encouraged disaffection in the lower Chesapeake. Eastern Shore rebel authorities feared that watermen raiders would join with Collier's squadron while it was in the Tangier Sound. Collier apologized for his privateers when they were accused of burning four Loyalist plantations in Northampton County. He wanted to make it clear to Loyalists that their property would not be mistakenly harmed by his ships, even his privateers. To compensate for the burning, he sent a truce sloop, loaded with precious salt, to Northampton. Isaac Avery, the county lieutenant, thanked Collier for his 'show of humanity' and four other residents acknowledged his good will by sending him eight lambs.[5]

Collier was elated by his success and informed Clinton that 'Portsmouth is an exceeding safe and secure asylum for ships against the enemy.'[6] He wanted to remain, but Mathew followed his orders to conduct a time-limited raid and Clinton, while he saw the advantage of Portsmouth as a Chesapeake base, needed more troops on the Hudson River above the city. Thus, the expedition stayed for only twenty-four days.

Overall, Collier's squadron encountered no serious opposition and returned to New York having suffered no casualties and having destroyed an estimated £2 million-worth of supplies. It also carried over 500 runaway slaves, chiefly families, whom Clinton would welcome with his Philipsburg Proclamation. Additionally, there were 500 whites, many of them shipwrights. Of Collier's Chesapeake exploits, George III wrote to Lord Sandwich, in September 1779, 'It is rather remarkable that Sir G. Collier, with so scanty a force, should have been during the five weeks able to effect more objects against the rebels than the admirals that commanded such large fleets.'[7]

Precedents were set for Clinton's later expeditions to the Chesapeake. Despite the fact it would often be discussed, no permanent British naval base would be established in the Chesapeake. This situation made it difficult to sustain the blockade, causing ships to be sent back and forth to New York from the Capes. While Clinton wanted to prolong British actions in the Chesapeake, he did not have the military strength of General Howe and was forced to act without reinforcements from home, because the American War had now been sidelined.[8] Regardless of these limitations, three more expeditions would be sent from New York to the Chesapeake.

Gayton and Leslie

After an absence of about a year, Clinton decided to send another expedition to the Chesapeake. He felt that a force was needed to relieve Lord Cornwallis's army, which was being forced to abandon South Carolina and move into North Carolina. The Chesapeake effort was meant to prevent supplies from getting from Virginia to the rebel army in the Carolinas. On October

20, 1780, Captain George Gayton's task force of the 44-gun *Romulus*, 32-gun *Blonde*, 18-gun *Delight*, the new 14-gun *Otter*, and one of Goodrich's privateers, arrived in the Chesapeake. They carried 2,500 soldiers under the command of General Alexander Leslie, who described how, 'We anchored in Chesapeake, after a most favorable passage, and the next day proceeded up as high as Lynnhaven.'[9] Orders from Clinton directed them to focus on the James River and destroy rebel munitions' supplies at Richmond and Petersburg, establishing a permanent post on the Elizabeth River at the Gosport shipyard.

For the tidewater Loyalists of Maryland and Virginia, the presence of the Gayton's naval squadron rekindled loyalties to the crown. Worcester and Somerset County Loyalists petitioned Leslie explaining their predicament:

> [We] have suffered in person and property, so as to have all taken ... and dragged about from jail to jail, though at last set at liberty, and now are willing to supply His majesty's troops and navy with provisions and forage, but cannot by means of those now in rebellion, that stop numbers of boats now loaded to come down [to Portsmouth].'[10]

Fearing for their lives if they traded with Gayton, they had Watts Traverse of Snow Hill carry their petition, but he was arrested trying to deliver it.

Still, with Gayton's arrival, the lower and central Chesapeake swarmed with Loyalist barges, galleys and privateers. His ships began to probe as high as the Patuxent River on the Western Shore, while others contented themselves with penetration raids, plundering, and foraging into the heart of the Eastern Shore.[11] They aimed not only to take ships but to destroy the plantations and country seats of the rebel elite.

Leslie found it necessary to fortify Portsmouth before he went further and, like Collier, he offered the opinion that a base at Portsmouth was 'the key to the wealth of Virginia and Maryland'.[12] However, after only twenty-three days in the Portsmouth–Hampton Roads area, Gayton's and Leslie's stay was cut, and the idea of making Portsmouth into a permanent naval base was curtailed. Clinton had placed Leslie's expedition under the overall command of Lord Cornwallis and Leslie kept him abreast of his Chesapeake success. Cornwallis was in difficulty after the defeat of his Loyalists at King's Mountain and he needed Leslie's army to reinforce him, regardless of its Chesapeake achievements. Cornwallis ordered Leslie south and he arrived at Charleston in mid-December.

Arnold and Symonds

Clinton continued to believe in the Chesapeake's importance and after only a month, he sent an expedition to continue what Gayton and Leslie had started. Twenty-seven ships conveyed an army, under the newly infamous Brigadier General Benedict Arnold, focused on destroying Virginia's ability to support the Continental war effort. The squadron included the 44-gun *Charon*, commanded by Commodore Thomas Symonds, four frigates, and the veteran *Fowey*. Symonds already had experience in the Chesapeake, having served in April 1778 as commander of the frigate *Solebay* at Tangier Sound and in Collier's foray. Arnold's force of 1,800 was largely made up of Loyalist corps: Simcoe's Queen's Rangers, New

York Volunteers, Pennsylvania Volunteers from Bucks County, though Hessian Jaegers and British regulars were also present. His highest priority still was to establish a permanent base at Portsmouth, 'which ought not afterward to be quitted'.[13] He also was placed under Cornwallis's orders, but Clinton made it clear that he wanted him to stay in Virginia and wrote to Cornwallis suggesting that he eventually reinforce Arnold in Virginia.

Washington had warned Virginia's Governor Thomas Jefferson about the imminent invasion; nonetheless, Jefferson was ill-prepared and doubtful of initial reports that British ships were sailing into the Chesapeake. Symonds' squadron arrived in Hampton Roads on December 30, 1780 and then moved up the James River in the direction of Richmond, foraging for or destroying the pork, corn and barrel staves the river plantations were known to export.[14]

On January 5, 1781, Arnold advanced on Richmond, now Virginia's capital, where Jefferson was too late in calling out the militia, so the city was undefended.[15] With barely time for a last-ditch effort to cart away supplies and public records, the governor fled. Arnold marched in at noon and remained in Richmond only a day. From his headquarters at Main Street's City Tavern, he sent Jefferson a message offering to spare the capital if Jefferson would allow him to remove stores to his ships without molestation. Jefferson refused and Arnold plundered public buildings, burned warehouses, destroyed records, and looted dozens of ships full of tobacco, wine and West Indian goods. Arnold claimed that he had not intended to destroy private buildings and merchandise, but a change in the wind caused the flames to spread randomly. Actually, Virginia's greatest loss was 6 miles upriver where the Westham cannon foundry and powder manufactory were destroyed. In Chesterfield, below the city, Arnold's men torched more buildings and military supplies and then worked their way back down the James River. The frigate *Iris* ended the careers of three rebel privateers: the brigs *Hawke* and *Cato* and the schooner *Nautilus*. The brigs were burnt, while the schooner was salvaged, after her guns and cargo were landed.

On both Arnold's advance and return down the James in the first week of January, he docked at Westover, the plantation of Mary Willing Byrd, the politically uncommitted widow of suspected Loyalist William Byrd III and first cousin of Peggy Shippen, Arnold's wife. Arnold's force would encamp at Westover as Mary watched from the windows of her mansion, and when they finally left on January 10, forty-nine slaves would go with them as freemen.[16] Four days later, forty tobacco hogsheads were destroyed at Smithfield, and at Mackay's Mill, 100 seamen acquired enough 'forage to serve the *Charon*'s entire company for two days'. While Arnold followed his orders to fortify Portsmouth, the squadron and prizes were gathered by Symonds, who joined him at Portsmouth.

From late January into February, Arnold disputed with Symonds over the prizes taken by the expedition. This should come as no surprise since Clinton and Arbuthnot had disagreed over the same issue after the fall of Charleston. No doubt Arnold expected the commander-in-chief would support him. Arnold claimed that when they embarked from New York, he and Symonds had agreed that the expedition should divide the proceeds of prizes evenly. On January 24, when Arnold asked the navy's Lieutenant James Bartholomew to carry dispatches to New York along with some of the prizes, Symonds found out about it. He counteracted the order, to which Arnold replied he was planning to take 'the Army's half of the prize goods', and accused Symonds of violating their agreement.[17] The problem was that in taking the prizes, the navy held all the cards because it had the ability to seize valuable vessels and their cargos and escort them to New York, where the prizes were adjudicated by Admiralty courts, resulting in prize money. Many ships were not worth the effort because their cargo was not valuable or they were in ballast. These ships were normally taken into the navy as tenders or even scuttled. Arnold seems to have referred to goods taken on land, which were a gray area. On February 7, a convoy, including many prizes, did leave for New York, following Symonds' orders. The dispute hardened the relationship between the navy's officers and Arnold, making them suspicious of each other.

Phillips and Arbuthnot

The French were now aware of Clinton's effort to control the Chesapeake, and Congress encouraged them to counteract it. On March 8, the French fleet at Newport sailed under Chevalier Destouches, destined for Chesapeake Bay. In the ships were troops commanded by Baron de Viomenil, who hoped to establish a French presence in Virginia. At the eastern end of Long Island, Admiral Marriot Arbuthnot, now based in New York, applied 'for a general press both afloat and ashore to raise seaman for the fleet' in preparation to carry Clinton's additional reinforcements for the Chesapeake.[18] This was fortuitous as Arbuthnot became aware of Destouches' sailing for the Chesapeake and within two days he decided to follow him. Clinton feared that he would denude New York's naval defenses, but he was able to outsail Destouches, arriving outside of the Chesapeake Capes ahead of him.

Because of the wind, neither fleet could head into the bay so the action took place just outside the entrance. The two fleets were equal in numbers with eight ships of the line on each side and they attacked each other in line, the classic manner. The French had the best of it, although they ended up out to sea. With strategy in mind, Arbuthnot entered Lynnhaven Bay and made contact with Arnold and Symonds at Portsmouth. Stuck outside the bay, Destouches' only option was to return to Newport. Regardless of specific ship action, it was the fleet that held the bay that was the victor.[19] As a result, Captain Charles Hudson escorted reinforcements of 2,000 men from New York under Major General William Phillips, who replaced Arnold as army commander, although Arnold remained to work with him. They arrived in late March and were charged with cutting supplies from the James River basin to Greene's Continental Army in the Carolinas that faced Lord Cornwallis.

Virginia Navy at Osborne's

On April 18, the Phillips–Arnold force moved up the James River on barges, taking Williamsburg and the Virginia Naval Yard on the Chickahominy River and again anchoring at Westover. Some of the Virginia ships were able to escape up the James and anchor further north at Osborne's, 10 miles above Petersburg. There on April 27, Arnold won a victory over the Virginia navy, ignoring Royal Navy support, using only his land forces. Osborne's was the rendezvous where Jefferson had collected the remaining Virginia warships to protect private tobacco vessels, with the intention of cooperating with Destouches in a projected attempt against Portsmouth.[20] While General Philips occupied Chesterfield Court House, Arnold at Osborne's, commanded the 76th and 80th regiments, Jaegers, and the Loyalist

Queen's Rangers and American Legion. Arnold summoned the American naval commander to surrender, 'offering one half the contents of their cargoes in case they did not destroy any part'.[21] Commodore James Maxwell's answer was we are 'determined and ready to defend [our] ships, and would sink in them rather than surrender'. This was regardless of the fact his ships were undermanned.

With the reply, Arnold ordered two 3-pounders, under Lieutenant Josias Rogers, to fire on the stern of 20-gun state *Tempest*. Additionally, Captain Page, with two 6-pounders, 'opened from an unexpected quarter, with great effect' on the *Tempest*.[22] At the same time, Lieutenant George Spencer led a party of Jaegers 'by a route partly covered with ditches, within thirty yards of her stern', so that all who showed themselves on deck might be picked off. The *Tempest*, 18-gun Apollo, 16-gun *Renown*, 14-gun *Jefferson,* 12-gun *Willing Lass,* 12-gun *Wilkes,* 8-gun *Mars* and smaller vessels, as well as Virginia militia, who occupied the northern bank of the river, all opened a brisk fire. A shot from one of the British pieces cut *Tempest*'s cable; she sheered around and exposed herself to a raking fire from Lieutenant Rogers' guns; its crew took to their boats. Panic spread throughout the squadron as crews attempted to scuttle or set fire to their ships.

Arnold was able to capture two ships, three brigs, two schooners, and five sloops, laden with tobacco, flour, and cordage.[23] His troops attempted to save as many vessels as possible, but four ships, five brigs, and several smaller vessels, similarly laden, were burnt or sunk. On twelve private vessels, upwards of 2,000 tobacco hogsheads, besides other stores, were destroyed, without any loss in British lives. It was a terrible blow to Virginia, not just in naval terms but economically because tobacco remained the mainstay of her trade and thus defense. This action added more luster to Arnold's reputation than his defeat on Lake Champlain against Carleton's squadron. Phillips and Arnold also recommend that further work on Portsmouth's defenses be discontinued and effort instead be directed toward Petersburg, rather than Richmond or Williamsburg, as it was the strategic center of supply produced along the James River.

Meanwhile in the Chesapeake, Loyalist privateers and watermen foraged for the British expedition, seizing corn at Vienna on the Eastern Shore's Nanticoke River. The port of Annapolis was blockaded by British warships.[24] The raids reached the upper bay as the Elk River area was threatened. Landings were carried out on Poole's Island and in Harford County, Virginia. The Maryland government called out militia as plantations were burnt and water-borne commerce disrupted. In late May, Lord Cornwallis's veteran army arrived at Petersburg, reinforcing Phillips' army, making a combined British force in Virginia of over 7,000 troops.

Chesapeake Bay between the Patuxent River and the Tangier Sound had become a virtual British lake so that rebel shipping ventured at great risk. The fear of invasion lingered throughout the early summer of 1781. County militia were held in readiness to march at a moment's notice, and commissaries were directed to purchase or seize stock to prevent them from falling into enemy hands. Loyalist privateers appeared in the Potomac in early June, dispatching armed barges to conduct foraging raids and plunder the inhabitants. The Loyalists remained on the river after the Royal Navy left. In July, Joseph Dashiell of Worcester identified John Travers – 'an only child of a worthy man' – and Samuel Garrick as having gone to Portsmouth in a schooner to trade with the British, furnishing them with flour and iron. In Portsmouth, Travers was advised by Jacob Hayward, a Quaker, to take British protection, which he did.[25]

As a result of support from these four expeditions, Loyalism grew as raids destroyed the rebel gentry's plantations and shipyards, cutting into their ability to supply the war effort. Loyalism had developed as the lower orders decided not to support the planters' revolutionary government. The success of their raids depended upon naval control of the rivers, streams, islands and coasts of the Chesapeake. The presence of the Royal Navy in these expeditions is a crucial part of this story, but the success also belonged to island watermen, Loyalist privateers and runaway blacks in their crews. This was exactly what Lord Germain expected Clinton to exploit.

PART 7

NEW ENGLAND AND NOVA SCOTIA IN CONFLICT

Chapter 24

Massachusetts' Hubris

Early in the war, Massachusetts authorities had asked Washington to send an invasion force against Halifax and Nova Scotia in an effort to add it to the colonies supporting the Revolution. Halifax had almost no garrison and it was estimated that 1,000 men, four armed vessels and eight transports were all that was needed to subdue the colony.[1] Washington, who was besieging Boston, knew that he did not have the resources for such an effort, and while it was often planned, no amphibious rebel expedition would ever be formed against Nova Scotia. Instead, its future would be determined in naval action in what is today Maine, which then belonged to Massachusetts.

In New York, as Sir Henry Clinton was preparing his expedition to Charleston, ever ambitious Lord Germain also asked him to support the expansion of Loyalism in Maine. A new post on Penobscot Bay was to be a place where Loyalists driven from their habitations 'may be enabled to support themselves and their families without being a continued burden upon the revenue of Great Britain'.[2] It also would secure Nova Scotia and provide mast timber and naval stores for the Halifax careening yard. Just as on Lake Champlain, the British found that their best defense was an aggressive offense against New England's borderlands.

Bagaduce Peninsula

In June 1779, word came to Boston of British activity in Maine. They had begun to erect Fort George on the Bagaduce River side of a spit of land that jutted out into Penobscot Bay, the Bagaduce Peninsula, today's Castine. Secondary batteries would be located on a nearby island and on the bluff overlooking the landing. Although it was 150 miles north of Boston, it was, from the British standpoint, conveniently located halfway between their naval bases at Halifax and New York.[3] From Halifax, Brigadier General Francis McClean came to occupy Bagaduce with a force of almost 700, consisting of the 74th and 82nd regiments and an artillery company. McClean's force was transported and escorted by a squadron under command of Captain Andrew Barkley, led by the 32-gun French prize *Blonde,* supported by three sloops, the *Albany*, the *Nautilus* and the *North,* the former under the familiar Captain Henry Mowat. Several locals came aboard the *Blonde* and assured the captains of 'their peaceable dis-position' and a proclamation was drawn up by which the locals would 'receive gratuitous grants … of all lands they may have actually cultivated and improved'. Barkley then sailed to New York, leaving Mowat in charge of the three sloops. He had been serving in Nova Scotia since the Falmouth incident.

A Massachusetts Enterprise

On news of the nearby British threat, the Massachusetts General Court proposed an amphibious operation against Bagaduce's emerging fortifications. The state's merchants were ready, as they already had an important stake in the Continental and state navies and were the sponsors of numerous privateers. They would support the raising of a fleet, commanded by Connecticut's Dudley Saltonstall, and almost 900 militia, serving under Massachusetts' Brigadier General Solomon Lovell. The latter was a veteran of the Seven Years' War at Lake George and a gentleman farmer who had represented Weymouth in the assembly for eight years, certainly politically well connected.[4]

Forty-one-year-old Saltonstall had gone to sea as a youngster and had commanded a privateer in the Seven Years' War. He had been in charge of the *Alfred* in Commodore Hopkins' ill-fated attack on the *Glasgow* and although charged with incompetence, he was exonerated. His lieutenant had been John Paul Jones, who found him to be a snob, with a 'rude unhappy temper'.[5] Late in 1776, Congress named Saltonstall its fourth-ranking captain after Nicholson, Manley and McNeill. Saltonstall had spent a frustrating 1777 trying to get the frigate *Trumbull* over the Connecticut River bar and into open water. Even those who felt his talents were underestimated, have described him as 'a curt, gloomy, surly man who kept to himself'.[6]

Massachusetts would accept contributions. From nearby New Hampshire came the 20-gun *Hampden*, a dozen privateers and twenty-one transports.[7] In Boston, the Eastern Navy Board would offer three Continental warships, the 12-gun *Providence* (participant in the *Glasgow* affair), the *Diligent,* and the most powerful ship of all: the 32-gun frigate *Warren.* It was now available because its captain, John Hopkins, had been charged with being a prize agent and suspended.

Saltonstall would use the *Warren* as his flagship, while the *Providence* was commanded by the other notable Continental captain, Hoysteed Hacker, sixteenth on the Continental captains' list.[8] In 1775, Hacker had been a mere lieutenant, commanding the schooner *Fly.* From a Providence, Rhode Island merchant family, he had been willing to take charge of a ship that John Paul Jones turned down, the *Hamden,* and as a result moved ahead of Jones in seniority. We will see that he and Jones served together in a squadron sent in late 1776 to raid the Cape Breton coal mines, in which Jones thought Hacker's conduct deserving of a court martial. Jones, of course, was known to be jealous of rival New Englanders, but it appears that Hacker had shortcomings.

In Boston, the same enterprising spirit pervaded as in 1745, when Massachusetts had enthusiastically raised a force that had been promised plunder as a reward for taking the French fortress of Louisbourg on Cape Breton Island. Massachusetts leaders seem to have forgotten that the plunder never reached expectations because a requested Royal Navy squadron under Commodore Peter Warren had blockaded Louisbourg and taken all of the valuable prizes. Still, Massachusetts authorities now gathered a fleet of at least thirty-seven ships from various sources, including at least twenty privateers and several transports. Its navy contributed the brigs *Hazard* and *Tyrannicide,* and the brigantine *Active.* The Massachusetts authorities were concerned that it be regarded as an exclusive state enterprise; they even failed to inform Washington of their intentions as they did not want Continental soldiers serving as marines, for they feared 'If but ten Continental soldiers are concerned, the Continent will take all the honor.'[9]

The strength of Massachusetts naval contribution actually lay in the fleet's largest segment, its privateers. In 1778, they had been active, bringing thirty-five prizes from Nova Scotia waters before their vice-admiralty courts. The names of the privateer captains included Nathaniel West, Nathan Brown, Thomas Alexander Holms and William Buke. Six of the privateers carried twenty guns and two more were at eighteen, only the *Warren* could compete with them in armament.[10] The marines were commanded by captains John Welsh and Thomas Jenner Carnes. During the siege, seamen outnumbered Lovell's men, easily forming parties of 1,000 men or more. The warships were to escort twenty transports with Lovell's militia to Penobscot. Both in terms of ships and men, this would be the largest fleet produced by the rebels at any time during the war.

At first it was thought that less than a week would be needed to put the expedition together. Speed was crucial because they feared that the fort would be completed or that Bagaduce would be reinforced. In reality it took six weeks to organize. The Massachusetts Commissary General impressed provisions for the expedition, and its agents spread throughout the state to acquire kettles and bowls for food preparation as well barrels of pork and flour, tierces of beef and tons of bread. On July 3, press warrants were issued to officers to procure men for service on their vessels for two months. They were to take any able-bodied seamen found in their precinct. Officers were 'authorized to enter on board & search any ship ... or to break upon and search any dwelling house ... in which you shall suspect [they are] concealed'.[11] Men were to be delivered over to be assigned among the fleet's vessels. At least 300 Marines were recruited, to be evenly divided between Massachusetts and Continental ships. The Massachusetts Council was forced to impress not only seamen to serve in the fleet but transports from Boston, Salem, Beverly and Newburyport.

Assault and Siege

The Eastern Naval Board ordered Saltonstall 'to captivate, kill or destroy the enemies whole force both by sea and land ...'[12] On July 19, 1779, he sailed out of Nantasket Roads bound for Penobscot Bay. When the fleet arrived at the bay, it seemed invincible for it greatly outnumbered Mowat's three sloops and Fort George was less than half finished. While the militia landed and a battery was erected to bombard the fort, the steep cliffs along the bay made it difficult for them to get close enough to confront Mowat's ships. The Massachusetts captains were mostly privateers, unwilling to have their ships damaged in an artillery duel and hoping for a quick victory rather than a protracted siege.

Meanwhile, the British garrison and seamen from Mowat's squadron constantly improved their defenses. Mowat was able to prevent the rebels from entering the harbor by placing his ships across its entrance and backing them up with possible fireships. On his own, he sent parties ashore to build an additional square redoubt, in which he placed eight of his ships' guns to be manned by fifty sailors.[13] When besieged, these British land and sea forces would cooperate on a daily basis, swapping ordnance back and forth, while Mowat's ships would send up to 140 seamen and marines ashore to reinforce McClean.

Lovell, having suffered heavy casualties among his militia and realizing that they were not capable of attacking Fort George alone, asked Saltonstall to risk his ships in an attack on Mowat's squadron before he would send his troops further. Saltonstall seemed unsure of how to cooperate with Lovell. A petition to him of July 27 by the fleet's ship masters complained that a prolonged siege was not what was needed. They contended 'delays in the present case are extremely dangerous: as our enemies are daily strengthening ... and are stimulated to do so being in daily expectation of a reinforcement.'[14] However, Saltonstall replied to Lovell that the continuing desertions of the fleet's impressed seamen were so extensive that he could no longer trust his ships. This impasse between Saltonstall and Lovell fatally delayed the expedition from acting.

Collier to the Rescue

Finally, plans were laid for a dawn land and sea assault on August 13, but before firing began, news came from a lookout ship that Sir George Collier was returning to the area, rapidly approaching with a relief squadron from New York. We have seen Collier at Chesapeake Bay in May 1779, but before this he had been in command of the North American squadron at Halifax. In 1778, he had led a squadron from Halifax to New England that took forty prizes and recaptured nine.[15] Collier's success from Halifax had resulted in his promotion in March 1779 to the acting command of the North American station in New York.

While the relief squadron may have had more firepower, it had fewer ships than the Massachusetts fleet. It was made up of his *Raisonable*, frigates *Blonde* (under Barkley), *Virginia* and *Greyhound*, and the sloops *Camilla, Galatea* and *Otter*, familiar names from Collier's Chesapeake expedition three months before.[16] In addition, Mowat would reconstitute his squadron, returning the guns that he had lent to the fort, sending a list of the rebel fleet to Collier, warping his vessels down the Bagaduce River and out to the bay, where he joined the *Blonde* in moving up the Penobscot River.

In Collier's words, the rebel fleet seemed 'inclined to dispute the passage. Their resolution, however, soon failed them; and an unexpected and ignominious flight took place.'[17] Saltonstall's captains had voted not to meet Collier, instead retreating up the narrowing Penobscot River, which emptied into Penobscot Bay. In the rout, fourteen vessels were burnt or scuttled by their own crews, while twenty-eight fell into Collier's hands. The *Warren*, one of the original thirteen frigates commissioned in 1775, was burnt to avoid capture, while the *Providence, Delight* and Massachusetts warships were abandoned to the British. Having lost all of their ships, the New England sailors were forced to join their soldiers on land, retreating in the wildest confusion. Falmouth's Committee of Safety reported the arrival of Penobscot seamen, who wandered in and were without officers and order 'under the greatest distress imaginable obliging us to furnish them with necessary provisions and relive their distresses'.[18] Nearly 500 New Englanders were killed or taken prisoner, while the British lost only fifteen. Collier had decisively destroyed the Massachusetts and New Hampshire navies along with some of the last Continental ships.

Assessing the blame

The most recent account of the debacle has claimed that Massachusetts authorities and Lovell conspired to put the full blame on Saltonstall. A late September investigation by the Massachusetts General Court asserted that expedition had failed 'owing ... to the lateness of our arrival before the enemy, the smallness of our land forces, & the uniform backwardness of the Commander of the fleet'.[19] The General Court was most concerned to spread the $7 million cost of the debacle to its partners so that it would not be caught bearing the entire expense. After the fact, Congress was coaxed to contribute $2 million toward the overall cost.

For the General Court, Saltonstall, a Continental naval officer, was a convenient scapegoat. However, it hard to see Saltonstall as an inspiring or decisive leader. Under oath, he admitted he was 'totally unacquainted with the [Penobscot] river'. A court martial would dismiss him from the Continental Navy and he would never hold a command in it again. Still, his influential Connecticut family, which included Silas Deane, saw to it that he was not brought to trial. Like so many ex-Continental officers, he was offered the captaincy of the newly refitted privateer, the *Minerva,* in which from May to July 1781, he had modest success.

In putting the emphasis on Saltonstall, the General Court ignored the fact that while the privateers were the largest segment of the fleet, they were not prepared for the siege and were less effective than their numbers suggest. Surely Lovell's militia should also share the blame for the failed amphibious operation? In Congress, the dominance that New England had exercised in the founding of the Continental Navy was tarnished, as leaders from Pennsylvania like Benjamin Franklin and Robert Morris moved to the forefront of naval administration.

The Bagaduce defenses would remain in British hands until 1784. Even before the Massachusetts expedition, McClean had sent out a call to the surrounding settlements for volunteers to work on the Fort George's defenses. At least 100 had responded and although at first they worked for free, McClean soon offered them hard currency, something that had not been seen in years.[20] As a result, Loyalism grew and many sought the creation of a new province around the new defenses, dubbed New Ireland. As agent for the Penobscot Loyalists, Dr John Calef, an Ipswich Loyalist, went to England and petitioned the king, extolling the virtues of the Penobscot area. In London, the cabinet responded favorably, outlining the usual colonial administration, including an assembly. The ministry, however, found itself overwhelmed by the demands of a transatlantic war and was unable to provide the resources for the new colony.

New England Retaliates

Meanwhile, some Continental ships had not been involved in the Massachusetts buildup for the Penobscot expedition and were free to seek prizes. Back from Europe, Captain Thomas Simpson was able to put aside his earlier disobedience to the Marine Committee and undertake a cruise, with the familiar *Ranger,* joined with the 28-gun *Providence* under Abraham Whipple and again the *Queen of France*, now under John Rathburn. From Boston, they went north to the Newfoundland's Banks, where in July 1779, flying a British flag as a ruse, by chance fell in with the British Jamaica convoy homeward bound, consisting of 150 sail protected by a ship of the line. They succeeded in capturing and retaining seven transports, which were brought into Boston Harbor. Those prizes had cargoes of 'rum, sugar, logwood, pimento, &c., were sold and the proceeds split between the government and the officers and crews'.[21] It was the richest haul that Continental ships took during the war, showing that their most lucrative targets were large convoys, where it was impossible for a few Royal Navy escorts to keep track of their charges. It contrasted a few months later with John Paul Jones' failure to take the

Baltic Convoy at Flamborough Head. Still this Continental success was exceptional, for both the *Ranger* and *Queen of France* would soon be lost at the surrender of Charleston in 1780.

With its navy destroyed at Penobscot, New England authorities would never again attempt to coordinate a large fleet with an army. As Continental ships disappeared, the war effort was left to privateers like Saltonstall's *Minerva,* which sailed in small squadrons or singly. Among their motives, they claimed it was revenge for the Penobscot debacle.[22]

On Nova Scotia's south coast, west of Halifax, Liverpool was a special target of New England privateers because it had sent out its own privateers against them. The last New England privateer raid on Liverpool occurred about a year after the Penobscot debacle. At night, the privateers, *Surprize* under Captain Benjamin Cole, and *Delight*, under Captain Lane, unloaded seventy men at Ballast Cove. By early morning they had captured the fort and taken most of the garrison as prisoner. However, Colonel Simon Perkins called out the militia, and captured Cole and negotiated with Lane for the recovery of the fort and the release of the prisoners. Within a few hours 'every thing [was] restored to its former Situation without any Blood Shed'.[23] While Liverpool would not be bothered by rebel privateers for the remainder of the war, other places in Nova Scotia were.

The use of privateers in the region was now controversial even among rebels. Hostility to privateering came on two levels. In June 1778, William Whipple, a New Hampshire delegate to Congress and a signer of the Declaration of Independence, felt the true culprit for the lack of Continental seamen were the privateers that attracted seamen in devious ways. In Portsmouth, he complained that privateers 'introduce luxury, extravagance, and every kind of dissipation that tend to the destruction of the morals of a people ...'[24] He asserted that they not only attacked enemy ships but any ship so long as the taking was lucrative.

Other local leaders felt that the privateers' plundering was heartless to the point of alienating people who might be their friends. Colonel John Allen of Massachusetts, who had previously lived in Nova Scotia, complained of Massachusetts privateers 'depredations committed on the coast of Nova Scotia [that] is cruel, robing [*sic*] the very people who ... are secreting & spiriting prisoner subjects of the States in getting to [Maine], others go with an excuse to rob certain Tories & to take revenge for private injury'.[25] To Allen, these raiding privateers were not part of the war effort, simply treating Nova Scotia's towns as sources of booty for their personal profit and revenge. He felt that destruction by privateers ended any thought of Nova Scotians joining the New England colonies in rebellion. To see this more clearly, we must now turn to Halifax and Nova Scotia.

Chapter 25

Halifax's Crucial Careening Yard

Halifax was the origin of Brigadier General McClean's troops and Captain Mowat's ships that established Fort George and the Loyalist settlement at Penobscot. It was also the most crucial naval base for a broad area, including the Gulf of St Lawrence, Newfoundland's Grand Banks and the Gulf of Maine. Since the Seven Years' War, it had been part of the Atlantic supply and defense chain with convoys sailing to Halifax and then New York, where a surplus of supplies was maintained for further distribution.[1]

Early in the war, New Englanders hoped to coax Nova Scotia into becoming the fourteenth colony of their rebellion. As with Canada, however, Nova Scotians remained within the British Empire during the war. This was because Nova Scotia was dominated by a strong British military presence, in which many owed their livelihood to Halifax's careening yard and its related facilities. Unlike most of the colonies to the south, Nova Scotia's economy had lost what little agrarian basis it had, when the Acadians were deported in 1755. Halifax became Nova Scotia's chief economic engine as it was the only naval careening yard for the mainland colonies of British North America.[2] Nova Scotia farmers provided fresh beef, spruce beer, hay and cordwood for the navy base. British dominance was not only economic, but also political and social. While Nova Scotia had an elected assembly like the rebellious colonies and after the Seven Years' War was settled by New Englanders, it was controlled by Halifax merchants, whose interests were tied to the naval and mercantile establishment. Nova Scotia's people were not about to give up the prosperity they had achieved because of the Royal Navy's presence in Halifax.

Halifax's Careening Yard

Halifax port is a result of the Sackville River emptying into a basin, divided between an inner and outer harbor, along Nova Scotia's Atlantic coast. It was the closest to Europe of any North American port. During the Seven Years' War, it had served as a naval counter to the French fortress of Louisbourg on Cape Breton Island, which had been restored to the French at the peace table in 1748. Ten years later, Louisbourg was taken by the British and systematically razed. From then on Halifax became popular with the Navy Board because of the 'convenient situation of His Majesty's yard …, its utility for heaving down ships stationed in North America, and supplying them with stores, and the preservation of the wharfs, storehouses, and other works erected there in the course of the war'.[3] In October 1764, an Admiralty court opened in Halifax for the adjudication of prizes. By the 1780s, Halifax's careening yard would actually be capable of copper bottoming ships. Still, it never reached the importance of English dockyards as it failed to have the required dry docks for building ships and this detracted from its ability to support the navy during a war.

Located a mile north of the town, the Halifax careening yard initially consisted of a capstan house with a rotating machine for hauling, along with a careening wharf, a mast house and associated mast and spar ponds, and a boathouse and storehouses.[4] A sail loft was added in 1769 and three years later a dockyard clock was installed. Ultimately, a stone wall would enclose the whole. The commissioner of the yard verified workers' attendance and approved extended work hours. After a new hospital was built, dockyard workers told the commissioner that they would be willing to have a deduction made from their pay to give them access to the assistant surgeon when they were sick. This became the basis of the yard's medical system. During the Revolution, the dockyard employed just under 200 men, only a fraction of a Royal Navy dockyard in England, but considering that Halifax's civilian population was only 3,500, those jobs were economically significant.

Halifax's dockyard jobs had long been monopolized by white British immigrant families, who perpetuated their control by apprenticing their sons and relatives, and through intermarriage.[5] As in the British dockyards, positions were meant to be held for lifetime, so that it was difficult for outsiders to gain jobs, especially if they did not have the requisite skills. When the war broke out, skilled workers were lacking at Halifax and 142 smiths, shipwrights and caulkers were recruited from the dockyards at Deptford, Woolwich, Chatham, Portsmouth and Plymouth. They formed the nucleus of the workforce and mounted guard every night for the protection of the careening yard. After five years, when the contracts for these English artificers expired, as they could not be replaced locally, the commissioner was forced to request that 'ten shipwrights, four joiners, and a block maker' be sent from England. The Navy Board replied that while it would advertise the positions, it could not 'keep pace with the wants of the fleet', and it was unable to fill the request.[6] Obviously, the lack of these skills in Halifax perpetuated the influence of British families over the yard's positions. Acadians before their expulsion and blacks during the Revolution were never employed at the dockyard. It was not only them; most whites were also shut out of the low-paying but secure jobs at the yard.

One aspect unique to the naval yard was the excursion of shipwrights directly into the woods to obtain spars or timber when supplies were exhausted. They could cut and haul trees to the nearest stream to be floated to the yard's mast pond.[7] Parties from ships' companies assisted them in doing this. During the Revolution, Halifax was able to send so-called sticks to other Royal Navy dockyards like New York and even to the West Indies.

To tie Nova Scotia's economy to the careening yard, commissioners noted that Halifax was surrounded by ample quantities of trees for masts and other sticks, so that its dockyard did not have to import these items from England, Scandinavia or Russia. An effort had been made to supply masts to the Royal Navy dockyards from Cape Breton Island. When the first shipment of masts reached England in 1779, however, the Navy Board found them 'so knotty' that they declined to order any more of similar quality.[8] The Saint John River valley, New Brunswick, proved to be a better source of masts, yards, bowsprits and small spars for both the Halifax and New York dockyards. In 1781, a contract was concluded with the newly created local partnership of Franklin, Hazen and White to supply masts for English dockyards. It helped that the new firm also dealt in furs, which were sent to the London firm of Brook Watson and Robert Rashleigh. Halifax would become the firm's entrepôt for overseas trade.

Early in the war, Halifax's defenses lacked troops. In 1776, it was thought necessary to reinforce Halifax to support the rescue of besieged Quebec. When Marriot Arbuthnot arrived at Halifax to be the new commissioner of the dockyard, he found it so poorly defended that he had to take marines from and delay the departure of the *Roebuck* that carried him there.[9] He attempted to get along with his Assembly and to defend Fort Cumberland, Liverpool and Yarmouth, but it turned out that some Nova Scotia communities actually sheltered New England privateers. When he left in August 1778, Halifax was secure, but the Nova Scotia coast remained open to privateers.

By mid-1780, when George Washington evaluated a map of Halifax Harbor and its defenses, made by Boston merchant James Bowdoin, he concluded, '[Halifax] appears to be very strong and to have had much attention [paid] to its security latterly.'[10] Still, while Halifax itself had impressive fortifications on paper, mounting 150 guns, only eighty-five artillerymen existed to man them.

Town of Halifax

Halifax developed two interrelated communities: the military and the civilian, which often were at odds with each other. Specifically, a large population of poor camp followers had been abandoned there when the Seven Years' War ceased, and they continued in need of feeding, clothing and shelter.[11] Smallpox had also been introduced by troops in the Seven Years' War and it reappeared at the beginning of the Revolution and continued to be a problem.

These problems were enhanced in late March 1776, when Admiral Molyneux Shuldham successfully evacuated Boston and carried General Howe's army to Halifax. Briefly, the town was the center of British activity to quell rebellious Massachusetts. It, however, was unable to meet the strain of Howe's 8,900 soldiers, 1,100 Loyalists and 553 children.[12] Rents and the price of provisions skyrocketed, especially for the civilian Loyalists. In support of the navy, but to the dismay of upstanding Loyalists, the town exploded with brewers, taverns, inns and bawdy houses, some of them at the very entrance to the careening yard. The streets swarmed with military recruits and the town was described as filthy and riddled with disease, providing every known vice to those who could afford it. The respectable, who could fund their passage, quickly moved to England. Luckily, Howe was anxious to leave and carry the war to New York so that the army was transported there in June.

Howe's departure renewed a problem which had plagued Halifax since its founding, as every time a major expedition left, a large number of transient women and children remained to be charges on the community's fledgling workhouse and poor house. Howe left 2,030 women and children when he embarked.[13] Halifax authorities approached the Lords of Trade for relief, but they were refused additional support for these indigents, as the Board defended the right of ship captains to rid themselves of the burden by leaving them. Some relief for transient military wives was provided by employing them to prepare oakum, a tarred fiber used to caulk seams.

Improving Halifax

Admiral Howe's favorite captain, Andrew Hamond, was named resident commissioner and lieutenant governor of Nova Scotia. He had come to Halifax because he was not ready to retire from the American War, which he believed could still be won. While visiting England, he had set his sights on the Halifax and Nova Scotia posts.[14] The authorities had promised him that he would ultimately succeed to the governorship of Nova Scotia and on this basis he accepted the positions. He arrived in Halifax during the night of July 29, 1781, with Lady Anne and his son Graham Eden, who was only a year and half old. Hamond was sworn into office five days later. It was the first time he had brought his family with him to America, as he was now shore based. Although permission was possible, the navy frowned on taking one's wife aboard a warship and he had never done it, so their presence was a pleasant perk of his new position.

Health care in Halifax's civilian, military, naval and prisoner hospitals was improving, supported by the arrival of numerous Loyalist surgeons. Hamond specifically needed to improve Halifax's naval hospital, which he found to be a disgrace. It was located in a deteriorating commercial warehouse, built on piles over the water, with scarce a roof or floors to it. He saw it was 'absolutely necessary to prepare for building a hospital in the spring'.[15] He found a 3-acre site north of the naval yard and on the harbor but away from the town and the naval burial yard. Bids were called for in December 1781 and John Loader, the yard's master shipwright, was placed in charge of the construction. Funded by the Navy Board, the new facility eventually cost almost £8,000, and when opened at Christmas 1782, it accommodated 200 patients in four wards. The staff consisted of a surgeon, a purveyor, a dispenser who acted as assistant surgeon, nurses for every ten to twelve patients, a matron, cook and porter, and two laborers. Its first physician was the Rhode Island Loyalist John Halliburton.

Another problem was the hundreds of enemy prisoners who arrived in Halifax, where no prison was large enough to hold them. Hamond had to hire a transport, the prison ship *Stanislaus*, that was fitted out to hold 400 prisoners in decent conditions.[16] A bulkhead with doors and loopholes was erected to separate the prisoners from the guard and the main deck was covered against the weather as it contained the necessary house. The captured seamen had clothes and blankets brought to them, to prevent the prison ship from becoming a watery grave. This contrasted with the situation of prison ships in New York.

Manning in Halifax

Manning ships in Halifax was a continuous burden. In the winter of 1780–81 a Halifax grand jury and the Court of Quarter Sessions protested against the navy's impressment of seamen from Lunenburg, Liverpool and Chester, who had been pressed when they innocently came to Halifax to purchase provisions and fuel. They asked Governor Sir Richard Hughes to intervene and he issued a proclamation in January 1781 reminding all that 'impressing Men for the Kings Service, without permission of the Civil Authorities, is contrary to, and an Outrageous breach of Law'.[17]

Seven months later, Hamond could only meet naval manpower needs by discreet impressment, showing respect for local laws governing the controversial activity. When Captain Thomas Russell of the *Hussar* attempted to fill his crew, he went to Hamond, who allowed him to press 'old Countrymen' among deserters. However, as the army could not spare soldiers to serve as his marines, Russell still came up short and had no alternative, but further impressment.[18] Hamond was willing to let Russell do it in Halifax, but only if he received the town's permission. Halifax authorities were willing, but limited the press to 'an early hour of the evening', and the press gang had to be accompanied by local peace officers, who would supervise its activities. Russell also had to ensure that 'none of the Inhabitants, People belonging to market Boats, or Fishermen are allowed to be impressed.'

Given the restrictions on the press, Hamond was forced to take additional steps to man his ships and transports. He encouraged crew sharing between vessels to avoid impressment. After granting Russell permission to press in Halifax, he ordered the sloop *Albany* to anchor off Mauger's Beach 'for the purpose of impressing seamen out of the merchant Ships inward bound, and to search all those that go out for Deserters from the Navy'.[19] As a result of these strategies, Hamond's tenure saw no further disturbances over impressment.

In September 1782, Hamond found that because of desertion from his transports 'the Ships now ordered for Spanish River [coal mines] cannot proceed for want of hands.'[20] One reason for these desertions was that American prisoners working in the Cape Breton Island coal mines had volunteered to serve in the Royal Navy to get out of the mines. British authorities knew they were likely to desert. Another cause of desertions was competition with the King's Orange Rangers, a Loyalist unit based in Halifax. Its commander, Major John Bayard, claimed he had 'a right to enlist any seamen that does not belong to any of His Majesty's Ships'. Hamond had to ask the military commander in Halifax to intervene with Bayard, so as to discharge two transport seamen who had enlisted in the Rangers and prevent further transport seamen from being lured away.

Despite its problems, Halifax grew as a naval base during the Revolutionary War. It sustained the greater part of Nova Scotia's economy, which made the province loyal to the crown. No serious rebel effort was ever made to attack it, as its naval defenses were too strong. The greatest challenge for Halifax's commanders would be to protect the Nova Scotia coast.

Chapter 26

Defending Nova Scotia

Nova Scotia's importance was shown in the spring of 1778, when d'Estaing proposed to Washington a joint expedition against Halifax and Newfoundland, which the American general had no resources to support. The possibility of d'Estaing attacking Halifax would continue into the next year. To meet such threats, the resident commissioner's priority would be defense of Nova Scotia's sea lanes from French or New England naval attacks. He also had to protect convoys that sailed into and from the Halifax and the British fishing fleets at nearby Newfoundland.

Continental Targets

A tempting target for the Continental Navy was Cape Breton's coal mines, which exported their production chiefly to Halifax's and New York's military establishments. As early as October 1776, Robert Morris and Esek Hopkins, following the Marine Committee's over-ambitious instructions, had sent Captain John Paul Jones of the *Alfred* with a squadron of three warships to destroy the British Newfoundland fishery, prevent storeships from reaching Quebec, capture convoys and the Hudson Bay fleet returning to England, and free American prisoners working in the Cape Breton coal mines![1] Actually only the *Alfred* and *Providence*, the latter commanded by Jones' rival Hoysteed Hacker, sailed on the mission, but the officers of the *Providence* soon felt they had to return to Rhode Island because the ship was leaking. Before Jones even got to Nova Scotia, he had run in with the Rhode Island privateer *Eagle* as he still needed to fill his crew, and in searching the *Eagle* for deserters, he impressed twenty men. The *Eagle*'s owners promptly sued him for damages.

Regardless of the Committee's objectives, Jones would only be able to take and lose prizes, raid the British base at Canso, and capture three colliers. He never reached Cape Breton to destroy the colliers loading in Sydney harbor. Upon being informed that the American prisoners working in the coal mines had solved their problem by enlisting in the Royal Navy, he gave up the effort to free them.[2] He headed for Boston, losing four of his prizes, including two colliers, on the way. As noted, Jones blamed Hacker for the failure of the expedition and sought to have him court-martialed.

As a reaction to the threat Jones had posed, an annual convoy of private transports was escorted by warships from the Cape Breton coal mines to Halifax. Upon arrival at its wharf, laborers speedily unloaded and distributed the coal. In 1781, a coal convoy of eighteen sail was scattered and the escorts heavily damaged by two French frigates.[3] Most of the coal convoys were able to arrive in Halifax.

North of Nova Scotia, another target was Newfoundland's Grand Banks, an immense fishing ground, where annually, from the sixteenth century, fishing fleets from Europe and America caught and dried their catch on land, which they then brought home.[4] You will remember in July 1777, on their way to the Grand Banks, the frigates *Handcock* and *Boston* and a prize had made landfall in Nova Scotia, where they encountered George Collier's frigates *Rainbow* and the *Flora*. It was decided that the best way of avoiding Collier was for the three ships to disperse in different directions. After a thirty-nine-hour chase, Collier's disciplined crews captured the *Hancock* and recaptured the prize crewed *Fox*.

Commodore George Collier had been sent to organize the naval defense of Nova Scotia, and his squadron was particularly successful in taking American vessels. By the end of 1777, some seventy-six enemy ships had been captured or burnt, perhaps a third of them British vessels that had previously been seized by the Americans.[5] In August 1777, Collier led a squadron to Machias to prevent the Maine town from being a base for a New England expedition against Nova Scotia. He carried no troops in his ships, using only 123 marines to overrun a fort, take an 80-ton sloop with a cargo of lumber, set adrift the timber boom across the Machias River, and destroy flour, rice, corn, 300 pairs of shoes, and ammunition. He did not attack Machias town. From there he raided to the southwest along the New England coast and among prizes he took a French mastship which he burnt, but only after four masts had been transferred to his ships and sent to Halifax, where they were much needed. Later, Collier issued a declaration to the inhabitants of coastal New England, including Machias, in which he urged that they remain neutral, not attacking their 'peaceable neighbors' in Nova Scotia, and in return he would spare their ports from destruction. Eastern Maine now understood that the Royal Navy could descend with impunity on their coast.

To support these efforts in 1779, Governor Richard Hughes persuaded Nova Scotia's reluctant House of Assembly to raise £5,000 for defense by a series of new taxes. He was able to construct blockhouses at various points along Nova Scotia's coast and he tried unsuccessfully to get permission from the Assembly to equip two small vessels to protect the Canso fishery.[6] Hamond would find that his efforts were not enough and that the Assembly was not inclined to support programs that required new taxes.

Hamond's Task

When Captain Hamond arrived in 1781, he learned that a convoy of eighteen sail, including colliers from Cape Breton Island and victuallers bound for Quebec, had been attacked by two French frigates and the four ships of the escort were badly mauled.[7] He was able to scrape together three frigates, the *Assurance, Danae* and *Surprise,* to search for the French frigates, but they were gone.

Hamond also had to meet the challenge of Massachusetts privateers along the Nova Scotia coast. Outside of Halifax, he was at a disadvantage, for he had only two sloops to regularly cover the entire coast. He faced an enemy that had escalated their privateer raiding far beyond previous bounds. Rather than seizing ships, the Massachusetts privateers now found it more lucrative to attack entire coastal communities. This was a type of warfare that had previously been frowned upon by both sides as smacking of piracy.[8] Hamond would find that he lacked the resources to protect both Halifax and the Nova Scotia coast.

By 1781, New England privateers had renewed raiding towns on the Nova Scotia coast, stimulated by the same desire for British manufactures that we saw with commissioned raiders on Long Island Sound. Previously, Collier had been aware of the swollen English imports to Nova Scotia, which were mostly smuggled to the New England coast. He made little effort to stop it 'because if they were not supplied by us, the Americans would get the commoditys they wanted from the French'.[9] While these privateers were not above attacking a convoy, it was coastal communities that now attracted them as their shops and homes held English manufactures that had become rare in New England. The privateers now demanded ransoms for important leaders, which were usually impossible to raise, so the sale of these goods might be the only profit from a voyage. An element of revenge for those who had served at Penobscot also moved some. Nova Scotians themselves deserve some blame because they had fallen into a false sense of security, even though the coast had been raided by privateers before. Places did not lack fortifications and barracks' houses for militia gatherings, but the militia failed to permanently man them and defense was neglected.

Annapolis Royal Attacked

To the northeast of Halifax, the Bay of Fundy became a Massachusetts privateer target. A militia barracks had been built in 1778 to serve as a temporary residence for musters to the northeast of Annapolis Royal at Starrs Point, overlooking the Cornwallis River, but by 1781 the government had sold the structure as uneccessary.[10]

On August 29, 1781, two Massachusetts privateers, the *Resolution* under Captain William Morgan and the *Reprisal* under Captain John Custis, appeared before Annapolis Royal.[11] Morgan and the rest of the *Resolution*'s crew had been anxious to avenge the capture, two years before, of Lieutenant Amos Potter, who was still languishing in a Halifax prison, by the navy frigate *Blonde*. Of the three forts protecting Annapolis Royal, none was occupied by militia. The surprise was so complete that resistance by Lieutenant Colonel Phineas Lovett and his militia was impossible. The town was sacked of its silverware, provisions, furniture, bedding and dry goods. The only casualty was an Acadian who had conducted the privateers into the town. Prominent hostages included merchant and militia captain John Ritchie. One of the hostages was later released on parole in exchange for Amos Potter.

Hamond responded to the attack by sending the veteran *Blonde* to cruise off Massachusetts and it took the privateer *Lion* with masts and spars bound for Spain.[12] After sending her prize to Halifax, the *Blonde* was wrecked on a reef in January 1782, although ultimately the crew survived and made its way back to Halifax. This was due to the generosity of rebel privateer captains Daniel Adams of the *Lively* and Noah Stoddard of the *Scammell*, who rescued the officers and crew and took them to the mainland. The captains were praised for their humanity by the *Blonde*'s Captain Edward Thornbrough, who promised that in the future 'we will treat rebel privateers with the utmost lenity.'

However, this goodwill would be tested off Halifax harbor, when the brig *Observer* inflicted heavy casualties on and took the rebel privateer *Jack* of Salem. The *Jack*'s lieutenant claimed that it was the addition of the *Blonde*'s crew members to the *Observer* that gave it an edge over the *Jack,* ensuring its capture. When Adams returned to Boston, the *Lively* was banished for letting the *Blonde*'s crew go and ultimately he and his family were so badly treated, they decided to become Loyalists and immigrate to Nova Scotia.

Lunenburg attacked

The most serious assault on the Nova Scotia coast took place on July 1, 1782 when a wolf pack of four rebel privateers, manned by 170 men, seized coastal Lunenburg, Nova Scotia's second city with a population of 1,400. Commanded by the aforementioned Noah Stoddard of Fairhaven, Massachusetts, his compatriots were Captain Herbert Woodbury, Captain Ballcock and Captain John Tibbets. Ninety men under Lieutenant Bateman came ashore at Red Head. As in Annapolis Royal, the forts and defenses were empty.[13] When the privateers advanced, local militia commander, Colonel John Creighton dashed from his house to the nearby blockhouse, hoping to stop their advance. The rebels seized two blockhouses after token resistance. They plundered the chief homes and shops, taking dry goods, silver, beef, pork, flour and rum, limiting their destruction to burning the homes of two local militia officers and the block houses. They demanded a ransom of £1,000 to leave. When no answer came, they took Creighton and two of his men hostage aboard their ships, threatening that they would burn the town if Major Dettlieb Jessen, commanding the local militia, offered resistance.

When news of the attack on Lunenburg reached Hamond, he found that only the storeship *Cornwallis* was available.[14] He sent militia after the raiders, but they were unable to confront them, as the enemy continued to threaten that resistance would lead to burning Lunenburg. Hamond now turned to his nephew's ships.

Andrew Snape Douglas had continued his promising career in North America. In mid-1781, he had been promoted to command the 54-gun ship of the line *Chatham*. With his knowledge of New England's coast, in August he led Admiral Thomas Graves' fleet on a three-week cruise from New York to Boston Bay. While Graves then went to the Chesapeake, Douglas was given command of a squadron of frigates on the New England coast, where reputedly he took fifty vessels from the enemy.[15] Among his prizes above Boston was the 36-gun French frigate *Magicienne*, in which the French lost thirty-two men killed and fifty-four wounded, while the *Chatham* had only two killed and four wounded. This capture was daring because he took the ship under the nose of privateers, anchored in Boston Harbor. The *Chatham*'s action thwarted a planned French assault on British ships in the St John River, today's New Brunswick.

The *Magicienne* was sent to Halifax to be recommissioned HMS *Magicienne,* while the *Chatham* was refitted. This is how Douglas was serving with his uncle Andrew. When word came of the Lunenburg raid in July 1782, Douglas' ships were still being refitted, thus unable to lead a rescue. However, Hamond took the *Chatham*'s crew and placed them on three brigs, which he dispatched under Douglas' command, with one of them also carrying 200 Hessian soldiers.[16] Rebel Captain Stoddard was forced to retreat and Douglas followed him as far as Liverpool. Despite not receiving the demanded ransom, after he returned to Boston, Stoddard released Colonel Creighton and his other prisoners.

While never seriously threatened, Halifax harbor did require constant vigilance. On August 8, 1782 a privateer was seen off Halifax harbor. Halifax merchants asked for protection of their ships, store ships and victuallers, who were expected to arrive.[17] Hamond sent ships to protect the mouth of the harbor. To further defend the harbor, he commissioned six row galleys, following the design of those he used in Chesapeake Bay.

Loyalist Migration

Hamond's duties coincided with the beginning of the white and black Loyalist migration from the British-occupied ports to the south. Only merchants and professionals went to Halifax, most being dispersed to new settlements on the Nova Scotia coast. Halifax initially welcomed the migrants with exorbitant prices and one Loyalist referred to it as 'this stupid insipid, extravagantly dear and horrid rainy stormy hole'.[18] Many settled in the part of Nova Scotia that became New Brunswick. By mid-November 1782, Hamond had organized transports and escorts to be sent to New York for its evacuation. Douglas' *Chatham* was to be the main escort, but it had to return to port when it collided with a storeship, which carried away her bowsprit.

As soon as the New York convoy left Halifax, the first of the Charleston, South Carolina Loyalists arrived. Hamond had sent a convoy of twenty-five ships to Charleston under guard of the *Belisarius* and *Emerald* in late September. On the return voyage to Halifax, the Charleston convoy carried 420 men, women and children and fifty-three blacks.[19] To receive them, he unloaded and stored the contents of his victuallers in warehouses and then converted as many as possible into transports. The stored victuals would sustain the Loyalists over the winter. Thus, Halifax was ready to accept the growing number of white and black Loyalists.

In New York, the Port Roseway Association received Hamond's blessing for settling at the undeveloped harbor of Port Roseway, about a 100 miles from Halifax. They later wrote to Hamond, thanking him for supporting their cause in England and asking that he continue his efforts on their behalf.[20] They eventually created the largest Loyalist community at Port Roseway, known as Shelburne, Nova Scotia.

The number of Loyalist transplants to Nova Scotia ultimately exceed 20,000 and the transport experience varied.[21] In September 1783, the transport *Martha* left New York and made its way to Nova Scotia. Onboard were officers of the Maryland Loyalists: Patrick Kennedy, Caleb Jones, John Sterling, Levin Townsend, Philip Barton Key, with their families. The *Martha* was undermanned and the sails were rotten, so that in a storm she floundered on rocks between Cape Sable and the Seal Islands. The captain abandoned his ship in its cutter, leaving most of the passengers in the water as the *Martha* broke up. Over the next several days, forty-five Marylanders out of over a hundred transported were rescued and taken to St Johns. While they had lost almost everything, land was granted to them up the St John River, opposite Fredericton. Many settled there and by 1788 Caleb Jones had become the area's leading land holder.

A New Governor

In the midst of these frenzied activities, Hamond received unexpected news. On July 8, 1782 the Home Secretary wrote informing him that John Parr had been appointed to succeed absentee Francis Legge as Governor of Nova Scotia. Hamond was surprised, having accepted the office of lieutenant governor 'on the strongest assurances of succeeding to the government'.[22] Parr had been an army officer in the Seven Years' War, but resigned in 1776 just before his regiment embarked for Quebec. Two years later, he exploited his government connections to secure the comfortable sinecure of major in the Tower of London. In July 1782, through the influence of the Earl of Shelburne, Parr had wangled the appointment of Governor of Nova Scotia. The pretext for superseding Hamond was that the office of governor was incompatible with the defensive duties, which Hamond was handling so well. Clearly Parr was more adept at political intrigue than Hamond.

Parr arrived in Halifax when Hamond was busy elsewhere and promptly moved into the governor's house, thus getting relations off to a bad start. Hamond realized that the province could not contain both of them and he resigned on October 8, 1782.[23] The news of his resignation was greeted with genuine regret by Nova Scotians. Five counties presented him with an 'addresses of approbation', and the Council voted him a grant of 10,000 acres at the mouth of the Kennebecasis River, New Brunswick. The Hamond family name was given to two locations in Halifax town and county. A road begun by Hamond 'from the foot of house hill to the North Farm' eventually became known as Lady Hamond Road.[24] Moreover, in 1786, 9,000 acres between Birch Cove and the head of St Margaret's Bay were granted to forty-five proprietors, who voted to call their settlement Hamond Plains. Hamond had hired carpenter William Lee to superintend the building of his house and barn at North Farm, Halifax, which his resignation forced him to abandon. In 1787, the Nova Scotia Assembly reimbursed Lee for the cost of constructing the house. These were tokens of the high esteem in which Hamond and his wife were held.

Hamond remained in Nova Scotia performing his naval duties as no successor to his positions had been named. Finally, in late January 1783, he and his family embarked for England. He offered passage to yard workers who wished to return and several families of carpenters, watchmen and laborers responded. The *Caton* set out from Halifax, carrying his entire family, including the wife and sister of Douglas, and all their servants.[25] It had been a French ship, captured at the Battle of the Saints, which on account of leakiness had progressed no further than Halifax, in a convoy destined for England. The return passage to England was anything but uneventful. Dismasted off Newfoundland, after five weeks at the mercy of the weather, the *Caton* was blown off course and ended up in Antigua. Then a further arduous and storm-filled voyage of almost four months followed, until they finally reached England. It turned out to be the closest that Hamond would come to death during his long naval career.

At a time when the British Empire had lost at least thirteen colonies, Hamond had made certain that Nova Scotia was not added to them. Despite New England's disaster at Penobscot, Nova Scotia had faced a renewed Massachusetts privateer effort to sack its coastal towns. This destroyed the last hope that Nova Scotia might join the rebellious colonies. The migration of Loyalists secured Nova Scotia's place in the British Empire, preparing the way for modern Canada.

PART 8

THE SIEGE OF GIBRALTAR

Chapter 27

The Spanish Obsession with Gibraltar

Spain's possession of Gibraltar was tied to broad episodes in its history. In 711, a Moslem army first crossed from North Africa into the Iberian Peninsula at Gibraltar.[1] The town, built against the Rock that jutted out 3 miles into the Mediterranean, was taken and retaken during Christian Reconquest from the Moslems. Finally in 1462, Gibraltar was captured for good by King Henry IV of Castile, who gave the town a charter. In the sixteenth century, as a town on the Spanish coast, it was constantly threatened by Algerians and Turks, until in 1540 it was pillaged, although its castle withstood them. In 1702, the War of the Spanish Succession broke out between the Bourbons and Hapsburgs over which dynasty would rule Spain. Britain supported the Hapsburgs and having failed to take strongly defended Cadiz or Barcelona, Admiral George Rooke tried his luck against Gibraltar, which was in ruins and garrisoned only by 150 Spaniards. His Anglo-Dutch marines, sailors and troops took it easily on July 24, 1704. It was far from being a prize, for its trade was minimal and its anchorage was unprotected. From then on, however, through the War of Austrian Succession and the Seven Years' War, Spain passionately sought the return of this sleepy port.

In 1782, English political caricaturist James Gillray satirized the Spanish obsession for Gibraltar with an etching entitled 'The Castle in the Moon, A new Adventure not mentioned by Cervantes'.[2] Don Quixote and Sancho are there, but they are not tilting against windmills, rather it is against an unreachable moon, upon which is embossed Gibraltar's fortifications. Their characters were well known in eighteenth-century Britain thanks to translations of Cervantes' novel, showing Don Quixote as the idealist and his squire Sancho as the realist. In the etching, when Don Quixote asserts that the castle of Gibraltar should be starved into surrender, Sancho the realist replies, 'We're like to be starved out first. There's not a mouthful left in the wallet.' The publisher, Hannah Humphrey, placed the print in the window of her London shop during the time it was besieged. The etching's distribution would not be limited to London as the trade in prints extended to the British Isles, the Continent and even America.

Spain's idealistic focus on Gibraltar was unique. In 1778, Spain was not as anxious as France to help the new United States because she feared its example might inspire upheaval in her own American colonies. Rebellions against Spanish authority actually would happen in 1781 in Peru and New Granada, during which it seemed that the Spanish treasure convoys would not be able to deliver the bullion necessary to finance, among other priorities, the siege of Gibraltar.[3] In the Seven Years' War, Spain had set a pattern of being reluctant to use its considerable navy. It did not enter that war against Britain until its final year, although it did offer courtesies to French ships, such as the use of St Augustine, Florida's harbor, for prizes taken by French privateers.

From the thirteen colonies' standpoint, the one bright spot in their Spanish relations was the happenstance of Gustavus Conyngham's raiders on its coast from 1777 to 1778. Local Spanish authorities had allowed his ships to supply and refit at Spanish ports. He used La Coruna, Bilbao, Ferrol and Cadiz as bases, cruising as far as the Canary Islands. Conyngham claimed to have taken as many as twenty prizes, although many were recaptured or disappeared with their prize crews.[4] By February 1778, his activities were too much for the Spanish court and Conyngham was expelled from Spanish ports.

Despite the effort of diplomats like John Jay, who came to Spain late in 1779, Spain would never form an alliance with the United States or offer substantial financial support. Jay was so disappointed with the lack of Spanish cooperation that towards the end of the war he encouraged the British to retake West Florida, which had fallen to them. Spain would only abandon her studied neutrality if it could be France's ally in its war with Britain. France in contrast could not make peace until American independence had been achieved. Early in 1779, France desperately needed Spanish naval support to carry on the war against Britain.[5] After a year of participation, the Franco-American alliance had only setbacks to its name. D'Estaing's fleet had escaped to America, but his efforts against the British at Sandy Hook and Newport had failed and after he had left for the West Indies, the British had seized Savannah and continued to hold it.

It was against these setbacks that France was willing to let Spain dominate the strategy of a proposed alliance. The Spaniards had substantial objectives: the capture of Gibraltar, for which they demanded extensive French support for a prolonged siege; an invasion of England, something that had not been seriously attempted since the defeat of Spanish Armada; the capture from the British of Minora in the Mediterranean and Florida and Jamaica in America.[6] In contrast, France sought Spain's support only to recover Senegal in West Africa and Dominica in the West Indies, as well as securing a place in the Newfoundland fishery. Spain also wanted to achieve its goals quickly so as to avoid a prolonged war in which Britain would have the edge. Actually, Spanish officials were not above dickering with British diplomats, seeking to gain Gibraltar as a price for their continued neutrality.

French diplomacy ultimately was able to craft an alliance between Spain and France in April 1779, and two months later Spain declared war on Britain. King Charles III and his minister the Conde de Floridablanca were especially concerned to emphasize France's obligations, including the timing and supply for a siege of Gibraltar.[7] Charles had experienced British sea power when he came to the throne at the end of the Seven Years' War, long enough to be stung by the fall of Havana to the British. Now Spain was to be feared as it had a navy equal to that of France and, when combined, the two nation's eighty ships of the line outnumbered those of Britain. Its Havana yard now built one-third of Spanish warships from tropical hardwoods, which coupled with investment in naval yards like Ferrol gave their ships a superior longevity. However, the status of American independence continued to be in jeopardy as the Franco-American siege of Savannah had failed. As noted, in August the Franco-Spanish alliance had its first test with the expedition to invade Britain, but sickness, weather and a lack of organization prevented it from landing on the British coast. In this test, the Spanish ships appeared to be better prepared than those of France.

The Siege

The 1,350-foot Rock of Gibraltar guarded navigation of the Mediterranean Straits into and from the Atlantic Ocean. The thread of land on which the Rock rose formed the eastside of Spain's Algeciras Bay. The town of that name was 5 miles away on the bay's west side and would be the chief Spanish naval base during the siege. Two important Spanish naval bases, Ceuta and Cadiz, would figure in the siege; Ceuta was on the North African coast opposite Gibraltar, while Cadiz was on the Atlantic and sheltered Spain's largest battle fleet under Admiral Luis de Cordova.[8] The Rock was thus surrounded by Spanish territory while Gibraltar's garrison was much on its own, without places of firm support within its immediate region.

On June 1, 1779, the allies began their siege of Gibraltar, which would go on for more than three years. While the Rock was prepared to withstand a siege, the longer it was without supplies penetrating the Franco-Spanish blockade, the more precarious its situation became. The blockade was in place by mid-July, but the border with Spain was sealed more slowly and the allied forces did not reach a respectable 14,000 besiegers, about twice the size of the British garrison, until October. Late in 1782, over 30,000 French and Spanish troops would be arrayed against the garrison.[9]

The Spaniards completed an elaborate series of fortification across the isthmus that connected the Rock to the mainland, denying the British access to Spanish territory and bombarding Gibraltar's northern and middle fortifications. Advancing slowly along the isthmus, the Spaniards extended their trenches closer to the British lines. The Spanish lines were anchored by two forts, St Philip and St Barbara, limiting British movement to the narrow isthmus.[10] Magazines were built among their trenches, as were fascines put up to establish mortar and gun-batteries. Behind the lines along Algeciras Bay was an extensive camp for the thousands of allied soldiers. Here a laboratory existed for the preparation of shells, fuses and powder.

The closer the Spanish lines came, the more difficult it was for the British to aim their cannon down into them.[11] The near-vertical cliff of the north front of the Rock greatly restricted the space in which the British cannon could be deployed. By May 1782, the Spanish had been able to knock out several British batteries on the north front without the British being able to adequately return fire. The only respite for the British came from 1 to 5 p.m. because the Spaniards took their traditional siesta.

Barcelo and the Blockade

The Spanish blockade was an alternative to an assault on the fortifications, as they hoped to starve the garrison into submission. Responsible for the blockade was the chief Spanish naval officer at the siege, Admiral Antonio Barceló y Pont de la Terra. His squadron was limited to two 74-gun ships of the line, two or three frigates and a number felucca-rigged craft, as ships of the line were not effective against Gibraltar's defenses.[12] His most useful vessels were smaller and more maneuverable gunboats, Mediterranean galleys and zebecs (a three-masted ship with lateen and square sails). His 70-foot-long gunboats harassed British ships and positions at night.[13] They had been quickly constructed to be fast, strongly built, flat-bottomed galleys. Each had a small mast with a lateen yard and sail. Their bows contained a single 24- or 32-pound gun, which was designed with a long barrel so that it threw the ball further than the English equivalent. Dependent on their oars, they could easily move in the morning mists or during flat calms. As many as 6,000 sailors manned these ships. Still, Barcelo never felt he had enough ships to effectively blockade Gibraltar.

Conditions in Algeciras Bay were not always conducive to Barcelo's blockade. Gibraltar's western shore fortifications were heavily entrenched and proved to be difficult to approach because of currents, shallows and wind. Single relief ships could survive his efforts to intercept them by maneuvering in the bay, especially at night. A constant penetration by small local merchant ships and privateers ensured that Gibraltar's garrison would be able to feed itself for another day. When, in November 1779, Barcelo's entire squadron confronted the British privateer *Buck,* the single ship was able to get through. By clever tacking, the *Buck* eluded its pursuers and was able to head straight for Gibraltar, where the batteries joined in to stop Barcelo's pursuit. After a week, the *Buck* sailed out of Gibraltar, easily avoiding Barcelo's squadron.[14]

Still his blockade had some success, for three months later the British reported that 'no vessel has got in here, the Spanish cruisers are so vigilant, consequently no supplies … many inhabitants are near starvation.'[15] Barcelo's gunboats were able to go anywhere and caused many civilian casualties. In May 1781, it was reported: 'About midnight a shell fell into a house … and buried about 16 people for 2 or 3 hours, but they got out . . . At between 1 and 2 a.m. came the gunboats, 7th time and fired as before.'

Born in Palma de Majorca on January l, 1717, Barcelo was not of the nobility, being barely literate, although a consummate seaman.[16] He began his career on a lowly privateer, which caused discrimination against him. Still, he was popular with the lower deck and crucially with his monarch, Charles III. His successful attacks on Algerian privateers and pirates had made him an admiral of the Spanish Royal Armada. After the Siege of Gibraltar, he would make a further name for himself leading privateers against Algiers, which he bombarded in 1783 and 1784, destroying the ability of its corsairs to ravage.

In June 1780, Barcelo's effort at Gibraltar peaked when he organized an attack of fireships against the warships and transports anchored before the Rock's New Mole. At night, the British *Enterprise* challenged an unknown vessel, which answered that it carried 'fresh beef from Barbary'.[17] Suddenly it burst into a blaze of fire, followed by two others, until nine fireships headed toward the New Mole. The fireship crews moved off and joined Barcelo's squadron, which followed them. Royal Navy seamen knew the drill for pushing fireships out of harm's way and Barcelo had failed to place gunpowder on them, which would have made them more dangerous. While his fireships burned fiercely, by morning it had begun to rain and most of the fires were extinguished. The remains of the fireships were eagerly sought by Gibraltar's civilians for scarce firewood.

While Barcelo was maintaining his blockade, the Sultan of Morocco added to the garrison's difficulties. The sultan had once been a friend to the British because he wished to expel the Spanish from Ceuta. However, Spanish diplomats convinced him that the British would not be able to hold the Rock. He reversed his policy, allowing Spaniards to seize British vessels in his ports and British citizens were ordered to leave Morocco.[18] The British consul in Tangier, Charles Logie, and all British subjects were forced out and arrived at Gibraltar without their belongings. Not only was this an additional burden on Gibraltar's food supplies but it also cut the garrison's chief source of mail, which Logie had been forwarding from Tangier, now that the Spanish border with Gibraltar was closed. For the rest of the siege, Tuscany's free port of Leghorn (Livorno) would be the closest consul and chief source of mail from Britain.

French Cooperation

From the beginning, France's Louis de Balbe de Berton, Duc de Crillon, was placed in overall command of the Franco-Spanish forces besieging Gibraltar. Born in Avignon, he had begun his military career in the French army, but during the Seven Years' War he joined the Spanish army and later received the Order of Charles III. Crillon was an excellent administrator who had long supported the idea of sending a French army across the Channel to invade England.[19] Thus, his background earned him the respect of both the French and Spanish forces.

Spain had made the return of Menorca almost as important as Gibraltar to the Franco-Spanish alliance. The French Mediterranean naval base at Toulon became the source of ships and war material for both objectives. Early in 1782, Crillon left Gibraltar to lead a Franco-Spanish expedition against Menorca that overran the island with the exception of Fort St Philip, which finally capitulated in February – a blow because Menorca was the center of the British Mediterranean privateering. The capture had symbolic value to the allies because Menorca had been in British hands since 1708.[20]

Having taken Menorca, Crillon's reputation would now be on the line at Gibraltar because his options had narrowed. No hope existed of taking Gibraltar by storm or bombardment.[21] Time to starve the garrison was now limited because peace negotiations had begun in which Gibraltar's ownership would be a bargaining chip between Britain and Spain. Crillon had to plan for a 'Grand Assault' on the Rock using a combination of his land batteries, squadron and newly developed floating batteries.

A French engineer, Jean-Claude-Eleonore Le Michaud, Chevalier d'Arcon, had designed these floating batteries of timber so thick that it was impenetrable by shot or bombs and was protected from catching fire by a pump-driven circulation of water.[22] Ten were built, carrying 152 heavy cannon and they were to be coordinated with Spanish gunboats and land batteries to overwhelm British guns. This activity on Algeciras Bay was followed intently by the British who could see the buildup for the assault.

Still, the floating batteries would have their problems. Their water circulation system was defective and had to be turned off. On September 13, 1782, the assault went ahead anyway, with a line of ten floating batteries leading, supported by Barcelo's squadron and the land batteries. At first, the floating batteries did well, even British 32-pound shot seemingly bounced off their reinforced sides.[23] As the day wore on, however, the heat within their enclosures became too stifling for the gun crews to operate and their fire slackened. British gunners began to aim red-hot shot against them, their artificers having built kilns to heat 100 pieces of shot at a time. Despite the Spanish crews' efforts, the batteries caught fire. The line of them became over extended and they had difficulty sailing as they had never had been equipped to maneuver. All night, Spanish crews made efforts to save the burning batteries, but nine of them blew up at their anchors and the last was boarded. In the morning, a dozen British gunboats destroyed their remains, which were unprotected. The Grand Assault died with a whimper as the massed Franco-Spanish armies paraded along the beach, but made no effort to attack.

D'Arcon defended his design for the batteries in publications that followed.[24] He noted the water systems were not working when the attack was ordered and that the heat of fire ultimately caused their failure. Neither the Spanish gunboats nor squadron had been directed to support the batteries. Crillon had made no preparations for towing the damaged batteries out of action and therefore they were completely destroyed. D'Arcon felt the floating batteries' crews deserved credit for their courageous effort to use and save them. As overall commander, Crillon received most of the criticism for the disaster. Certainly, only he could have coordinated a combined attack of the floating batteries, squadron and land batteries.

Opinions

During the siege, as many as 80,000 Spaniards watched the action from the hills. In September 1782, for the Grand Assault of floating batteries, a grandstand was built on shore to observe the spectacle. The spectators included notables like the Comte d'Artois, Louis XVI's brother, and the Duke of Bourbon.[25] Upon their arrival in August, Crillon had sent Gibraltar's commander George Eliott a truce boat with a present of ice, fruit, game and vegetables as well as the defenders' mail. These courtesies were meant to convince Eliott that the princes should not be singled out by British gunners or marksmen. Eliott regarded the gifts as propaganda to undermine his garrison's morale and returned them.

A few weeks earlier in London, Thomas Colley designed a caricature of Crillon, making fun of his outdated chivalry. This joined an explosion of print sales brought on by Parliamentary changes.[26] The fall of Lord North's enduring government in early 1782 had resulted in a flurry of prints to support the political campaigns for the succeeding governments of Rockingham, Shelburne and Charles James Fox-Lord North. This critical print of Crillon was meant to be a warning to Shelburne not to offer up Gibraltar as means to gain peace with Spain.

The Spanish obsession for Gibraltar was not unlike Congress's desire for Canada. The Siege of Gibraltar would be the largest and by far the longest action of the war. It would carry the war into 1783 and it would figure prominently in negotiations for the Peace of Paris. To further explain this, we have to look at the stubborn British defense of Gibraltar.

Chapter 28

The Defenders Succeed

Gibraltar's military and civilian defenders would suffer from starvation, fire, disease and bombardment. Clearly, the deciding factor in the siege would be the continuous supply of food and reinforcement for the Rock's defenders. In this, the Royal Navy would play a prominent part, but it should not be forgotten that private Mediterranean ships also contributed.

The Resources

On the Rock, little arable land existed for growing crops and it had long ago been denuded of trees, making driftwood precious.[1] The dockyard's activities remained limited unless timber was imported. Coal was the best fuel, but it had to be imported from Britain and was soon in short supply. No springs existed so fresh water had to be collected in cisterns during the rainy winter and spring, but the hot and dry summers consumed every drop. A damp, hot and sticky wind, known as the Levanter, was constant, accompanied by a lowering mass of cloud, which clung to the summit of the Rock, making the climate uncomfortable. Like a ship, Gibraltar was completely dependent on outside supplies of food and water. The garrison in June 1779 amounted to 5,382 English and Hanoverian soldiers, 760 sailors, with 1,500 dependents, mostly wives and children.[2] Later in the siege, a regiment of Corsican troops appeared, recruited as the result of their revolt against the French. In all, fewer than 8,000 combatants were available at any one time.

Despite the Spanish declaration of war in June 1779, fighting seemed delayed and it took a while to separate the contending military forces. Many British officers had homes and families on the Spanish mainland and the declaration forced them to bring their dependents to Gibraltar.[3] On the Rock, as the siege continued, soldiers moved their families away from the town, as it was soon destroyed by the Spanish guns. Families that stayed took refuge further south on the Rock at the less exposed Windmill Hill, where they erected tents and huts for temporary shelter.

The majority of the additional 3,500 civilians were of Mediterranean origin from Portugal, Genoa, Spain and the Rock itself. Among them were 1,819 Catholics, 863 Jews and 300 to 400 Moslems. Britons numbered only 519.[4] During the siege, civilians who had property and would defend it were allowed to stay. They were also encouraged to raise vegetables. From June 1779, the Genoese and Jews were asked to level the sands and garden the isthmus' northern neutral ground, dangerously located between the two sides' fortifications.

To prevent civilian and military families from suffering and being a burden on food supplies, women and children were encouraged to leave as the siege continued. British families were sent to England, 150 women went to nearby Malaga, Spain and about forty Jewesses sailed for the island of Menorca.[5] Many Jews remained and suffered accordingly. Most of them saw their homes destroyed by the allied bombardment and either left or moved to the south end of the Rock to avoid it. By September 1779, above the South Barracks, many were concentrated in 'New Jerusalem', laid out for them to build on. Their synagogues in town had been destroyed, although their burial ground was in the south and they were able to celebrate Yom Kippur there. However, as the siege grew more desperate, in July 1781 their burial ground was taken by the garrison and turned into a garden.

The Defenses

Gibraltar's fortifications were in charge of Lieutenant Colonel William Green of the Royal Engineers. He had been posted to the fortress in 1761 as its senior engineer. Eight years later, he explained the Rock's vulnerabilities to a Parliamentary commission of enquiry.[6] He felt the Rock needed a bastion and battery about halfway between the extremes of the Old and New Moles. When constructed from 1773, the King's Bastion became the town's chief defense from an Algeciras Bay attack. While these defenses stretched along the west side of Rock, the east side was so steep that no defenses were needed. During the siege, the first efforts would be made to extend the northern defenses by tunneling into the Rock at high elevation.

The Squadron

A small naval yard had come into existence in 1739, but anchorage facilities were limited, as was the Royal Navy's presence. During the siege, the defensive squadron consisted of Rear Admiral Robert Duff's 64-gun *Panther*, the frigate *Enterprise* and the sloop *Childers*.[7] Governor Eliott found Duff to be uncooperative and many a blockade runner was taken by the Spaniards because Duff would not help them. He complained of having too few large ships to be active and early in 1780 he was recalled. Duff's complaint about lacking larger ships was not well founded as smaller vessels were what was needed in Algeciras Bay. By 1782, the Admiralty recognized the value of smaller craft for the defense of the Rock and later naval commanders were able to use them effectively.

Artificer Company

Following Green's suggestion, in October 1770, the government had authorized a major program of construction at the Rock. The work was initially carried out by civilians recruited from England and elsewhere in Europe, much as the Royal Navy dockyards did. They were not subject to military discipline, which made them difficult to manage. The only punishments for misconduct were reprimands, suspension and dismissal. This caused significant delays and extra expense in completing the defenses.[8]

To create a different workforce, a unique organization was suggested by Green, which combined the duties of artificers at Royal Navy dockyards with the defensive duties of a strategic naval base. He proposed that a company of military artificers should be raised from the garrison to work on the construction of fortifications.[9] His suggestion was welcomed by the Governor Eliott and accepted in March 1772. A warrant was issued to raise a sixty-eight-man company consisting of one sergeant-adjutant, three sergeants, three corporals, one drummer and sixty privates working variously as stonecutters, masons, miners, lime-burners, carpenters, smiths, gardeners and wheel-makers. Officers of the existing Corps of Engineers were put in command of the new company, which was named the Soldier Artificer Company.

Men from the garrison were easily recruited to join. The Company proved to be a great improvement and it was expanded to ninety-three men. At first, progress on the King's Bastion had been slow because of manpower shortages, but when the Company was expanded, it worked on the bastion 'from gun-fire in the morning to gun-fire in the evening, and also on Sundays'.[10] By 1776, the completed bastion mounted over twenty guns and had bombproof casemates capable of housing 800 men. At the height of the siege, nearly 2,000 men of the garrison would be at work on the fortifications under the direction of the Soldier Artificers.

Preparations

In 1777, Gibraltar's defense had been placed in the hands of Lieutenant General George August Eliott, the new Governor of Gibraltar. He would command Gibraltar during the entire siege and be honored with the nickname, 'Cock of the Rock'.[11] As the siege began, he made efforts to feed everyone from his limited supplies. He rationed all fresh meat and forbade his soldiers to powder their hair with flour.[12] Officers who were able to cultivate small patches for their own vegetables and fruit were ordered to sell any surplus at Gibraltar's public market. The number of horses was restricted to only those households that could adequately feed them. Eliott expanded his administration by appointing four aides-de-camp for unmet tasks like quartermaster general and hospital director. As the siege progressed, gunners would be under more fatigue than any other members of the garrison. At first, he had been forced to move artillerymen from one threatened spot to another. To meet the need, he trained 180 infantrymen in the use of the guns.

By 1782, General Eliott would offer a bounty of 1,000 Spanish dollars to 'anyone who can suggest how I am to get a flanking fire upon the enemy's works'.[13] In response, the Artificer Company's Sergeant-Major Henry Ince proposed to tunnel a gallery through the North Front of the Rock to reach an outcrop called the Notch, so that a cannon could be mounted there to cover the entire front. His suggestion was accepted and the Soldier Artificers began tunneling on May 25, 1782. As the works progressed, the tunnelers decided to create an opening in the cliff face to provide ventilation. Immediately it was realized that this would offer an excellent firing position. By the end of the siege, the newly created Upper Gallery housed four guns, mounted on specially developed 'depressing carriages' to allow them to fire downwards into the allied positions.

Relief Convoys

In London, it was questioned as to whether the defense of Gibraltar was worth the cost, for England had only minimal trade with the Mediterranean, which was not yet its route to India.[14] The garrison's survival depended upon outside help. From England, this required supply convoys guarded by a battle fleet that could pass through the allied blockade of Gibraltar. The relief forces had to be drawn from the Channel Fleet, weakening efforts to monitor the French coast. As the navy's resources were finite, the relief expeditions would be broken up to achieve multiple goals and be required to return rapidly to defend the Channel.[15]

Rodney's Relief in the Moonlight

Late in 1779, Lord Sandwich took the risk of appointing George Rodney commander of the first Gibraltar rescue fleet sent from England. It had been five years since Rodney had been to sea and the year before he was actually living in France in an attempt to escape his creditors. His secret multifaceted orders were to take much of the Channel Fleet to the Bay of Biscay, there to split it, with most transports and a small escort heading for Barbados, while the warships and some transports would aim for Gibraltar.[16] A few warships were also sent directly to reinforce Menorca. After this, the bulk of the fleet would return rapidly to the Channel, while Rodney with only four warships would go to the West Indies. Gibraltar's relief was most important, but the fleet had other objectives.

Word that the relief fleet was sailing from England reached Gibraltar in mid-January 1780.[17] The Spanish fleets of Admiral Luis de Cordova and Admiral Juan de Langara were aware of Rodney, but thought his fleet to be weaker than his twenty-one ships of the line. Upon receiving this intelligence, de Cordova promptly turned around and returned to his base at Cadiz. De Langara, unaware of Rodney's strength, went out into the Atlantic to oppose him, assuming that de Cordova was nearby to support him. Rodney's and de Langara's fleets met off Cape St Vincent, Portugal, where de Langara realized he was outnumbered and turned to escape to Cadiz. Rodney was in bed suffering from gout aboard his flagship the *Sandwich* and he hesitated, but then signaled to his fleet to chase the Spaniards to their leeward. His ships were faster because they were copper-bottomed and they pursued the Spanish fleet into the night, illuminated by the moon, so that his action was called the 'Moonlight Battle'. Heavy seas appeared and the Spanish ships were unable to use their lower-deck gunports on the lee side. De Langara was taken in his flagship, the *Fenix*, and six more ships were seized or blown up, only two escaping. Many of the captured ships were sent to Gibraltar where their ordnance and powder were appropriated. Rodney's role in the victory was limited, the *Sandwich* fired only a single broadside, on their own his captains playing a significant part in the success.

Rodney's relief fleet with his prizes arrived at Gibraltar on January 19, and over the following three weeks, transports and reinforcements came in and were unloaded. Rodney came on shore at Gibraltar and was saluted by the New Mole's guns. Eliott reported he now had bread and flour for 607 days, pork for 487 days, beef for 291 days, butter for 183 days, dried peas for 164 days, salt fish for 160 days and oatmeal for 104 days.[18] Still, once Rodney left for the Leeward Islands and sent other ships back to the Channel, the allied blockade resumed.

Darby's relief

More than a year passed before the next relief force of twenty-eight Channel Fleet ships and 400 transports was sent, commanded by George Darby. After organizing difficulties, it sailed in March 1781. As Darby moved toward Gibraltar, at intervals he sent off transports destined for the West and East Indies. The ministry hoped that Darby would be able to confront a French fleet, but none was there, as de Grasse's fleet had missed him on their way to America. Darby passed the Cape St Vincent and the great Spanish fleet at Cadiz, arriving at Gibraltar on April 12, 1781.[19] Barcelo's squadron and eighteen gunboats were on the alert at Algeciras, but no coordinated effort was made against Darby. Instead, the Spanish land batteries opened up with an enormous barrage, which continued the destruction of the town. As long as Darby's ships tacked backwards and forwards, his transports were able to deliver their supplies, take on non-combatants, and regroup for the return home. His fleet was back in the Channel at the beginning of May. On the return, Sir George Collier captured the Spanish frigate *Santa Leocadia* and when he put into Cork with his prize, the newspapers claimed that overall he had been the navy's most successful prize-taker, his captures totaling near £80,000. Collier never commanded a battle fleet, but his example shows that an aggressive navy commodore could accumulate wealth to match the most successful privateer captain.

Howe's Relief

Although the allied 'Grand Assault' had been destroyed, the siege continued as the night forays of the Spanish gunboats were incessant. De Cordova's fleet of forty-four ships of the line had actually been in the English Channel until the end of July 1782, challenging convoys and Royal Navy escorts.[20] They then returned to Algeciras Bay and became part of the blockade.

In September, a Gibraltar relief force of 34 ships and 140 transports sailed under the command of Richard Howe. He had returned to England from his North American post and in 1779 defended his and his brother's conduct, causing his alienation from the North ministry. With the fall of North's government in March 1782, Howe was returned to command of the Channel Fleet on his flagship, the famous *Victory*. His relief fleet arrived in the vicinity of Gibraltar on October 11, but was only able to land a few ships, as most missed Gibraltar's harbor.[21]

This was because de Cordova had situated his fleet between Howe and Gibraltar. A storm disorganized de Cordova's ships, and Howe hid his transports on the North African coast and then passed by de Cordova into Gibraltar.[22] Over a week, Howe's transports landed food, ammunition and troops, ensuring that Gibraltar could hold out indefinitely. Howe took his fleet back to the Atlantic, avoiding combat in the Straits, followed by de Cordova, who was unable to bring about a confrontation. By mid-November, Howe was back in Spithead, his relief of Gibraltar having ended the last hope of de Cordova to starve the garrison into surrender. Howe's tactics sustained the Royal Navy's reputation for invincibility.

Beyond these formal Royal Navy relief fleets, smaller vessels from the region got through the blockade with necessities on a weekly basis.[23] In 1779, a large boat from Spain brought fruit to exchange for tobacco, and a month later a Jew's boat brought in a Dutch Dogger laden with wheat and cheese. Ships like this slipped in and out of Gibraltar's harbor from Portuguese, Italian and North African ports. Privateers also brought their prizes to the Rock with captured cargos of food.[24] These ships carried fresh produce like lemons, oranges and onions that were crucial to the prevention of scurvy in the garrison and which were not found in the relief fleets' naval stores. Upon return, these ships carried Gibraltar refugees, as more of the civilian population sought to live elsewhere during the protracted siege.

Roger Curtis' Gunboats

The best commander of the Rock's smaller warships was Captain Roger Curtis. Now 35 years old, he was from an old Wiltshire naval family.[25] He had served in America at the capture of New York in 1776, a year later in the Philadelphia campaign, and was present at Sandy Hook when Admiral Howe foiled d'Estaing's fleet. He returned to England with Howe in late October 1778.

By 1780, Curtis commanded the 28-gun frigate *Brilliant* and assembled the 24-gun *Porcupine*, 18-gun *Minorca* and a small convoy of store ships to relieve Gibraltar and Menorca.[26] Upon reaching the Mediterranean, Curtis' squadron was chased into Menorca by two Spanish frigates and a xebec, and they were blockaded for five weeks. Still, Curtis was able to slip back into Gibraltar's harbor with a few ships and supply transports loaded in Menorca. Much later, he was charged by First Lieutenant Colin Campbell for failing to attack the blockaders, claiming that his squadron had the greater firepower. Although the accusations had some substance, the naval establishment remained solidly behind Curtis and nothing came of the charges.

At Gibraltar, Eliott recognized Curtis' ability and immediately placed him in command of its naval squadron for the remaining siege.[27] On November 27, 1781, Curtis volunteered for Eliott's sortie, commanding two seamen brigades, attacking the Spanish siege lines. The sortie demolished Spanish entrenchments and spiked their mortars and cannons, also destroying their carriages, beds and platforms. As the fire spread, Spanish magazines blew up one after another.

Like Barcelo, Curtis would become a master of gunboat warfare in Algeciras Bay. In July 1781, he built his first two gunboats, converting and cutting down a couple of brigs, mounting 24-pounders in them. In late February 1782, the *St Ann* arrived from the Admiralty carrying timbers and frames, ready-made but unassembled, for two gunboats and with news that timbers for another ten gunboats would follow.[28] These gunboats were quickly assembled; the first was in the water by mid-April. They would be instrumental in meeting the assault of the floating batteries.

By April 1782, Curtis had organized a naval brigade of a dozen gunboats, all of them having been assembled or refurbished at Gibraltar.[29] They patrolled the shores of Gibraltar, often at night, to gain intelligence. On August 7, he personally commanded two gun boats which covered the arrival of the 14-gun sloop *Helena*, fighting off fourteen Spanish gunboats from Algeciras.

Each gunboat had a crew of twenty-one, taken from the larger ships. They were diverse, one man was Benjamin Whitecuff, a free black born on Long Island, New York. He had sailed to Gibraltar and joined Curtis in February 1782, after the British garrison surrendered Menorca. Previously in the New York area, he had served Sir Henry Clinton as a spy and was condemned by the rebels to death and sent to Boston to be hanged. On the way to Massachusetts, a Liverpool privateer, the brig *Eagle*, took his ship.[30] He was carried to Tortola and from there he sailed to England. He volunteered for the Royal Navy brig *St Philips Castle,* which sailed to and participated in the defense of Mahon, Menorca. When the Gibraltar siege ended, Whitecuff was discharged and he settled in Deptford, the navy dockyard community, where many Loyalist black sailors made their homes. He had prize money and wages due him, a naval pension of £4 a year and the Claims Commission awarded him £10 for his services and losses.

In September, Governor Eliott asked Curtis to help to repulse the allied floating batteries. Curtis brought 900 sailors ashore to form a marine brigade.[31] During the allied attack, he earned praise for his command of the gunboats. His life was endangered when his pinnace was caught in an explosion and his coxswain killed. Still, he rescued 400 Spaniards from their blazing hulks, a show of humanity toward his enemy.

A month later, when a storm struck de Cordoba's fleet, the Spanish *San Miguel* of seventy-four guns, crew of 650, was washed up at the King's Bastion, helpless as she had lost her foremast and bowsprit.[32] Curtis went aboard her and took possession; she would be refitted and commissioned as the *St Michael.*

During Howe's relief, after going aboard the *Victory* to greet his old commander, Curtis was unable to get back to Gibraltar, being obliged to return to England with Howe's fleet.[33] Upon reaching London, Curtis was knighted for his part in the defense of Gibraltar, had his memoirs published and he was feted by society. He was awarded the thanks of Parliament and given a 500-guinea pension.

At the request of the beleaguered Governor Eliott, however, Curtis was again sent back to Gibraltar, sailing in January 1783 with the rank of commodore aboard the 38-gun *Thetis,* arriving at the Rock in March.[34] By then the siege had ended, so he used his diplomatic talents, visiting Tangiers aboard the *Brilliant* to restore friendly relations. He asked for the release of all captive British subjects and delivered gifts to the Court of Morocco, including four brass guns taken from the allies.

The Siege and Peace Negotiations Continue

While Curtis was in England, the Franco-Spanish siege waned as it was becoming evident that the Rock could not be taken. Diplomacy took over as Lord Shelburne's government sought to end the war both in America and Europe. To the American commissioners, peace was especially vital because they lacked the resources to continue the war.[35] Willing to ignore their European allies, the American diplomats had approved a preliminary peace agreement with Shelburne at the end of 1782. Still, Gibraltar remained an important concern in British negotiations with Spain and France. Again, British representatives discussed exchanging Gibraltar for concessions from Spain, like Menorca and West Florida. When Shelburne suggested to the French and Spanish ministers that Gibraltar be dropped from further negotiations, they both agreed, evidently being weary of the siege.

While these negotiations continued, Gibraltar remained under siege as Spanish gunboats attacked. The allied guns were so slack, however, that seamen began to salvage abandoned cannon from the bay and refurbish them. At the beginning of February 1783, the Spaniards suddenly announced that 'We are all friends', and Duc de Crillon told Eliott that the blockade was formally ended.[36] While peace treaties had not yet been signed, the guns were at last silent. Moreover, Eliott and the garrison received assurances that Gibraltar would remain British. It had been a heavy price for Britain to pay, but the national instinct had been to retain Gibraltar.

British Public Opinion

During the siege, British public opinion had become captivated by the supposed invincibility of the Rock and hostile to any idea of it being lost at the peace table. Certainly, Eliott's defense of the Rock against the formidable Spanish and French forces was much admired in Britain. The Rock was highly defensible and the British garrison was well led by Eliott. The Royal Navy's admirals showed they had the ability to provide relief for the Rock, while at the same time maintaining commitments elsewhere. Captain Roger Curtis cooperated with the army in Algeciras Bay to foil the besiegers. Despite the allied superiority in ships and troops, they did not seem united, implementing their plans singly, never bringing to bear all of their forces at once.[37]

This led the British public opinion to see the prolonged defense of Gibraltar as a great victory.[38] Rewards to the defenders of Gibraltar reflected British respect for the defense. Parliament granted prize money not only to the ships' crews but to the entire garrison for the destruction of the floating batteries and the capture of the *San Miguel*. The grants totaled £46,000, so even privates received about £4. For those who would re-enlist a generous bounty was offered.

In the decade following the siege, history painters would take up the commemoration of the victory, as the subject was popular with a wide audience.

Surprisingly, American artists led the way in commemorating the siege. Boston-born John Singleton Copley had moved to England in 1774, developing a career as a history painter and he never returned to America. When it was first exhibited in 1783, 60,000 people came to see his *Destruction of the Floating Batteries*. According to *Arnold's Magazine of Fine Arts*, the painting was 'an instance perhaps not to be paralleled by any age or nations'.[39] An engraving by William Sharp popularized the painting. Another American artist, John Trumbull, who was best known for his heroic views of American successes, evidently could not resist the subject's popularity and in 1789 he did a view of Eliott's sortie, which was engraved by C.W. Metz.

A favorite subject of the public became Curtis risking his life to drag Spaniards from the fiery inferno of the floating batteries. William Hamilton did a 1783 painting of Curtis and Eliott in action, which was popularized by Scottish painter Archibald Robertson's engraving.[40] Much later, a more modest etching enforced Curtis' reputation for saving Spanish sailors from the burning floating batteries. The honoring of Curtis' humanitarian acts toward the enemy made Britain's siege role more sympathetic.

Rebuilding

With the war concluded, the Artificer Company secured a permanent place in Gibraltar's defense. It began a large-scale program of further tunneling, leading to 4,000 feet of tunnels being excavated by 1790.[41] The Artificers were instrumental in rebuilding Gibraltar's town and repairing and strengthening the fortifications. The Company's numbers were replenished with men transferred from regiments stationed at Gibraltar. They were uniquely privileged among the garrison's lower ranks, being exempted from guard duty and having their cleaning and cooking provided by regulars.

PART 9

THE CONTINENTAL NAVY IN TROUBLE

Chapter 29

Loyalist Privateers Expand the War

While it is accepted that rebel privateers combined war with profit to make up for a lack of Continental warships, it is less recognized that in the later years of the war privateers became crucial to the British war effort.[1] Privateers played a part in the long siege of Gibraltar. The Rock's merchants had at least seven privateers based there from 1777 to 1783. In February 1782, the privateer *Mercury* delivered welcome supplies to the garrison, demonstrating that privateers could be a supplement to navy transports.

In past wars, British privateers had appeared when private ships of war and armed merchantmen were outfitted to sail under Admiralty licenses to seize enemy property. Letters of marque were issued by the High Court of Admiralty, in which a ship's captain had to identify his ship and post a bond.[2] The letters were meant to enhance armed trading voyages so that ships might be able to take a prize in addition to selling their cargo. Privateer licenses were also given to purpose-built warships that were fully armed and cruised extensively. These private warships were further divided between those that cruised in 'deep water', throughout the Atlantic, and those smaller vessels that sailed in coastal bays and rivers.

During the colonial wars, privateering had been a business enterprise meant to offer a financial return on the investment of the ship's owners. Prizes had to be presented to Admiralty courts sitting throughout the empire, which decided how the prize's proceeds were to be distributed between the crown, officers, crew and ship owners. The 1768 Vice Admiralty Court Act created four district courts in the North American colonies, located at New York, Boston, Philadelphia and Charleston, adding to the existing, but remote, court at Halifax.[3] The Admiralty courts also helped customs officials to prosecute smugglers like those in Rhode Island, and they were the one place where the rights of sailors were recognized and protected. Some colonial critics claimed the Admiralty courts were high handed because they did not use juries, but such a procedure would have jammed the courts and made them inoperable.

British American privateers were only gradually accepted as an essential part of the British naval effort. They had been regulated since a 1692 statute, chiefly because privateers competed with the Royal Navy for skilled seamen. Five years later, Maryland's Governor Francis Nicholson experienced a 'great encouragement for illegal traders and privateers, or rather pirates, which causes many men to run from the king's ships in the convoys and from merchant ships'.[4] He made certain that privateer owners post substantial bonds for good behavior, which were forfeited if looting occurred. Piratical behavior by privateers was not tolerated because privateering laws were enforced by the world's most extensive naval police force, the Royal Navy.

Delay in Privateering

At first in the Revolution, the licensing of Loyalist privateers was ambiguous because in the eyes of Parliament, the rebels were technically not an enemy, remaining His Majesty's subjects. This delayed privateering, but could be circumvented by using the 1775 Prohibitory of Trade Act, which authorized the seizure of goods carried by the ships of the thirteen colonies. It prohibited the American colonies from 'all manner of trade and commerce' and declared that any ships found trading with the colonies 'shall be forfeited to his Majesty, as if the same were the ships and effects of open enemies'.[5] This allowed for the *Roebuck*'s prize activity in the early years of the war, when the Royal Navy had little competition from privateers, taking the bulk of rebel prizes.

Before Parliament withdrew its opposition to privateering, Admiral James Young, Commander of the Leeward Islands Station in English Harbor, Antigua, felt it was his duty to prevent merchant privateers from sailing. He feared that they might act with the rebels or prey on the ships of then neutral France and Spain, which would cause them to declare war on Britain. This actually led Antigua's merchants, who owned many privateers, to have Young arrested and sued. By April 1777, this was no longer a problem as Parliament had withdrawn its opposition and the Admiralty was commissioning privateers, even in Bermuda and the Leeward Islands.[6] In occupied places, privateers were now licensed by royal governors to take rebel prizes as had been done in the past.

The Royal Navy was not anxious to work with privateers. In the race to recruit seamen, privateers had advantages over it. Privateers' amount of prize money was probably larger as they focused only on obtaining prizes, while the navy ships had limited time for such diversions.[7] Still, drawbacks existed for recruits. Crews of private warships received no wages and most privateers deducted the cost of their food and medical care from their prize money. Privateer ships were built for speed, thus usually smaller and overcrowded – conditions that spread vermin. A seaman who served on a privateer had to gamble that a string of valuable prizes would be taken. In contrast, life in the navy was more secure as a seaman's livelihood did not depend on circumstance, for even if his ship was lost or he were taken prisoner, he still was compensated.

Eventually, Loyalist privateers became the wild card in the makeup of British naval forces, supplementing the Royal Navy in maintaining the long-standing blockade. In North America, privateers rarely came from distant Britain, rather appearing from closer Bermuda, Norfolk and Portsmouth, Virginia, and New York. The Chesapeake remained an important place to recruit privateer crews. In 1776, the privateer *Rodney* recruited its crew around Deal Island, Somerset County, Maryland.[8]

While rebel naval forces came to act almost exclusively as privateers and did considerable damage to British merchant shipping, the balance sheet of prizes favored the Royal Navy supported by Loyalist privateers. They destroyed over 1,000 rebel vessels and crews. An American historian has concluded that 'British privateers and warships had a greater impact on the American economy than did the American privateers on the economy of Great Britain.'[9]

New York

In North America, New York was the most consistent origin of Loyalist privateers. Its merchants had become experienced as privateers during the Seven Years' War, when they had obtained letters of marque and purchased shares in privateering ventures. The city was occupied by the British from its conquest by the Howes in 1776 until the very end of the war, and it became a magnet for Loyalist refugees. It was the seat of an Admiralty court to clear prizes and its careening yard and maritime enterprises supported privateers. Robert Bayard, descendant of a Huguenot family and judge of the Admiralty court, authorized privateers broadly

> to attack, surprise, seize and take all ships and vessels, goods, wares and merchandises, chattels and effects whatever, belonging to the inhabitants of the said colonies now in rebellion, and all ships and vessels with their cargos, apparel and furniture, belonging to our subjects in Great Britain and Ireland, which shall be found of from the said colonies.[10]

In the early years of the war, New York's merchant community claimed to have suffered a lost opportunity because of Parliament's Prohibitory of Trade Act. These restrictions were gradually whittled away by Sir Henry Clinton and Parliament, so that a New York privateer could go to Delaware Bay to support Sussex County Loyalists. By the summer of 1777, members of the Chesapeake Goodrich family – Bartlet, William and Bridger – were reunited in New York and joined Willie and Robert Shedden to form Shedden & Goodrich, a company dedicated to privateering and supply of the British. A year later, the new commander of the New York naval station, Rear Admiral James Gambier, was praised for his support of privateers. It was said, his 'astonishing exertion to the private ships of war' and 'the success of the enterprisers ... seems indeed to have given a hard blow to the rebellion.'[11]

New York Governor William Tryon sought permission to issue commissions and letters of marque for privateers, as he could charge a fee for issuing them. From March 1777, he licensed 185 privateers and five months later, he was given the authority to provide more. Even the ministry's peace commissioners authorized an expansion of privateering to meet the French challenge on the high seas. By 1779, Tryon was promising generous bounties for 'seamen, shipcarpenters and other landsmen' to man privateers.[12] Between August 1778 and April 1779, 121 privateers were fitted out in New York to challenge the rebels. As a result, the number of ship's libels taken by privateers at New York's Vice Admiralty Court rose to two-thirds of the total, the remainder belonging to the Royal Navy.

In May 1779, Sir George Collier's expedition to Chesapeake Bay contained many New York privateers. When Collier returned from the Chesapeake to New York, however, he found that his seamen were deserting to privateers because of lucrative bounties. To make up for the competition, New York City merchants were willing to donate ships to the Royal Navy. Still, crews would remain more difficult to come by than ships. In 1780, regulars of the 82nd Regiment were lured to a privateer because they were offered a share in the prizes.[13] As a result, inspections were put into effect to prevent regulars and Royal Navy sailors from joining privateer crews.

A few months after Colliers' expedition, the New York privateer *Irish Hero* came into the Chesapeake on its own, but while chasing prizes it ran aground on the Northampton coast and the crew set her afire. The plucky captain and some of the crew set out in a longboat and eventually made New York. At the same time, the privateer *Charlotte* arrived in New York with the captured prize *Success,* taken off the Virginia Capes. The overall take of such New York privateers was estimated by Tryon at £600,000 and a list of prizes published in *Rivington's*

Gazette show that many came from the Chesapeake.[14] New York owners of privateers, such as John Watts, John Armory and Theophilact Bache, and captains like William Bayard's son, Samuel, profited from the goods taken by the privateers and sold in New York.[15]

Actually, many rebel merchant cargos ended up in British-held New York rather than their supposed destination, usually the West Indies. The diversion of rebel cargos to New York was the result of a captain deciding he could do better with the British. In 1780, Captain James Anderson, a former lieutenant in the Maryland navy, cleared Baltimore with a destination of the West Indies.[16] However, once out of the bay, Anderson headed his ship for New York, sold his cargo there, and returned to the Chesapeake as a Loyalist privateer. Similarly, Captain John Stump, an assistant to supply Commissioner Henry Hollingsworth, procured flour and sailed out of the bay. He pretended that his flour had been captured en route to Boston, but actually he went to New York, where he sold the flour to the British army. Once this illicit trade was discovered, captains had to become Loyalist privateers.

Late in the war, when combat continued in New York's waterways, special Loyalist units supplemented privateers. By 1780, a series of British blockhouses on the New Jersey side of the Hudson River and at Sandy Hook served as collecting points for livestock and firewood for New York City, as well as intelligence gathering as they watched Washington's army and supporting militia. They were garrisoned by Loyalists, many of them free blacks. In July 1780, Anthony Wayne's Continentals were driven back from the Bull's Ferry blockhouse, with heavy losses.

A year later, Sir Henry Clinton authorized William Luce, New Jersey Loyalist, to create a raiding force 'for his Majesty's Service. One Company of Able Bodied Men, to be employed in Whale Boats & other Armed Vessels.'[17] They were to receive the same pay as Marines on armed vessels and be clothed and armed as Provincial forces. In 1782, they grew from 80 to 125 men, raiding by water against rebel strongholds. On January 8, they joined about 300 British regulars in attacking rebel whaleboats at New Brunswick. Another foray was authorized by the Board of the Associated Loyalists, who targeted Toms River as a nest of rebel privateers and the site of valuable salt works. On March 23, the Armed Boat Company, joined by forty Associated Loyalists, attacked the Toms River blockhouse. Several were killed and wounded on each side, but the Loyalists took the blockhouse and the bulk of the rebel garrison. Among the captives was Captain Joshua Huddy, who ultimately was hung by Loyalists, making the incident a cause célèbre to the rebels. In June, forty whites and forty blacks of the Armed Boat Company landed at Forked River and burnt homes and salt works. In March 1783, the Company numbered seventy at the East River Boat Yard and Fort Kniphausen on the Hudson, formerly Fort Washington.

The Goodrich Transatlantic Family

From 1775, the most active Loyalist privateers were those of John Goodrich, his sons, William, John Jr., Bartlet, Bridger and Edward, and his associates in Robert Shedden's family. Most of the six privateers in Governor Dunmore's fleet belonged to the Goodrich family. By 1779, the Goodrich privateer fleet, now based in New York and Bermuda, was so successful in Chesapeake Bay that Virginia's Governor Thomas Jefferson admitted that, 'Our trade has never been so distressed since the time of Lord Dunmore.'[18]

The patriarch John Goodrich was a wealthy merchant and planter whose family had come to Virginia's Norfolk–Portsmouth area in the late seventeenth century. He owned over 2,000 acres of developed land in Nansemond and Isle of Wight Counties and five town lots in Portsmouth for his residences, as well as an extensive wharf, warehouses, dry goods stores and other shops.[19] By 1774, the family owned twelve trading ships, which went chiefly to the West Indies, but were also involved in costal shipping.

During the Stamp Act crisis, the Goodrich family had been as active as any Whig in protesting British efforts to regulate imperial trade. In 1774, John had been elected to the Committee of Correspondence of Norfolk and Portsmouth, which communicated with merchants in other ports and sent aid to beleaguered Boston.[20] He also subscribed to the Continental Association, although this did not stop his family from continuing to smuggle British manufactures into their stores. With his adult sons, John Jr., William and Bartlett, he contracted with rebel authorities to procure gunpowder in the French or Dutch West Indies, to replace what Governor Dunmore had taken from the Williamsburg arsenal. William returned in October 1775 with the gunpowder purchased in Dutch St Eustatius, which was unloaded in North Carolina and transported overland to Williamsburg to avoid the Royal Navy. True, other Goodrich ships had gone with William, who had also made purchases to the financial advantage of the family. In January 1776, William and John Jr. were accused by a committee of violating the Continental Association, which aimed to prevent British imports, threatening confiscation of concealed manufactures.

In November 1775, however, Dunmore got wind of the Goodrich family's gunpowder deal and he arrested John Goodrich Jr. and Goodrich's son-in-law and partner, Robert Shedden. This led the senior Goodrich to repent the gunpowder enterprise and intervene, asking to see Dunmore. At the meeting on the *Otter*, Goodrich claimed 'that he and his son had no other motive for engaging in this business but the prospect of a good freight for their vessel'.[21] He offered to go to St Eustatius and purchase gunpowder for Dunmore, leaving his son William in the governor's hands for security. Instead, William went back to St Eustatius and obtained a note for his costs in the service of Virginia and then returned to Dunmore's custody.

Despite William's confinement, the Goodrich family were becoming Loyalists. The senior Goodrich now agreed to work with Dunmore, offering his ships as Loyalist privateers, and in March 1776, serving as a pilot on the *Otter*.[22] John Jr. was released, and from this moment forward the Goodrich family served as Loyalist privateers, taking prizes and raiding rebel plantations. Five of the family's ships patrolled the coasts and rivers, in league with Royal Navy tenders, gathering provisions like pork and bacon for Dunmore. Captain Hamond advised Captain Matthew Squire to seek the advice of Bridger, John Goodrich's younger son, who commanded a tender, in procuring fresh meat for navy ships. The Goodrichs' ships would now be under navy supervision and he and his sons were regarded by the rebels as traitors.

The Goodrichs' evolving Loyalism did not go unnoticed by the rebels. In revenge, the senior Goodrich and his four eldest sons would be sought out and imprisoned. When Portsmouth was taken by rebels, the Goodrich homes and property were looted and destroyed, fortifying their loyalty to the crown. Soon the extended Goodrich family of ships' masters, wives, clerks and slaves joined the Hamond-Dunmore fleet in seven sloops.[23] William was able to bring his wife and newborn child aboard one of the family's sloops. At Gwynn's

Island, William commanded the *James* and sloop *Lady Susan*, John Sr., the *Lilly* and *Peggy*, and Bridger, the tenders, *Edward, Samuel* and *Lady Susan*.

In June 1776 near Ocracoke, North Carolina, John Sr., having taken two prizes in a rebel harbor, was unable to escape and was seized and sent to Williamsburg, where he was placed in heavy irons. He was incarcerated in several jails and finally in Charlottesville, where he met Midshipman Josias Rogers of the *Roebuck,* who was released as a military prisoner while Goodrich remained. John Sr. escaped from Charlottesville and eventually was picked up by HMS *St Albans* in Chesapeake Bay and taken to New York. He reported 'that 130 Men from Somerset County in Maryland are now on board the Virginia enlisted into the British service ... & that [he] at pleasure, could fetch of 170 more who had agreed to enter into the king's servise'.[24] Goodrich found Rogers in New York and, according to Rogers, offered him the command of his privateer fleet, although he turned him down. Whether in the Chesapeake or New York, John Sr. was a persuasive privateersman.

After Dunmore sailed to New York in August 1776, John Sr., William, Bartlet and Bridger, along with the Sheddens, were established there. However, William and Bridger would gravitate toward Bermuda. Bridger was described as 'a stoop shouldered, genteel, well-looking young man of about twenty-four years, with a daring, bold countenance, light colored hair and a little freckly'.[25] In 1776, he had captained the *Molly* and sailed toward Bermuda, carrying 15,000 bushels of wheat confiscated by Dunmore, which ultimately would be sent to Halifax. Off Bermuda, however, the *Molly* was intercepted by the Continental ship *Andrew Doria,* and Bridger's heavily laden ship could not make a resistance; its crew of Loyalists and slaves was taken to Philadelphia. The captured brothers, Bridger and William, were placed in a Baltimore prison but escaped at the end of 1776. Both served briefly in the crew of the *Roebuck* in the spring of 1777 before going to Bermuda and conducting privateering from the mid-Atlantic. Before the war, the British island was known for the construction of sloops of speed and weatherliness, which made ideal privateers. In 1777, Bridger bought a fine Bermuda sloop and refitted her as a privateer. On his initial voyage he took five prizes, two of which belonged to Bermudians, which he brought back to the island, accusing their owners of trading with the enemy.

Meanwhile, Margaret, John Sr.'s wife, remained in Virginia at the family's Nansemond plantation, living with her children on a modest stipend provided by the Virginia Commissioners of Sequestration.[26] In 1778, she petitioned them for an increase in her stipend in order to rehire her slaves to cultivate her lands, but was refused. In May 1779, when Collier's squadron landed at Portsmouth, the Goodrich privateers *Dunmore, Hamond, Lord North* and *Fincastle* were among the ships. Commanded by Bartlet Goodrich, the *Hamond* was able to carry John Jr.'s wife and children to New York. A year later, John Goodrich Sr. was back in a privateer with Gayton's expedition to the Chesapeake and it was then that he rescued Margaret and the children and took them to New York.

After the war, John Sr. and most family members migrated to London, where Bartlet had made connections in 1778. John Sr.'s referees for his Loyalist claim indicated his service: Lord Dunmore, Captain Hamond, Sir Henry Clinton, Admiral Gambier, Admiral Collier, Admiral Arbuthnot, General Mathew, General Leslie and Captain Gayton. After a brief stay in Bristol, he moved to the port of Topsham, Devonshire, where he resided in Grove House. The war and imprisonment had taken its toll and he died in 1785. He claimed he 'took and destroyed five hundred vessels ... while giving employment to more than one thousand Americans or other Loyalists'.[27]

In Bermuda – where Henry Tucker, formerly of Somerset County Maryland, had continued to trade with the rebels and formed an association to boycott Bridger's privateering – Bridger's seizure of Bermudian vessels raised a storm of indignation.[28] In 1779, Bridger's fleet of Bermuda privateers blockaded the Chesapeake and took prizes at Fox Island. Back in Bermuda, he blatantly became engaged to Elizabeth Tucker, a kinswoman of Henry Tucker's and the association's opposition to his privateering momentarily became confused.

Bridger would not be the only privateer captain from Bermuda. The war would disrupt Bermuda's traditional reliance upon trade with the rebellious North American colonies. With the appearance of new fortifications and British troops, as well as Bridger's privateers, Bermuda's economy was altered. As reconstituted, it depended on the proceeds of privateering to sell goods to the beefed-up British military.[29] Ultimately, Bridger took so many prizes he could afford to live at elegant Goodrich Hall in Bermuda's Orange Grove. In 1788, he sold Goodrich Hall and went to England for a prolonged visit to his family. He later returned to Bermuda, where he resided at the Bridge House, St George's. Overall, the Goodrichs succeeded in the war, continuing the ideal of a prosperous transatlantic family.

Other Privateers

During the British occupation of Charleston, privateers cruised as far as St Augustine. Its location, convenient to Savannah, the Bahamas and Havana, Cuba, offered opportunities for privateers. St Augustine also had an Admiralty court, where privateers sought judgements. Headed by Reverend John Forbes, the court was known for verdicts of condemnation, which meant that scarce items like foodstuffs, powder and slaves were for sale in St Augustine. Royal Navy vessels were few and on their way to other destinations. Thus, Governor Tonyn followed the example of Virginia's Governor Dunmore by creating his own provincial navy as well as issuing letters of marque. In 1776, letters were given to Captain John Mowbray of the 10-gun *Rebecca*, who would later become commander of all armed vessels protecting East Florida.[30]

Elsewhere in the South, analysis of British privateering on Chesapeake Bay in 1776 has identified seventeen ships commanded and manned by Loyalists.[31] Of those, ten were sloops and five schooners, indicating a preference for vessels suitable for close inshore combat. Their small size is further affirmed by their typical armament of two to six carriage guns. Only the sloop *Fincastle,* the pride of Portsmouth merchants Robert and Roger Stewart, had as many as eight to ten guns. Its career began in Dunmore's fleet at Gwyn's Island and it followed Dunmore to New York. In June 1779, it was one of the privateers that remained behind when Collier left and it joined Captain Richard Creyk's *Otter* in raiding the Wicomico River, Virginia. At least three of the sloops and one schooner also carried an average of six swivel guns. Most of these ships were 100–250 tons. Compared to navy ships, the crews of these vessels were diminutive, ranging from a schooner of roughly ten men to a sloop with as many as twenty-four. In July, the combined crews of Joseph Wayland's three schooners numbered only twenty, all but one described as 'Country born'. While many Loyalist mariners were volunteers, others were pressed and those mariners signing articles on Dunmore's vessels were officially taken into government service, receiving modest pay.

On their own, Loyalist privateers perfected hit and run tactics and frustrated the ability of rebel militia to catch them. In Maryland, County Lieutenant Joseph Dashiell noted that the port of Sinepuxent was not vulnerable because it was on Worcester County's Atlantic side and not well known to the British. This changed in June 1777, when six Loyalist privateers appeared at Sinepuxent Inlet and captured the sloop *Independence's* boat, which, unawares, had been sent out to provide them with a pilot.[32] The militia were called up to oppose them, but wind caused the privateers to put to sea the next day. However, the privateers returned and were unopposed because the militia had refused to go over to guard the beach. The privateers left again but returned, still looking for a tempting target. Dashiell felt that a proper guard drafted from the militia was needed to protect the inlet from marauding.

Loyalist privateer activity increased later in the war. In 1780, Loyalist privateers attempted to seize tobacco warehouses at Benoni's Point, Maryland's Eastern Shore, but were driven off by Talbot County militia.[33] The privateers then took possession of Matthew Tilghman's Choptank Island and looted it. The privateer *Spitefire* with thirty-two oars and thirty-three men rowed up the Choptank River as far as Castle-Haven in Dorchester County and took possession of the rebel schooner *Mayflower*, smaller boats, cattle and sheep. Here the privateer tried to release the captives it had taken, but the militia fired on them.

In July 1780, Loyalist privateers captured two vessels at the mouth of Virginia's Patuxent River and continued to take rebel privateers. In September, Simon Lambard, sailor on Captain John Dashiell's schooner, *The Secretary*, deserted to Captain Daniel Collier's Connecticut Loyalist privateer. A month later, the residents of Vienna, Maryland feared the 'probable return of enemy crews from New York privateers ...'[34] In November, the rebel privateer *Luzerne*, which had escaped in previous encounters, was taken by the New York privateer *Trimmer* under Captain Phillips. One Baltimore merchant in particular, James Carey, found as late as 1783 that he could not return home because 'the Chesapeake has been so blocked by New York and Bermudian [privateers] that business in Maryland has been almost annihilated.'

Raiding the Gentry's Plantations

In 1780 in New York, Clinton approved instructions from the Board of Associated Loyalists, which encouraged privateers to attack rebel property. It read that Loyalist raiders should be provided with appropriate shipping, 'not commanded by the King's officers ... to be manned by themselves, and that their mariners shall not be impressed into any other service'. It also said that Loyalists 'may ... form conjunct expeditions, in any quarter, with such [privateers], as may ... be for the future under one general direction and regulation'.[35] Here was authority for Loyalist privateers to organize raiding parties on their own initiative.

A combination of indigenous watermen, Loyalists privateers and perhaps a Royal Navy tender carried on forays against rebel plantations. As with rebel privateers in Nova Scotia, Loyalist privateers in the Chesapeake turned increasingly to attacking land-based objectives rather than ships at sea because they seemed more lucrative. Loyalist raiders, supported by watermen, viewed plantations and their owners as centers of luxury, peopled by fine gentlemen who had little in common with them, which had been demonstrated by the gentry's earlier hoarding of scarce salt.[36] The Chesapeake gentry saw anyone who opposed their leadership as outlaws. British privateer warfare not only hurt a planter's pocketbook, but it left him insecure, uncertain of how much influence he still exercised in his local bailiwick. As officers of the militia, could planters turn them out to oppose the privateers in a timely fashion? The planters blamed the lower orders for the destructive raids on their plantations, and in turn the lower orders felt the planters exploited them when they demanded supplies, taxes and service in the military.

Loyalist privateers were the backbone of the raids on the gentry's Chesapeake plantations. The privateers encouraged watermen to serve with them. In February 1781, while Benedict Arnold's army occupied the western shore of Virginia, Thomas Seon Sudler's Back Creek plantation was ransacked by, in the words of the victim, 'British barges and neighbors'.[37] Three months later, Somerset's George Dashiell was more specific, 'The inhabitants of this county … have suffered much by parties either from British Cruisers or the inhabitants of the Tangier Islands (tho' I believe the latter) as a number of them are well known by persons that they have plundered.' These water-borne raids seemed to the gentry to be coordinated, aimed at the homes and slaves of militia officers, who supported the Revolution.

In presenting Loyalist merchants and ship owners with the opportunity for profit, Loyalist privateers expanded the war into the narrowest waterways, while also sustaining trade. Despite the competition privateers created, the Royal Navy came to accept their ability to add to naval resources necessary to carry on the war.

Chapter 30

Demise of the Continental Navy

Congress lacked its own naval dockyards, yet it had to sustain an Atlantic-wide war effort. To do this it appointed agents to represent its naval interests, usually in French ports. You will remember that in mid-1776, Wickes had carried William Bingham to Martinique where he would serve as Congress's agent until 1779. One of his duties was to pass on information from Congress to Silas Deane, the commissioner in France. When Robert Morris informed Deane of this, he described Bingham as having 'a good deal of fanciful young man in [him], but experience will cure him of this, and upon the whole, I think he has abilities & merit'.[1] In Martinique, Bingham became experienced. He learned that while Congress wanted him to send munitions from the island, they were difficult to come by. He would soon find that Congress had almost no credit to refit or buy ships so he had to use his own resources and those of Willing, Morris and Company or be dunned by Martinique's merchants. Most of his efforts happened before the French alliance so he found Martinique's French authorities to be unpredictable and occasionally even hostile to Congress's interests. Considering his responsibilities, agents like Bingham were as crucial to the American cause as a worthy sea captain.

Robert Morris had worked with Bingham and as Congress's Secretary of the Treasury in the later years of the war, he would replace the various naval committees. He alone had the wearisome job of figuring out what financial support Congress could expect from the states to carry on the war. In mid-1781, typically, he sent Caesar Rodney, president of Delaware, a certified copy of what was due to the United States' government both in terms of money and supplies from the previous year. Rodney was to present Congress's requisition to his legislature as he 'must be sensible of the impracticability of carrying on the war unless the states will cheerfully furnish the means'.[2] Morris would follow up with a request for information from Rodney focusing on 1781, including the amount of money in the state treasury, when taxes were to be collected, and by what process. He also needed to know when the Delaware legislature would meet to offer approval. Morris's approach was regarded as more efficient than previous committee efforts, but he still had to cope with realities of the war.

Previously, to fund the Continental Navy and Army, Congress had borrowed large sums at first at home and then from European bankers. It also extracted large sums from the states, which were forced to increase taxes. Still this was not enough. Congress began to cover bounties and buy supplies by printing paper currency, which it backed by a pledge of redemption from future tax receipts. However, the states were never able to collect enough tax receipts to retire the $191 million in Continental currency that Congress had issued by 1779, when it stopped. Lack of confidence in the value of the currency led to a steady depreciation in its purchasing power. As Maryland planter and representative to Congress, John Henry put it, 'The [printing] press is at work ... and has been for some time, and nearly a million a week is now made, and yet our demands are greater than we can answer.'[3] Typically in 1780, the state of Maryland added to depreciation by printing its own paper currency to cover the cost of the war. The result was a dramatic rise in the cost of living, which fell heaviest on the lower orders because they had least resources to cope with these economic pressures. Ultimately, state funding of the navy and army was at best sporadic.

Providing for the navies was exacerbated by the worthlessness of Continental currency. By April 1781, the value of Continental currency had reached the point that the Pennsylvania Assembly declared it could not be used to pay the debts and taxes due it, only gold, silver and its latest paper emission being acceptable. During the preceding two months, vessels had arrived from the West Indies and filled Philadelphia with discharged sailors whose wages had been paid in Continental currency. When the paper money stopped circulating on May 5, the sailors and other laboring poor 'with paper dollars in their hats ... paraded the streets ... carrying colors flying, with a DOG TARRED ... his back covered with Congress paper dollars'. They refused to work 'unless paid in hard Money'.[4] This protest destroyed the last vestige of respect for paper currencies in Philadelphia.

During these upheavals, Morris and a few others, such as Silas Deane and William Bingham, were able to build fortunes, despite privateering losses. Those who suffered financially during the war saw their mixing of public funds and private gains as corruption. Morris shored up public credit with his private wealth and created the Bank of North America through private investment, but saw its principal function as providing financial assistance to the government.[5] Both Morris and Dean would be investigated by Congress. In Commissioner Dean's case, he had been honored by Louis XVI and carried letters of commendation from Franklin and Vergennes when he returned to Philadelphia in 1778 to find that Congress charged him with financial impropriety. He would fight the charges, but by the time he returned to Paris in 1780, his investments had soured and ships with his merchandise had been captured by the British. Morris and Bingham were more fortunate.

Continental Navy Problems

Against this lack of financial resources, it should be no surprise that gradually Continental Navy ships and captains disappeared. You will remember Captain Nicholas Biddle who had commanded the *Andrea Doria* in Hopkins' ill-fated clash with the *Glasgow*. He was born into a prominent Philadelphia family in 1750 and went to sea at the age of 13, as a ship's boy aboard a merchant vessel trading to the West Indies.[6] At 20, he joined the Royal Navy and served three years until resigning in 1773 to participate in Captain Constantine Phipps' exploratory expedition toward the North Pole. After the *Andrea Doria*, on June 6, 1776, Biddle had been appointed by Congress to command 32-gun frigate *Randolph*, then being built in Philadelphia. She was launched at the end of the year and in 1778 the *Randolph* sailed from Charleston to the West Indies with four ships of the South Carolina navy: *General Moultrie, Notre Dame, Polly* and *Fair American*. They cruised quietly as far as Barbados, when they were confronted by an unknown ship which turned out to be the 64-gun *Yarmouth* under Captain Nicholas Vincent. The *Randolph* alone passed the *Yarmouth* with guns firing, when with a thunderous roar it blew up with the loss of 311 crew members, including Biddle. The South Carolina ships scattered. Four days later, the *Yarmouth* found four survivors clinging to wreckage. The explosion of the *Randolph* was the largest single loss the Continental Navy suffered during the war.

By the spring of 1779, Congress's Marine Committee regrouped and planned a long-term cruise with ships based in New England, the objective being to disrupt British shipping from the Chesapeake all the way to Charleston, South Carolina, and with a diversion toward Bermuda – that nest of Loyalist privateers. They were to contest Loyalist privateers and take merchant prizes to finance the navy. The New England warships' cruise was meant to placate Southerners in Congress, who felt that New Englanders had been too anxious to gain prizes, which they sailed to their home courts for favorable distribution of prize money.[7] This pattern had been established earlier by Esek Hopkins. To prevent a repeat of this, the Committee required the cruising ships to be at sea for as long as their supplies lasted, not returning immediately after taking a few prizes, which had become the usual New England practice.

Back from Europe, the *Ranger,* under Captain Thomas Simpson was ready to join the Marine Committee's proposed squadron. It had left France for New Hampshire in August 1778, arriving in late September. Over the winter and spring, it would again be rerigged, reballasted and refitted, including mast work, smithwork, new water casks, new spars and roping.[8] Gaps in the European crew were to be filled by a rendezvous or recruitment party. Items were appropriated for the *Ranger* from the 74-gun *America,* a ship that had been under construction at John Langdon's shipyard since May 1777 but would languish incomplete for three more years. When finally finished, Robert Morris and Congress would give the ship to the French, where it had only three years of service because of dry rot caused by the use of green timber in its construction.

The rest of the squadron consisted of the 32-gun *Warren,* Captain John Burroughs Hopkins – the son of the infamous Esek – and the 28-gun *Queen of France,* Captain John Olney. The latter, named for Marie Antoinette, was a French ship which had been purchased at Nantes for Congress.[9] Olney was placed in command, but Hopkins would dispute the choice. The fleet left Boston, arriving at Cape Henry, Virginia and hoisted British colors to lure the unwary into its clutches. It was able to take several Loyalist privateers and navy transports operating out of New York.

After only three weeks, however, the squadron returned all the way to Boston to redeem its prizes, a blatant disregard of its orders, which required a more extensive voyage in the South.[10] It also turned out that Olney and Hopkins had a lively business, acting as prize agents by buying their crews' prize money shares at much discounted prices. As a result, at their court martial Olney and Hopkins were suspended from the navy, never again holding a Continental command. Simpson survived, although he had also disobeyed orders, only because he did not buy up his crew's shares. Clearly, New England ships could not be depended upon to defend Southern waters.

The lack of Continental crews continued to delay naval action because their officers and seamen spent long periods incarcerated in British prisons or prison ships. When he reviewed the prison situation in New York in October 1780, Admiral George Rodney was quite aware of the rebels' need for experienced crews. He commented:

> The ships I stationed upon the coast have been very successful against the enemy's privateers and ships of war ... By the great number of prisoners taken [perhaps 1400,] the rebels will find it difficult to man the Continental

> ships now in the Delaware and at Boston … I am fully persuaded that if their prisoners are not released it will be to the greatest advantage of the commerce of His Majesty's loyal subjects.[11]

Rodney was ruthless in his belief that the imprisonment of seamen crippled the efforts of the Continental Navy as well as rebel privateers.

Losses

Analysis of Continental ships has concluded that by mid-1781 the navy 'was capable of little more than running errands and raiding commerce for the remainder of the war'.[12] Of the original frigates authorized in 1775, none got to sea until 1777 and eight of those rendered no service while incurring considerable expense. Four were destroyed or captured before they could put to sea. Losses in the defense of Philadelphia in 1777 included a frigate and three smaller ships. A year later, other frigates were lost before they could leave Chesapeake Bay. The next year, it was expected that the few remaining Continental ships would benefit from the arrival of d'Estaing's fleet. As we have seen, the French presence was disappointing and three more frigates were lost in the unsuccessful defense of Charleston. In 1781, two more frigates were lost off the Capes of Delaware and the newly launched sloop *Saratoga* foundered in a gale off the Bahamas with the loss of all hands.

In a final effort to sustain the Continental Navy, in July 1782, Robert Morris proposed to fund the navy by completing two ships being constructed in New England, the aforementioned *America* and 28-gun *Bourbon*, and by building six more ships in the future. Congress slashed the proposal by 90 per cent, causing Morris to offer the unfinished *America* to the French.[13] The completed *Bourbon* and another ship were sold, effectively ending the Continental Navy.

State Navies Survive

While state navies proved to be an alternative to the Continental Navy and privateering, they never had stable funding. They tended to be put together in reaction to Loyalist raids and it proved impossible to permanently maintain them. In 1777, for instance, the Pennsylvania navy suffered heavy casualties in the defense and occupation of Philadelphia, leading to Washington's recommendation that its remains be scuttled.[14]

South Carolina had the potential to create the South's most active navy. It had shipbuilding yards at Charleston and Beaufort and an abundance of live oak timbers and naval stores. In 1776, the legislature set up a board of commissioners to administer the new navy. While a few ships were built, the problem was the inability to fill crews. It was necessary to switch crews from one vessel to another in order for a ship to sail. South Carolina's slaves were a majority of the population and the legislature feared them, not allowing them to be armed to serve in its navy. White sailors were few so the state had to look elsewhere. In December 1775, Charleston's Captain Robert Cochran received permission from Congress to recruit up to 500 mariners from Massachusetts, as long as it did not interfere with existing recruiting.[15] Three months later, Cochran left Boston for Charleston with nowhere near that number.

Another source of mariners was nearby Savannah. The South Carolina navy could only sail by recruiting its crews in other states.

The Maryland navy's situation is equally instructive. Like its counterparts in Pennsylvania and Virginia, the Maryland navy decided to use its resources to focus on smaller vessels which could operate in the shallows, at first chiefly galleys, which combined a removable sail with oared propolsion.[16] Its Council of Safety originally proposed eight galleys, but when it sent a representative to investigate the Pennsylvania navy's galleys, the report was negative. We have seen their uneven response to the advance of Hamond's squadron up the Delaware River. The representative noted that the Pennsylvania galleys were too small for their heavy bow gun, which was only used at a distance from the enemy, and the galley was unseaworthy in the midst of river currents. A larger galley was recommended, which also could serve as a transport. Thus, Maryland's galleys were to be larger and more seaworthy, but as a result only four could be afforded, which were to be completed by the end of 1776.

One of these original Maryland galleys, the *Chester*, was built at the request of the Committee of Safety in Thomas Smyth's shipyard near Chestertown.[17] Among the occupations exempt from Maryland militia service were ship carpenters employed in building vessels like the *Chester*. It was rigged in lateen with three masts and was meant to carry eighty men. Its armament was to be twenty guns, but that number could not be found. Stores on the *Chester* were divided between the boatswain, gunners, carpenters and cook. As with other state ships, however, when construction was completed, it still lacked cordage, cables and anchors, and despite the Maryland Council's threats, it was delayed in sailing under Captain Thomas Coursey until June 1778. Forty-eight-year-old Coursey had the qualification of being married to Mary Wickes, a relative of the famed Lambert Wickes.

Maryland's finances could not bear the cost of even a few galleys like the *Chester*. Finally, in March 1779, it would be part of Commodore Thomas Grason's squadron sent to protect trade around the Virginia Capes. By the end of the year, however, the state had begun to sell its galleys because they were too expensive to maintain. Useful as the *Chester* had become, in March 1780 a buyer was found, ending its career.[18] Some of this parsimony was attributed to the failure of Grason's squadron to prevent Collier's invasion of the bay in May 1779. When the Maryland navy was revived in 1781, it would build barges similar to those used by Collier rather than galleys.

Virginia's galley experience was similar to that of Maryland. Its galleys had also failed to stop Collier, resulting in their being scheduled to be sold. By 1780, however, the Virginia Assembly recognized that it needed a renewed navy and it initiated a press for new crews in its best vessels. Virginia captains were authorized to take 20 per cent of the sailors on merchant vessels, excepting those of Virginia and Maryland.[19] County Courts were to apprentice at least half of the orphans in their care to the navy. However, the Assembly also reiterated that vessels not subject to this press were to be sold.

The failure of the Maryland and Virginia governments and their county lieutenants to maintain a navy meant that the Chesapeake's plantations were undefended against Loyalist incursion. In 1777, Attorney Luther Martin, living near Maryland's Princess Anne, surmised, 'There was a period of considerable duration throughout which, not only myself but many others, did not lay down one night in our beds without the hazard of waking on board a British armed ship, or in the other world.'[20] Constant raids had put fear into the hearts of the rebels and weakened their commitment to the Revolutionary cause. It was not just a matter of the Royal Navy, for even when it was not present, Loyalist privateers and watermen continued their raids. Late in the war it was warned, 'Invasion without the power of resistance, however strong the inclination, will and really has, sapped the whiggism of our common people ... They have frequently been at the mercy of a cruel enemy without any weapon to defend themselves but those which nature gave them.'[21] As these conditions became the norm, these state governments were frustrated in their attempts to defend Chesapeake Bay.

Gentlemen Organize Their Defense

The decline of the state navies caused leading private citizens to take on the defense burden by building their own vessels. Chesapeake planters decided to take their defense into their own hands. They had been involved in shipbuilding before the war, constructing six- to eight-oared barges, rowed by their liveried slaves, which carried them to church. They regarded flat-bottomed barges as the best craft for travel not only in shallows, but also in the choppy waters crossing the bay. On the Eastern Shore in 1779, planter and commissioner Colonel James Murray and three other wealthy friends wanted to invest in building a barge to be used as a privateer against Loyalists in Hooper Straits.[22] Proceeds from the sale of the prizes were to support the fatherless families of soldiers who died in the state's Continental regiments. However, they would need state support and the state did not take up this early private offer.

On March 21, 1781, twenty-six of Somerset County's leading planters proposed a scheme developed by naval Captain Zedekiah Walley to the Maryland Council.[23] Walley's plan was to build a barge with a 50-foot keel, capable of carrying sixty men and a 24-pound bow gun to protect Somerset's waters. He argued that such a vessel might be built for less than £150 and he volunteered to superintend the construction. While the state was sympathetic to the proposal, no money existed in the treasury; Somerset's gentry, therefore, went ahead on their own with the project. Built at Snow Hill, the barge was dubbed *Protector*. She was destined to sail with initial success, on one occasion driving Loyalist raiders from the Pocomoke region and capturing several prizes.

Simultaneously, reacting to the continued destruction of Maryland plantations, forty-seven wealthy Queen Annes and Talbot County gentry, with plantations along the Wye and St Michaels Rivers, decided to take defense into their own hands.[24] They paid for the recruitment and operating costs of officers and twenty men to patrol in the barge *Experiment* and also built several more barges for their protection. In May 1781, the list of subscribers included many victims of Loyalist raids. Stationed on the Eastern Shore, the barges would cruise between Kent Point and Tilghman Island.

In August, Talbot County planter and slaveholder Colonel William Webb Haddaway was the victim of Loyalist raiders. To pursue the Loyalists, he raised an armed force of 'spirited young fellows' from his 38th Maryland battalion. Following in a row boat, they were able to retake 'the hindmost' of the vessels.[25] Maryland political leader Matthew Tilghman described Haddaway's experience to the Governor Thomas Sim Lee and suggested that he 'enable these brave fellows for doing more'. Tilghman proposed to have a vessel, crewed by them, commissioned to rout the Loyalists and regain lost property. He assured the governor that if he could provide a vessel, Haddaway would raise the crew. However, the governor had no resources.

Soon planters in Dorchester County followed the example of their brethren by completing the barge *Defence*. They wished to punish the raiders, and to this end the Maryland Council commissioned Matthias Travers as captain. Still, it was one thing to construct barges but quite another to find the rope, rigging and naval stores necessary for a launching, or the time necessary to recruit and train a crew, without state support. Eventually, more barges, either captured from the enemy, constructed privately, or built for the state government, began to appear in the Chesapeake, with names like *Intrepid, Terrible* and *Fearnaught*.[26]

As a result of private gentlemen's efforts, a revived Maryland navy of barges rather than galleys was created. The arrival of the Gayton-Leslie expedition from New York, forced the Maryland Assembly to pass a series of Acts for Defense of the Bay from 1780 to 1781. It was proposed in July 1781 that four well-armed barges be built and equipped with swivels, using bounties and wages to attract twenty-five sailors for each barge.[27] These barges followed the design of Loyalist privateer barges. The government would also raise companies of marines for defense of its Chesapeake and Atlantic coasts. Thus, a revived Maryland navy would now use shallow-draft barges and marines to patrol the coastal waterways. What had not entered into their thinking was the appearance in the Chesapeake of a French fleet and how this would affect their needs.

Chapter 31

French Assistance

Until now, Sir Henry Clinton's expeditions had continued to dominate Virginia and Maryland through naval control of the Chesapeake. In mid-March 1781, Admiral Marriot Arbuthnot had prevented a French fleet from cutting off support of Benedict Arnold's Virginia army. It seemed to Clinton that the Royal Navy was capable of rescuing any British army that was in trouble in the Southern colonies. It appeared the revived state navies and Chesapeake gentlemen could not possibly change this situation.

However, events elsewhere began to unravel these assumptions. To the north in May 1781, the two army commanders, George Washington and the Comte de Rochambeau, gravitated toward a joint effort to oppose the British.[1] Rochambeau was in Newport, Rhode Island, his troops and small fleet bottled up by the Royal Navy, while Washington's army of only 4,500 was at the Hudson Highlands. For some time, Washington had contemplated attacking New York City and sought Rochambeau's cooperation for this. Rochambeau, however, felt that their forces were not adequate to attack the strongly fortified city and instead he suggested that they look to joint operations in the Chesapeake. The problem was getting there, especially as both armies had so little naval transport. It would also be necessary to have a strong French fleet in the Chesapeake to prevent the Royal Navy from reinforcing their army in Virginia.

In late May, Rochambeau wrote to Admiral Francois de Grasse in the West Indies asking him to come to the Chesapeake, bringing troops and money as well as his ships because 'none of the means within our control can be made available without your cooperation and without the naval superiority which you can bring here.'[2]

De Grasse was a career navy officer who had been serving under d'Estaing since 1779. By now almost 60, Francois Joseph Paul, Comte de Grasse was born in the seaside Alps at the outlet of the Gorges du Loup. He grew to be over 6 feet tall. Of a noble family, from his thirteenth birthday until age 41, he was a Knight of Malta, that medieval military religious order founded to defend the Holy Land, but in later centuries a bulwark against the expanding Ottoman Turks and North African pirates. France's Louis XIV had allied with the Knights in the Mediterranean, as they were experts in galley warfare. Command of an old-fashioned galley offered de Grasse the opportunity for chivalric hand-to-hand fighting to gain recognition, a great contrast to the artillery duels of fleet actions, in which the wind gauge was the determining factor. Still, de Grasse must have tired of monastic life for when he left the order it was to marry. In his new naval career he was not popular, reputedly, 'Few men are more feared and less loved in the entire [French] navy.'[3]

Putting aside his instructions from France, de Grasse agreed to leave the West Indies and come north to free the French squadron at Newport.[4] Meanwhile in July, the allied armies came together at White Plains above New York City, preparing for Washington's desired assault on Clinton's fortifications. However, the New York defenses proved formidable and thus Washington was forced to return to Rochambeau's Chesapeake suggestion. De Grasse's fleet of twenty-six ships of the line sailed in early August by way of Havana, where they were able to raise considerable cash.

The West Indies

The West Indies had continued to be a focal point of Atlantic trade. St Eustatius, a small unproductive island that flew the Dutch flag, had become the war's great trading entrepot, an open port following the Dutch belief in free trade.[5] Even before the war, ships of all nations had gathered there, refitting as they exchanged their cargos for sugar, molasses and slaves. Cut off from British manufactures, rebel ships made for St Eustatius to gain what was needed for war and trade. At first, most ships were sent to the island by Councils of Safety, especially from Maryland and Virginia, which established island agents to protect their trade. This activity was carried on despite the fact that Britain and the Dutch Republic were bound as allies by several treaties. The British ambassador protested the situation to no avail; indeed, British merchant ships were at St Eustatius, as it offered them protection from French naval patrols. Finally in December 1780, frustrated by this continuing illicit trade, Britain declared war on the Dutch Republic.

The same day as the declaration, orders were sent to Admiral Rodney and Major General Vaughan of Hudson River fame to seize St Eustatius. You will remember that after Rodney had defeated the Spanish in the Moonlight Battle and relieved Gibraltar, he went to the West Indies to command the British fleet.[6] He was at Barbados on December 6 and after embarking Vaughan's men, on February 3, 1781, he arrived and demanded St Eustatius' surrender. The island had minimal fortifications so defense was impossible. Rodney viewed the island as 'a nest of villains', so that 'they shall be scouraged'.[7] All of its inhabitants were to be held as prisoners of war, and property, whether of friend or foe, was to be confiscated for the king. The governor and the Dutch, American, Bermudian and British merchants were compelled to retire and take with them their household goods. Congress's agent Samuel Curzon and his partner Isaac Gouverneu Jr. were sent to England and confined for thirteen months. Reverberations in American ports like Philadelphia caused renewed decline in Continental currency and a search for an alternative to St Eustatius, in which Spain's Havana, with its precious coin and demand for flour, came up first. Rodney would spend three months at St Eustatius conducting a gigantic auction of its properties and putting together a fleet to carry the spoils to England, rather than following de Grasse's fleet.

Rodney had his good points. He was an aggressive admiral and a stern disciplinarian with high professional standards, who was ruthless in combating Britain's enemies. Rodney had been heartless in imprisoning Continental seamen to cripple the recruiting of their navy as well as rebel privateers. His advice to his son, on the duties of a Royal Navy captain, show his command of shipboard procedures.[8]

Rodney also had a dark side. He was cold and arrogant toward his fellow officers, making him unpopular. He was constantly in debt and bankrupt, forcing him to flagrantly misappropriate public money and abuse his powers of patronage.[9] At St Eustatius, he confiscated goods that had no military purpose. He was arbitrary with the island's 101 Jews, whose personal possessions were seized and they were banished without their families. They were imprisoned and stripped in a search for money secreted in their clothes, and their cemetery was dug up for jewelry in his frenzy for riches. Rodney's conduct at St Eustatius seemed overly vindictive, so that the opposition in Parliament demanded an inquiry.

North American Station

In August 1781, Rodney decided to return to England with a few ships for the winter as he was exhausted and needed to defend his conduct, leaving Admiral Samuel Hood with only ten ships of the line, with orders to reinforce the North American station at New York. Arbuthnot had retired and his successor was Admiral Thomas Graves. He was slow to respond to the situation because, like Clinton, he thought that Washington and Rochambeau were still about to attack New York, when in fact they were moving toward the Chesapeake by stages.[10] Hood's reinforcements arrived at Sandy Hook in late August, having scouted the Chesapeake on the way, but found no French fleet, missing the arrival of de Grasse by five days. It appeared to the British that an attack on Newport would prevent the unification of the French fleets from Newport and the West Indies. The Newport attack was delayed, however, allowing the new commander of the Newport fleet, Jacques-Melchoir Comte de Barras, to sail to meet de Grasse's fleet at the Virginia Capes, carrying crucial heavy siege guns. Leaving Sandy Hook, Graves' and Hood's combined fleet of nineteen ships sought to arrive at the Chesapeake before French ships combined in overwhelming strength.

The Virginia Capes

At the Virginia Capes, the confrontation between the French fleet and the Royal Navy would be a classic battle, following rules instilled in admirals that ships should be formed into lines, which in passing, fired broadsides into each other. Ships with enough heavy ordnance and size qualified for the maneuver and were designated 'ships of the line'.[11] This situation was meant to create order in naval battles, prevent collisions of ships on the same side, and give the advantage to the fleet with the greatest firepower. As usually both fleets suffered damage and the confrontations were often draws, it was rare for either side to claim outright victory.

De Grasse's fleet, totaling twenty-six ships of the line, entered the Chesapeake. It was in Lynnhaven Bay gathering wood and water when admirals Graves and Hood arrived at the Virginia Capes on September 5. They needed to enter the bay to rescue Cornwallis, who was entrenched at Yorktown in the mid-Chesapeake. The two fleets confronted each other and despite considerable maneuvering and firing, only one ship was lost on either side.[12] At the end, Barras' Newport fleet arrived to reinforce de Grasse and land troops and artillery at Jamestown. In the face of this strength, Graves and Hood had to return to New York to refit, leaving the French inside the Capes, in control of the entrance to the bay.

While the Royal Navy had lost control of the Chesapeake's mouth, the siege of Yorktown was never a sure thing. In September, when the Washington-Rochambeau army of 7,500 arrived at the Head of Elk military depot, in the northern Chesapeake, their secret journey was stalled because there was insufficient craft to carry them over the bay toward Yorktown.

The Maryland council responded that 'since the enemy has had possession of the bay, our number of sea vessels and craft have been so reduced by captures that we are apprehensive that what remains will not transport so considerable a detachment.'[13] A few ships came from de Grasse, but Washington had to split the allied forces between ships that could carry the artillery and fewer than 2,500 men to Annapolis, while the bulk of the armies, including the horses of the French cavalry, marched overland. The chief obstacle to the marchers was crossing the wide Susquehanna River, which they succeeded in doing, later joining the water-borne force. Despite their lack of transport, the two armies were finally on their way to Virginia.

De Grasse never actually set foot on the shore, remaining aboard his flagship, the *Ville de Paris*, poised to leave. On September 24, he was looking toward New York, fearing that a Royal Navy rescue fleet was on the way, so that as soon as the weather permitted, he would go to sea and 'remain outside the bay to prevent the enemy from entering'.[14] He would disembark the troops he brought with him, but he would not participate in the Yorktown siege or surrender of Cornwallis. De Grasse left the Chesapeake completely on November 4 to pursue more demanding Franco-Spanish interests in the West Indies. Washington made every effort to keep de Grasse's fleet in the Chesapeake, to bring about 'the total extirpation of the British force in the Carolinas and Georgia, if Comte de Grasse could have extended his cooperation two months longer'.[15] Instead, Washington would be forced to disperse his Continental and state forces as he had limited supplies to sustain them.

Back in New York, Graves and Hood were reinforced with three ships arriving from England under Admiral Robert Digby. It took time to refit their damaged vessels and to recruit for a relief fleet of twenty-five ships. The city's Chamber of Commerce offered a bounty and accepted a proposal for raising volunteer seamen and able-bodied landsmen, who were to serve only for the duration of the relief but would receive full navy health benefits, and for those on transports, navy pay above that of their existing compensation. To top it off, the new recruits were to be protected from future impresses; 240 were recruited.[16] The fleet sailed on October 19, but Cornwallis had surrendered the previous day. Hood blamed Graves because he failed to respond more rapidly. As the naval war had now shifted to the West Indies, de Grasse would be pursued there by Graves and Hood.

War Continues

Without a significant French naval presence, the war in the South would continue for another two years, a conflict which would be decided by naval action. The long-standing British blockade by warships and privateers in the Chesapeake and Delaware would reach its apex.[17] They aimed to cut American trade with the French and Spanish ports in the West Indies. At the end of 1781, the Royal Navy had four warships off the Delaware Capes, which were active until the river froze. Philadelphia shipping fared badly as at least forty merchant ships were taken.[18] By March 1782, the blockade was strengthened because navy ships were no longer required for army operations. Robert Morris informed Admiral de Grasse in May that 'It is only by a kind of Miracle that any vessel can get in or out' of the Delaware River or Chesapeake Bay. Morris himself had lost all of his personal shipping and privateer investments.[19] The effectiveness of the blockade was a major reason the states had failed to meet the financial quotas Morris had requested. Foreign trade was gone, leaving the American's only source of revenue to be unpopular taxes. The war effort was dependent on begging for loans from the French and Dutch, who became increasingly reluctant.

Congress attempted to continue the naval war by supporting privateers. Late in 1782, its pride was a privateer named for the state of South Carolina. She had originally been built as a new 40-gun French frigate *L'Indien*, whose command John Paul Jones had coveted. When completed, however, she was granted to Chevalier de Luxembourg, who leased her for three years to the state of South Carolina. She was the strongest vessel in the war to fly the Stars and Stripes and 'was commissioned by the Continental Congress to seize and take British property'.[20]

The *South Carolina* put into Philadelphia for repairs and raised a crew of 430, including many German and British deserters who were not really experienced seamen. She left Philadelphia under Captain John Joyner guarding three smaller ships: the 10-gun brig *Hope*, carrying tobacco and flour, another brig *Constance*, and the 6-gun schooner *Seagrove*. As the *South Carolina* came out of Delaware Bay, three Royal Navy ships – the 58-gun *Diomede* and 38-guns *Astrea* and *Quebec* – cornered them. Joyner tried to escape, but after six of his men were killed and wounded, he struck his colors. Only the *Seagrove* got away. Altogether, 530 crew members were taken and *South Carolina*'s short career was ended.[21] It, the *Hope* and *Constance* were sailed by prize crews to New York where the ships were condemned as prizes. The navy was not tempted to refit *South Carolina* and she was sold to be a merchantman.

Meanwhile, with de Grasse's fleet gone, the defense of the Chesapeake was left to the Maryland and Virginia navies. They faced the continued operations of Royal Navy ships, Loyalist privateers and watermen barges, frustrating their efforts to control the bay. Insurrection on the lower Chesapeake continued as late as March 1783, although Washington begged the new British commander-in-chief, Guy Carleton, to bring an end to the enduring conflict. It was a barge conflict around its islands which would ultimately decide the fate of the Chesapeake.

PART 10

FINAL CONFRONTATIONS

Chapter 32

Rodney Humiliates France

The West Indies may have been rich in sugar, coffee, molasses and rum, but it was notorious as a place for ships and sailors to avoid a prolonged stay. Officers and men alike tried to circumvent service in its warm waters and tropical shores because of the risk of fever. The Royal Navy dockyard at Antigua was fatal to crews as the surrounding marshes were infested by yellow fever mosquitos.[1] On account of its climate, a crew could not be worked as hard and the usual drinking had to be strictly limited because of heat exhaustion. Unless a ship were copper-bottomed, the teredo worm played havoc with its wooden sheathing and weeds accumulated, cutting down the speed of a ship. The hurricane season, lasting from the end of July to the beginning of November, forced fleets to escape from the Indies altogether, heading for North America or Europe.

In 1782, France's Caribbean strategy aimed to take the weakly defended English islands one at a time, avoiding a fleet confrontation with the Royal Navy.[2] While the French were dedicated to this, it remained difficult to avoid a single fleet action that could seal the fate

The West Indies.

of the Indies. The British island garrisons were certainly weak because they had been established to protect their planters from slave or indigenous Carib uprisings, rather than a naval war. The Royal Navy divided the islands into two areas of operation: the Lesser Antilles, with its dockyard at English Harbor, Antigua, and 1,000 miles to the west, Jamaica, with its dockyard at Port Royal. It soon became clear to the Admiralty that it could not afford to maintain a fleet for each area and therefore it was decided to base its fleet at English Harbor and hope that Jamaica could fend for itself, clearly a risky business after Spain entered the war. Thus Franco-Spanish strategy came to focus on adding vulnerable Jamaica to its conquests.

By the end of 1781, de Grasse, Barras, Hood and Graves were commanding their ships in the Caribbean. Coming from the Chesapeake, Hood had arrived at Barbados in early December 1781. He learned that the Marquis de Bouille, Governor of Martinique, had captured St Eustatius from its English garrison, restoring the island to the Dutch. With Rodney in England, Hood took acting command of the Leeward Islands Station. He made up for his difficulties at the Chesapeake by using his smaller fleet to shadow and find de Grasse in late January at British St Kits. Hood lured de Grasse from his anchorage and inserted his fleet between de Grasse and the island, in a strong line that the French were unable to break. However, the situation was altered when the besieged British garrison surrendered to the French army on February 18. Hood was able to stealthily abandon his defensive position at night, leaving decoy lights burning.[3]

De Grasse and the Spanish authorities began to plan for the attack on Jamaica.[4] His ships were to rendezvous at St Domingo with Spanish ships, which would carry an army to invade Jamaica. Spanish concerns now dominated his thinking.

With the focus now on the Caribbean, a race developed between Britain and France to reinforce their navies, the British Cabinet aiming to prevent the allies from coming together to threaten Jamaica.[5] De Grasse had come with twenty-three ships and a further five ships had joined him from Barras' squadron. French reinforcements from Europe were ultimately limited to only four ships because the Royal Navy and contrary weather in the Bay of Biscay drove reinforcements back to France. Meanwhile, Hood's fourteen ships were lent five more by Digby in New York and he picked up more in the West Indies. To this, the Cabinet added Rodney's seventeen ships, which left Portsmouth and Plymouth and joined Hood on February 25. When the two fleets were gathered in the West Indies, for the first time the Royal Navy enjoyed a slight superiority in ships of the line over de Grasse, thirty-seven to thirty-three. With his combined fleet, Rodney took up a position at St Lucia to watch de Grasse.

Rodney's Crucial Subordinates

Rodney had three outstanding subordinates serving under him who would ensure that his fleet was ready for battle. The first was obviously Samuel Hood. He was born in 1724 at Burleigh, Somerset, the son of a humble clergyman who was not anxious to have his son enter the navy, so Samuel was 17 when he went to sea as a midshipman, serving on the ship his younger brother Alexander was already on.[6] Two years later, he was in the Channel, aboard a ship under Captain George Rodney, the first meeting of the future admirals. When the Revolutionary War commenced, he was 52 and based at Portsmouth from where he successfully conducted the blockade against American privateers and Continental ships heading for North America. Still at Portsmouth when France entered the war, he gained the favor of George III and was elevated to flag rank in 1780.

Hood had avoided the political fallout swirling around the outcome of the Battle of Ushant, and after reconsideration accepted the command of a squadron sent by Sandwich to the Leeward Islands to supplement's Rodney's fleet. With eight sail of the line he joined Rodney at the beginning of 1781.[7] Rodney ordered him to patrol between Montserrat and Nevis so that he could invade St Eustatius, thus Hood was not directly involved in its capture, although he would criticize Rodney's handling of the island's riches. Rodney sent him to blockade Martinique, but Hood felt it to be unwise if a French fleet was coming, a prediction which became reality when de Grasse arrived in late April. He escorted a convoy successfully into Martinique because Hood's fleet was stranded to leeward of the island. Four of Hood's van ships were damaged and he rejoined Rodney at Antigua. As noted, when Rodney went to England, Hood was sent to New York and then the Chesapeake. While Hood was critical of Rodney as a commander, ultimately he did his duty, and no obvious animosity existed between the two admirals.

Another of Rodney's subordinates was Charles Douglas, Rodney's captain of the fleet, a position which gave him the authority of a Rear Admiral. Earlier he commanded the relief of Quebec and supported the building of the squadron that still dominated Lake Champlain. Douglas had become an advocate for the improvement of firepower in Royal Navy ships.[8] As commander of the 98-gun *Duke,* he had ordered the ship's guns be fitted with flintlocks and when the Admiralty refused, he funded the improvement from his own pocket. He also advocated better gun carriages and revived drilling by gun crews to give the ships an edge in fleet actions. He introduced perforated goose quills to be prefilled with powder, which were safer and tidier than tin priming pans. In mid-1779, he requested that carronades be added to the *Duke*'s poop deck. These short, smashing guns were destructive at close range to a ship and its crew. Douglas would apply these measures to Rodney's flagship, *Formidable*, and to the *Arrogant*. In confrontations with the French, these improvements would cause heavy losses to their crews.

The third subordinate was Rodney's personal physician Gilbert Blane. From a respectable middling family, he had studied medicine at Edinburgh University and graduated from Glasgow Medical School. Rodney was concerned about the health of his crews and he hoped Blane's diagnosis would sustain them in the unhealthy West Indies. Rodney made him 'physician to his fleet' before it crossed the Atlantic.[9] While Blane approached the task comprehensively, his most lasting contribution was to resurrect the use of lemons and oranges to prevent scurvy. Surgeons had remarked since the seventeenth century that lemon juice was an effective treatment for scurvy, but in the 1700s it had lost favor among the medical establishment and thus the Admiralty. This was not because lemons were ineffective, but rather they were too expensive for the Admiralty to consider on a fleet-wide basis. Yet in mid-winter at Halifax, the *Roebuck* took on oranges and lemons. Still, the medical establishment sought substitute antiscorbutics like portable soup, sauerkraut, and malt of wort, none of which contained much of the necessary Vitamin C to treat scurvy. They were, however, cheap enough for the Admiralty to afford and adopt.

Before sailing, Blane had studied the work of another Scotsman, ship's surgeon James Lind, who in 1747 experimented with several cures for scorbutic sailors, in which lemons and oranges won easily, cider coming in a distant second.[10] Realizing that the expense of the citrus fruit was prohibitive, Lind was able to produce a mixture of the citrus fruits called 'rob', which could be stored in bottles or vials, which lasted for a long time. However, rob remained expensive and its amount of Vitamin C deteriorated rapidly the longer it was kept. Still, Blane found Lind's work useful and he recommended citrus juice among other remedies to treat and prevent scurvy in a pamphlet distributed to the fleet's surgeons. He also asked that fleets' surgeons collect statistics on illness and deaths and report them to him on a monthly basis. Back in England, he presented his findings to the Admiralty stating that a supply of lemons, oranges and fresh vegetables should be on every ship and offered daily to build up immunity to scurvy. The Admiralty still clung its belief in the cheaper wort of malt, which Blane had found worthless and stopped using. To his credit, Rodney ignored the Admiralty and supported Blane's innovations within his fleet. Rodney's seamen would be in a robust state of the health, giving him another advantage over the French fleet.

Fleets Collide

From St Lucia, Rodney began to chase de Grasse, missing a French convoy with reinforcements and provisions. Rodney continued his pursuit in April and Hood's advanced squadron, actually overtook de Grasse, who united his ships and began an artillery duel, but kept his distance because he wished to avoid the British carronades.[11] By the time the rest of Rodney's fleet caught up with exposed Hood, de Grasse had withdrawn, missing an opportunity to destroy Hood. Based at Dominica three days later, de Grasse continued to avoid Rodney's fleet, as his fleet moved north, close to the Saints island chain. After maneuvers with little wind, three of de Grasse's ships collided or suffered damage and were left for repair, reducing his fleet to thirty. Rodney continued to pursue him with thirty-seven ships.

In what followed, de Grasse would stick to the established rules of naval warfare, which he had demonstrated at the Virginia Capes. It was left to Rodney and his subordinates to put them aside. On April 12, the two fleets closed on each other and passed on opposite tacks, but a shift in the wind caused confusion in both lines. Royal Navy ships found three openings in the French line and brazenly went through. This broke with tradition, but it has been debated as to whether it was intentional or a result of sailing conditions. It led to the French line being broken and the portion with de Grasse's flagship and its supporting ships being ravaged by superior firepower, although the dispersal of the line also allowed the bulk of the French fleet to escape.[12] At end of the day, de Grasse and five French ships, including the 100-gun flagship *Ville de Paris*, were Rodney's prisoners. The planned allied attack on Jamaica would be abandoned and de Grasse was taken to England as a prisoner.

As might be expected, Douglas felt that his artillery improvements had been the deciding factor in the battle:

> ships as have their guns fitted accordingly, derived unspeakable advantage from improvements lately made in the use of naval artillery, their fire having been so very quick and so very well directed, and extending so far to the right and left, that the French cannot comprehend how they came to lose so many men, and we so few, on the late bloody day.[13]

Afterwards, Douglas and Hood would criticize Rodney for not pursuing the remains of the French fleet. Still, the British ships were heavily damaged and after five days at Jamaica, Rodney allowed Hood to pursue and he took the *Jason* and *Caton*, ships of the line, as well as a frigate and corvette in the Mona Passage, between Hispaniola and Puerto Rico.[14] Despite their losses, the French were soon able to bring together twenty-six ships and continue individual ship confrontations until the end of the year.

The voyage to Britain by the captured French ships, including the *Ville de Paris,* would be ill-fated. Early in August, a convoy and escort left Jamaica under Admiral Thomas Graves destined for England with the French prizes.[15] Hit by a gale in the vicinity of Halifax, the *Caton* sprang a leak and had to be towed to Halifax. Later in a hurricane, The *Ville de Paris* and *Glorieux* sank off the coast of Europe as did one of Graves' escorts and his flagship, *Ramilles*, was badly damaged.

In Britain, a new government headed by the Marquis of Rockingham had replaced the North ministry and the new First Lord, Augustus Keppel, had dismissed Rodney while he was in the West Indies.[16] A ship was sent out with the dismissal, but when word of Rodney's victory arrived, the British public was so congratulatory that the new ministry was forced to offer Rodney insincere praise. Rockingham's brief ministry ended when he died of influenza on July 1, 1782.

In July, Rodney was replaced by Hugh Pigot and he returned to Britain, where he was feted with honors. The British delight with Rodney continued a movement that had begun in reaction to the French alliance in 1778.[17] It emphasized the idea that arbitrary and Catholic France was the enemy of Whig and Protestant Britain. Rodney was voted a £2,000 pension from the Commons and created a peer, Baron Rodney of Stoke-Rodney. In Bristol, he had a dinner at the Merchant's Hall, followed by a ball, while in Winchester, the militia fired a *feu-de-joie* and then the populace took the horses from his carriage and drew it up the High Street to the Guildhall, where he received the freedom of the city. In Newcastle, bell ringing, bonfires and illuminations demonstrated their joy in the victory. Not to be outdone by the provinces, in London, after numerous toasts at the London Tavern, Rodney's 'horses were forcibly taken up, and the coach drawn by the mob to Hertford Street'.[18] Renowned Thomas Gainsborough would complete a portrait of Rodney, with the naval ensign of the *Ville de Paris* at his side. In these events, a popular sense of Britishness brought Britons together, not just in England, but from throughout the Atlantic world, including white and black Loyalists in America. Britain's position seemed far brighter after the Battle of the Saints and the Defense of Gibraltar than it had been before.

In France, Rodney's victory was seen as a restoration of the Royal Navy's superiority at sea. A series of courts martial sought to discredit those French officers who had supposedly been responsible for the defeat at the Saints. This bolstered the British position as preliminary peace terms were being discussed in Paris with the French, Spanish and Americans. Lord Shelburne, who was keen to revive peace negotiations with France, released de Grasse, sending him to France where he arrived in Paris with an understanding of Shelburne's priorities in negotiating with France and Spain.[19] De Grasse's opinions were sought by Vergennes as he still hoped for another Franco-Spanish expedition against Jamaica. Neither Shelburne nor Vergennes trusted each other and negotiations continued until Shelburne was ousted as chief minister in mid-February 1783 over his unpopular preliminaries.

Chapter 33

Maryland and Virginia Humiliated

After de Grasse left the Chesapeake, its naval defense reverted once more to the Maryland and Virginia navies. The continued war would not go well for the Chesapeake planters who supported the state navies. Seven months after the Battle of the Saints, another naval confrontation would take place which would justify the confidence British officers and ministers had put in the commitment of Loyalists.

Before the war, many landless and poor Chesapeake farmers could not make a living from the traditional agricultural staples of tobacco and wheat. They became refugees by gravitating to the coastal marshes, then to the adjacent islands and finally to islands distant from the mainland. Here their only need was a canoe to allow them to navigate the water. The abundance of shellfish, fish and wild fowl, along with a patch of corn, sustained them and their families. Most of these islands and marshland farmers failed to develop plantation agriculture and thus they were outside of the great planter's economy and influence. Instead, these marginal lands would become the home of an independent breed of watermen who would contribute to the Loyalist insurrection that had been going on. The most famous of them was Joseph Whaland Jr.

Whaland's Return

Early in the war, as a Loyalist, Whaland had been taken from the Chesapeake's Eastern Shore and imprisoned in Frederick and Baltimore, Maryland. He finally returned to the Eastern Shore in mid-1780, when his galley was once more recognized on the Chesapeake. He was elated by the appearance of Leslie and Gayton in October 1780. He had been discharged on a bond, in which his bondsmen, Samuel Covington and Thomas Holbrook, acknowledged themselves to be indebted to the State of Maryland for £5–10,000 each, if Whaland failed to appear before Governor Thomas Sim Lee and his Council 'to answer a charge of high treason'.[1] His bond was presumably forfeited.

Before his confinement, the Eastern Shore's Smith Island had been Whaland's earliest center of operations, from where in 1776 he had cooperated with Virginia's Governor Dunmore. The 'tall, slim, gallows looking' waterman had used the island as a base from which to recruit ships to join Dunmore.[2] In league with Smith Island's inhabitants, Whaland was able to bring in prizes, distribute their cargos on the island, refit ships and form crews from the mixed population. In late June, working with Dunmore's tenders, he participated in a Hopkins Island raid, taking sixty head of cattle, two young men, and 'everything else that was valuable'. Later, the Accomack County Committee described Whaland as one who 'was then bound to the Kings fleet with 20 or 30 people of his own stamp'.

While Whaland joined the Dunmore–Hamond fleet, he did not stay for long. Smallpox was raging in the ships and he and some of his crew caught it. By chance at Hooper Straits in July 1776, thirty Dorchester militia under Major Daniel Fallin found him among his Smith Island crew recuperating from smallpox. The rebels were able to easily take his schooner.[3] Brought before the Dorchester County Committee of Observation, his previous activities were revealed. For these offenses the Committee sent Whaland across the bay for safe-keeping to the distant Frederick County jail.

Now out of confinement, Whaland was seen in a pilot boat near Popular Island, Maryland.[4] From Holland and Tangier Islands a majority of his crews were blacks or mulattoes, probably runaway slaves. They had mariner backgrounds, were refugees on the islands and had become watermen. They had continued operating while Whaland was imprisoned.

Upon his return, Whaland superficially appeared willing to put aside his Loyalism. In December 1780, he met with Somerset County Lieutenant George Dashiell and sought to explain away his former treasonous actions.[5] His involvement in attacking rebel shipping, he claimed, was actually forced as he had been a captive in irons, locked up below decks during the actual raiding. Now he wanted to come up the Wicomico River with his family, removing them from possible Loyalist raiders. To prove his newfound change of heart, he told Dashiell he would contribute to the expense of building a barge to be used against Loyalists. Dashiell was completely taken in by his story and sent a letter to Governor Lee expressing his belief in Whaland's sincerity.

Immediately afterward, however, Dashiell received an express letter from Colonel Henry Hooper of Dorchester, requesting that he arrest Whaland, enclosing an affidavit from Captain Valentine Peyton of Stafford County, Virginia.[6] Peyton had been captured by Whaland in August off Poplar Island. Whaland had returned to his former activities without batting an eyelid, in command of a pilot barge fitted with a jib and a crew of veteran Loyalists. Soon, Captain Oakley Haddaway's vessel was also taken, as was one belonging to William Barnes. Seeking revenge, Haddaway would become a first lieutenant on Robert Dashiell's barge *Terrible,* and Barnes would have the same rank on Levin Spedden's *Revenge,* Maryland navy vessels.

By February 1781, Whaland was in command of four barges that raided Benedict on the Patuxent River, Virginia. As Whaland reappeared, from Cambridge in Dorchester, Captain John Smoot wrote that rebel transports had been seized with supplies destined for the Continental army and sent to the British. His own tobacco-loaded vessels had been taken, so in retaliation he wanted the raiders hanged and their homes burned.[7] Soon after, a letter sent from Salisbury to Governor Lee reported:

> From every appearance we are in much worse situation than we have been in this war. A great majority of our people seem determined to give over [to the British] ... It is with great difficulty we can keep a guard of thirty men together and many have refused expressly to march against the enemy. I am sorry to inform that very few people will take a shilling of the new [state paper] money.[8]

In March, petitioners sent a request to the state council to defend 'those who live contiguous to navigation' in Somerset County.[9] George Dashiell's brother, Joseph, at first unaware of Whaland's release, was more than a little upset over his reappearance. Dashiell complained to Governor Lee that Whaland should not have been released:

> Joseph [Whaland] that old offender was down in Somerset plundering again and we have reason to believe that the Gaoler in Baltimore is alone to blame … If this practice is followed no one will venture to take any of them up and send them forward as they will be there to suffer for it. If I had directions to go into Somerset, I think I could apprehend him, as he has lately robed a certain Thomas Reuker who I think would assist me to trap him.[10]

Whaland's Lieutenants

In the Chesapeake's narrow waters, the barge had replaced the galley because while slower, its flat bottom provided more stability for heavy caliber artillery. Whaland had worked with the Royal Navy's armed barges, tenders and Loyalist privateers, learning secret signals of recognition: three successive hoistings and lowerings of the mainsail, and then an English jack raised at the masthead. In June, his barge *Resolution* and four others invaded the Shore's Wicomico and Pocomoke Rivers.[11] While he commanded the *Resolution*, the other barges were under his trusted lieutenants: Shadrack Horsman, Jonathan Robinson, and the brothers Michael and William Timmons Jr. of Hooper's Straits. Up the Wicomico they plundered widow Elsey and Captain Elijah Evans at the lower ferry in Worcester and then gathered at Courtney Island.

By mid-July 1781, wealthy Somerset militia Captain Henry Gale – a descendant of George Gale of Whitehaven – was hauled from his bed in his Whitehaven, Maryland home by Whaland's protégé, Captain John McMullen. He was commander of the barge *Restoration*, leading a band of four white and nine black watermen. Gale's house was ransacked and he was hauled off to Sandy Island at the mouth of the Nanticoke River, where he was accused of having participated in the court martial that had sentenced Loyalist Marmaduke Mister to death. They tied Gale to a post 'where he was most inhumanly whipt six lashes' and then hung by a rope around his neck from a tree, until they believed him dead.[12] Soon after, he was cut down and revived by Loyalist John Timmons. McMullen attempted to persuade his crew to hang their victim again, but they refused. McMullen proposed drowning Gale, but again they refused. Later, Gale wrote a letter to Governor Lee asking for a reprieve of Timmons for his brave act of mercy.

After Whaland's return, the Timmons brothers of Hooper's Strait – John, Michael and William – served as officers of his crew.[13] William commanded a barge. William and Michael were with him in the 1781 raid of the Wicomico River, and when Whaland left Chesapeake Bay in a British squadron, Michael accompanied him to North Carolina. Whaland, John McMullen and Jonathan Robinson frequently acted in concert, occasionally gathering at Courtney's Island before setting out upon a cruise. They often employed black slaves as crewmen, whom they freed during their attacks. McMullen would be captured in July 1781 by Commodore Grason's fleet.

While Yorktown was besieged by the allies, Whaland's *Rover* and a smaller galley captained by a 'mulatoo, named George, six feet high' captured Captain John Greenwood's schooner, placed a prize crew on it commanded by George, and made Greenwood and his crew prisoners.[14] The *Rover* then removed a cargo Greenwood had left at Gwynn's warehouse, including a hogshead of rum. Enraged Greenwood described watermen as:

> A set of gallows-marked rascals, fit for nothing but thieves; hellbounds and plunderers from inoffensive, unarmed people, they seemed to be without any kind of principle and I really believe that ten honest, religious, determined men could intimidate or drive a hundred such villains.[15]

Despite Greenwood's views, many in Whaland's crews came from respectable local middling families, although the war forced them to become refugees and earn a living as watermen. Whaland himself had lived on Garden Island, Straights Hundred, Dorchester.[16] He held 500 acres, a lot in Norfolk, an interest in several vessels and was a recognized pilot. His father, Joseph Sr., was a Dorchester planter, and his brother, Thomas, jointly owned a schooner with him. In 1777, Joseph Sr. and Thomas turned the tables on Major Daniel Fallin by protesting the seizure a year earlier of their vessel by his militia, appealing in writing to the Committee of Safety for the return of their vessel. Fallin had claimed the boat belonged to Joseph Jr., who had been detained because it was allegedly in the service of the enemy. On the contrary, Joseph Sr. claimed it was not his son's vessel, who at the time was respectably employed as a mariner on the Potomac River by William Geahagan, a Somerset merchant. This was an untruth; in reality, Whaland was trading with Governor Dunmore at Gwynn's Island, but it showed how the family protected its own.

Watermen at Tangier Island

Tangier Island off Pocomoke Sound had been patented in the early eighteenth century by Virginia planter families, but no evidence of settlement exists and it is assumed it was used to graze cattle.[17] Thus Tangier was not settled until the Revolution, populated chiefly by white and black Loyalist refugees, most of them watermen. Its combination of difficult access and yet a strategic location at the mouths of several Eastern Shore rivers, not far from the Norfolk–Portsmouth area, made it an ideal location for these refugees.

Early in 1781, Joseph Dashiell was distraught over the nest of Loyalists found on Tangier Sound. Citing the recent robbery of Planner Williams, by a band of nine island watermen, whom he suspected operated 'under the color of belonging to the British cruisers',[18] Dashiell offered help to Governor Lee 'that whenever your excellency & council propose to remove the people and stock of the islands [of Tangier Sound] I should be glad to assist with all my heart as I consider them at this time the most dangerous enemy we have to watch the motions of ...'

A year later, the British flag still flew over Tangier Island. In reaction, the state governments aimed 'to depopulate the Tangier Islands'. In April, the Maryland Council ordered Commodore Thomas Grason to remove the inhabitants, including the old men, women and children.[19] Here was a threat that would motivate the islanders to defend themselves.

Thomas Grason's fate

Thomas Grason was a worthy opponent for Whaland. In March 1779, with a squadron of Maryland galleys and tenders, he had first cruised off Cape Charles to protect rebel ships. Three months later, in the same waters, with the sloop *Hannah* and the galleys *Conqueror* and *Chester*, he opposed a mysterious British ship, but it easily outdistanced his squadron.[20] After this encounter, the fleet was not sent out again, for the state was beginning to dispose of its navy.

A native of Talbot County, Grason had inherited the plantation, Grason's Discovery, from his father Richard. He was also an experienced sailor. In 1761, at the age of 27, he had served in a Royal Navy frigate off the coast of France.[21] By 1773, he was master of HMS *Somerset* and he deeded his Talbot land to his brother Richard, a sign of his inability to pay attention to it. However, five years later we find him commodore of the Maryland navy in command of the *Dolphin.*

By July 1781, the Maryland navy was revived and Grason again cruised, commanding the *Revenge*, supported by captains Robert Dashiell's and Levin Spedden's ships, a bateau and two smaller vessels. They took the Loyalist barge *Restoration* and two tenders, while a second barge and bateau escaped. 'The event has given general joy,' wrote planter Matthew Tilghman, 'And if we cannot flatter ourselves with peace, we begin to think we have a chance of remaining safe from the plunderers that have late infested us.'[22] The captured Loyalist vessels were displayed at Haddaway's Ferry to demonstrate that the bay could be secure. Tilghman boasted the rebel barges would attack any vessel, except a British fleet. Months later, Grason commanded several vessels transporting part of Washington's army from the Head of Elk to Virginia, and provided provisions for the army besieging Yorktown.

In April 1782, Grason was ordered to the Miles River in Talbot County to supervise the outfitting of four barges, enlist seamen and marines and, as noted, expel the inhabitants of Tangier Islands.[23] He commanded the *Revenge,* and with him were the *Intrepid, Terrible* and tender *Planter*. Grason's squadron was a family affair as son George was his second lieutenant on the *Revenge*, while the tender *Nancy* was commanded by Thomas Grason Jr., and Richard Grason served as second lieutenant on the *Terrible*.

On May 10, when Grason approached Janes Island with his flagship barge the *Revenge* and three other vessels, he was confronted by three to five Loyalist barges. In the battle that followed, the *Revenge* was taken and Robert Dashiell's barge *Terrible* was blown up. In the words of James Bryant, a seaman on the *Terrible,* 'most parts of the crew was lost'.[24] Grason and several of his men were killed, ending his naval career at age of 49. The Loyalist barges took the survivors prisoner, including his son George. Whaland had returned from imprisonment in North Carolina, but it is not evident that he was involved in this action. Grason's defeat showed that the islanders did not take threats to their existence lightly.

Raids by Loyalist watermen were now unopposed and even rebel privateers feared them. In July, two Loyalist barges under John Anderson attacked the Massachusetts privateer *Ranger* off St George's Island. After three hours of fighting, the ships disengaged to care for their wounded. Three days later, Loyalist barges seized the privateer schooner *Greyhound* in Hooper Straits, a 'boat laden with Salt, Peas, Pork, Bacon and some Dry Goods'.[25] The captain and his crew were detained for twenty-four hours aboard Whaland's barge, during which time a passenger, Mr Furnival, claimed he was robbed of his money and watch. The captain and his crew were set ashore at the Loyalist enclave of Dames Quarter. Before he was released, Furnival later reported that he 'saw several other Bay craft fall into the Fangs of the same Vultures'. On Smith Island, Loyalist watermen attacked George Pruitt's house and burnt it to the ground, so that he was financially ruined; it was said he took to drinking for the rest of his life.

Whaland's Greatest Victory

Against this background, the Chesapeake's last great naval confrontation came in late November 1782, more than a year after Cornwallis' surrender at Yorktown. The battle involved armed barges, in which five from the Maryland navy, plus a tender from the Virginia navy, sought to take on six Loyalist barges in the straits north of Tangier Island.[26]

Commodore Zedekiah Walley, a native of Worcester County and merchant captain trading in the British Isles before the war, now commanded the Maryland squadron of five sail- and oar-driven barges. He was given full authority to command, so long as 'your operations are not to be extended beyond the Capes of this Bay'.[27] The Assembly had diverted funds from the recruitment of its Continental army quota, in order to build four barges for defense of the bay. As noted, the largest and most heavily armed of these ships, Walley's *Protector*, was constructed under his direction at Snow Hill. It needed a crew of sixty to service the 24- and 18-pound guns, and required a captain in charge of its marine company. The barge had been financed and built by Somerset County gentlemen and donated to the Maryland navy. Robert Dashiell, a cousin of George and Joseph, represented the family in Walley's squadron, commanding the new barge, *Terrible*.

Walley had been Grason's second in command, and Maryland's Governor Thomas Johnson ordered him to take up where Grason had left off and destroy the bay's watermen Loyalists. His foray began auspiciously, as he was able to chase Loyalist barges from Gwynn's Island southward toward Cape Charles.[28] In mid-November near Smith Island, his fleet caught the slowest Loyalist privateer *Jolly Tar*, commanded by Captain Daniel Brooks of Somerset. In the crew were five blacks and several leading Loyalists, Jacob Extine, Samuel Outten and Peter Franks, a Portuguese, known for his raiding exploits. Outten had previously served as captain of the privateer barge *Trimmer*. After his capture, he was paroled and restricted to Annapolis by the Maryland Council. He was allowed, however, to return home, visiting friends and passing through the site of his exploits on his way to see them.

Finding the Loyalist navy too strong for his lightly manned barges, Walley took his squadron, including the *Jolly Tar*, into Virginia's Onancock Creek to get reinforcements. At the port of Onancock, he found a barge and asked Onancock citizens to fit and man it. On November 28, Colonel John Cropper received a letter from Walley explaining his proposed attack on Whaland's barges, then in the bay off Onancock Creek, and asking for volunteers from Accomack to serve in his fleet as marines.[29] Cropper gathered twenty-five to fifty local men, who went on the Onancock barge, although it turned out to be unseaworthy and was forced to return. Most were then transferred to the Virginia tender *Flying Fish*, but Cropper and nine 'gentlemen' boarded Walley's flagship, *Protector*. All told, Walley's squadron now consisted of four barges, a galley and the captured sloop *Jolly Tar*, now renamed *Languedoc*.

Joseph Whaland Jr. had established a rendezvous for his barges at Hog Island in the Hooper Straits, a place where their plunder could be disposed of. His squadron consisted of five barge-rigged vessels, one of which was a galley. His flagship was the *Kidnapper.* His known captains were Fling of the *Victory*, Young of the *Ranger,* William Perrey of the *Peryorge* and Nathan Adams of the *Ladies Revenge.*[30] From there he moved north by Tangier Island and then into Tangier Sound and finally westward under easy sail to Kedges Straits, where to the north the water divides Smith Island from South Marsh Island.

The Battle

Walley's squadron anchored off Janes Island, the site of Grason's defeat only seven months earlier, and then followed Whaland. On the morning of November 30, Walley pushed the *Protector* to the head of Kedges Straits, so that it soon outdistanced the rest of his squadron. Whaland spied the *Protector* and he directed his entire squadron to drop their sails and row in a line toward the *Protector*. When they were within 200 yards, Whaland's squadron opened with a unified cannonade.[31] The *Protector* was now joined by the *Defence* and the *Fearnaught,* but the latter at the first salvo shattered its bow gun and thereafter had only swivels. As the firing continued, one of the *Protector*'s gunners broke a cartridge, spilling powder on the deck and in the succeeding cannon shots a flashback occurred, igniting the powder and stacked ammunition chests. These exploded, burning three or four crew members to death, the rest, including the gentlemen, being forced to leap overboard. This was followed by a second explosion of ammunition chests, encouraging the Loyalist barges to advance.

Captain Whaland, in the *Kidnapper* with two other Loyalist barges, surrounded the *Protector*, while the other Loyalist barges continued to fire. According to Cropper, 'There was one continual shower of musket balls, boarding pikes, cutlasses, cold shot and iron stantials for eight or ten minutes, till greatly overpowered by numbers, and having all the officers killed and wounded, we struck to them.'[32] Captain Levin Handy, of a wealthy plantation family, commanded the marines aboard the flagship, and believed the casualties so devastating that he attempted to strike its flag, but Walley prevented him. Subordinate Captain Joseph Handy fought on, despite losing an arm, from which injury he died. Cropper had at least four wounds on his body and was rescued by two Loyalists: an Irishman and a former slave of his father's. Walley was killed and twenty-five crew members were killed or drowned, while twenty-nine were wounded, only eleven being able to save themselves by leaping in the water. Whaland's vessel had eight killed and eight wounded out of a crew of forty-three blacks and whites. In a bloody ten minutes the *Protector* belonged to Whaland.

Meanwhile, the other four Maryland barges, including the *Defence* and *Fearnaught,* and the Virginia tender, after maneuvering with their oars, turned tail and ran as the *Protector* was seen to be on fire. In fact, the rebel fleet had never formed a unified line of battle. Some would be pursued by Loyalist barges for nearly 30 miles, as they attempted to hide in the Annemessex or the mouth of the Choptank River, and all ultimately escaped. The flight of most of the Maryland barges led Governor William Paca to initiate an inquiry into the conduct of the other four captains. Cropper blamed the defeat on the 'dastardly conduct of our comrades'.[33] He, Levin Handy and George Dashiell were highly critical of the conduct of Walley's subordinates. After investigation, captains Levin Spedden of the *Fearnaught* and

Solomon Frazier of the *Defence* were absolved and reinstated in the Maryland navy. Captains Robert Dashiell, of the *Terrible*, and Botfield were charged with 'highly unbecoming and improper conduct', and suspended. Botfield got off, but for his conduct, Robert Dashiell was cashiered from the Maryland navy, a blot on the family's reputation. Dashiell was clearly a better shipbuilder than a naval officer. The bloody battle had left wounds in the prestige of the Eastern Shore's leading families.

Whaland dictated terms to Cropper and he agreed to take the Loyalist wounded to Onancock to have them attended at the public expense, upon condition that Whaland would parole all of his prisoners, both unhurt and wounded.[34] The agreement required approval by the Virginia governor in Council and the Assembly. The *Kidnapper* took the wounded of both sides to Onancock, where they were treated. Whaland's barges also took forty prisoners and he insisted that the crew of the captured *Jolly Tar* be released to Hog Island. By December 3, Cropper was back in Onancock to recover, although he was not free until almost two months later when he was exchanged for Samuel Outten of the *Jolly Tar's* crew. It took longer for others to be exchanged. Cropper's honoring of this agreement would cause him financial difficulty.

George Corbin, the Accomack County Lieutenant, arranged the funeral of Walley in Onancock. His body was carried around the square and through the streets by a procession of Accomack County militiamen. He was buried on December 3, 1782, probably in the Corbin family cemetery by Scott Hall, although this burial place may not have been established until later.[35] The Maryland and Virginia navies were defeated, a victim of Loyalist barges in the bloodiest confrontation on the Chesapeake's Eastern Shore, a situation that continued to inspire Loyalism.

Aftermath

In early December, the defense of the bay was now limited to militia. According to Maryland Governor William Paca, the enemy now had thirteen barges, one sloop and two schooners in the bay. Worcester's Colonel Henry Dennis observed that the Loyalists had created a situation that was 'truly distressing, for the enemy are now able to continue their depredations in any part of [Worcester or Somerset Counties], and ... there is neither arms nor ammunition were the militia disposed to make use of them ...'[36]

Paca's first hope for assistance was the three ships of the French squadron commanded by Jacques-Aime, Le Saige de la Villesbrunne, left by de Grasse, but they were no longer present. In February 1783, Paca wrote Washington desperately hoping that preliminary peace negotiations would put an immediate end to the watermen's activities, but the response was not encouraging.[37] On March 24, Congress directed Robert Morris to revoke the commissions of all American armed vessels and authorized an approach to Carleton and Digby in New York to cease hostilities. However, they had no instructions from London and refused to respond so that their ships continued to operate at war. Anyone who thinks the war in the Chesapeake ended with the siege of Yorktown should note the situation faced by Paca and Washington in 1783.

Paca was left to refit his remaining barges, but during the winter, crews refused to re-enlist or volunteer. He was promised a 14-gun brig from the French, the *Pole Cat*, which was to be sent to the Eastern Shore, but no money existed in the treasury to outfit it. He was forced to appeal, as had been done in the past, to Baltimore merchants to raise ships, claiming 'there is no force belonging to the government able to oppose [the watermen]. Were our barges completely armed and fitted, they would be quite insufficient to the purpose ...'[38] However, the merchants replied with conditions that he could not meet.

Without the *Pole Cat*, Paca was able to put together a schooner and two barges under command Captain John Lynn, a soldier in charge of the marines, lacking naval experience. He was to sail to '[Deal] Island, one of the upper Tangier Islands, the Place of [Whaland's] Rendezvous, where they have collected their Plunder, and ... they have become so confident by Success, that they think any Precaution for their Security, unnecessary.'[39] It was hoped that the number of prizes taken and sent to New York had weakened their force considerably.

To offset Lynn's inexperience, the exonerated Captain Frazier was asked to go with him. Lynn was warned that if a confrontation appeared he should defer to Frazier's barge 'as he is a man of sense ...' in naval matters.[40] Remembering the *Protector*'s fate, Frazier was also advised to watch his ammunition chests. The explosions on the *Protector,* and earlier on Dashiell's *Terrible* at Janes Island, were the result of inexperience, where too much powder was massed on a barge's single deck. On Royal Navy ships, powder was kept below and brought up by boys in sparkproof containers in small amounts, only enough to fire a gun. Paca's expedition, however, never got underway as the crew members of the Frazier's *Defence* were charged with disobedience and court-martialed, making it impossible to embark.

Meanwhile, Whaland established winter quarters for his five barges and sloop on Tangier and Hog Islands. In February 1783, he commanded them as they landed at Benedict on the Patuxent River, Maryland and raided Philip Ferguson's farm, taking 12,000 pounds of salt pork. It was reported that when asked who led the raiders, he scrolled his signature with a piece of red chalk: 'Joseph Whaland, Commander of the Sloop Rover'.[41]

Peace between Britain and the United States was not signed until September 3, 1783 and official recognition of it did not reach America until 1784.[42] That year, both the Maryland and Virginia navies were eliminated, making it impossible for further naval action against Whaland and his watermen. With peace, Whaland remained at large. Watermen claimed that he had retired to the marshes of Dorchester County. Apparently, this is where he spent the last years of his life.

Chapter 34

Evacuation Becomes Migration

The evacuation, which at first seemed a humiliating conclusion to the war, now became a logistical feat for the Royal Navy – using its ability to carry thousands of black and white Loyalists to widely dispersed parts of the British Empire. It gave a new start to Loyalists who faced persecution if they stayed in the thirteen colonies. Crucially, it fulfilled the pledge of British officers to protect their black allies and see to it that they had a place in an evacuating ship. Blacks rarely feared going on board a British ship because their preachers emphasized the Old Testament perspective that they were leaving the threat of bondage for a promised land.[1] This process would continue, even after the peace was signed and thus the transporting of Loyalists was a means to 'begin the world anew' in many areas of the British Empire.

By April 1782, the normal flow of white and black Loyalists to New York was enhanced as the evacuation of all British North American garrisons seemed imminent. The Navy Board's Charles Middleton sent the new First Lord August Keppel an estimate of the transports necessary for the task. Were New York and Charleston to be evacuated simultaneously, 60,000 tons of shipping would be required for the troops alone, with 25,000 additional tons for ordnance, provisions and stores, and no more than a third of this was on hand.[2] Middleton felt that because of a possible West Indies strategy, New York should be evacuated first, rather than Charleston, which was closer to the Indies. He would have New York's garrison removed by September.

Middleton's proposal was too narrowly conceived because he was chiefly concerned with returning troops to Europe. In fact, the effort would not just require the removal of garrisons but the migration of thousands of civilians. As white and black Loyalists often outnumbered the garrisons, of which sometimes they made up a majority anyway, they would contribute the greater number of any embarkation. Military authorities agreed: they could not be abandoned, regardless of their demands on shipping. The civilians and even some garrisons were to be evacuated to diverse locations, where the goal was to resettle them. Thus, the evacuation become a migration to new homes in the British Empire, rather than a purely military operation.[3]

Replacing Clinton as commander, Sir Guy Carleton arrived in New York on May 5, 1782 to carry out the evacuations.[4] Rear Admiral Robert Digby, who had succeeded Marriot Arbuthnot as commander of the North American Station, gathered transports and warships for evacuation of Savannah, Charleston and New York, although lack of transports would cause the evacuations to be spread over two years. Carleton designated Savannah as first place for removal as it did not require extensive naval support. On July 11, a minority of Loyalists left Savannah and moved to Tybee Island at the mouth of the Savannah River to await transports to New York or Jamaica. In fact, most white and black Loyalists would go by coastal barge or overland, southward to St Augustine or northward to Charleston. Two-thirds of the garrison of 1,000 were Loyalist units, while the civilian exodus numbered over 5,000, more than a third of the entire state population. General Alexander Leslie, who earlier had invaded the Chesapeake, was in charge of both Savannah's and Charleston's evacuations. Shadowing the evacuation, Continental General Anthony Wayne had tried to prevent these high numbers by convincing Georgia Governor John Martin to offer deserters 200 acres of land, a cow and two breeding swine, as well as a pardon and protection. Still, few Loyalists took the bait.

Charleston was next, where blacks substantially outnumbered whites as a result of rebel estates around the city being seized and their slaves liberated in Charleston. Officers of the army and navy had adopted black families as servants, promising them their freedom, so that they required removal. Additionally, Savannah whites and free blacks who went to Charleston would have to be taken. Leslie began the evacuation in August 1782, and it continued until December. He was willing to allow rebel masters to search the departing vessels for their slaves, but British naval commanders refused to let them search their ships. A squabble over a prisoner exchange led Leslie to decide to have an all-British board screen the embarkees, taking those who could prove their service to the British. The board sent some evacuees to New York, although others sailed to England, Halifax and St Lucia. Cooperating with Digby, Andrew Hamond sent a convoy of twenty-five ships from Halifax to Charleston in late September and it returned in mid-November, bringing Charleston Loyalists to Nova Scotia. A month later, 3,794 whites and 5,333 blacks went chiefly to Jamaica and St Augustine.[5]

Charleston would send Jamaica its largest number of emigrants. These included nearly 5,000 slaves and 200 free blacks. The latter were asked to register at church vestries and provide information about their emancipation. Black Pioneers had been recruited in Charleston and Savannah for work in Jamaica. While slaves were by far the majority, Jamaica already had a free black community that numbered 4,000.

Altogether it is estimated that 14,000 migrants would depart Charleston on 130 Royal Navy ships. A majority were probably enslaved people held by Loyalists, who continued a life of bondage in new locales. Some blacks, however, had been given their freedom by the military for serving behind the British lines, or claimed freedom from their previous rebel masters, or had been appropriated by the military. The day after the evacuation was completed, nineteen jovial British sailors had remained to see 'the end of the frolic'.[6] They were escorted to their ships by Continental troops, who took the opportunity to congratulate Leslie on the manner in which he conducted the removal.

In New York, Carleton would be the final British officer to turn away rebel or neutral masters who visited the city to reclaim their slaves, spreading the fear of re-enslavement among blacks. Of the many confrontations with masters, his most notable was with slaveholder George Washington. With the preliminaries of the peace now signed, on May 6, 1783, Washington proposed he and Carleton meet to discuss the 'true intent and spirit' of Article VII in the preliminaries.[7] He had been surprised to hear that a large number of Negroes had already embarked, since his purpose was to seek the return of runaway slaves to their rebel masters. He personally felt this violated the spirit of the preliminaries, but he was ready to sit down and discuss how to prevent the further carrying away of Negroes belonging to citizens of the republic.

Carleton answered quickly that it was impossible to tell when his evacuation would be completed, but that already he had requested of Congress that inspectors be appointed to come to New York and help superintend the embarkations. Three had been appointed. When these inspectors were present no conflict existed, 'except in the case of negroes who had been declared free previous to my arrival: as I had no right to deprive them of that liberty I found them possessed of...'[8] He judged that those he 'found free when I arrived at New York, I had therefore no right, to prevent their going to any part of the world they thought proper.' Had they been denied permission to embark, he argued, they would simply have run away and it would be impossible for a former master to find. Carleton later claimed that Article VII of the preliminaries affected only blacks who come after the articles had been signed, late in 1782.

Admiral Digby allied with Carleton as they did not wait for formal permission from London authorities to evacuate blacks along with whites. A New York Association had planned the largest black Loyalist community for Port Roseway, known as Shelburne, Nova Scotia. From New York in April 1783, Carleton sent the first free blacks to Nova Scotia, and in mid-August he received word from London to evacuate all of the city's military and Loyalists, a task carried on by transports and navy ships for the rest of the year. His 'Book of Negros' records black evacuees from April to November 1783, covering 1,336 men, 914 women and 750 children who largely went to Nova Scotia, although some were destined for Quebec, the Bahamas and England. Two-thirds of them had originally come from Virginia, Georgia and the Carolinas, while the rest were from the middle colonies.[9]

From New York in early June 1783, a fleet of transports carrying 1,500 Loyalists headed to Nova Scotia. They arrived in Conway (renamed 'Digby' in 1787), with Admiral Digby commanding the *Atalanta*. He returned to New York in July and continued to direct the evacuation of blacks from the city. He ordered Lieutenant Philips of L'Abondance and Lieutenant Trounce of an armed storeship into the Hudson to receive blacks from Captain Henry Chads and after inspection proceed with them immediately to Port Roseway, Annapolis and St. Johns.[10]

New York's final evacuation fleet left for Halifax on November 25, 1783. Ten days later, Carleton departed from Staten Island to return to England, where Lord North praised him for his 'act of justice'.[11] As noted, the Treaty of Paris was not signed by the Americans until September 3, 1783 and was not ratified by Britain until April 9, 1784.

Evacuations actually continued after the Treaty of Paris was signed, involving Spain not the United States. From 1784 to 1785, East Florida was evacuated from St Augustine and the St Mary's River by the British, as Spain had won the Floridas in the peace negotiations. However, the colony had absorbed 4,581 black and 2,998 white Loyalist refugees from South Carolina and Georgia, adding to a population of only 4,000. This influx caused its evacuation to be frequently postponed. While the Spanish Governor Manuel de Zespedes arrived in St Augustine in July 1784, it was not until November 1785 that Governor Tryon left, as Loyalists sought to delay implementation of the treaty.[12] The refugees finally went to the Bahamas, Jamaica, Nova Scotia and Britain.

The Bahamas had become St Augustine's chief destination as result of an effort by its Loyalists. When Charleston was evacuated at the end of 1782, Colonel Andrew Deveaux and his irregulars went to St Augustine with other refugees.[13] He had previously led privateers taking Beaufort, and in St Augustine he became aware that a Spanish force had seized the nearby Bahama Islands. He financed an expedition to return them to the British fold. He fitted out five or six privateers with sixty-five men and was joined at Harbor Island, the Bahamas, by 170 more, making an armed force of 235 provincials, volunteers and blacks. Nassau's Spanish garrison, under Don Antonio Claraco Sauz, comprised 600 troops, seventy cannon and six galleys, certainly outnumbering the attackers. However, Deveaux blockaded the harbor, making it appear that his force was larger, and after a few well-directed shots, on April 18, 1783, Sauz surrendered without putting up a defense. Deveaux became temporary Governor of the Bahamas and established a cotton plantation on Cat Island. In the Treaty of Paris, the Bahamas had been given to Britain, whose dominion over the islands would never again be challenged. This was the last major naval action of the war.

Wherever the Loyalists went, their voyage out of the thirteen colonies was a fresh beginning and it carried them into a dynamic, if uncertain, world. The black refugees who were transported by the Royal Navy no longer saw themselves as property when offered the possibility of freedom within a new British Empire. They would have the additional support of Britain's growing Abolitionist movement, which would end the slave trade throughout the empire in 1807.[14]

Affirmations

At the end of the war, Britain was saved from invasion; thirteen of its twenty-six British American colonies remained; it retained control of Chesapeake Bay and Lake Champlain; and Gibraltar was saved. How had the Royal Navy salvaged victory from admitted defeat on land? Our Maritime perspective has uncovered the reasons, which are usually neglected in accounts of the war.

Most American military historians have avoided investigating these final years of the war, after Cornwallis' surrender at Yorktown.[1] They miss the Battle at the Saints, the Battle of the Barges, the relief of Gibraltar, and the recapture of the Bahamas. The British emerged from these successes more powerful than had earlier seemed possible. Americans found themselves without naval resources to continue the war and desperately hoped that their commissioners in Europe could end the hostilities immediately. Maryland's Governor Paca wrote to Washington hoping that Whaland's barges were somehow unauthorized by the British, but found that no peace treaty had been signed. It is evident that naval conflict had continued and that the Yorktown Siege was a memory.

The longest and largest confrontation of the war was the Siege of Gibraltar. This siege is almost never mentioned by American historians, although it was appreciated by contemporary American painters. The allied blockade was meant as a long-term alternative to an assault on Gibraltar's fortifications, as it was hoped the garrison could be starved into surrender. To do this, the allies collected vast resources. They completed an elaborate series of fortification at the northern extreme of Gibraltar's isthmus, denying the British access to the mainland and reducing their northern fortifications. Admiral Barcelo also commanded a fleet of smaller craft to control Algeciras Bay. Despite these preparations, admirals Rodney, Darby and Howe were able to avoid the blockade and provide relief to the garrison. The allied blockade was also undermined by continuous supplies from regional ships. Naval supply defeated the best efforts of the allies. The Franco-Spanish blockade of Gibraltar was a failure in comparison with the British blockade of the American coast.

Still, some histories claim that the Royal Navy's North American blockade was an ultimate failure.[2] I believe this is a hasty judgement. Too often the impossibility of patrolling the long Atlantic coast has been overemphasized because the blockade depended more on daily preparation and evasive tactics rather than combat at sea. Captain Hamond continued to believe that the best means of ending the war was an economic solution, putting a stop to as much American trade as possible. When in 1776, the *Roebuck* first blockaded the Delaware River under orders from London, it was the beginning of an effort which would be a long-term activity. It would also provide the navy with invaluable knowledge of navigating the coastal waters and attract Loyalists to their cause. It can be argued the effect of the blockade's many small encounters was to strangle the American economy and eliminate the Continental Navy.

The Royal Navy blockade also extended the war beyond the major Atlantic ports to less-familiar islands, inland lakes, rivers and coastal streams and marshes. It was in the narrow waters of Lake Champlain or Chesapeake Bay that naval conflict had some of its most enduring results. Conforming to conditions in the Chesapeake, Royal Navy commanders saw that their frigates needed smaller tenders and barges to control these waters. Tenders and support vessels multiplied by taking prizes, which were refitted and manned by the navy. The crews of the prizes were a source of sailors, making a land-based impress unnecessary, as those pressed at sea were most likely to be the desired seamen. In the narrow waters, local watermen came to support the navy and significant battles would be won by barges and galleys.

Another reason the Siege of Gibraltar is instructive is that it demonstrates that what started as a localized Massachusetts' rebellion became an Atlantic conflict. While today this view is commonplace, we should recognize Piers Mackesy and Admiral Alfred Mahan, who first introduced it. Only the navy with its warships and transports could carry British infantry throughout the Atlantic. The ability of the British state, Navy Board and Admiralty to sustain such far-flung assignments must be recognized.

The maritime perspective shows how crucial American diplomacy in Europe was to the cause of independence. The arrival of Continental ships in Europe in 1776, bringing together the American commissioners, led to European support. It was the commissioners' efforts that ultimately brought the alliance with France, and help from Spain and the Dutch Republic. The entry of these states into the conflict made the British naval position in the English Channel precarious for the first time in the war. By the end of the war, it was American diplomats, who succeeded where their military had failed, bringing about independence and peace.

The American commissioners opened up another naval front in the waters around the British Isles. While they would never have adequate funding to meet the extensive diplomatic and naval duties that Congress gave them, the commissioners would encourage a few American ships to carry the war to the British Isles. Wickes, Conyngham and Jones would have got nowhere without the intrigue and support of Benjamin Franklin. His belief in John Paul Jones' raiding voyages show that he deserves to be honored as founder of the Continental Navy in Europe. His leadership in the negotiations for the peace in Europe continuously kept the ideal of the thirteen colonies' independence foremost.

Naval action measured how well these European relationships were working. While at first Franco-American efforts against the Royal Navy in America were failures, the French navy finally succeeded in confronting the Royal Navy with superior force. In 1781, at the entrance to the Chesapeake, de Grasse confronted Graves, and in a standoff the damage to the British fleet was enough to force him to return to New York. This gave the French fleet a temporary control of the Chesapeake, allowing a Franco-American army to arrive and besiege Yorktown, where Cornwallis eventually surrendered. While de Grasse then left the Chesapeake and gave the Americans no further support, the loss of this British army affected war-weary British opinion.

Throughout the war, Congress entertained the illusion that Quebec and Nova Scotia were ripe for the picking, hoping that freedom-craving Canadians would rally to the American cause and expel their British governments. Early in the war, the rebels tried to dominate

Lake Champlain and used it to invade Canada. The building of a Royal Navy squadron and destruction of Arnold's ships in 1776 put an end to armed rebel presence on the lake. While Congress continued to desire Canada, it lacked the ships necessary to support an expedition over Lake Champlain.

Investigations of the role of supply in the Continental Navy and among American privateers has not been forthcoming.[3] It has been assumed by American historians that the Continental Navy and Army were self-sufficient, drawing abundant supplies from the local populace. In truth, the rebellious colonies were dependent on European and indirectly West Indies trade for munitions, arms, ships' outfitting and war materials. Even in terms of food, Washington's and other Continental armies were never secure; in fact, they were subject to freezing weather, starving every winter, despite their purposely reduced numbers.

The role of trade is fundamental to understanding why some colonies rebelled and others did not. The organization of supply convoys or blockades of trade were as effective as battles between warships in deciding this war. The British Empire before the Revolution had been built on trade. To an extent the war dislocated trade, making British-occupied New York the center of illicit trade because it had the best prices on British goods. In this endeavor, Halifax and occupied Charleston and Savannah joined New York.

Unaffected by the war was the American desire for British manufactures as all forms of illicit trade became necessary to obtain these goods. At best, illicit trade offered the rebels a means of funding the war, which both Congress and the states were unable to do with taxes. At worst, illicit trade made rebel embargoes impossible and deceived many innocent victims.

As the bulk of the King's troops had to be raised and equipped in Europe, the Navy Board faced the task of Atlantic transport and supply services. Convoys carrying troops, their gear and munitions from the British Isles to the American coast were necessary, despite delays in forming them. Royal Navy ships protected these convoys, holding them together in the face of danger, especially from rebel raiders that cut out stragglers. Considering the obstacles, the Navy Board had relative success in putting together the Atlantic convoys.

The Continental Navy developed differently from the Royal Navy. An important duty of their warships was to carry cargo to establish credit to purchase the munitions necessary for the war. Congress did not ask its navy to confront the Royal Navy, but rather to avoid its superior ships, instead serving primarily to protect and participate in needed trade. Congress placed the duty of supplying its armed forces ahead of naval combat. Yet, Congress hoped that a substantial portion of the navy's revenue would somehow come from its ships taking prizes. At its birth, then, confusion existed as to whether the Continental Navy was primarily a military or a financial endeavor.

Popular accounts of the American navies tend to focus on privateers since they sustained themselves through economic success. In the last years of the war, privateers would be the chief means for Congress to carry on war. It was no accident that leading Continental captains John Manley and Hector McNeill ended their careers as privateer captains. The vast majority of privateers were letters of marque from Congress or the states, where the objective of their voyages was trade, privateering being only one possibility of enriching a voyage. While Congress attempted to regulate the taking of prizes to its financial benefit, the effort failed because the crews of its ships and privateers sailed with the expectation of rewards – and mutinied or deserted when they did not readily appear.

While privateers became more numerous as the war continued, they did not perform well when joined with the Continental or state ships. Privateers were best when operating singly or with one or two compatriots, rather than in a squadron, especially if it was not devoted to taking prizes. They were at pains to avoid warships so as not to damage or lose their investors' property, and they were useless in a prolonged siege, as little opportunity to take prizes existed. This is seen in 1779 when Massachusetts formed a fleet to conduct amphibious operations against a small British force fortifying Penobscot. The ample rebel expedition of mostly privateers proved incapable of carrying out a siege and of confronting a Royal Navy relief squadron. It showed the limitations, not just of Massachusetts authorities but of Congress's Continental ships, in opposing the British. The debacle revealed the cracks within the American war effort: the Continental Navy alone could not create a fleet, and the states were jealous of the possibility that the Continent would receive the lion's share of the credit.

In contrast, the Royal Navy conducted many complicated amphibious operations, which allowed the British army to bring New York, Philadelphia and Charleston under its control. Its success did have long-term limitations, for in New York's case, Washington's army escaped to fight another day. In the occupations that followed, the British had difficulty in expanding their control into each city's hinterland. From the naval perspective, the true challenge came during the occupation. It was then the navy was charged not only with defense but also maintaining supply and contact with the outside world. Keeping trade and supply lines opened would go a long way to pacifying these cities.

In forming ships' companies, the competition for experienced seamen was fierce. The demands of merchant ships and the army, in addition to privateers, cut into the pool of seamen. Inevitably, captains were forced to turn to unpopular but necessary impressment. We have seen that in 1777 Continental Captain James Nicholson used the press on the Baltimore waterfront to fill the *Virginia*'s crew. When Maryland's Governor Johnson demanded that the pressed men be released, Nicholson replied sharply that he was under pressure from Congress to get his ship underway. Congress backtracked and suspended Nicholson from his command, but he was reinstated after grudgingly making an apology to Johnson. Nicholson's situation was not unique.

The British sought to promote Loyalism by offering opportunities for whites and blacks to serve. At first, the Royal Navy's dealings with Loyalists were inconsistent and even unrealistic. Loyalism could not be sustained when British military forces were evacuated, leaving Loyalists open to persecution by rebels. Navy ships and Loyalist privateers had to continuously support Loyalists on a local basis, providing them with arms, ammunition and salt. They also would carry recruits for Loyalist regiments to places where they could be organized and trained. The civil war that emerged in the Chesapeake and elsewhere, made it impossible for rebel authorities to stop Loyalist depredations against their water accessible plantations.

Watermen existed in the lower Chesapeake's shoals and rivers and had mastered amphibious warfare by using their armed barges. Their most renowned captain, Joseph Whaland Jr., returned to the Chesapeake in mid-1780 and kept Tangier Sound in the control of Loyalist barges. In 1782, watermen would have two complete victories over the Maryland navy, showing they were inspired and disciplined enough to continue the war. This was not the end of their insurrection. When the Royal Navy returned to the Chesapeake in the War of

1812, its officers would capitalize on the past by establishing a fortified base at Tangier Island for training black marines and supplying Royal Navy ships.

Overall, a new British Empire was in the making. Loyalists in New York, Charleston, Savannah and St Augustine were not stranded at the war's end, instead migrating on navy transports to other parts of the British Empire. This was not a matter of consistent policy from London or the Admiralty, rather it was formed on the spot as military officers decided to carry as many white and black Loyalists as possible to the far corners of Britain's Atlantic possessions. As the thirteen rebellious colonies set out on a path as a new republic, Britain forged a new empire, which had free blacks as an important constituency.

Notes

Abbreviations

AA   Force, Peter, ed., *American Archives-1790–1868*. Washington, DC, 1837–1853

BL   British Library, London

CVSP   *Calendar of Virginia State Papers and Other Manuscripts*. Palmer et al., eds., Richmond, 1875–1893, vols. 1–3

DCB   *Dictionary of Canadian Biography*, University of Toronto/Université Laval, 1959– to date 15 vols.

DNB   *Dictionary of National Biography*, ed. Leslie Stephen and Sidney Lee, London, 1885–1900, 63 vols. plus. In 2004 the *Oxford Dictionary of National Biography* replaced it.

DPA   Delaware Public Archives, Dover, Del.

HP   Hamond Naval Papers, 1766–1825, University of Virginia Library, Charlottesville, Va., Microfilm edition

JE   *The American Journals of Lt John Enys*, ed. Elizabeth Cometti, Syracuse, 1976

JPJ   *John Paul Jones and the Ranger*. ed. Joseph Sawtelle, Portsmouth, N.H., 1994

MA   William Brown et al., eds., *Archives of Maryland*. Baltimore, 1883–, to date 864 vols.

MS   *Memoir and Official Correspondence of General John Stark,* ed. Caleb Stark, Concord, N.H., 1860

NABB   Edward H. Nabb Research Center, Salisbury, Md.

NDAR   *Naval Documents of the American Revolution*, eds., William Bell Clark et al., Washington, DC, 1964–, to date 12 vols.

NMM   Caird Library, National Maritime Museum, Greenwich, London

NRSP   Naval Records Society Publications, a series of original research and edited rare documents on naval history published since 1894 by the Navy Records Society of Great Britain. More than 150 vols.

RB   Red Books, 1748–1827, 33 Volumes. The Red Books are described and partially indexed in *Calendar of Maryland State Papers*. Annapolis, Md.

RV   Scribner, Robert, and Tarter, Brent, eds., *Revolutionary Virginia: The Road to Independence*, Charlottesville, Va., 1978

TNA   The National Archives, Kew, London

Preface

1. Ward, Christopher, *The War of the Revolution*. New York, 1952.
2. Fowler, William, *Rebels under Sail, The American Navy during the Revolution*. New York, 1976, viii–ix.

Introduction

1. John Shy's *Toward Lexington: The Role of the British Army in the Coming of the American Revolution*, Princeton, 1965 and Richard Ketchum's *Divided Loyalties: How the Revolution Came to New York,* New York, 2002 go no further than their titles suggest.

Chapter 1

1. Brewer, John, *The Sinews of Power, War, Money and the English State 1688–1788*. Cambridge, Mass., 1988, 34–36.
2. Morriss, Roger, *The Royal Dockyards during the Revolutionary and Napoleonic Wars*. Leicester, UK, 1983, 1–9.
3. Lord Sandwich to Philip Stephens, June 29, 1775; Philip Stephens to Samuel Graves, July 6, 1775, NDAR, 1: 1305–1306, 1318; Rodger, N. A.M., *Command of the Ocean, A Naval History of Britain, 1649–1815*. New York, 2006, 417; Morriss, 79; Winfield, Rif, *British Warships in the Age of Sail, 1714 to 1792: Design, Construction, Careers and Fates*. Barnsley, UK, 2007, 9.
4. Rodger, *Command of the Ocean*, 371; Rodger, *Insatiable Earl, A Life of John Montagu, 4th Earl of Sandwich*. New York, 1993, 149–154.
5. Winfield, 62–67.
6. Ibid., 126.
7. George McKinly, Logbook of the Roebuck, July 20, 1803–1809, Aug 1, 1805–Jan. 30, 1806, NMM, ADM L/R 164; William O'Byrne, *A Naval Biographical Dictionary,* Lincoln, 45–47.
8. Rodger, *Insatiable Earl,* 150–153.
9. Haas, J.M., 'The Introduction of Task Work into the Royal Dockyards, 1775', *Journal of British Studies*, 8: 44–68; MacDougall, Philip, *Royal Dockyards*. London, 1982, 87–89.
10. Warner, Jessica, *The Incendiary, The Misadventures of John Painter.* New York, 2004, 85–104.
11. Ibid., 105–116.
12. Warner, 117–128; MacDougall, 112–116.
13. Warner, 145–168; MacDougall, 117; Press, Jonathan, *The Merchant Seamen of Bristol 1747–1789*. Bristol, 1976, 1–2.
14. Warner, 105–116, 132–144; MacDougall, 118–119.
15. Rodger, 'A Little Navy of Your Own Making' Admiral Boscawen and the Cornish Connection in the Royal Navy', Duffy, Michael, ed., *Parameters of British Naval Power 1650–1850*. Exeter, UK, 1992. 84–85.
16. Rodger, *Insatiable Earl*, 62–63.

17. Rodger, 'A Little Navy', 83–87.
18. Rodger, *The Wooden World: An Anatomy of the Georgian Navy*. New York, 1996, 109, 183–187.
19. Ibid., 158.
20. Pietsch, Roland, *the Real Jim Hawkins, Ships' Boys in the Georgian Navy*, Barnsley, UK, 2010; A Sea-Officer, 'Some hints for the more effectually regulating and disciplining his majesty's navy', NRSP, no. 119, *The Manning of the Royal Navy, Selected Public Pamphlets 1693–1873*, ed. J.S. Bromely, 1974, 120–121.
21. Earl, Peter, *Sailors, English Merchant Seamen 1650–1775*. London, 1998, 189–194, 199–205.
22. Rodger, *The Wooden World*, 149–152, 164–182; O'Riordan, Christopher, *The Thames Watermen in the Century of Revolution*. 1992. np.
23. Rodger, *The Wooden World*, 145–156 provides a corrective for Hutchinson, John, *Press Gang, Afloat and Ashore*. Middletown, Del., 2010, 1–44, 304.
24. Andrew Snape Hamond, Roebuck Log, July 14, 1775-July 14, 1776. NMM, ADM L/R 159.
25. An Account of the Progress and Proceedings of his majesty's frigate Arethusa between 17 June and 28 Nov. 1773, Hans Stanley to Hamond, July 13, 1775, HP, 3: 1–92; At the time, the commander-in-chief in North America was John Montagu, whose flag was on the 70-gun *Captain*, commanded by Thomas Symonds.
26. Hamond autobiography, HP, 1: 60.
27. Philip Stephens to Samuel Graves, July 6, 1775; Abstract of the Most Material Proceedings for this Department Relative to North America, July 6, 1775, NDAR, 1:1314, 1318.
28. Matthew Squire to Lord Dunmore, Sept. 18, 1775; Journal of HMS Otter, Sept. 24, 1775, NDAR, 2: 140,195.
29. Condemnation Proceedings against the Brigantine Betsy, June 11, 1776, NDAR, 5: 477.
30. Lord Dunmore to Lord Germain, June 26, 1776, Ibid., 5: 342–343; 5: 477.

Chapter 2

1. Rodger, *Command of the Ocean*, 331–333.
2. Rodger, *Insatiable Earl*, 23–25.
3. Syrett, David, *Shipping and the American War 1775–83*. London, 1970, 139–150.
4. Syrett, *Shipping and the American War*, 154–160, 178; Roebuck Log, July 5, 1779, NMM, ADM/N/249.
5. Rodger, *Insatiable Earl*, 228–229; Syrett, *Shipping and the American War*, 9–10.
6. Syrett, Shipping and the American War, 17, 20–30.
7. Ibid., 42–47, 151.
8. Syrett, *Shipping and the American War*, 22–24, 31–32, 196–198; Talbott, John, *The Pen & Ink Sailor, Charles Middleton and the King's Navy, 1778–1813*. London, 1998. 36–39.
9. Syrett, *Shipping and the American War*, 38–57.
10. Rodger, Insatiable Earl, 228–229; Syrett, *Shipping and the American War*, 78, 136
11. Syrett, *Shipping and the American War*, 154–157, 160–170.

12. Ibid., 37–46.
13. Ibid., 168–171.
14. Ibid., 182–192.
15. Narrative of Andrew Snape Hamond, Oct. 31, 1775; Hamond to Samuel Graves, Nov. 3, 1775, NDAR, 2: 869.
16. Address of the Nova Scotia General Assembly to Francis Legge, Nov. 4, 1775; Arbuthnot to Hamond, Nov. 6, 1775. Ibid, 2; 655, 900.
17. Samuel Graves to Hamond, Dec. 25, 1775; Marriot Arbuthnot to Hamond, Jan. 5, 1776, Ibid., 3: 235–236, 3: 625.
18. Hamond to James Montagu, Feb. 14, 1776, *Purdie's Virginia Gazette*, Feb. 16, 1776, Ibid., 3: 1293, 1323.
19. Rodger, *The Wooden World*, 87–98.
20. Ibid., 22–27, 36, 40–41.
21. Narrative of Andrew Snape Hamond, June 1–30, 1776, NDAR, 5: 839.
22. Journal of H.M.S. Roebuck, May 10, 1776, Ibid. 5: 37.
23. [James] Cunningham's Examination, July 18, 1776, Ibid., 5: 1136–1139.
24. Clement, J. and Sigourney, Lydia, eds., *Noble Deeds of American Women with Biographical Sketches*. New York, 1855, 164–165.

Chapter 3

1. *The Papers of Alexander Hamilton, 1768–1778*, ed., Syrett, Harold, New York, 1961, 1: 81–165.
2. Rodger, *The Command of the Ocean*, 330–331.
3. Miller, 35–41.
4. DNB, 1885–1900, 59 by John Knox Laughton.
5. Yerxa, Donald, *The Burning of Falmouth, 1775: A Case Study in British Imperial Pacification.* Portland, 1975, 120–121.
6. Yerxa, 121, 123–126; Kevitt, Chester, *General Solomon Lovell and The Penobscot Expedition.* Weymouth, Mass. 1976, 173; Leamon, James, *Revolution Downeast: The War for American Independence in Maine.* Amherst, Mass, 1995, 62–67.
7. Yerxa, 127.
8. Ibid., 127–130.
9. Ibid., 130–133.
10. Ibid., 133–137.
11. Ibid., 137–143.
12. Orderly Book of Major Daniel Isley, Feb. 10, 1776, NDAR, 3: 1193; Rodger, *The Insatiable Earl*, 225–227; Yerxa, 144–148.
13. Parramore, Thomas, Bogger, Tommy, Stewart, Peter, *Norfolk, The First Four Centuries.* Charlottesville, VA, 2000, 78; Mullin, Gerald, *Flight and Rebellion, Slave Resistance in Eighteenth-Century Virginia.* New York, 1974, 105, 119; Wertenbaker, Thomas and Schlegel, Marvin, *Norfolk, Historic Southern Port.* Durham, NC, 1962, 17–18.
14. Extract of a letter from Colonel Charles Scott to Captain Southall, Dec. 17, 1775, NDAR, 3: 140; Selby, John, *The Revolution in Virginia 1775–1783.* Williamsburg, Va., 1988, 81–84.

15. Journal of the Liverpool, Feb. 5, 1775, NDAR, 3: 1139; Hast, Adele, *Loyalism in Revolutionary Virginia, The Norfolk Area and the Eastern Shore.* Ann Arbor, Mic. 1979, 57–59. The figures come from the official report, which John Selby (Selby, 84) contends, 'was not made public until sixty years later, ... and then was buried in a legislative journal from which historians did not unearth it for another hundred years'.

Chapter 4

1. Middleton, *Tobacco Coast: A Maritime History of Chesapeake Bay in the Colonial Era.* Baltimore, 1984, 148–149.
2. Ibid., 313.
3. Doerflinger, Thomas, *A Vigorous Spirit of Enterprise: Merchants and Economic Development in Revolutionary Philadelphia.* Chapel Hill, 1986, 112–114, 123–124.
4. Ibid., 49, 236–240.
5. Morgan, Kenneth, *Bristol & Atlantic Trade in the Eighteenth Century.* New York, 2004, 70, 75, 78, 96–98, 113,130, 209.
6. Van Schaack, Henry Cruger, *The Life of Peter Van Schaack LLD: Embracing Selections from His Correspondence and Other Writings during the American Revolution.* New York, 1842, 30–31, 43–45, 51–66; Underdown, P.T., 'Henry Cruger and Edmund Burke: Colleagues and Rivals at the Election of 1774', *William and Mary Quarterly,* 15: 1, 14–34.
7. Crane, Elaine, *A Dependent People: Newport, Rhode Island in the Revolutionary Era.* New York, 1992, 16–46, 69–75.
8. Fowler, 2.
9. Clark, Charles, *The Eastern Frontier: The Settlement of Northern New England 1610– 1763.* New York, 1970, 154–162, 335–341.
10. Fowler, 8.
11. Clark, Charles, 293–341; Main, Jackson Turner, *The Social Structure of Revolutionary America.* Princeton, NJ, 1965, 37–38, 74.
12. Fowler, 6–10.
13. Hollett, Dave, *From Cumberland to Cape Horn.* London, 1984, 11, 20.
14. Ibid. 21.
15. *County Court Records of Accomack-Northampton, Virginia 1640–1645.* ed., Ames, Susie, Charlottesville, Va., 1973, 242.
16. Middleton, *Tobacco Coast*, 287–309, quote on 287.
17. Ibid., 288–289.
18. Ibid., 305–306.
19. Middleton, *Tobacco Coast*, 137–140; McKey, JoAnn, ed., *Accomack County Virginia Court Order Abstracts*, 1731–1736, Westminster, Md., 2007, 16: 289.
20. Middleton, *Tobacco Coast*, 294–297, 305–306.
21. To Robert Henry & Bedingfield Hands from the Grand Jury of Kent County, April 29, 1757, MA, 31: 205–208, 221–222; Middleton, *Tobacco Coast*, 305–306; Rediker, Marcus, *Between the Devil and the Deep Blue Sea.* New York, 1989 is devoted to mariners in the major ports.

22. Middleton, *Tobacco Coast*, 112–116.
23. Ibid., 89–95.
24. Rediker, *Between the Devil and the Deep Blue Sea,* 51–53.
25. Governor Sharpe to Alexander Colvill, Jan. 28, 1758, MA, 9: 137.
26. Wertenbaker and Schlegel, 17–18; Hast, 10.
27. Nash, Gary, *The Unknown American Revolution*, New York, 2005, 423–455; Young, Alfred, 'Afterward', *The American Revolution,* Young, ed., DeKalb, Ill., 1976, 450–452.

Chapter 5

1. Buel, Richard, *In Irons: Britain's Naval Supremacy and the American Revolutionary Economy*. New Haven, Ct., 1998, 77–84.
2. Fowler, 54–90.
3. Clark, Charles, 154–162, 335–341.
4. Building Accounts from the Langdon Ledger-Daybook, April 18- Nov. 11, 1777, JPJ, 216.
5. Ibid., 216–220.
6. Ibid.,
7. Buel, 86–89.
8. Fowler, 21–25.
9. Smith, Philip, *Captain Samuel Tucker (1747–1833) Continental Navy*. Salem, Mass., 1976, 1–19.
10. Magra, Christopher, 'Soldiers ... Bred to the Sea': Maritime Marblehead, Massachusetts and the Origins and Progress of the American Revolution', *New England Quarterly*, 78, 4: 554.
11. Fowler, 287–289; Miller, 'Chesapeake Bay Ships and Seamen in the Continental Navy', Eller, Ernst, ed., *Chesapeake Bay in the American Revolution.* Centreville, Md., 1981, 147–151.
12. Fowler, 272–278.
13. Norton, Louis, *Captains Contentions: The Dysfunctional Sons of the Brine.* Columbia, S.C., 2009, 1–6, 17–18, 133–146; Fowler, 57–58.
14. Fowler, 278.
15. Ibid., 274–276.
16. Stephen Hopkins to Esek Hopkins, Nov. 6, 1775, Beck, Alverda, ed., *The Correspondence of Esek Hopkins: Commander in Chief of the United States Navy.* 2011, 22.
17. Field, Edward, *Esek Hopkins, Commander-in-Chief of the Continental Navy During the American Revolution, 1775 to1778.* Providence, R.I., 1898.
18. Naval Committee to Esek Hopkins, Jan. 5, first draft of Jan. 5 and Jan. 10, 1776, Beck 23–26.
19. Naval Committee to Esek Hopkins, Jan. 5, 1776; Esek Hopkins in answer to the Report of the Committee, Aug. 1777, Ibid., 23–24, 57.
20. Buel, *In Irons*, 84–85.
21. Inventory of stores taken at Fort Nassau, March 3, 1776, Beck, 35.
22. Tyringham Howe to Philip Stephens, April, 27, 1776, NDAR, 4: 1281.
23. *Connecticut Gazette*, Apr 12, 1776; James Wallace to Molyneux Shuldham, April 10, 1776, Ibid., 4: 784–786, 746–747.

24. Abraham Whipple to Esek Hopkins, April 30, 1776, Beck, 42–43; Morison, Samuel, *John Paul Jones, A Sailor's Biography*. Boston, 1959, 56.

25. In the Marine Committee Resolved, March 25, 1777, Beck, 77.

26. Officers of the Continental frigate Warren to Robert Treat Paine, Feb. 11, 1777; Officers of the Continental Frigate Warren to the Continental Marine Committee, Feb. 19, 1777; Statement of Richard Marvin and others, Feb. 24, 1777; Statement of gunner, carpenter and midshipmen of the Warren, Feb. 24, 1777; Statement of John Reed, Chaplain of the Warren, Feb. 24, 1777, NDAR, 7: 1167–1168, 1234–1235, 1275.

27. Rank of Captains in the Navy, Oct. 10, 1776, JPJ, 225.

28. Bourne, Michael, *Historic Houses of Kent County*. Chestertown, Md., 1998, 48,107–108, 136, 339.

29. Bourne, 107-108; Peden, Henry, *Inhabitants of Kent County Maryland 1637–1787*. Westminster, Md., 1994, 174, 176–177.

30. Peden, 174.

31. Norton, 95–96, 128.

32. Marine Committee to James Nicholson, April 8, 1777; Marine Committee to James Nicholson, Nov. 6, 1777; Marine Committee to James Nicholson, Dec. 2, 1777; Marine Committee to James Nicholson, Dec. 20, 1777; Paullin, Charles, *Out-Letters of the Continental Marine Committee and Board of Admiralty, August, 1776 to September, 1780*. New York, 1914, 93, 167–168, 182–183, 186–187.

33. Marine Committee to James Nicholson, Jan. 28, 1778; Marine Committee to James Nicholson, March 4, 1778; Paullin, *Out-letters*, 197–198, 207–208.

34. Smith, Philip, *Fired by Manley Zeal, A Naval Fiasco of the American Revolution*. Salem, Mass., 1977, 3–12.

35. John Paul Jones to Thomas Bell, Nov. 15, 1778 and Memorial, Feb. 14, 1779, Allen, Gardner, *Captain Hector McNeill of the Continental Navy*. New Delhi, 2013, 93–95, 99–101.

36. Marine Committee to Captain McNeill, Sept. 21, 1776, Allen, 29–31.

37. Smith, Philip, 4–7.

38. Ibid., 49–73.

39. Ibid., 75–89.

40. John Paul Jones to Hector McNeill, Nov. 17, 1778, Allen, 95–96.

Chapter 6

1. Patton, Robert, *Patriot Pirates: The Privateer War for Freedom and Fortune in the American Revolution*. New York, 2008, 19, 49, 55, 61, 91, 106, 114–121, 180–81.

2. Fish, Stuyvesant, *The New York Privateers 1756–1763*. New York, 1945, 12–17; Lydon, James, *Pirates, Privateers and Imperial Warfare, 1739–1748*. Upper Saddle River, N.J., 1970, 43–45; Middleton, *Tobacco Coast*, 377.

3. Miller, 255–260.

4. George Washington to the states, Nov. 25–Dec. 19, 1775, *Red Books*, no. 4, part 5; Tilghman, Oswald, *History of Talbot County*. Baltimore, 1967, 2; 79.

5. Clarkson, Paul and Jett, Samuel, *Luther Martin of Maryland*. Baltimore, 1970, 48–50.

6. George Read to President of Congress, Jan. 16, 1778, DPA, RG 1800. 066, box 3, folder 332; Miller, 260; Foy, Charles, 'Eighteenth Century Prize Negros: From Britain to America', *Slavery & Abolition*, 31: 3, 379–393.

7. See Chapter 14.

8. Stokes, Durward, 'The Narrative of John Kilby', *Maryland Historical Magazine*. 67: 21–53; Middleton, 'Ships and Ship Building in Chesapeake Bay and Tributaries', Eller, 98–132.

9. Robert Morris to William Hooper, Jan. 24, 1777, NDAR, 7: 1031–1032.

10. Fowler, 280–283.

11. Buel, *In Irons*, 91–96; Van Buskirk, Judith, *Generous Enemies, Patriots and Loyalists in Revolutionary New York*. Philadelphia, 2002, 122–124; Usilton, Fred, *History of Kent County, 1630–1916*. Kent County, 1916, 124–125; on the British American desire for British manufactures see Breen, T.H., *The Marketplace of Revolution*. New York, 2004, 33–192.

12. Smith, *Fired by Manley Zeal*. 52–53; See Chapter 27.

13. Huntington Historical Society, *Mustering and Parading: Two Hundred Years of Militia on Long Island*, Huntington, NY, 1982, 16–19.

14. Overton, Albert, *Plunders From Across the Sound*. Florissant, Mo., 1980, 3, 5. Most of the local court decisions are today found among Congress's Court of Appeals papers.

15. Ibid., 3–4, 7–10.

16. Ibid., 49–50, 69.

17. Ibid., 51–53.

18. Buel, *Dear Liberty: Connecticut's Mobilization for the Revolutionary War*. Middleton, Ct., 1980, 266.

19. Overton, 11–14.

20. Ibid., 2, 14, 53,

21. Overton, 19–20; Buel, *Dear Liberty*, 260–261.

22. Buel, *In Irons*, 226–228; Bailyn, Bernard, *Atlantic History, Concept and Contours*. Cambridge, Mass. 2005, 88.

Chapter 7

1. Lanctot, Gustave, *Canada and the American Revolution,* trans. Cameron, Margaret, Cambridge, Mass, 1967.

2. Bigham, Clarence, *Paul Revere's Engravings*. New York, 1969, 124–125.

3. Stanley, George, *Canada Invaded, 1775–1776*. Ottawa, 1973; Mackesy, 57–60.

4. Reynolds, Paul, *Guy Carleton, A Biography*, Toronto, 1980, 8–26.

5. Ibid., 27–55.

6. Ibid., 56–75.

7. Gaumond, Michel, *Place Royal, Its Houses and their Occupants*. Quebec, 1977, 52–56.

8. Desloges, Yvon, *A Tenant's Town*. Ottawa, 1991, 57–60.

9. *Canada Preserved, The Journal of Captain Thomas Ainslie*. ed. Cohen, Sheldon, New York, 1968, 23–24.

10. Ibid., 21–22.

11. 'Orders of the New York provincial Congress', Aug. 15, 1775 and P.V.B. Livingston to Philip Schuyler, Aug. 7, 1775, New York Public Library.
12. Gerlach, Don, *Proud Patriot: Philip Schuyler and the War of Independence, 1775–1783*. Syracuse, 1987, 59–65; Higginbotham, Don, *Daniel Morgan*, Chapel Hill, NC, 1961, 27–53.
13. Nelson, James, *Benedict Arnold's Navy*. Camden, Me., 2006, 159–161.
14. Rodger, *The Insatiable Earl*. 221–223.
15. Extract of a Letter from Gosport, Nov. 9, 1775; Alan Gardner to Clark Gaton, Feb. 3, 1776, *London Chronicle*, Feb. 3–6; Admiralty to Douglas, NDAR, 3: 356, 882, 912–913, 1121; Rodger, *The Insatiable Earl*, 227.
16. Charles Douglas to Philip Stephens, May 8, 1776, NDAR, 4: 1451.
17. Charles Douglas to Philip Stephens, May 8, 1776, NDAR, 4: 1451; *Ainslie Journal*, 88–89.
18. *The Acland Journal, Lady Harriet Acland and the American War*, Thorp, Jennifer, ed., Winchester, UK, 1994, 16–17; Fryer, Mary, *King's Men, the Soldier Founders of Ontario*. Toronto, 1980, 48–50; Charles Douglas to Philip Stevens, May 15, 1776, NDAR, 5: 99–100; Dalin, Christopher, *Fortune's Favorite, Sir Charles Douglas and the Breaking of the Line*. Tucson, Az., 2009, 25–27.
19. Journal of the Blonde, Captain Philemon Pownoll, June 13, 1776, NDAR, 5; 502.
20. Journal of schooner Magdalen, Lt. Joseph Num, June 1, 1776, NDAR 5: 367–368; Thorp, 20; Digby, William, *The British Invasion from the North: Digby's Journal of Generals Carleton and Burgoyne from Canada, 1776–1777*. ed. James Baxter, New York, 1970, 88, 98, 102–103.
21. Digby, 113, 119, 141.
22. Beebe, Lewis, *Journal of Dr. Lewis Beebe*. New York, 1971, 337–339.

Chapter 8

1. Mahan, *The Influence of Seapower on History*. 30–31.
2. Guy Carleton to Charles Douglas, June 21, 1776; Journal of the Blonde, Captain Philemon Pownoll, June 14, 1776, NDAR, 5: 657, 522–523.
3. Extract of a Letter from Gosport, Nov. 9, 1775; Capt. Alan Gardner to Clark Gaton, Feb. 3, 1776; Guy Carleton to Philemon Pownoll, July 1, 1776; Charles Douglas to Philemon Pownoll, Sept. 23, 1776, Ibid., 3: 356, 1121, 4; 951, 5: 845.
4. Charles Douglas to Lord Howe, Aug. 4, 1776, Ibid.,6: 45–47.
5. Charles Douglas to Philip Stephenson, June 27, 1776, Ibid., 5: 762–763.
6. Charles Douglas to Lord Howe, Aug. 4, 1776, Ibid., 6: 45–47.
7. Charles Douglas to Philemon Pownoll, Sept. 23, 1776, Ibid., 5: 951.
8. Force on the Lake Tolerably Exact on September 18, 1776, NDAR, 6: 883–884; JE, 18–19.
9. Charles Douglas to Philip Stephenson July 21, 1776; Douglas to Lord Howe, Aug. 4, 1776, NDAR, 5: 1167, 6: 43.
10. Charles Douglas to Philemon Pownoll, Sept. 23, 1776; Guy Carleton to Hector Cramahe, Oct. 9, 1776; Charles Douglas to Philemon Pownoll, Oct. 10, 1776; Ibid., 6: 951, 1178, 1193.

11. Horatio Gates to John Hancock, July 16, 1776, NDAR, 5: 1099–1101; Gerlach, 120.

12. *Parole: Quebec; Countersign: Ticonderoga, Second New Jersey Regimental Orderly Book 1776.* Salsig, Doyen, ed., Toronto, 1980, 179; Morton, Doris, *Philip Skene of Skenesborough*, Granville, NY, 1959, 48–51.

13. Bielinski, Stefen, The Colonial Albany Social History Project is a community history program of the New York State Museum, Albany. Since 1981, over 16,000 individuals who lived in the city of Albany have been identified and analyzed. It is maintained through its website: https://exhibitions.nysm.nysed.gov//albany/whoarewe.html, Feb. 13/ 21.

14. Corbett, Theodore, *No Turning Point: The Saratoga Campaign in Perspective.* Norman, Okla., 2012, 63–65; Morton, 46–48.

15. Philip Schuyler to John Hancock Jan. 27, 1776, NDAR, 3: 917–18; Harmanus Schuyler from Bielinski, https://exhibitions.nysm.nysed.gov//albany/whoarewe.html, Feb. 13/ 21.

16. Horatio Gates to John Hancock, July 16, 1776, NDAR, 5: 1099–1101; Nelson, 228–247.

17. Benedict Arnold to Philip Schuyler, July 24, 1776, NDAR, 5: 1197.

18. A list of the Navy of the United States on Lake Champlain, Aug. 7, 1776, Ibid., 6: 96–98.

19. Horatio Gates to Benedict Arnold, July 13, 1776, NDAR, 5: 1057–58; Nelson, 246–247.

20. 'Accounts, Money owed him by the U.S.', Jan. 27-April 29, 1776, Cherry Hill Papers, 3/22, 3/30, Albany, NY.

21. Gerlach, 134–35.

22. Philip Schuyler to Jonathan Trumbull, June 25, 1776; Horatio Gates to John Hancock, July16, 1776, NDAR, 5: 733, 1101.

23. Journal of the Continental Congress, Feb. 5, 1776; Philip Schuyler to Hancock, Jan. 24, 1776, Ibid., 3: 1137, 957.

24. 'Schuyler's Letter Book', 3: 345–346,482, 485, New York Public Library.

25. Gerlach, 157, 166, 189.

26. Nelson, 259–262

Chapter 9

1. Charles Douglas to Philip Stephenson and enclosure, Oct. 21, 1776, NDAR, 6: 340–343. The figures for both squadrons vary; one reason being that while some ships were in the process of building, they were not yet fitted out. The Admiralty Collection of the National Maritime Museum, Greenwich has draughts not only of Royal Navy vessels but those of captured American ships; see Gardiner, Robert, ed., *Navies and the American Revolution 1775–1783*. London, 1996, 34–35.

2. Benedict Arnold to Horatio Gates, Oct. 12, 1776, NDAR, 6: 1235–1237; Digby, 162–63.

3. Benedict Arnold to Horatio Gates, Oct. 12, 1776; John Burgoyne to Charles Douglas, Oct. 12, 1776, NDAR, 6: 1235–1237, 1229; JE, 18–20; Digby, 158–159.

4. Benedict Arnold to Horatio Gates, Oct. 12, 1776, NDAR, 6: 1235–37; JE, 20; Digby, 148–164.

5. Charles Douglas to Philip Stephenson and enclosure, Oct. 21, 1776, NDAR, 6: 340–343; JE, 20.

6. Benedict Arnold to Horatio Gates, Oct. 12, 1776, NDAR, 6: 1235–37; JE, 21–22; Digby, 160–162.

7. Benedict Arnold to Horatio Gates, Oct. 12, 1776; Charles Douglas to Philip Stephenson and enclosure, Oct. 21, 1776, NDAR, 6: 340-343, 1235–1237.

8. Guy Carleton to Charles Douglas, Oct. 22, 1776, NDAR, 6: 1365; Nelson, 322–327.

9. Digby, 174–178.

10. Bowler, Richard, *Logistics and the Failure of the British Army in America.* Princeton, N.J., 1975, 214–216, 224–225.

11. Guy Carleton to Charles Douglas, Nov. 8, 1776; Guy Carleton to William Philips, Nov. 8, 1776; A List of His Majesty's Armed Vessels with Dimensions, Jan. 1, 1777, NDAR, 7: 88, 82–83, 830.

12. First Campaign of the Brunswickers in Canada in the year 1776, Stone, William, ed., *Letters of Brunswick and Hessian Officers During the American Revolution.* New York, 1970, 48.

13. Mintz, Max, *The General of Saratoga: John Burgoyne & Horatio Gates.* New Haven, Ct., 1990, 69–74.

14. Charles Douglas to Capt. Richard Pearson of the *Garland*, Nov. 3, 1776, NDAR, 7: 26–27.

15. Corbett, *No Turning Point,* 127–129.

16. Lord Howe to Philip Stephens, June 29, 1777, NDAR, 9: 187; Morton, 52–54.

17. Richard Pearson to Philip Stephens, Aug. 12, 1777, NDAR, 9: 735–736.

18. Roll of Captain Munro's Company, National Library and Archives of Canada, MG21, Bi67, 91–93; Abstract of Captain Munro's Company, ibid., 94–95, 130–135; Miscellaneous Papers pertaining to the service of Captain Hugh Munro, ibid., 242–245.

19. John Starke to Guy Carleton, Sept. 17, 1777, NDAR, 9: 935.

20. John Starke to Guy Carleton, Sept. 17, 1777, NDAR, 9: 935; Hughes, Thomas, *A Journal.* Port Washington, NY, 1970, 11–14; Anburey, Thomas, *Travels through the Interior parts of America, 1776–1781.* Toronto, 1963, 158–159, 161; Thomas Wood, Pension Deposition, Dann, John. ed., *The Revolution Remembered.* Chicago, 1980, 94–95.

21. Richard Pearson to Guy Carleton, Sept. 24, 1777, NDAR, 9: 957.

22. Henry Powell to Guy Carleton, Oct. 19, 1777, Ibid., 10: 212.

23. Instructions to Captain Samuel Graves, Oct. 3, 1777, NDAR, 10: 20; Hille, Julius Friedrich von, *The American Revolution: Garrison Life in French Canada and New York, Journal of an officer in Prinz Friedrich Regiment, 1776–1783.* Trans. Helga Doblin, Westport, Ct., 1993, 85–87.

Chapter 10

1. Higginbotham, *The War of American Independence*, Boston, 1983, 198.

2. Transcript of Articles of Confederation (1777), https://www.ourdocuments.gov accessed Feb. 18, 2012.

3. Dull, Jonathan, *A Diplomatic History of the American Revolution*. New Haven, 1985, 59, 89–96.
4. Ibid., 114–118.
5. Gates to Stark, July 14, 1778, MS, 181.
6. Thomas Johnson to Maryland Council, Jan. 20, 1778, NDAR, 11: 175.
7. James Duane to Stark, Dec. 16, 1777, Stark to Duane, Jan. 14, 1778, MS, 11–46, 79–80.
8. Gates to Stark, Jan. 24, 1778, MS, 142.
9. Stark to the President of Congress, May 24, 1778, MS, 150; Burnett, *Letters of the Members of the Continental Congress*, Washington, DC, 1921–1936, 261–267.
10. Gates to Stark, Jan. 24, 1778, MS, 142.
11. Lafayette to Washington, Feb. 23, 1778, *The Papers of George Washington*, Revolutionary War Series, 26 December 1777–28 February 1778, ed. Lengel, Edward, Charlottesville, Va, 2003, 13: 648–650.
12. Lafayette to Washington, Feb. 19, 1778, Ibid., 13: 594–597.
13. Washington to Lafayette, Mar. 10, 1778, *The Papers of George Washington*, Revolutionary War Series, 1 March 1778–30 April 1778, ed. Hoth, David, Charlottesville, Va, 2004, 14: 132–133; Dull, 114–115.
14. Stark to Gates, May 24, 1778; Stark to President of New Hampshire Congress, June 28, 1778; Gates to Stark, July 14, 1778; Stark to Washington, July 31, 1778, MS, 151, 172, 181, 183.
15. Stark to Washington, Oct. 29, 1778, MS, 170–171.
16. Stark to Gates, June 29, 1778; Stark to Gates, July 7, 1776, MS, 166, 179.
17. Washington to Schuyler, Nov. 20, 1778, *Papers of Alexander Hamilton*, ed. Syrett, Harold, New York, 1961, 1: 585; Washington to Schuyler, Dec. 18, 1778, George Washington Papers, Library of Congress, Washington, DC.
18. Watt, Gavin, *Burning of the Valleys: Daring Raids from Canada against the New York Frontier in the Fall of 1780*. Toronto, 1997, 75–80; Herwig, Miriam and Wes Herwig, eds., *Jonathan Carpenter's Journal*. Randolph Center, Vt. 1994, 73–74, 76–78, 80.
19. Carleton's Journal, Oct. 24-Nov. 8, Washington, Ida and Paul, *Carleton's Raid*, Canaan, NH, 1977, 85–92.
20. JE, 24–35;
21. JE, 26–35.
22. Carleton's Journal, Nov. 9-Nov. 13, Washington & Washington, 7–11, 27, 91–93.
23. Corbett, *No Turning Point*, 299–311.
24. Dull, 140, 145.
25. Hutchinson, Bruce, *The Struggle for the Border*. New York, 1955, 187.

Chapter 11

1. Rodger, *Command of the Ocean*, 331.
2. Rodger, *Insatiable Earl*, 225–226; The idea that the study of coastal warfare is an important approach to maritime history is treated in Pearce, Cathryn, 'Is Coastal History Maritime History', *Topmasts:* Special issue 2017, 25–28.

3. 'General Introduction', Hoffman, Paul, ed., *Guide to the Naval Papers of Sir Andrew Snape Hamond and Sir Graham Eden Hamond.* Charlottesville, Va., 1966, 11–12, 13, 20; Shomette, Donald, *Shipwrecks, Sea Raiders, and Maritime Disasters along the Delmarva Coast 1632–2004.* Baltimore, 2007, 41–43.

4. Syrett, *Admiral Lord Howe*, Annapolis, Md., 2006, 61–66, 73–76; Rodger, *The Insatiable Earl*, 230–231; for a different view of Lord Howe's blockade see Mackesy, *The War for America*, 100–102.

5. Account of A.S. Hamond's part in the America Revolution, HP, 2: 27–30; Buel, *In Irons*, 43; Comtois, George, 'The British Navy in the Delaware, 1775 to 1777', *American Neptune*, 40: 7–22.

6. Hamond to Hans Stanley, Aug. 5 and Sept. 24, 1776, HP, 1; On the Royal Navy's amphibious warfare in the Revolution see Harrington, Hugh, 'Invading America: The Flatboats that Landed Thousands of British Troops on American Beaches', *Journal of the American Revolution*, March 16, 2015, 3–9.

7. Specie was money in the form of coins, more trusted than paper notes. Buel, *In Irons*, 39–40, 217–234; Doerflinger, 214–215.

8. Account of A.S. Hamond's part in the America Revolution, HP, 2: 27–30.

9. Ibid.

10. Journal of the Roebuck, March 20, 1776, 97, NDAR, 4: 427.

11. Journal of Roebuck, March 25, 1776, 729; Hamond to Henry Bellew, April 8, 1776, Ibid., 4: 595, 729.

12. Journal of Andrew Hamond, March 20, 1776; Deposition of William Barry, June 11, 1776, NDAR, 4: 427–428, 5: 481–483.

13. Journal of Roebuck, April 29, 1776, Ibid., 4: 596.

14. Journal of Roebuck, March 11, 1776 and April 9–10, Ibid., 4: 315, 756.

15. Hamond to Henry Bellew, April 8, 1776; Journal of the Roebuck, April 9, 1776, Ibid., 4: 729, 756.

16. Journal of Roebuck, March 20, 1776, Ibid., 4: 427.

17. Journal of Roebuck, April 14, 1776, Ibid., 4: 821.

18. Hamond narrative, April 22, 1776, HP; Journal of Roebuck, April 22, 1776, NDAR, 4: 1218.

19. Journal of Roebuck, April 24, 1776, Ibid., 4: 1225–1227.

20. Journal of Roebuck, April 28, 1776, April 30, 1776, Ibid., 4: 1297, 1383.

21. Journal of Roebuck, April 28. 1776, Ibid., 4: 1297.

22. Hamond to Henry Bellew, April 8, 1776, Ibid., 4: 729.

23. Prizes Power of Attorney Granted by the Officers and Crew of the Liverpool, October, 1776, Ibid., 6: 1143–1144.

24. Support came to Lewes in April 1776 when two companies of John Haslet's newly formed Delaware Regiment arrived to overawe the Loyalists. Anderson, Enoch, 'Person Recollections … in the Revolutionary War', ed. Ballas, Henry, *Papers of the Historical Society of Delaware*. 1896: 1–20; Ward, *The Delaware Continentals*. Wilmington, De., 1946, 8–10.

25. Molyneux Shuldham to Hamond, Jan. 17, 1776, NDAR, 3: 384.

26. Henry Fisher to Pennsylvania Committee of Safety, April 1, 1776; Journal of the Roebuck, March 28 and 29, 1776, Ibid., 4: 596–597.

27. Hamond to Henry Clinton, May 4, 1776, Ibid., 4: 1407–1408.

28. Narrative of Andrew Snape Hamond, May 5–9, 1776; Journal of Roebuck, May 5, 6, 7, Ibid., 5: 15–16, 4: 1446–1447.
29. Journal of Roebuck, May 8, 1776; Narrative of Andrew Snape Hamond, May 5–9, 1776, Ibid., 4: 1470, 5: 15; George Read to Caesar Rodney, May 10, 1776, Ryden, George, ed., *Letters to and from Caesar Rodney, 1756–1784*. Philadelphia, 1933, 66.
30. Healing is the dangerous situation in which the ship tilts to its side and does not return to an upright position. Journal of Roebuck, May 8–9, 1776; Journal of Liverpool, May 8, 1776, NDAR, 4: 1470, 4: 1471.
31. Narrative of Andrew Snape Hamond, May 5–9, 1776, Ibid., 5: 18.
32. Hamond to Peter Parker, June 10, 1776; Deposition of William Berry, June 11, 1776, Ibid., 5: 460–461, 5: 481–485.
33. George Read to Caesar Rodney, May 10, 1776, Ryden, 66.
34. Thomas Read to Pennsylvania Committee of Safety, May 9, 1776, NDAR, 5: 17; Plummer, Norman, *Lambert Wickes Pirate or Patriot?* St Michaels, Md., 1991, 6–7.
35. *Middelburgsche Courant*, Sept. 10, 1776.
36. Jackson, John, *The Pennsylvania Navy, 1775–1781, The Defense of the Delaware.* New Brunswick, N.J., 1974, 138–147, 225–244; Jackson, *With the British Army in Philadelphia*. San Rafael, Calif., 1979, 147–157.

Chapter 12

1. Hamond to Hans Stanley, Sept. 24, 1776; William Fielding to Lord Denbigh, Aug. 17, 1776, NDAR, 6: 973 and 6: 184; Balderston, Marion and Syrett, eds., *The Lost War: Letters from British Officers during the American Revolution.* New York, 1975, 96; Gallagher, John, *The Battle of Brooklyn.* New York, 1995; Schecter, Barnet, *The Battle for New York.* New York, 2002. 129–130.
2. Hamond to Hans Stanley, Sept. 24, 1776, NDAR, 6: 973; Gallagher, 91.
3. Hamond to Hans Stanley, Sept. 24, 1776, NDAR, 6: 973.
4. Narrative of Andrew Snape Hamond, Aug. 14–29, 1776, Admiral Howe to Philip Stephens, Aug. 31, 1776, NDAR, 6: 351–352, 375–376; Black, Jeremy, *War for America: The Fight for Independence 1775–1783*. New York, 1991, 102–104.
5. Journal of Ambrose Serle, Sept. 13, 1776, NDAR, 6: 805–806.
6. Clinton, Henry, *Sir Henry Clinton's Narrative of His Campaigns, 1775–1782*. ed. William Wilcox, New Haven, Ct., 1954. 45; Gallagher, 160.
7. Master Log of the Roebuck, Sept. 23, 1776, NDAR, 6: 965.
8. Journal of Ambrose Serle, Oct. 9, 1776; Hamond to Molyneux Shuldham, Nov. 7, 1776; Narrative of Andrew Snape Hamond, October 3 to October 9, 1776, NDAR, 6: 1186, 7: 76–77, 6: 1182–1183; Clinton, 47–48.
9. George Washington to John Hancock, Oct. 9, 1776, NDAR, 6: 1185; [George Collier], "To my inexpressible astonishment': Admiral Sir George Collier's observations on the battle of Long Island', ed. Tucker, L. L., *New York Historical Society Quarterly*, 48: 292–305; Black, 107–108.
10. Libel filed in Vice Admiralty Court of New York, Mar. 18, 1778, NDAR, 11: 687–688.

11. Van Buskirk, 23.
12. Ernst, Robert, 'Andrew Elliot, Forgotten Loyalist of Occupied New York', *New York History*, 57: 285–320.
13. Matson, Cathy, *Merchants & Empire: Trading in Colonial New York.* Baltimore, 1998, 313; James Robertson to Isaac Low, May 11, 1780, *The New York Letter Book of General James Robertson 1780–1783*. Klein, Milton and Howard, Ronald, eds. Cooperstown, N.Y., 1983, 109; Burrows, Edwin and Wallace, Mike, *Gotham, A History of New York City to 1898.* New York, 2000, 245–247.
14. Van Buskirk, 147–148.
15. Gwyn, Julian, *Ashore and Afloat*, Ottawa, 2004, 23; Foy, 'The Royal Navy's Employment of Back Mariners and Maritime Workers, 1754–1783', *International Maritime History Journal*, 28:1, 20–21.

Chapter 13

1. Report from Henry Clinton to Sir William Howe, Oct. 9, 1777, NDAR, 10: 345–47, 350; Gruber, Ira, *The Howe Brothers and the American Revolution.* Chapel Hill, N.C., 1972, 266.
2. Willcox, William, *Portrait of a General: Sir Henry Clinton in the War for Independence.* New York, 1964.
3. George Clinton to Pierre Van Cortlandt, June 5, 1777, NDAR, 9: 24.
4. Israel Putnam to New York Council of Safety, June 5, 1777, Ibid., 9: 23–24.
5. Journal of the New York Council of Safety, June 5, June 6, 1777, Ibid., 9: 23–24, 41.
6. Clinton, 64–66.
7. Ibid., 73–75.
8. Ibid., 77.
9. Clinton 75–76; Diamant, Lincoln, *Chaining the Hudson: The Fight for the River in the American Revolution.* New York, 1994, 115–120.
10. Clinton, 76.
11. Clinton, 76–77; Henry Clinton to William Howe, Oct. 9, 1777, NDAR, 10: 98–100.
12. Ibid.
13. Henry Clinton to Burgoyne, Oct. 6, 1777, Clinton, 379–380
14. Ibid., 79–80.
15. George Clinton to New York Committee of Safety, Oct. 12, 1777, NDAR, 10: 126–127.
16. Journal of galley Dependence, Oct. 16, 1777 and Journal of brig Diligent, Oct. 16, 1777, Ibid., 10: 183–84.
17. John Vaughan to Henry Clinton, 17. Oct. 1777; James Wallace to William Hotham, Oct. 17, Ibid., 10: 192–193.
18. Wermuth, Thomas, *Rip Van Winkle's Neighbors.* Albany, 2001, 70, 73–74, 77.
19. John Vaughan to Henry Clinton, Oct. 17, 1777, NDAR, 10: 192.
20. Journal of brig Diligent, Oct. 18, 1777, NDAR, 10: 203; *New York Gazette and Weekly Mercury*, Nov. 3, 1777, NYHS; Lynd, Staughton, 'The Tenant Rising at Livingston Manor, 1777', in *Anti-Federalism in Dutchess County.* Chicago, 1962, 37–54; Smith,

Helen, *Colonial Days and Ways,* New York, 1900, 250–260; Kierner, Cynthia, *Traders and Gentlefolk: The Livingstons of New York, 1675–1790.* Ithaca, N.Y., 119–120, 228–29.

21. Clinton, 81; William Hotham to Lord Howe, Oct. 21, 1777, NDAR, 10: 232–233.

22. Sullivan, James, ed., *Minutes of the Albany Committee of Correspondence, 1775–1778.* Albany, NY, 1923, 853.

23. William Hotham to Lord Howe, Oct. 9, 1777, NDAR, 10: 96–97; Clinton, 81.

24. George Clinton to Israel Putnam, Oct. 18, 1777, NDAR 10: 204.

25. Israel Putnam to George Washington, Oct. 16, 1777, Ibid., 10: 185–186.

26. *General Orders issued by Major-General Israel Putnam,* Ford, Worthington, ed., Brooklyn, NY, 1893, 82–83; Israel Putnam to George Washington, Oct. 25, 1777, Ibid., 10: 282.

27. Washington to George Clinton, Feb. 16, 1778, *The Papers of George Washington.* Charlottesville, Va., 2003, 13: 552–554; George Clinton to Washington, March 5, 1778, Ibid., 1992, 2: 408–409.

28. Mahan, 302.

Chapter 14

1. Dull, 82–88.

2. Continental Marine Committee to Lambert Wickes, Oct. 24, 1776, NDAR, 6: 1400–1403; Plummer, 19.

3. Fowler, 129; Hendrick, Burton, *The Lee's of Virginia.* Boston, 1935, 279.

4. Dull, 78–85.

5. Some American historians believe French neutrality was a façade, for they really wished to support the American rebellion. Miller thinks that Vergennes wanted to help Wickes and Conyngham, 286–288, but Fowler, 134–35, disagrees.

6. Miller, 283

7. Fowler, 53–54.

8. Isaacson, Walter, *Benjamin Franklin: An American Life.* New York, 2003, 330–333, 382–383.

9. Clark, William Bell, *Lambert Wickes: Sea Raider and Diplomat,* New Haven, Ct., 1932, 12–13, 373; Plummer, 1–4.

10. Captain Thomas Read to the Pennsylvania Committee of Safety, May 9, 1776, NDAR 5: 17; Plummer, 7.

11. Marine Committee of the Continental Congress to Wickes June 10, 1776; Wickes to the Committee of Secret Correspondence of the Continental Congress, July 11, 1776; Baron de Corky to Count d'Argout, July 28, 1776 & July 29, 1776, Ibid., 5: 454, 1030, 1263–6, 1276–9; Plummer, 12, 15.

12. Plummer, 19.

13. Lambert Wickes to American Commissioners in France, Feb. 14, 1777, NDAR, 8: 589.

14. Lambert Wickes to the American Commissioners, April 27, 1777, Ibid., 8: 797.

15. Benjamin Franklin to John Bradford, May 1, 1777; Captain Samuel Nicholson to Silas Dean, May 15, 1777, NDAR, 8: 810–811, 847–48, 9: 443–444; Plummer, 26–28.

16. Lambert Wickes to the American Commissioners in France, June 27, 1777, NDAR 9: 440–441; London, Philip, *Captain Samuel Nicholson: A Monograph*, 2012, 1–8.

17. *General Advertiser*, July 4, 1777; Vergennes to Benjamin Franklin and Silas Dean, July 16, 1777; Lambert Wickes to the American Commissioners in France, Aug. 12, 1777 and Aug. 22, 1777, NDAR, 9: 446, 502, 567, 594, 598, 610, 617, 651–652, 663; Plummer, 30–33.

18. Captain George Bowyer to Philip Stephens, June 29, 1777, NDAR 9: 443–44; Fowler, 130–132.

19. Plummer, 33–34.

20. Attestation of Gustavus Conyngham, Nesser, Robert, ed., *Letters and Papers Relative to the Cruises of Gustavus Conyngham 1777–1779.* New York, 1915, 104; Malo, Henri, 'American Privateers at Dunkirk', *United States Naval Institute Proceedings,* 37: 934.

21. Nesser, xxxiii–xxxv, 68–79.

22. Malo, 938; Nesser, 1–2, 60.

23. Extract of a Letter from Harwich, May 9, [1777]; Vergennes to Marquis de Noailles, May 9, 1777; Prince de Robeco Montmorency to Vergennes, May 31, 1777, NDAR, 8: 833–834, 834–835, 880–881; Lord Stormont to Lord Weymouth, Aug. 9, 1777, Nesser, 88.

24. American Commissioners to Committee of Foreign Affairs, Oct. 7, 1777, NDAR, 10: 880–881; Nesser, 37–38.

25. William Carmichael to Conyngham, July 15, 1777, Nesser, 64–65.

26. Ibid.

27. Deposition of John Hutchinson, Prize Master of the Brig Venus, Oct. 15, 1777, NDAR, 10: 199; Fowler, 139–140.

28. John Hancock to Conyngham, May 2, 1777; Attestation of Gustavus Conyngham, Nesser, 104.

29. Nesser, 97–98.

30. Lord Grantham to Lord Weymouth, Oct. 6, 1777; Silas Dean to Miguel Lagounere & Company, Oct. 19, 1777; Gustavus Conyngham to Arthur Lee, Jan. 32, 1778; Floridablanca to Francisco de Escarano, Feb. 16, 1778; Lord Weymouth to Lord Grantham, Feb. 20, 1778, NDAR, 10: 923, 11: 957, 11: 1013, 11: 1026; Nesser, 64–65; Norton, 'Captain Gustavus Conyngham: America's Successful Naval Captain or Accidental Pirate', Journal of the American Revolution, April 15, 2015, 6/4/20.

31. Marine Committee to Joseph Reed, March 12, 1779, Paullin, *Out-letters*, 52; Benjamin Franklin to Conyngham, June 20, 1781, *Founders Online,* National Archives, https://founders.archives.gov/documents/Franklin/01-35-02-0130, 6/4/20.

32. Benjamin Franklin to Lebrun, Oct. 25, 1779; Franklin to Conyngham, June 20, 1781, Nesser, 189, 203.

33. Fowler, 145.

34. Ibid., 282–287.

35. Lambert Wickes to Captain Henry Johnson, Sept. 5, 1777; American Commissioners in France to Lambert Wickes, Sept. 9, 1777, NDAR, 9: 629–630, 636–637.

36. Benjamin Franklin to John Bradford, May 1, 1777; Captain George Bonyer to Philip Stephens, June 29, 1777; NDAR, 8: 810–811, 9: 443–444; Plummer, 26–28.

37. Robert Morris to William Hooper, Jan. 24, 1777, NDAR, 7: 1031–1032.

38. Franklin to Conyngham, June 20, 1781, Nesser, 203.
39. Dull, 87–88.

Chapter 15

1. Morison, 5–9
2. Morison, 9–11; Manceron, Claude, *The Wind from America 1778–1781*. New York, 1989, 2: 5–6.
3. Morison, 12–15; *The Morning Post and Daily Advertiser*, April 28, 1778, JPJ, 210.
4. Morison, 15–20
5. Ibid., 21–23.
6. Ibid., 23–25.
7. Royal Commission on the Ancient and Historical Monuments of Scotland, *Tollbooths and Town-Houses: Civic Architecture in Scotland to 1833*, Edinburgh, 1996, 122–126.
8. Morison, 26–27.
9. Ibid., 28–31.
10. Jones to Robert Morris, Aug. 24, 1777; Rank of Captains in the Navy, Oct. 10, 1776, JPJ, 33–34, 225.
11. Fischer, Julian, 'The Ranger, 1777', Ibid., 1–2.
12. Jones to the American Commissioners, Dec. 5, 1777, Ibid., 106.
13. Jones to Matthew Parke, July 2, 1777; John Fraser to Jones, Oct. 29, 1777, Ibid., 19–20, 45–46.
14. *Journal of the Continental Congress*, Ford, 8: 463–465; John Wendell to Jones, Oct. 29, 1777, JPJ, 45–46.
15. Jones to Samuel Wallingford, July 15, 1777, JPJ, 23–24.
16. *Advertisement for Seamen for Continental Navy Ship Ranger*, March 29, 1777, JPJ, 27; Morison, 102–111.
17. Jones to Lieutenant Elijah Hall, July 29, 1777 and Jones to Joseph Hewes, Aug. 17, 1777, JPJ, 2933; Ranger Crew members to the Commissioners, June 3, 1778, JPJ, 182.
18. Ranger Crew members to the Commissioners, June 3, 1778, JPJ, 182; De Koven, Anna, *The Life and Letters of John Paul Jones,* New York, 1913, 272–286.
19. Manceron, 2: 1.
20. Lewis, James, *Neptune's Militia, The Frigate South Carolina during the American Revolution.* Kent, Oh., 1999, 22, 23, 81, 120; Fowler, 150–151.
21. Thomas Simpson to Jones, Dec. 19, 1777, JPJ, 109.
22. John Frazer to Jones, Sept. 1, 1777; Matthew Parke to Jones, Feb. 19, 1778, JPJ, 39, 123–124; Jones to the Continental Navy Board of the Eastern Department, Feb. 23, 1778, NDAR, 11:1037.
23. Jones to Silas Deane, March 25, 1778, JPJ, 126–128.
24. Syrett, *The Royal Navy in European Waters during the American Revolutionary War.* Columbia, SC, 1998, 9–10; Gibbon, Ronald, *'To the King's deceit' A Study of Smuggling in the Solway.* Carlisle, UK, 1983, 17.
25. *The Cumberland Chronicle and Whitehaven Public Advertiser, Ap. 25, 1778*; Surgeon Green commented, 'had the Captain ...permitted the Marines to fire on them when they

first came under our lee Quarter [we] might have taken Her with great Ease,' Diary of Dr. Ezra Green, April 19, 1778, JPJ, 203; Fowler, 152.

26. Jones to the American Commissioners, May 27, 1778; Diary of Dr. Ezra Green, April 21, 1778, JPJ, 160–161, 204; Fowler, 153.

27. Beckett, J.V., *Coal & Tobacco, The Lowthers and the Economic Development of West Cumberland 1660–1760.* Cambridge, UK, 1981, 62–101, 142–174; Routledge, Alan, *Whitehaven Harbour through Time.* Gloucestershire, 2012, 4–11.

Chapter 16

1. *The Cumberland Chronicle and Whitehaven Public Advertiser,* Mar. 7 and 21, Apr. 25, 1778; Manceron, 2: 14.

2. Beckett, J.V., *Coal & Tobacco, The Lowthers and the Economic Development of West Cumberland 1660–1760.* Cambridge, UK, 1981, 62–101, 142–174; Routledge, Alan, *Whitehaven Harbour through Time.* Gloucestershire, 2012, 4–11.

3. Beckett, 199.

4. Ibid., 200.

5. Jones to Robert Morris, Dec.11, 1777, JPJ, 107–108.

6. Jones to the American Commissioners, May 27, 1778, Ibid., 161–163.

7. Ibid.

8. Ibid.

9. Ibid.

10. *The Cumberland Chronicle and Whitehaven Public Advertiser,* Mar. 7 and 21, Apr. 25, 1778; Morison, 140.

11. *The Cumberland Chronicle and Whitehaven Public Advertiser,* Mar. 7 and 21, Apr. 25, 1778.

12. Ibid.

13. *The Cumberland Chronicle and Whitehaven Public Advertiser,* Mar. 7 and 21, Apr. 25, 1778; MacDougall, 120.

14. *The Morning Post and Daily Advertiser*, Apr. 28, 1778, JPJ, 210.

15. Fischer, 8.

16. Ibid.

17. Ibid.

18. Jones to the American Commissioners, May 27, 1778, JPJ, 161–163

19. Balfour Paul, James, *Scots Peerage*, Edinburgh, 1902, 7: 520–522.

20. *The Cumberland Chronicle and Whitehaven Public Advertiser,* Mar. 7 and 21, Apr. 25, 1778; Jones to the American Commissioners, May 27, 1778, JPJ, 163; Morison, 145.

21. Manceron, 2: 7–9; *Gazetteer and Daily Advertiser,* May 1, 1778, Seitz, Don, ed., *Paul Jones, his exploits in English seas, during 1778–1780, Contemporary accounts collected from English newspapers.* New York, 1917, 11–12; Young Thomas became the 5th Earl of Selkirk and went on to play a role in the expansion of Canada.

22. *The Cumberland Chronicle and Whitehaven Public Advertiser,* Apr. 25, 1778.

23. Jones to the Countess of Selkirk, May 8, 1778, JPJ, 167–170. During 1782, Lord Selkirk would support the renewed effort to create a Scottish militia, contributing to

national defense. A radical Whig, he joined John Cartwright, Granville Sharp and Josiah Wedgwood in the Society for Constitutional Information, which aimed to reform the way in which representatives were elected to the Commons. Morison, 151–154; Robertson, John, *The Scottish Enlightenment and the Militia Issue*. Edinburgh, 1985, 128, 141.
24. Diary of Dr Ezra Green, April 24, 1778, JPJ, 204.
25. Fowler, 170.

Chapter 17

1. Morison, 142; Lorenz, Lincoln, *John Paul Jones: Fighter for Freedom and Glory*. Annapolis, 1943, 144–149; Jones Memorandum to Benjamin Franklin, July 4–5, 1778, *The Papers of Benjamin Franklin*, New Haven, Ct. 1959-, 27: 45.
2. Rodger, *The Command of the Ocean*, 76–79.
3. Milton, Giles, *White Gold: The Extraordinary Story of Thomas Pellow and North Africa's One Million European Slaves*. London, 2004, 13–37, 58–61, 113.
4. Captain George Bonyer to Philip Stephens, June 29, 1777, NDAR 9: 443–444.
5. Wilson, Kathleen, *The Sense of the People: Politics, Culture and Imperialism in England, 1715–1785*. Cambridge, UK, 1998, 237–284; Rude, George, '"Mother Gin" and the London Riots of 1736', and 'Wilkes and Liberty, 1768–9', *Paris and London in the Eighteenth Century*, New York, 1970, 201–267.
6. MacDougall, 118; Warner, 169, 207, 212.
7. A miniature of Wickes exists by late eighteenth-century French artist Louis Marie Sicardi.
8. *The Cumberland Chronicle and Whitehaven Public Advertiser*, Apr. 25, 1778.
9. *Gazetteer and New Daily Advertiser*, Apr. 28, 1778, JPJ, 211.
10. *The Cumberland Chronicle and Whitehaven Public Advertiser*, Jan. 6, 1778.
11. *Morning Post and Daily Advertiser*, Apr. 28, 1778.
12. *Morning Chronicle and London Advertiser*, Apr 29, 1778, Seitz, 8–9.
13. Jones to Robert Morris, Dec.11, 1777, JPJ, 107–108.
14. Jones to Benjamin Franklin, May 18, 1778, JPJ, 167; *The Cumberland Chronicle and Whitehaven Public Advertiser*, Apr. 25, 1778; *Morning Chronicle and London Advertiser*, May 8, 1778, Seitz, 19; Wilson, Andrew, 'He raided the fleet but gave back the Teapot', *Christian Science Monitor*, Apr. 23, 1987. Wilson says that today the teapot is in a Kirkcudbright bank vault, although that is not evidence that Jones ever had it.
15. JPJ, 153.
16. Sperry, Armstrong, *John Paul Jones: The Pirate Patriot*. New York, 2016 contends that the British thought Jones was a pirate. Another portrait of Jones is said have been done in 1780 by Charles Willson Peale, but Jones was in Europe at the time and Charles Coleman Sellers' exhaustive study, *Charles Willson Peal*, New York, 1969 does not mention this portrait.
17. Morrison, 391–406.
18. Proceedings in the Lords respecting the Commercial Losses occasioned by the American War, Feb. 6, 1778, NDAR, 11: 968, 971; Conway, *The British Isles*, 64–65; Buel, 96; Fowler, 134.

Chapter 18

1. *The Cumberland Chronicle and Whitehaven Public Advertiser,* Apr. 4, 11, 25, 1778; *Morning Chronicle and London Advertiser*, May 5, 1778, JPJ, 212.
2. *The Cumberland Chronicle and Whitehaven Public Advertiser,* Apr. 25, 1778.
3. *Morning Chronicle and London Advertiser*, May 9, 1778, *Gazetteer and Daily Advertiser,* May 11, 1778, JPJ, 212–214.
4. 'The 18th century defenses of Whitehaven', 2007, http: whitehavenandwesternlakeland. co.uk, accessed 10/30/21.
5. Ibid.
6. Starkey, 194–195.
7. Memorial of the Merchants, Traders, and Ship Owners of London to Lord Weymouth, Nov. 24, 1777; Extract of a Letter from a Gentleman on Board the Roebuck ... to his father in Edinburgh, March 8, 1777, NDAR, 10: 1024, 8: 61; Bristol, England was active in privateering during the Revolution: Morgan, 220–221; Press, 15–17; Buel, 56–57.
8. Archive Centre, Liverpool Maritime Museum, *B/BROC;* Hollet, 21–23.
9. *The Cumberland Chronicle and Whitehaven Public Advertiser,* Apr. 11, 1778; Hay, 65–67; Wilson, 269.
10. Hay, 30; Virginia Calendar of State Papers for April 3 and 16, 1779 in Charles, Joan, *Mid-Atlantic Shipwreck Accounts to 1899.* Hampton, VA, 1997, 19–20.
11. Pool, Bernard, *Navy Board Contracts 1660–1832.* London, 1966, 77–110.
12. Hollet, 23.
13. Hollet, 24. By 1795 Brocklebank's had a merchant fleet consisted of eleven vessels. Five years later, the yard had completed seven brigs, two full-rigged ships, one cutter and a snow. The plans and specifications of the vessels built by his yard, provide an important source for the construction of eighteenth and early nineteenth century merchant ships. Brocklebank retired at 59 years of age, and died the following year at his home, No. 25 Roper Street. His company was renamed for his remaining sons Thomas and John, who took over the business.

Chapter 19

1. 'He Bought HMS Drake', *Seacoast New Hampshire*, 2012, 4/4/20.
2. O Baoill, Ruairi, *Carrickfergus, the Story of the Castle and Walled Town.* Belfast, 2008, 58–78.
3. McConnell, Charles, *The French are Landing! The Forgotten Invasion of Carrickfergus in 1760,* 1–14.
4. Ibid., 15–38
5. McConnell, 39–49; Tildesley, Jim, *'I am Determined to Live or Die on Board My Ship' The life of Admiral John Inglis: An American in the Georgian Navy.* Kibworth Beauchamp, UK, 2019, 43–72.
6. *Morning Chronicle and London Advertiser*, May 1, 1778; Diary of Dr Ezra Green, April 24, 1778, *Morning Chronicle and London Advertiser*, May 9, 1778; *Gazetteer and New Daily Advertiser*, May 11, 1778, JPJ, 204–205, 212–214.

7. Building Accounts from Langdon Ledger-Daybook, Feb. 1, 1779-July 14, 1779, Ibid., 223–224.
8. Fisher, Epilogue: The Ranger leaves France under Command of Thomas Simpson, Ibid., 189; Fowler, 104–107.
9. JPG, 189–190.
10. Morison, 167–172; Syrett, *Royal Navy in European Waters*, 61–79.
11. Jones to Thomas Simpson, April 26, 1778; Jones to Thomas Simpson, May 7, 1778; Jones to Elijah Hall, May 7, 1778, JPJ, 144, 154; Gawalt, Gerald and Sellers, John, eds., *John Paul Jones' Memoir of the American Revolution Presented to King Louis XVI of France*. Washington, DC, 1979, 8; Morison, 171.
12. American Commissioners to Jones, May 25, 1778, From Benjamin Franklin to Jones, May 27, 1778, JPJ, 170–171; *John Adams Diary and Autobiography*, June 3, 1778, NDAR, 4: 123–124.
13. Diary of Dr Ezra Green, July 27, 1778, JPJ, 207.
14. Morison, 166–167.
15. Rodger, *Command of the Ocean*, 317–318.
16. Gilje, Paul, *Liberty on the Waterfront: American Maritime Culture in the Age of Revolution*. Philadelphia, 2004, 110–112; De Koven, 272–279.
17. Morison, 196–197.
18. Ranger Crew Members to the Commissioners, June 3, 1778; The Warrant and Petty Officers of the Ranger: Petition to the American Commissioners, June 15, 1778, JPJ, 181–185; Thomas, Evan, *John Paul Jones: Sailor, Hero, Father of the American Navy*. New York, 2004, 91,118. The latest analysis of Jones and his conflict with the *Ranger*'s crew is Jonathan Feld, 'John Paul Jones' Locker, The Mutinous Men of the Continental Ship Ranger and the Confinement of Lieutenant Thomas Simpson', Department of the Navy, Washington, DC., online June 11, 2019; Gilje, 97–129.

Chapter 20

1. Dull, 107–109.
2. Mackesy, 279–281; Paterson, A. T., *The Other Armada: The Franco-Spanish Attempt to Invade Britain in 1779*. Manchester, 1960.
3. Manceron, 2: 176–177.
4. Ibid., 2: 177–179.
5. Ibid., 2: 180–181.
6. Stokes, 32–33; Morison, 186–88, 200–206. John Kilby wrote a detailed account of his naval service as a member of the crew. Still, he wrote it more than thirty years after the events he describes and he mistakenly places Leith in Ireland and is a supporter of Jones, ignoring his flaws.
7. Morison, 188–191; Miller, 371–374.
8. Morison, 191–197.
9. Ibid., 197–212.
10. Ibid., 212–220.
11. Ibid., 213.
12. Ibid., 221–232.

13. Morison, 251–252; Miller, 378–385.
14. Barnes, John, ed., *The Logs of the 'Serapis', 'Alliance', 'Ariel' Under the Command of John Paul Jones, 1779–1780.* New York, 1911, 32, 36–39, 45, Stokes, 43–47.
15. Morison, 201, 256, 307–308.
16. Gardiner, 154, 189.
17. Morison, 266–68; Miller, 433–436.
18. Morison, 290–301.
19. Ibid., 269–279.
20. Ibid., 301–307.
21. Ibid., 307–308.
22. Fowler, 149.
23. Morison, 275–289; Martelle, Scott, *The Admiral and the Ambassador.* Chicago, 2014, 50.
24. Morison 401–408; Arnett, Earl, Brugger, Robert, Papenfuse, Edward, Maryland, *A New Guide to the Old Line State.* Baltimore, 1999, 56.

Chapter 21

1. Rodger, *Insatiable Earl*, 235–236.
2. Ibid., 238–239.
3. Manceron, 143.
4. Rodger, *Insatiable Earl*, 272–277.
5. Rodger, *Command of the Ocean.* 336–337, 342.
6. [O'Beirne, Thomas Lewis,] *Candid and Impartial Narrative of the Transactions of the Fleet: Under the Command of Lord Howe.* London, 1779, 5–10.
7. Hamond autobiography, HP. 1: 89–90; John Bowater to Lord Denbigh, Jul 31, 1778, Balderston and Syrett, 166–167; Marine Committee to Count d'Estaing, July 17 and Aug. 12, 1778, Paullin, 268–269, 284–285; O'Beirne, 11–15; Syrett, *Admiral Lord Howe*, 79–80.
8. James Payne, Logbook of the Roebuck, Aug. 27, 1778-May 12, 1779, NMM, ADM L/R 150; O'Beirne, 17–28.
9. O'Beirne, 30–31.
10. Clinton, 149–160; Smith, Paul, *Loyalists and Redcoats: A Study in British Revolutionary Policy.* New York, 1964, 79–125.
11. Wright, Leitch, *Florida in the American Revolution,* Gainesville, Fl., 1975, 5–6, 27–28, 44, 53, 103; Mowat, Charles, *East Florida as a British Province 1763–1784.* Gainesville, Fl., 1964, 108–123.
12. Wright, 43–44, 56–58.
13. Clinton, 116–117.
14. Clinton, 134; Comte d'Estaing, Journal of the Siege of Savannah; Anonymous naval officer, An English Journal of the Siege of Savannah 1779 in *Muskets Cannon Balls & Bombs*, ed. Kennedy, Benjamin, Savannah, 1974, 42–45, 83.
15. d'Estaing, 46–48; Augustine Prévost to George Germain, Nov. 1, 1779, Journal of the Siege of Savannah in Kennedy, 93; Major General Lincoln, Journal from Sept. 3 to Oct. 19, 1779 in Kennedy, 121–122.

16. d'Estaing; Prévost; Anonymous naval officer, Kennedy 46, 94, 81–82.
17. Prévost, Kennedy, 95–96; Lincoln, 123.
18. d'Estaing; Anonymous naval officer; Lincoln, Kennedy 67-68, 85-86, 127.
19. d'Estaing; Anonymous naval officer, Kennedy 74, 86–88.
20. d'Estaing, Kennedy, 69–70.
21. Boubacar, Barry, *Senegambia and the Atlantic Slave Trade*. Cambridge, UK, 1998, 55–126.

Chapter 22

1. Germain to Clinton, Sept. 27, 1779, Clinton, 423.
2. Clinton, 159-160; John Philips, Logbook of the Roebuck, Dec. 11, 1779-June 18, 1780, NMM, ADM L/R, 161.
3. Clinton, 160–161; Roebuck Captain's Log, Dec 25–26, 1779 and Apr. 8–10, 1780, NA, ADM 51/796; Black, 185.
4. Hamond autobiography, HP, 1: 18, 114; quote from Mackesy, *The War for America*, 341.
5. Harris, J. William, *The Hanging of Thomas Jeremiah*. New Haven, Ct., 2009, 7–10.
6. McCowen, George, *The British Occupation of Charleston, 1780–82*. Columbia, SC, 1972, 3, 6.
7. Hamond autobiography, HP, 1: 109–110; NA, ADM 1/486, f. 355; Black, 183–189.
8. John Philips, Logbook of the Roebuck, Dec. 11, 1779-June 18, 1780, NMM, ADM L/R, 161; Hamond autobiography, HP, 1: 111.
9. John Philips, Logbook of the Roebuck, Ibid.; Hamond autobiography, HP, 1: 112.
10. Clinton, 164; the observer was Peter Timothy, publisher of the *South Carolina Gazette*. After the British took Charleston, as a rebel he was sent to prison in St Augustine, Florida.
11. Borick, Carl, *A Gallant Defense, the Siege of Charleston, 1780*. Columbia, S.C., 2003, 136–137.
12. Gilpin, William, ed., *Memoirs of Josias Rogers*. London, 1808, 52–53; Hamond to George Keith Elphinstone, April 14, 1780, Elphinstone, George Keith, *The Keith Papers, selected from the Letters and Papers of Admiral Viscount Keith*. ed. W.G. Perrin, London, 1927, 1: 165–166.
13. Hamond autobiography, HP, 1: 113.
14. Clinton, 169; Tracy, Nicholas, Who's Who in Nelson's Navy. London, 2006, 273; Tarleton, Banastre, *A History of the Campaigns of 1780 and 1781 in the Southern Provinces of North America*, Dublin, 1787, 49.
15. Clinton, 171; Willis, Sam, *The Struggle for Sea Power: Naval History of the American Revolution*. New York, 2015, 352–355; Rodger, *Command of the Ocean*, 345.
16. George Scott, Logbook of the Roebuck, May 15, 1780-May 14, 1781, NMM, ADM L/R 150; Hamond autobiography, HP 114; Tracy, *Who's Who in Nelson's Navy*, 213; Tarleton, 53; Fowler, 110; Coker, P.C., *Charleston's Maritime Heritage 1670–1865*. Charleston, 1987, 110.
17. Smith, Paul, 126–133.

18. Clinton, 182, 186.
19. Clinton, 173–180; McCowen, 13- 42; Bull, Jr., Kinloch, *The Oligarchs in Colonial and Revolutionary Charleston.* Columbia, S.C., 1993, 293–296.
20. McCowen, 86.
21. Thomas Williams, Logbook of the Roebuck, May 15, 1780-June 2, 1781, NMM, ADM L/R 219; McCowen, 87–88. Captain James Gambier is not to be confused with his uncle Admiral James Gambier.
22. McCowen, 82–83; Coker, 125.
23. Fraser, Henry, 'The Memoranda of William Green, Secretary to Vice-Admiral Marriott Arbuthnot in the American Revolution', *Rhode Island Historical Society Collections*, 17: 59–64; Clinton, 181.

Chapter 23

1. Clinton, 149–160.
2. George Germain to Henry Clinton, Jan. 23, 1779, Clinton, 397–399 and 27, quote on 27; Smith, 109; O'Shaughnessy, Andrew, *The Men Who Lost America, British Leadership, the American Revolution, and the Fate of Empire.* New Haven 2013, 227–228. Sir Henry Clinton saw the long-term strategic value of the Chesapeake and also a place to cultivate Loyalists. However, Clinton's attitude toward Loyalists was more restrained than that of Lord Germain as he sought to limit the restoration of civil government and the forming of Loyalist combat units.
3. Collier, George, *A Detail of Some Particular Services Performed in America During the Years 1776–1779.* New York, 1835.
4. Collier to Clinton, May 16, 1779, Clinton, 406–7, quote on 406; Wilcox, *Portrait of a General*, 274–275; Fallaw, Robert and Stoer, Marion, 'The Old Dominion Under Fire', Eller, 443–452; Hast, 99–101; Selby, 204–209; Smith, Paul, 108–110; Wertenbaker and Schlegel, 70.
5. Edmund Pendleton to Woodford, June 21, 1779, *The Letters and Papers of Edmund Pendleton, 1734–1803.* Charlottesville, Va., 1967, 1: 290–1; Smith, Paul, 110–111; Northampton County Minute Book, May 1779; Hast, 138; Selby, 204–209.
6. Henry Clinton to George Mathew, May 20, 1779, Clinton, 406–407.
7. The fleet returned immediately to New York with all its refugees, 'Return of Persons that came off from Virginia with General Mathew in the Fleet August 24, 1779', NA, CO 5/52/63.
8. Germain to Clinton, Jan. 23, 1779, Clinton, 397–399; Smith, Paul, 109–111.
9. Clinton, 230–231, 235, quote on 235; Wilcox, *Portrait of a General,* 349–350; Wertenbaker and Schlegel, 71–72; Scharf, J. Thomas, *History of Delaware, 1609–1888.* Ann Arbor, Mich., 1972, 2: 386–387.
10. Petition of Somerset and Worcester Loyalists to General Leslie, before July 3, 1781, in Thomas, Roger, ed., *Brown Books.* Annapolis, 1948, 2: 481.
11. Selby, 216–217, 220–221; Fallow and Stoer, 453–457.
12. Clinton, 228–229; Selby, 220–221.

13. Instructions to Brigadier General Arnold, Dec. 13, 1780, Clinton, 482–483, 244; Wilcox, *Portrait of a General,* 354, 372–373; Selby, 221–223, Fallow and Stoer, 458–459; Benjamin Caldwell to William Hotham, April 18, 1778, NDAR, 12:135.

14. Kranish, Michael, *Flight from Monticello: Thomas Jefferson at War,* New York, 2010, 119–318; Fallow and Stoer, 464.

15. Simcoe, John Graves, *Simcoe's Military Journal,* Arno ed., New York, 1968, 93–95; Booker, Marshall, 'Privateering from the Bay, Including Admiralty Courts and Tory as well as Patriot Operations', Eller, 179.

16. Kranish, 141, 183–186; Selby, 223–224.

17. *Journal of Rear-Admiral Bartholomew James, 1752–1828,* eds. J. Laughton and J. Sullivan, Naval Records Society, 1896, 103–104.

18. Ferreiro, Larrie, 'The Race to the Chesapeake between Destouches and Arbuthnot, March 1781', *Mariner's Mirror,* 104: 477–481.

19. Mahan, 341–344; Benians, 111; Clinton, 254, 276.

20. Goldenberg, Joseph, and Stoer, Marion, 'The Virginia Navy', Eller, 194–195.

21. Arnold to Clinton, May 12, 1781, Clinton, 520.

22. Simcoe, 199; Clinton, 520.

23. Simcoe, 199; Goldenberg and Stoer, 202–203.

24. George Dashiell to Thomas Sim Lee, March 12, 1781; Joseph Dashiell to Thomas Sim lee, March 13, 1781, MA, 47: 118, 120-22; Stewart, Robert, *The History of Virginia's Navy of the Revolution.* Baltimore, 1934, 102.

25. Joseph Dashiell to Thomas Sim Lee, July 5, 1781 and Joseph Dashiell to Thomas Sim Lee, July 13, 1781, *Brown Books,* 3: 483, 488.

Chapter 24

1. Gwyn, *Ashore and Afloat,* 19–20.

2. George Germain to Henry Clinton, Sept. 2, 1778, Clinton, 390–391, 135.

3. Clinton to Francis McLean, Feb. 11, 1779 and Francis McLean to Clinton, May 28, 1779, Kevitt, 57, 60; Buker, George, *The Penobscot Expedition.* Lanham, Md., 2002, 6–14.

4. Buker, 19.

5. Morison, 38–39, 42–45, 59, 71, 87–89, 97.

6. Buker, 22.

7. Continental Navy Board in Boston to Massachusetts Council, June 30, 1779, Kevitt, 64.

8. Morison, 44–45, 77, 88–89; Kevitt, 5–8.

9. Peter Warren to Thomas Corbett, June 18, 1745, *The Royal Navy and North America: The Warren Papers, 1736–1752.* Gwyn, Julian, ed., London, 1973, 120–125; Rawlyk, George, *Yankees at Louisbourg,* Orono, Me., 1967, 44–57; Lovell's Journal, July 15, 1779 and July 19, 1779, Kevitt, 27–28; Buker, 24.

10. Continental Navy Board in Boston to Massachusetts Council, June 30, 1779, Kevitt, 64; Buker, 29.

11. Massachusetts Council, Warrant to Impress Seamen, July 3, 1779, Kevitt, 68–69; Buker, 23.

12. Continental Navy Board to Dudley Saltonstall, July 13, 1779; Lovell's Journal, July 26 and July 28, 1779, Kevitt, 72–73, 33, 35.
13. Buker, 39–40, 48, 68.
14. Petition from Ship Masters to Commodore Saltonstall, July 27, 1779, Kevitt, 78.
15. Major Lee to Major General Lord Stirling, August 1, 1779, Kevitt, 87–88.
16. Buker, 75–81, 91.
17. George Collier to Henry Clinton, Aug. 19, 1779, Clinton, 416–417; Council of War on Board the 'Warren', Aug. 14, 1779, and Falmouth Committee of Safety to Massachusetts Council, Aug. 30, 1779, Kevitt, 108–109, 114–115.
18. Statement of General Wadsworth, Sept. 29, 1779, Kevitt, 141–146.
19. Notes from Saltonstall's Defense, Penobscot Marine Museum, Me, LB2023.26.18; Buker, 114–135.
20. Kevitt, 174–175; Buker, 14–15.
21. Fischer, Julian, 'The Ranger leaves France under the Command of Thomas Simpson', Sawtelle, 189.
22. Kevitt, 171–172; Buker, 163.
23. C. Bruce Fergusson, 'Perkins, Simeon', in *DCB*, vol. 5, University of Toronto/ Université Laval, 2003–to date, accessed January 29, 2021, http://www.biographi.ca/en/ bio/perkins_simeon_5E.html.
24. Miller, 253, 281.
25. John Allen, Orders Given to Indians, Aug. 17, 1778, *Military Operations in Eastern Maine and Nova Scotia*, ed. Kidder, Frederic, Albany, 1867, 255–256. Gwyn, *Frigates and Foremasts*, 68.

Chapter 25

1. Syrett, *Shipping and the American War,* 17–36; Talbott, 36–39.
2. Gwyn, Julian, *Excessive Expectations: Maritime Commerce & the Economic Development of Nova Scotia, 1740–1870.* Montreal and Kingston, 1998, 16–30.
3. Navy Board to Philip Stephens, Dec. 9, 1762, NMM, ADM/B/170; Gwyn, *Ashore and Afloat*, 4–8, 10; Ubbelohde, Carl, *The Vice Admiralty Courts and the American Revolution.* Chapel Hill, NC, 1960, 3–4, 49–53.
4. Gwyn, *Ashore and Afloat*, 7–10, 231.
5. Navy Board to Arbuthnot, Oct. 3, 1775, TNA, ADM106/2470, fol. 211–212; Hamond to Navy Board, Nov. 25, 1781, HP, 7: 43, 47; Gwyn, *Ashore and Afloat*, 24–25, 101–121.
6. Hamond to Navy Board, Nov. 25, 1781, HP 7: 47; Navy Board to Hamond, NA, ADM106/2471, fol. 190; Hamond to George Thomas, Jan. 1, 1782, HP, 9: 106; Gwyn, *Ashore and Afloat*, 78, 106, 113–114, 244.
7. Gwyn, *Ashore and Afloat*, 170–174.
8. Marriot Arbuthnot to Philip Stephens, Oct. 29, 1780, NA, ADM1/486, fol. 443; Gwyn, 'The Halifax Naval Yard and Mast Contractors, 1775–1815', *The Northern Mariner – Le marin du nord*, 11: 1–25.

9. Gwyn, *Ashore and Afloat*, 20–21, 67, 69; Donald F. Chard, 'Arbuthnot, Marriot', in *DCB*, vol. 4, University of Toronto/Université Laval, 2003–, accessed October 31, 2021, http://www.biographi.ca/en/bio/arbuthnot_mariot_4E.html..

10. George Washington to James Bowdoin, June 14, 1780, George Washington Papers at the U.S. Library of Congress, Historical Collections for the U.S. National Digital Library, http://memory.loc.gov/mss/mgw/mgw3c/003/301298.gif, accessed May 15, 2019.

11. Marble, Allan Everett, *Surgeons, Smallpox, and the Poor: A History of Medicine and Social Conditions in Nova Scotia, 1749–1799*. Montreal, 1993, 45–48, 73–81, 103–108.

12. Blakeley, Phyllis and Grant, John, eds., *Eleven Exiles, Accounts of Loyalists in the American Revolution*. Toronto, 1982, 30–32, 71–72; Marble, 107–110.

13. Marble, 112.

14. Hamond autobiography, HP, 1: 124–125; Lincoln, 33–34.

15. Gwyn, *Ashore and Afloat,* 43–45; Cahill, J. B., 'Hamond, Sir Andrew Snape', *DCB*, vol. 6, University of Toronto/Université Laval, 2003–to date, http://www.biographi.ca/en/bio/hamond_andrew_snape_6E.html, accessed Nov. 4, 2016.

16. Hamond to Sick & Hurt Board, Nov. 25, 1781, HP, 8: 11–13, 9: 189–191.

17. Blakeley, 'Hughes, Sir Richard', DCB, vol. 5, University of Toronto/Université Laval, 2003–to date, http://www.biographi.ca/en/bio/hughes_richard_5E.html, accessed May 30, 2017.

18. Hamond to Capt. Russell, April 20, 23, 1782, HP, 7: 78–79; Mercer, Keith, North Atlantic Press Gangs: Impressment and Naval-Civilian Relations in Nova Scotia and Newfoundland 1749–1815, PhD thesis Dalhousie University, 2008, 82–83.

19. Hamond to Lt. Vardon, June 13, 1782, HP, 9: 13.

20. Hamond to Brigadier General Campbell, Sept. 12, 1781, HP, 7: 126–127.

Chapter 26

1. Morison, 76–80; Miller, 128–129.

2. Morison, 87.

3. Hamond to Thomas Graves, Dec. 6, 1781, HP 7: 51–52; Gwyn, *Ashore and Afloat*, 155–157.

4. Magra, *The Fisherman's Cause.* Cambridge, UK, 2011, 73–98.

5. Gwyn, *Frigates and Foremasts*, 64–66.

6. Blakeley, 'Hughes, Sir Richard', DCB, accessed May 30, 2017.

7. Hamond to Navy Board, Nov. 25, 1781, HP, 7: 43, 47.

8. Horwood, Harold, and Butts, Edward, eds., *Bandits and Privateers: Canada in the Age of Gunpowder.* Halifax, 1988, 39–42.

9. Mackesy, 37, 158; Gwyn, *Frigates and Foremasts*, 67.

10. 'The Barracks', Canada's Historic Places, Provincial Registry found at Heritage Property Program office, 1747 Summer Street, Halifax, NS B3H 3A6.

11. Moody, Barry, 'Ritchie, John', *DCB*, vol. 4, University of Toronto/Université Laval, 2003–, accessed November 20, 2017. The record on the *Resolution* and Captain Amos Potter is unclear. After the *Resolution* was captured in 1779, it appears that a second privateer *Resolution* was launched. Meanwhile in July 10, 1780, the refitted Loyalist privateer *Resolution* fought a hot engagement with the American privateer *Viper* to a draw.

12. Hamond to Robert Digby, June 2, 1782, HP, 7: 89–91; Gwyn, *Frigates and Foremasts*, 74–75; *Nova Scotia Gazette*, June 4, 1782 and Letter of Lieutenant William Gray, June 12, 1782, Paine, Ralph, *The Ships and Sailors of Old Salem, Massachusetts*. Salem, 2007, 72–75.

13. *Collections of the Nova Scotia Historical Society*, 123; Horwood and Butts, 42–44; Beck, J. Murray, 'Creighton, John (1721–1807)', DCB, vol. 5, University of Toronto/Université Laval, 2003–, accessed November 20, 2017.

14. Hamond to Alexander Breymer, July 1, 1782, HP, 7:22-23, 97; Gwyn, *Frigates and Foremasts*, 73, 75.

15. Hamond to the Admiralty, Sept. 10, 1781, HP, 7: 22–23. In November 1781, Douglas had taken time from his duties to marry Anne Burgess in New York. He was only twenty and his later portraits show him to be handsome and youthful. Anne was later painted as Lady Anne Douglass, in the simplest dress and hair style, reflecting classical taste. She would be a great favorite of Admiral Howe. The couple would eventually have two daughters and one son: Anne, Harriet, Andrew Snape Jr.

16. Hamond to Admiralty, Sept.10, 1781; Hamond to Graves, Sept.10, 1781, HP, 7: 22–23, 8: 1; Gwyn, *Frigates and Foremasts*, 80.

17. Hamond to John Crymes, Aug. 10, 1782, HP, 9: 152.

18. Hamond to the Admiralty, Nov. 13, 1782; Hamond to Robert Digby, Nov. 22, 1782, HP, 7: 152, 155.

19. Hamond to Robert Digby, September 24, 1782; Hamond to the Navy Board, Oct. 25, 1782, HP, 7: 131–132, 145–146; McCowen, 149.

20. MacKinnon, Neil, *This Unfriendly Soil: The Loyalist Experience in Nova Scotia, 1783–1791*. Montreal and Kingston, 1986, 13–18, 35–45.

21. Mackinnon, 8, 40, 68; Syrett, *Shipping and the American War*, 238; Jasanoff, Maya, *Liberty's Exiles: American Loyalists in the Revolutionary World*. New York, 2011, 86–87.

22. Peter Burroughs, 'Parr, John,' DCB, vol. 4, University of Toronto/Université Laval, 2003– to date, http://www.biographi.ca/en/bio/parr_john_4E.html, accessed July 13, 2022.

23. Hamond to Lord Shelburne, Oct. 9, 1782; Hamond to Philip Stephens, Oct. 30, 1782, HP, 8: 33, 7: 147–148.

24. Sir Andrew Snape Hamond, hamondplainshistoricalsociety.ca/our-history/ 11/ 5/ 2016; Gwyn, *Ashore and Afloat*, 334, 339.

25. Hamond to Captain Fisher, Dec. 4, 1782, HP, 9: 201, 204.

Chapter 27

1. Rodger, *The Command of the Ocean*. 169, 170, 179; Smith, C.T., *An Historical Geography of Western Europe*. New York, 1967, 146–153.

2. Donald, Diana, *The Age of Caricature: Satirical Prints in the Reign of George III*. New Haven, Ct., 1996, 20.

3. Elliott, John, *Empires of the Atlantic World: Britain and Spain in America 1492–1830*. New Haven, Ct., 2006, 353–366.

4. Silas Dean to Miguel Lagounere & Company, Oct. 19, 1777; Gustavus Conyngham to Arthur Lee, Jan. 31, 1778; Floridablanca to Francisco de Escarano, Feb. 16, 1778; Lord Weymouth to Lord Grantham, Feb. 20, 1778, NDAR, 11: 957, 11: 1013, 11: 1026.

5. Dull, 91–2, 107–109.
6. Ibid., 108–109.
7. Ibid., 110–112.
8. A Gentleman, *An accurate Description of Gibraltar: interspersed with a Pathetic Account of the Progress of the Siege*, reprint Uckfield, UK, 1–2, 21–22; McGuffie, T.H., *The Siege of Gibraltar*. London, 1965, 14–17.
9. 'Etat des forces employais au siege de Gibraltar au commencement de September 1782', *Seven Letters about siege of Gibraltar, Armee France, 1782*, Ashok Vilon, India, *17*.
10. McGuffie, 45, 54, 84.
11. Ibid., 45–46, 100, 117–118.
12. Ibid, 49, 73.
13. A Gentleman, 15–16.
14. Spilsbury, John, *A Journal of the Siege of Gibraltar, 1779–1783.* London, 1908, 10; A Gentleman, 6–7; Willis, 297–298.
15. Spilsbury, 33, 38, 82.
16. McGuffie, 49, 55.
17. Spilsbury, 19.
18. Spilsbury, 25, 63; A Gentleman, 23–24.
19. Courcells, Jean, *Dictionnaire historique et biographique des generaux francais.* Paris, 1820, 1: 291–295.
20. Rodger, *Command of the Ocean*, 349.
21. McGuffie, 13.
22. Le Michaud, Jean-Claude-Elenor, *Historie du Siege de Gibraltar, Fait Pendent L'ete de 1782 sous les Ordres du Captaine General Duc de Crillon* ...1783, 10–47; Etat des forces, Camp de Roche, Sept. 12, 1782, 7–10, 18.
23. Spilsbury, 77–78; Le Michaud, 55–66.
24. Spilsbury, 47; Le Michaud, 68–75.
25. Spilsbury, 71; Le Michaud, 77.
26. Donald, 60–63.

Chapter 28

1. Spilsbury, 11.
2. A Gentleman, 33.
3. McGuffie, 40, 44–45.
4. Spilsbury, 1, 11.
5. Ibid., 8, 17. 22, 27, 28, 38.
6. A Gentleman, 10–15.
7. McGuffie, 49, 54, 61.
8. Connolly, Thomas, *The History of the Corps of Royal Sappers and Mines*, London, 1857, 1: 1.
9. Ibid., 1: 4–8.
10. Ibid.,1: 7–8.
11. McGuffie, 23–27

12. Ibid., 41–43
13. Connolly, 1: 13–14; Spilsbury, 64.
14. Mackesy, 381–382.
15. Rodger, *Insatiable Earl*, 242–244.
16. Spinney, David, *Rodney*. London, 1969, 297–302; Rodger, *The Command of the Ocean*. 343.
17. Spinney, 304–310; Rodger, *The Command of the Ocean*. 344–345.
18. Spilsbury, 16.
19. Spilsbury, 92–102; McGuffie, 94–96.
20. Syrett, *Admiral Lord Howe*, 104–105.
21. A Gentleman, 27–28, 50–52; Rodger, *The Command of the Ocean*. 355–356.
22. Syrett, *Admiral Lord Howe*, 105–106.
23. Spilsbury, 5, 23; McGuffie, 48–49, 54, 132–136.
24. McGuffie, 40–54
25. Knight, Roger, 'Curtis, Sir Roger, First Baronet', *DNB*, https://doi.org/10.1093/ref: odnb/6961, accessed, Jan. 21, 2021; Syrett, *Admiral Lord Howe*, 66.
26. Knight.
27. Knight; McGuffie, 119–137.
28. McGuffie, 137–138.
29. Ibid., 160–164.
30. The Memorial of Benjamin Whitecuff a Black Man, NA, Audit Office, class 13, 56: 628.
31. McGuffie, 150.
32. Ibid., 173.
33. Ibid., 169, 174.
34. Ibid., 188, 194.
35. Dull, 147, 152, 156–157.
36. Spilsbury, 96; McGuffie, 189.
37. McGuffie, 173, 177, 181–183,
38. Ibid., 189–192.
39. Chipulina, Neville, The People of Gibraltar, https://gibraltar-intro.blogspot.com/2011/01/ chapter-17.html, accessed Feb. 12, 2021.
40. Ibid.
41. Connolly, 1: 32–41.

Chapter 29

1. Clark, William, *Benjamin Franklin's Privateers: A Naval Epic of the American Revolution*. Baton Rouge, 1956; Patton, 124, 114–121. A Gentleman, 27–28, 50–52; Rodger, *The Command of the Ocean*. 334; McGuffie, 49, 136.
2. Starkey, *British Privateering*. 35–38, 249–256; Ubbelohde, 2–4, 60–71, 179–201.
3. Ubbelohde, 128–147.
4. Starkey, *British Privateering*. 19–34; Ritchie, Robert, *Captain Kid and the War Against the Pirates*. Cambridge, Mass., 1986, 17–19, 151–152.
5. Starkey, *British Privateering*, 194–196.

6. Memorial of the Merchants, Traders, and Ship Owners of London to Lord Weymouth, Nov. 24, 1777; Extract of a Letter from a Gentleman on Board the Roebuck … to his father in Edinburgh, March 8, 1777, NDAR, 10: 1024, 8: 61; Crewe, 85–86, 131–140.

7. Rodger, *The Wooden World*, 63, 127–130.

8. Cronin, William, *The Disappearing Islands of the Chesapeake*. Baltimore, 2005, 107.

9. Norton, 16.

10. Pattison to Robert Bayard, July 16, 1779 in 'Letters of Major General James Pattison', in *Collections of the New-York Historical Society*. New York, 1876, 226–227; Ubbelohde, 172–178; Buel, 135–137.

11. Gambier, James, *A narrative of facts, relative to the conduct of Vice-Admiral Gambier.* London, 1782. 14. The comment was made by William Eden of the Carlisle Peace Commission in a letter of April 27, 1779 to Gambier; Hartley, 66–67; Van Buskirk, 112–114.

12. *Rivington's The Royal Gazette*, Mar. 21, 1778, NDAR, 11: 689; Adair, William, 'Revolutionary War Diary of William Adair', ed. Harold Hancock, DH, 13: 161; Chopra, Ruma, *Unnatural Rebellion, Loyalists in New York City during the Revolution*. Charlottesville, Va., 2011, 127; Starkey, *British Privateering*, 194, 201; Buel, *In Irons*, 136–137.

13. CMSP, *no. 5 Executive Miscellanea*, Annapolis, 1968, 137; *Rivington's The Royal Gazette*, Mar. 21, 1778, NDAR, 11: 689; Chopra, 130.

14. Chopra, 127–128.

15. Pattison to Magistrates of Police, Jan. 7, 1780, in 'Letters to Major General Pattison', 338–339; Chopra, 127–130.

16. Jameson, Edward, 'Tory Operations in the Bay', Eller, 388.

17. Armed Boat Company Warrant to William Luce, NA, Treasury Office, Class 1, Volume 647, folio 74; Hodges, Graham, *Root & Branch: African Americans in New York & East Jersey, 1613–1863.* Chapel Hill, N.C., 1999, 153.

18. Thomas Jefferson to John Jay, June 19, 1779, *The Papers of Thomas Jefferson*, 3: 4–6.

19. Hartley, 4–7; Pougher, Richard, '"Averse to Remaining Idle Spectators": the Emergence of Loyalist privateering During the American Revolution, 1775–1778,' Digital Commons @ University of Maine, 121–215, 218, 221–223, accessed Dec. 18, 2018.

20. Custis, George, 'The Goodrich family and the Revolution in Virginia, 1774–1776', *Virginia Magazine of History and Biography*, 84: 49–74; Edmund Pendleton to Richard Henry Lee, Nov. 27,1775, *Letters and Papers of Edmund Pendleton*, 133; Hartley, 9–18; Hast, 48.

21. Lord Dunmore to Lord Dartmouth, Jan. 4, 1776; *Dunlap's Maryland Gazette*, Mar 19, 1776; Andrew Hamond to Matthew Squire, Feb. 26, 1776, NDAR, 3: 617–619, 4: 92–93; Custis, 50–57; Hartley, 18–28; Hast, 48–50, 74–76.

22. Lord Dunmore to George Germain, June 26, 1776; John Lancaster to James Parker, April 27, 1778, NDAR, 5: 755–758, 12: 201; Hartley, 29–30.

23. Lord Dunmore to Lord George Germain, June 26, 1776, NDAR, 5: 755–758; Maryland Council to Robert Hooe, May 30, 1777, MA, 16: 268; Hartley, 31.

24. John Lancaster to James Parker, April 27, 1778, NDAR, 12: 201; Hartley, 44, 50–51.

25. James Calhoun to Thomas Johnson, April 23, 1777, RB, no. 4, part 2; Deposition of Lawrence Sanford, May 31, 1777, RB, no. 4, part 2, 1085; Josiah Bartlet to John

Langdon, Aug. 5, 1776, *The Papers of Josiah Bartlett*. ed. Myers, Frank, Hanover, NH, 1979, 102; Middleton, 'Ships and Shipbuilding in the Chesapeake and Tributaries', Eller, 100.

26. Hartley, 112–113.
27. Hartley, 137; Custis, 58–74; Hast, 50, 60, 64, 76, 100, 128–129; Wrike, 51, 53, 58, 66.
28. Hartley, 55, 69, 83, 90.
29. Jarvis, Michael, *In the Eye of all Trade: Bermuda, Bermudians, and the Maritime Atlantic World, 1680–1783*. Chapel Hill, 2010; Hartley, 89–108, 125.
30. Mowat, 114–115.
31. Pougher, 224–231.
32. Joseph Dashiell to Thomas Johnson, June 10, 1777, NDAR, 9: 84.
33. Truitt, 133–134.
34. James Carey to F. Steward, sent Oct. 10, 1783, NABB, E. Carey Collection, 2015, 180; Overfield, Richard, 'The Loyalists of Maryland during the American Revolution', Ph.D. dissertation, University of Maryland, 1968, 255.
35. Instructions and Regulations for the Board of Associated Loyalists, Oct. 28, 1780, *Sources of American Independence*, ed. Peckham, Howard, Chicago, 1978, 605–607.
36. Bushman, Richard, *The Refinement of America, Persons, Houses, Cities*. New York, 1992, 15–21, 110–112; Gikandi, Simon, *Slavery and the Culture of Taste*, Princeton, N.J., 2011, 145–187. Isaac, *Langdon Carter's Uneasy Kingdom: Revolution and Rebellion on a Virginia Plantation*. New York, 2004, 99–100, 105–120, 239; Hoffman, 'The 'Disaffected' in the Revolutionary South', *The American Revolution*. ed., Young, Alfred, DeKalb, Ill., 1976, 275–276.
37. Typed copy of Thomas S. Sudler diary in the possession of Mr & Mrs Joseph Eberly p. 3, entry dated Nov. 18, 1803.

Chapter 30

1. Alberts, Robert, *The Golden Voyage, The Life and Times of William Bingham 1752–1804*. Boston, 1969, 25–82, quote on 25.
2. Robert Morris to Caesar Rodney, July 16 and July 25, 1781, Ryden, 419–423.
3. John Henry to Thomas Johnson, Feb. 14, 1778, Henry, 3–4; Henretta, James, *The Evolution of American Society 1700–1815, An Interdisciplinary Analysis*. Lexington, Mass., 1973, 159–160.
4. Buel, *In Irons*, 192–196; Rosswurm, Steven, *Arms, Country and Class*. New Brunswick, N.J., 1989, 243.
5. Doerflinger, 236–239, 258–261.
6. Clark, William, *Captain Dauntless: The Story of Nicholas Biddle of the Continental Navy*. Baton Rouge, 1949; Fowler, 119–121.
7. Fowler, 104–107.
8. Ibid.
9. Marine Committee to Navy Board of the Eastern Department, July 24, 1778, Paullin, 270–274; Fowler, 104–107.
10. Fowler, 104–107.

11. George Rodney to Philip Stevens, Secretary of the Admiralty, Oct. 28,1780, *Letter-books and order-books of George, Lord Rodney, admiral of the White squadron, 1780–1782*. New York, 1932, 54–56; quotes on 55 and 56; Spinney, 362.

12. Buel, *In Irons*, 86–89.

13. Rappleye, Charles, *Robert Morris*. New York, 2010, 300.

14. Convention, Jan. 27, 1776 and June 25, 1776, RB, no. 4, part 3; Jackson, *Pennsylvania Navy*, 205–319; Buel, 79. 90.

15. Coker, 48–52, 77.

16. Smith and Earle, 226–229.

17. Ibid., 223–234, 247, 251–252.

18. Ibid., 228–229.

19. Selby, 255.

20. Luther Martin to Thomas Johnson, March 18, 1778, Executive Papers, folder 60z, Maryland Archives, Annapolis, Md.

21. Truitt, 151.

22. Ibid., 117.

23. Somerset County Gentlemen to the Maryland Council, March 21, 1781, MA, 47: 140–141; Tilghman, 2: 119.

24. Tilghman, 1: 306.

25. Ibid., 2: 126.

26. Truitt, 117.

27. 'An Act for the defense of the bay …, in Kilty, William, ed., *Laws of Maryland*, 1, Nov. 1782, chap. XXVI; *Maryland Journal and Baltimore Advertiser*, August 14, 1781; Buel, *In Irons*, 90; Smith and Earle, Eller, 236.

Chapter 31

1. Manceron, 2: 435–438.

2. Ibid., 2: 436.

3. Manceron, 2: 446–449; Bamford, Paul, *Fighting Ships and Prisons: The Mediterranean Galleys of France in the Age of Louis XIV.* Minneapolis, 1973, 95–99.

4. Manceron, 2: 436.

5. Rodney, *Command of the Ocean*, 348–349.

6. See Chapter 28.

7. Jameson, J. Franklin, 'St Eustatius in the American Revolution', *The American Revolution and the West Indies*, ed. Toth, Charles, Port Washington, NY, 1975, 87–94.

8. Trew, Peter, *Rodney and The Breaking of the Line*, Barnsley, UK, 2006, 4, 200–202; George Rodney to Philip Stevens, Secretary of the Admiralty, Oct. 28,1780, *Letter-books and order-books of George, Lord Rodney, admiral of the White squadron, 1780–1782*. New York, 1932, 54–56.

9. Rodger, *The Command of the Ocean*, 343–349, 382; Spinney, 206, 238, 343, 349, 385, 415; Trew, 4–11; Norton, Louis, 'Admiral Rodney ousts the Jews from St Eustatius', *Journal of the American Revolution*, March 6, 2017.

10. Rodger, *Command of the Ocean*, 351.
11. Mahan, 344; Larrabee, Harold, *Decision at the Chesapeake*. New York, 1964; Johnston, Henry, *The Yorktown Campaign and the Surrender of Cornwallis, 1781*. New York 1958.
12. Mahan, 345–346; Rodger, *Command of the Ocean*, 351–352.
13. Maryland Council to George Washington, Aug. 30, 1781, MA, 45: 588; Calderhead, William, 'Prelude to Yorktown', *Maryland Historical Magazine*, 77, 123–125; Batch, Thomas, ed., *The Journal of Claude Blanchard: Commissary of French Auxiliary Army sent to the United States during the American Revolution, 1780–1783*. Albany, 1876, 137–139; Manceron, 496–497.
14. Manceron, 2: 513.
15. Ibid, 2: 503–504.
16. Proposals for raising Volunteers to Man his Majesty's Ships ..., Oct. 4, 1781, Klein and Howard, 219–220; Thomas Graves to Henry Clinton, Aug. 21, 1781; Samuel Hood to Henry Clinton, Aug. 25, 1781, Clinton, 560–562.
17. Buel, *In Irons*, 217–234; Mahan, 346–348, 355; Rodger, *Command of the Ocean*, 352–353.
18. Buel, *In Irons*, 218–225.
19. Rappleye, 300, 371–373.
20. Middlebrook, Louis, *The Frigate South Carolina: A Famous Revolutionary War Ship*. Salem, Mass., 1929, 12–14, 15–18, 30, quote on 16.
21. Lewis, 83–95.

Chapter 32

1. Crewe, 5–8, 11–61, 297–302.
2. Miller, 389–391.
3. Rodger, *Command of the Ocean*, 353
4. Ibid.
5. Mackesy, 443–457; Mahan, 420–426.
6. Tracy, 186–188.
7. Trew, Peter, *Rodney and the Breaking of the Line*. Barnsley, UK, 2006, 89–115.
8. Dalin, 43–49; Spinney, 297.
9. Bown, Stephen, *Scurvy*. New York, 2003, 170–172.
10. Ibid., 172–175.
11. Mahan, 428–436.
12. Mahan, 436–444; Spinney, 393–405, 443–445.
13. Dalin, 51–59; Mahan, 445–446.
14. Trew, 170–171.
15. Ibid., 172.
16. Mackesy, 472–473, Spinney, 409–410.
17. Conway, '"A Joy Unknown for Years Past": The American War, Britishness and the Celebration of Rodney's Victory at the Saints', *History,* 86: 282, 180–199; Rodger, *The Command of the Ocean*, 354–355.

18. Spinney, 414–415; Conway, *The British Isles*, 201–202, 288, 299, 315–316; Wilson, 275.
19. Dull, 152–154, 159.

Chapter 33

1. Samuel Covington and Thomas Holbrook to State of Maryland, Dec. 11, 1780, RB, No.3, part 4, 757.
2. Shomette, *Pirates on the Chesapeake*, 256–260.
3. Truitt, 106–107.
4. Shomette, *Pirates on the Chesapeake*, 266.
5. George Dashiell to Maryland Council, Dec., 1780, MA, 45: 122–123.
6. Truitt, 107.
7. Ibid., 129.
8. Ibid., 158.
9. Joseph Dashiell to Thomas Sim Lee, March 4, 1781, MA, 47: 104.
10. Truitt, 107–108.
11. Information of John Anderson, July 2, 1781, AA, 47: 334; Truitt, 165.
12. Joseph Dashiell to Thomas Sim Lee, July 6, 1781, MA, 47: 338–339; Truitt. 167–168.
13. Truitt, 105, 108, 165, 168.
14. Shomette, *Pirates on the Chesapeake*, 277–282.
15. Ibid., 281.
16. Truitt, 106–107.
17. Crockett, Thomas, *Facts and Fun: Historical Outlines of Tangier Island*, Norfolk, Va., 1890.
18. Joseph Dashiell to Thomas Sim Lee, March 4, 1781, MA, 47: 104.
19. Governor's Council to Thomas Grason, April 13, 1782, MA, 48: 130–131.
20. Thomas Grason to Thomas Johnson, June 30, 1779, RB, no. 4, pt. 3.
21. emorys.inf/family-tree/thomas grason-96, accessed May 7, 2016.
22. Tilghman, 1: 306.
23. emorys.inf/family-tree/thomas grason-96, May, 7, 2016; *Brown Books, 1803*, Annapolis, Md., no. 561, 115.
24. Footner, 55–56; emorys.inf/family-tree/Thomas grason-96, May, 7, 2016; Statement of James Bryant to obtain benefit of act of Congress …, Aug. 4, 1840, Orphan's Court Queen Annes County; *Brown Books, 1775–1803*, Annapolis, Md., no. 561, 115; Council to Abraham Skinner, June 10, 1782; Maryland Council, Jan. 15, 1784, MA, 48: 188, 48: 507; Smith and Earl, 238–239, 259–260.
25. *Journal and Advertiser,* July 8, 1782; Footner, 56–57; RB, no. 4: 106.
26. Smith and Earle, 241–245.
27. Council to Zedekiah Walley, July 31, 1782, MA, 48: 226–229;
28. William Paca to Secretary at War, Jan. 4, 1783, MA, 48: 374; Shomette, *Pirates on the Chesapeake*, 291.
29. Zedekiah Walley to John Cropper, Nov. 28, 1779, Wise, 25–26.

30. The Loyalist commander at Kedges Straits was Joseph Whaland Jr. Rebel authorities would could not admit that Whaland could win such a decisive victory, so they concocted an alias, John Kidd. Footner, 63.

31. Wise, 26; Maryland Council, Nov. 8, 1787, MA, 71: 224; Smith and Earle, 242–243.

32. Smith and Earle, 243–244; Baits, Lawrence, 'The Principles of War and the "Battle of the Barges" Using the Principles of War Archeology for a Better Understanding of Behavior on the Battlefield', eds. Pertermann, Dana and Norton, Holly, *The Archaeology of Engagement: Conflict and Revolution in the United States*. College Station, Tex., 2015.

33. Truitt, Reginald and Les Callette, Millard, *Worcester County Maryland's Arcadia*, Snow Hill, Md. 1977, 449–450; Truitt, 184–185.

34. John Cropper to William Davies, Dec. 6, 1782, CVSP, 3: 391; Wise, 26–27.

35. Mariner, *Off 13, The Eastern Shore of Virginia Guidebook*, Onley, Va., 1987, 107, Truitt, 184.

36. William Paca to the merchants of Baltimore, Feb. 19, 1783, MA, 48: 361; Truitt, 181.

37. Paca in Council to Chevalier de la Ville Brune, Dec. 3, 1782, Paca to George Washington, Feb. 21, 1783, MA, 48: 312–313, 365–366.

38. Stiverson, Gregory and Jacobsen, Phebe, *William Paca, A Biography.* Baltimore, 1976, 86.

39. Paca to John Lynn, Mar. 21, 1783, 387–388; Scharf, 2: 481; Stiverson and Jacobsen, 86.

40. Paca to George and Joseph Dashiell, Feb. 20, 1783, MA 48: 364.

41. Depositions of Joseph Anderson, Philip Ferguson and John Senior, Feb 21, 1783, RB, no. 3, part 4, 1301–1305.

42. Dull, 150–151, 159–161.

Chapter 34

1. Jasanoff, *Liberty's Exiles*, 69; Schama, Simon, *Rough Crossings.* New York, 2006, 5, 150–154, 435.

2. Talbott 90–91.

3. Schama, 129-135.

4. Mitchell, Robert, 'After Yorktown: The Wayne-Greene Correspondence, 1782', Peckham, *Selected Manuscripts from the Collections of the William L. Clements Library,* Chicago, 1978, 2: 364; Wilson, Ellen, *The Loyal Blacks*. New York, 1976, 44–47; Syrett, *Shipping and the American War,* 236–237.

5. Hamond to Robert Digby, September 24, 1782, HP, 7: 131–132; Schama, 132–136; Wilson, 1976, 50–51, 68–69; McCowen, 149.

6. McCowen, 147–150.

7. 'Account of a Conference between Washington and Sir Guy Carleton, May 6, 1783', *Founders Online,* National Archives, https://founders.archives.gov/documents/ Washington/99-01-02-11217, accessed Jan.,15, 2022; Washington to Carleton, May 6, 1783, *Founders Online,* National Archives, https://founders.archives.gov/documents/ Washington/99-01-02-11218, accessed June 26, 2022; Schama, 145–146.

8. Carleton to Washington, May 12, 1783, *Founders Online,* National Archives, https:// founders.archives.gov/documents/Washington/99-01-02-11252, accessed June 26, 2022.

9. Schama, 150–156; Wilson, 53–55.
10. Admiral Robert Digby's Naval Order Book, July 23 and 29, 1783, Admiral Digby Museum, Digby, Nova Scotia; *Report on American Manuscripts in the Royal Institutions of Great Britain.* London, 1909, 297; Schama, 155, 435.
11. Dull, *A Diplomatic History,* 159–163.
12. Wright, 125–143; Mowat, 136–140.
13. A. Deveaux to Carleton, June 6, 1783, Crary, 354–357.
14. This topic is vast, but fundamental to it is Jasanoff's *Liberty's Exiles*.

Affirmations

1. Higginbotham, 383. At end of his chapter, 'Defeat and Victory in the South', he says after Yorktown, 'the war dragged on until 1783', and he fails to cover it.
2. In *Admiral Lord Howe*, Syrett emphasizes the blockade's shortcomings: 61–66, 73–76.
3. While not devoted to the Continental Navy's logistics, Buel, *In Irons*, has material on the topic, 81–88, 91–96; Bowler's, *Logistics and the Failure of the British Army in America*, occasionally touches on the Continental army's logistics.

Index

Adams, John, 116
Adams, Samuel, 44
Admiralty, 9–10
Aitken, James, 4–5, 87, 108
Albany, N.Y., 50–51
Alfred, USS, 31–2, 97
American Commissioners, 87–9, 221
Annapolis Royal, N.S., 159–60
Arbigland Estate, 95
Arbuthnot, Admiral Marriott, 12, 68, 132–5, 142, 154, 196
Arcon, Jean–Claude–Eleonore Le Michaud, Chevalier d', 168–9
Arnold, General Benedict, 45, 47–8, 52–4, 56–7, 140–3, 196
Articles of Confederation, 61

Bahamas, 32, 218–20
Bailyn, Bernard, 41
Barceló y Pont de la Terra, Admiral Antonio, 166–8, 220
Barges, Battle of the, 213–4, 220
Barras, Jacques–Melchoir Comte de, 198, 203
Barrington, Secretary at War William, 68
Bartlett, Josiah, 97
Beaufort, S.C., 136
Bebee, Dr. Lewis, 49
Biddle, Captain Nicholas, 32–3
Bingham, William, 34, 88, 189–90
Black Pioneers, 217
Blane, Dr. Gilbert, 204
Bonhomme Richard, 117, 119–21

British Empire, ix, 22, 152, 162, 216, 219, 222, 224
Bouille, Governor, Marquis de, 203
Brocklebank, Captain Daniel, 25, 111, 113
Brown, Colonel John, 59–60
Buel, Richard Jr., 69
Burgoyne, General John, 58–60, 79–80, 84

Campbell, Colonel Archibald, 129
Caribbean Sea, 202–4
Carleton, Major Christopher, 64–5
Carleton, General Guy, 44–9, 55–8, 60, 216–18
Carrickfergus, Ireland, 100, 102, 114–16
Chambly Rapids, 54
Charleston, S.C.,
    migration, 217
    occupation of, 135–7
    Prevost attack, 129
    siege of, 132–5
Chatham Dockyard, 2–4
Chesapeake Bay,
    British blockade, 69–74
    British initiatives, 138–44
    Loyalist initiatives, 207–15, 220
    privateers, 36, 183–6
    state initiatives, 193–5
    water employment, 25–7
Clinton, Governor George, 83–4
Clinton, General Henry, 72, 79–84, 127–9, 132–7, 138–44, 146, 196
Collier, Captain George, 35, 138–9, 149, 158–9

Congress's Naval Committees, 28, 36, 98, 191
Connecticut, 39
Continental Navy,
 demise of, 189–92, 200
 in Europe, 87–90, 221
 Jones in, 96–9, 114–7
 losses at Charleston, 135
 on Lake Champlain, 50–3
 organization of x, 28–38, 222
 Penobscot and the Grand Banks, 147, 150, 157–8
Convoys, 10–11, 22, 120–1, 222
Copley, John Singleton, 177
Cornwallis, Lord Charles, 63, 140, 142–3, 198–9, 220–1
Conyngham, Captain Gustavas, 37, 41, 86, 90–5, 99–100, 107–8, 110, 123, 165, 221
Cordoba y Cordoba, Admiral Don Luis de, 118
Coursey, Captain Thomas, 193
Crillon, Louis de Balbe de Berton, Duc de, 168–9
Crimps, 6
Cropper, Colonel John, 212–15
Crown Point, N.Y., 46, 57–8
Cruger, Henry Jr., 23
Curtis, Captain Roger, 175–7

Dashiell,
 Captain Robert, 211, 213–14
 George, 208
 Joseph, 209–10
Dean, Silas, 87–90, 93, 99, 109, 190
Delaware River, 69–74, 220
Deptford Dockyard, 2
Destouches, Captain Sochet, 142
Deveaux, Colonel Andrew, 136, 218–19
Digby, Admiral Robert, 203, 216–18
Digby, Lieutenant William, 49
Douglas, Commodore Charles, 48–9, 54–5, 204–6
Drake, HMS, 100, 115
Duff, Admiral Robert, 171

Dunkirk, France, 91, 93
Dunmore, Governor John Murray Lord, 8, 18–19, 70, 207–8

Eliott, General George, 169, 171–7
Elliott, Andrew, 77
Elphinstone, Captain George, 132–3, 137
English Harbor Dockyard, Antigua, 2, 202–3
Esopus (Kingston), N.Y., 82–3
Estaing, Admiral Charles–Henri–Hector d', 126–7, 129–30, 133, 157

Falmouth, Maine, 16–9, 25
Flamborough Head, Battle of, 120–1
Floridablanca, Conde de 93, 165
Fort Moultrie, 133–4
Forts Clinton and Montgomery, 80–1
Forts Washington and Lee, 77
France, ix–x, 64, 86–95, 99–115, 117–28, 165, 202–6
Franklin, Benjamin, x, 87, 89, 91, 109, 116, 119, 190
Fraser, General Simon, 49, 59
Freeman, David, 104, 108

Gage, General Thomas, 16
Gale, Captain Henry, 209
Gambier, Admiral James, 138
Gates, General Horatio, 23, 52–4, 62
Gayton, Captain George, 139–40, 207
George III, 137, 139
Germain, Lord George, 9, 11, 79, 128, 135, 144
Gibraltar,
 Artificer Company, 171–2, 177
 Darby relief, 173, 220
 Howe relief, 173–4, 176, 220
 Rodney relief, 172–3, 220
 siege of, 164–77, 220
Gillray, James, 164
Glasgow, HMS, 32, 135
Glover, Colonel John, 29

Goodrich family, 183–6
Goree, Senegal, 131
Grason, Captain Thomas, 193, 209–12
Grasse, Francois Joseph Paul, Comte de, 196–9, 203–7, 221
Graves, Admiral Samuel, 16, 18, 47, 68
Graves, Admiral Thomas, 198–9, 203
Green, Dr. Ezra, 98, 106
Green, Lt. Cornel William, 171

Hacker, Captain Hoysteed, 157
Haldimand, Governor Frederick, 64–5
Halifax, N.S.,
    careening yard, 2, 152–3
    lack of men, 12
    Maine threatened by, 146
    military and civilian base, 154–62
Hamilton, Colonel Alexander, 15, 44
Hamilton, William, 177
Hamond, Captain Andrew Snape, 7–8, 12–13, 68–77, 132–4, 154–6, 158–62, 217, 220
Handcock, John, 32, 92
Hood, Admiral Samuel, 198–9, 203–6
Hopkins, Captain Esek, 31–3, 97, 135,157, 191
Hopkins, Stephen, 31
Howe, Admiral Richard, 68, 74–8, 127, 220
Howe, Colonel Robert, 18
Howe, Captain Tryingham, 32
Howe, General William, 74–7, 154
Hudson River, 76, 79–84

Illicit Trade, 38–41, 167–8
Impressment, 6–8, 27, 148, 154–6
Inflexible, HMS, 54
Insurance rates, 110
Irish Sea, 100–11

Jacobites, 102
Jamaica, 96, 203, 217
Jay, John, 165
Jefferson, Governor Thomas, 141
Johnson, Captain Edward, 39

Jones, Captain John Paul, 30, 33–4, 93–117, 119–23, 147, 157, 200, 221
Judson, Captain Amos, 40

Keppel, Admiral, First Lord Augustus, 206, 216
Kilby, John, 37, 119, 121
Kirkcudbright, Scotland, 96

Lafayette, Marquise de, 61–3, 126
Lake Champlain,
    battle of, 56–7, 220, 222
    British control, 61–5
    British invasions, 57–60
    invasion route, 44
    rebel retreat, 47
Lake George, N.Y., 59–60
Landais, Captain Pierre, 119–21
Langara, Admiral Juan de, 173
Langdon, John, 97
Lee, Arthur, 87–88, 116
Leslie, General Alexander, 139–40, 207, 217
Lincoln, General Benjamin, 133, 135
Lind, Dr. James, 204
L'Indien (*South Carolina*), 99, 117, 119, 200
Livingston Manor, N.Y., 82–3
Long Island Sound, 39
Louis XVI, 122–3, 196
Lovell, General Solomon, 147–50
Lowther, Sir Christopher, 100
Loyalists,
    in Savannah, 130
    in the Chesapeake, 18–19, 138–44, 207–15
    migration, 161, 216–9, 223
    privateers, 180–89
Lunenburg, N.S., 160

Machias, Maine, 158
MacKenzie, Captain Thomas, 47
MacKesy, Piers, 221
Mahan, Alfred, 50, 84, 123, 221
Manley, Captain John, 34–6, 97, 222

Marblehead, Mass., 29–30
Martin, Governor John, 217
Marven, Lieutenant Richard, 32–3
Maryland Navy, 193–4, 210–14
Massachusetts General Court, 147–50
Massachusetts Navy, 147–50
Mathew, General Edward, 138–9
Maxwell, Ship's Carpenter Mungo, 96
McClean, General Francis, 146–9
McNeill, Captain Hector, 34–6, 97, 222
Middleton, Admiral Charles, 113, 216
Montgomery, General Richard, 44, 47
Morison, Samuel Eliot, 123
Morris, Robert Jr., 22, 38, 41, 88–9, 157,
    189–90, 199–200
Mowat, Captain Henry, 16–8, 148–9
Murray, Governor James, 46

Navy Board, 9–11, 113, 222
Newfoundland Grand Banks, 150, 157–8
Newport, RI, 23–4, 78
New Hampshire Navy, 147
New York,
    Chamber of Commerce, 78
    city captured, 75–8
    migration, 217–18
    navy, 80
    province, 146
Nicholson, Captain John, 30, 33–4, 97, 223
Nicholson, Captain Samuel, 33, 89, 94
Norfolk, Va., 18–19
North, Frederick Lord, 9
Nova Scotia, 157–62, 221

Ordnance Board, 13
Orvilliers, Admiral Louis d', 118
Osborne's, Va., 142–3
Otter, HMS, 8

Paca, Governor William, 213–14, 220
Parker, Captain Hyde, 76
Parr, Governor John, 161–2
Pattison, General James, 77
Pearson, Captain Richard, 58–60, 120–1

Penobscot Bay, Maine,
    Massachusetts attacks, 146–50
    siege, 148–9
Philadelphia, Pa., 69–74
Phillips, General William, 142
Plymouth Dockyard, UK, 2
Portsmouth, N.H., 24–5, 97
Portsmouth, Va., 139, 144
Portsmouth Dockyard, UK, 2
Powell, General Henry, 59–60
Prevost, General Augustine, 128–30
Pringle, Lieutenant Thomas, 48, 55, 56–7
Privateers,
    Britain–Loyalist, 112, 180–8
    United States, 36–9, 151, 222–3
Putnam, General Israel, 79–80, 83–4

Quebec,
    Congress wants, 44–9, 61, 221
    siege of city, 46–9
    Act, 44, 46

Ranger, USS, 28–9, 34, 97–111, 115–17, 150
Revere, Paul, 44
Revolutionary War, ix–x, 102, 203, 222
Rhode Island, 15–16, 39
Rochambeau, Comte de, 196–9
Roche, Captain John, 97
Rodney, Admiral George, 172–3, 191,
    197–8, 202–6, 220
Roebuck, HMS, 2–3, 8, 12–14, 70–7, 132–4,
    136, 220
Rooke, Admiral George, 164
Royal Navy,
    administration, 9–13, 16
    amphibious operations, 75–7, 220–3
    blockade and convoys, 10–11, 68–75,
        199, 220–1
    bombardment, 16–19
    dockyard,s 2–5, 13, 152–3, 203
    in British Isles, 90, 100
    in the Hudson, 81–3
    in the South, 126–44, 197–202
    in Maine, 146–52

in Nova Scotia, 158–60
in the Caribbean, 205–6
on Lake Champlain, 54–7

St. Augustine, 13, 128, 218–9
St. Eustatius, Dutch, 197
St. Johns, Que., 58
St. Lawrence River, 44–5, 48
Saints, Battle of, 205–6, 220
Sale Rovers, 107
Saltonstall, Captain Dudley, 31, 147–51
Sandwich, Earl of, First Lord, 2, 48
Sandy Hook, N.J., 127
Savannah, Ga.,
    capture and siege of, 128–30
    migration, 216–17
Schuyler, Hermanus, 51–2
Schuyler, General Philip, 47, 50–4, 64
Scurvy, 204
Selkirk Mansion, Scotland, 105–6, 108–9, 116
Serapis, HMS, 120–1
Seven Years' War, 6, 44–5, 114, 152
Sharp, William, 177
Shaw, Midshipman Samuel, 33
Simpson, Lieutenant Thomas,
    97–8, 150
Skene, Philip, 50
Skenesborough, N.Y., 51–3, 59, 64
Slave Trade, 23–4, 96
South Carolina Navy, 135, 192
Southern Strategy, 128
Spain, 93, 95, 118, 164–77, 203, 219
Squire, Captain Matthew, 8
Stamp Act, ix
Stark, General John, 62–4
Sturdy Beggar, US privateer, 37–8
Symonds, Captain Thomas ,140–2

Tenders, 8
Teredo worm, 202

Texel, The Netherlands, 121–2
Thomas, General John, 48
Thompson, Samuel, 17
Thurot, Francois, 114–15
Ticonderoga, 46, 49, 52, 57–8, 61
Trumbull, Governor John, 39, 52–3
Trumbull, John, 177
Tryon, Governor William, 80–1

Van Rensselaer, Philip, 52
Vaughan, General John, 81–3
Vergennes, Comte de, 87, 92, 126
Virginia Capes, Battle of, 198–9
Virginia Navy, 142–3, 212–14

Wallace, Captain James 15–6, 80–3
Walley, Captain Zedekiah, 212–13
Wallingford, Lieutenant Samuel, 98, 103–5
Warren, USS 147–9
Washington, General George, 13, 36, 61, 63,
    75–7, 79, 84, 128, 141, 146, 154, 157,
    196–9, 217, 220
Waterbury, General David 52–3
Watermen,
    Chesapeake, 200, 207–15, 223
    River Thames, 6
Wayne, General Anthony, 217
Wells, Captain Jeremiah, 40
Whaland, Captain Joseph Jr., 207–15,
    220, 223
Whipple, Captain Abraham, 31, 33, 135
Whitecuff, Benjamin, 175
Whitehaven, 96, 100–107
Wickes, Captain Lambert, 86–90, 92, 94,
    97, 99–100, 107–8, 221
Wynkoop, Captain Jacobus, 53–4

Yorktown, Siege of, 198–9, 220

Zebecs, 166